Leigh Hunt

A Book for a Corner

Selections in Prose and Verse

Leigh Hunt

A Book for a Corner
Selections in Prose and Verse

ISBN/EAN: 9783337098292

Printed in Europe, USA, Canada, Australia, Japan

Cover: Foto ©Thomas Meinert / pixelio.de

More available books at **www.hansebooks.com**

Leigh Hunt

A Book for a Corner
Selections in Prose and Verse

ISBN/EAN: 9783337098292

Printed in Europe, USA, Canada, Australia, Japan

Cover: Foto ©Thomas Meinert / pixelio.de

More available books at **www.hansebooks.com**

A BOOK FOR A CORNER;

OR,

Selections in Prose and Verse

FROM AUTHORS
THE BEST SUITED TO THAT MODE OF ENJOYMENT

WITH

COMMENTS ON EACH, AND A GENERAL INTRODUCTION,

BY LEIGH HUNT.

NEW YORK:
H. W. DERBY, 625 BROADWAY.
1861.

PFEFACE.

AN ample account of the nature of this work will be found in the *Introduction;* but to give a brief and more general idea of the entertainment which it is proposed to set before the purchaser, it may be as well to state in this place, that the book, for the most part, is a collection of passages from such authors as retain, if not the highest, yet the most friendly and as it were domestic hold upon us during life, and sympathize with us through all portions of it. Hence the first extract is a Letter addressed to an Infant, the last the Elegy in the Churchyard,* and the intermediate ones have something of an analogous reference to the successive stages of existence. It is therefore intended to be read by intelligent persons of all times of life, the youthful associations in it being such as the oldest readers love to call to mind, and the oldest such as all would gladly meet

* The last article of the Second Series.

with in their decline. It has no politics in it, no polemics, nothing to offend the delicatest mind. The innocentest boy and the most cautious of his seniors might alike be glad to look over the other's shoulder, and find him in his corner perusing it.

This may be speaking in a boastful manner; but an Editor has a right to boast of his originals, especially when they are such as have comforted and delighted him throughout his own life, and are for that reason recommended by him to others.

CONTENTS OF FIRST SERIES.

	PAGE
NATURE OF THE PRESENT WORK, AND A FEW REMARKS ON ITS READERS	9
LETTER TO A NEW-BORN CHILD . . . . . . *Catherine Talbot.*	27
THE SCHOOLMISTRESS . . . . *Shenstone.*	30
GROWN SCHOOLBOYS. A Letter to Geo. Montagu *Horace Walpole.*	42
ODE ON SOLITUDE. Written at twelve years of age . . *Pope.*	45
SIR BERTRAND—A Fragment . . . . *Dr. Aikin.*	47
ROBINSON CRUSOE. The Five Points in his History . . . *De Foe.*	53
Crusoe's Meditations and Mode of Life	56
He finds the Print of a Man's Foot on the Shore . . .	59
Sees Savages in the Island, and obtains a Servant . . .	63
PETER WILKINS'S DISCOVERY OF THE FLYING WOMAN. *Rob't Pultock.*	73
GIL BLAS AND THE PARASITE . . . . *Le Sage.*	96
LUDOVICO IN THE HAUNTED CHAMBER. From the "Mysteries of Udolpho". . . . . *Mrs. Radcliffe.*	104
THE WARNING. From the Novel of "Nature and Art" *Mrs. Inchbald.*	128
JOHN BUNCLE . . . . *Thomas Amory.*	137
DELIGHTS OF BOOKS OF TRAVEL	149
Wandering Tartars and their Chief Zagatai, in the Thirteenth Century . . . . . . *William de Rubruquis.*	154
Passage of the Desert of Lop . . . . . *Marco Polo.*	162
Kubla Khan . . . . " "	164
Kubla Khan's Palace at Xanadu . . . . . " "	165
Kubla Khan's Person and State . . . . . " "	168
Friar Oderic's Rich Man who was fed by Fifty Virgins . . . . " "	170
Of the Old Man of the Mountain . . . . " "	171

DELIGHTS OF BOOKS OF TRAVEL—*Continued.*

 How Prester John burnt up his Enemy's Men
  and Horses . . . . "   " 173
 Praise of Women . . . . *Ledyard.* 175
 Bed in the Desert . . . . *Mungo Park.* 177
 First Sight of the Niger . . . . . .   "   " 179
 Kindness of a Woman to him, and a Song
  over his Distress . . . .   "   " 180
 He passes a Lion . . . .   "   " 182
 Narrow Escape from another Lion . . .   "   " 184
 Moss in the Desert . . . .   "   " 184

A SHIPWRECK, A SEA VOYAGE, AND AN ADVENTURE BY THE WAY . 189
 Shipwreck of a Spanish Vessel . . . *Cyrus Redding.* 190
 A Sea Voyage, and Adventure by the Way . . . *Cook.* 193

BUSINESS, BOOKS, AND AMUSEMENT. Passages from his Autobiography . . . . *William Hutton.* 217

NATURE OF THE PRESENT WORK,

AND A

FEW REMARKS ON ITS READERS.

THIS compilation is intended for all lovers of books, at every time of life, from childhood to old age, particularly such as are fond of the authors it quotes, and who enjoy their perusal most in the quietest places. It is intended for the boy or girl who loves to get with a book into a corner—for the youth who on entering life finds his advantage in having become acquainted with books—for the man in the thick of life, to whose spare moments books are refreshments—and for persons in the decline of life, who reflect on what they have experienced, and to whom books and gardens afford their tranquillest pleasures.

It is a book (not to say it immodestly) intended to lie in old parlour windows, in studies, in cottages, in cabins aboard ship, in country-inns, in country-houses, in summer-houses, in any houses that have wit enough to like it, and are not the mere victims of a table covered with books for show.

When Shenstone was a child, he used to have a new book brought him from the next country-town, whenever any body went to market. If he had gone to bed and was asleep, it was put behind his pillow; and if it had been forgotten, and he was awake, his mother (more kindly than wisely) " wrapped up a piece of wood of the same form, and pacified him for the night." This is the sort of child we hope to be a reader of our volumes.

When Gray and Walpole were at Eton, they partitioned out the fields into territories of which they had read in books, and so ruled over them and sent ambassadors to one another. These are the sort of school-boys we look to entertain.

When Mrs. Inchbald, who was a farmer's daughter, first came to London, she was alone, and would have been subjected to no small perils but for the knowledge she had acquired from books; for she was poor, lovely, and sensitive. She turned the knowledge to the greatest account, and lived to add precious matter to the stock. We flatter ourselves, or rather we dare to aver, considering the authors who furnish our extracts, that nobody would have more approved of our book than Mrs. Inchbald.

Some of the most stirring men in the world, persons in the thick of business of all kinds, and indeed with the business of the world itself on their hands,—Lorenzo de Medici, for instance, who was at once the great merchant and the political arbiter of his time,—have combined with their other energies the greatest love of books, and found no recreation at once so wholesome and so useful. We hope many a man of business will refresh himself with the short pieces in these volumes, and return to his work the fitter to baffle craft, and yet retain a reverence for simplicity.

Every man who has a right sense of business, whether his business be that of the world or of himself, has a respect for all right things apart from it; because business with him is not a mindless and merely instinctive industry, like that of a beetle rolling its ball of clay, but an exercise of faculties congenial with the other powers of the human being, and all working to some social end. Hence he approves of judicious and reflecting leisure—of domestic and social evenings—of suburban retreats—of gardens—of ultimate retirement " for good"—of a reading and reflective old age. Such retirements have been longed for, and in many instances realized, by wise and great men of all classes, from the Diocletians of old to the Foxes and Burkes of our own days. Warren Hastings, who had ruled in India, yearned for the scenes of his boyhood; and lived to be happy in them. The wish to possess a country-house, a retreat, a nest, a harbour of some kind from the storms and even from the agitating pleasures of life, is as old as the sorrows and joys of civilization. The child feels it when he " plays at house;" the schoolboy, when he is reading in his corner; the lover, when he thinks of his mistress. Epicurus felt it in his garden; Horace and Virgil expressed their desire of it in passages which the sympathy of mankind has rendered immortal. It was the end of all the wisdom and experience of Shakspeare. He retired to his native town, and built himself a house in which he died. And who else does not occasionally " flit " somewhere meantime if he can? The country for many miles round London, and indeed in most other places, is adorned with houses and grounds of men of business, who are whirled to and fro on weekly or daily evenings, and who would all find something to approve in the closing chapters of our work. The greatest moneyed man of our time, Rothschild, who weighed kings in his balance, could not do without his house at Gunnersbury. Even the turbulent De Retz, according to Madame de Sévigné, became the sweetest of retired Signiors, and did nothing but read books and feed his trout. It is customary to jest upon such men, and indeed upon all retirement; to say that they would still meddle with affairs if they could, and that retirement is a failure and a " bore." Fox did not think so. It is possible that De Retz would have meddled fast enough ; nor are many energetic men superior, perhaps, to temptations of their spirit in this way, when such occur. But this does not hinder them from enjoying another and a seasonable pleasure meantime. On the contrary, this very energy is the thing which hinders it from palling ; that is to say, supposing their intellects are large enough to include a sense of it. De Retz, like Burke and Fox, was a lover of books. Sir Robert Walpole, who retired only to be sick and to die, did not care for books. Occupation is the necessary basis of all enjoyment; and he who cannot read, or botanize, or farm, or amuse himself with his neighbours, or exercise his brain with thinking, is in a bad way for the country at any time, much more for retiring into it. He has nothing to do but to get back as fast as he can, and be hustled into a sensation by a mob.

"Books, Venus, books." It is those that teach us to refine on our pleasures when young, and which, having so taught us, enable us to recall them with satisfaction when old. For let the half-witted say what they will of delusions, no thorough reader ever ceased to believe in his books, whatever doubts they might have taught him by the way. They are pleasures too palpable and habitual for him to deny. The habit itself is a pleasure. They contain his young dreams and his old discoveries; all that he has lost, as well as all that he has gained; and, as he is no surer of the gain than of the loss, except in proportion to the strength of his perceptions, the dreams, in being renewed, become truths again. He is again in communion with the past; again interested in its adventures, grieving with its griefs, laughing with its merriment, forgetting the very chair and room he is sitting in. Who, in the mysterious operation of things, shall dare to assert in what unreal corner of time and space that man's mind is; or what better proof he has of the existence of the poor goods and chattels about him, which at that moment (to him) are non-existent? "Oh!" people say, "but he wakes up, and sees them there." Well; he woke *down* then, and saw the rest. What we distinguish into dreams and realities, are, in both cases, but representatives of impressions. Who shall know what difference there is in them at all, save that of degree, till some higher state of existence help us to a criterion?

For our part, such real things to us are books, that, if habit and perception make the difference between real and unreal, we may say that we more frequently wake out of common life to *them*, than out of them to common life. Yet we do not find the life the less real. We only feel books to be a constituent part of it; a world, as the poet says,

> "Round which, with tendrils strong as flesh and blood,
> Our pastime and our happiness may grow."

What do readers care for "existing things" (except when Ireland is mentioned, or a child is grieving) compared with poetry and romance? What for Bonaparte and his pretences, compared with the honest jealousy of "Orlando," or the cakes of Alfred? What for all the parsons in the world (except Pius IX. or some Welsh curate) compared with Parson Adams or the Vicar of Wakefield? What men (generally speaking) are they so sure of? are so intimate with? can describe, quote, and talk of to one another with so much certainty of a mutual interest? And yet, when readers wake up to that other dream of life, called real life (and we do not mean to deny its palpability), they do not find their enjoyment of it diminished. It is increased—increased by the contrast—by the variety—by the call upon them to show the faith which books have originally given them in all true and good things, and which books, in spite of contradiction and disappointment, have constantly main tained. Mankind are the creatures of books, as well as of other circumstances; and such they eternally remain; proofs, that the race is a noble and a believing race, and capable of whatever books can stimulate.

The volumes now offered to our fellow readers originated in this kind of passion for books. They were suggested by a wish we had long felt to get up a book for our private enjoyment, and of a very particular and unambitious nature. It was to have consisted of favourite passages, not out of the authors we most admired, but those whom we most loved; and it was to have commenced, as the volumes do, with Shenstone's *Schoolmistress,* and ended with Gray's *Elegy.* It was to have contained indeed little which the volumes do not comprise, though not intended to be half so big, and it was to have proceeded on the same plan of beginning with childhood and ending with the church-yard. We did not intend to omit the greatest authors on account of their being the greatest, but because they moved the feelings too strongly. What we desired was not an excitement, but a balm. Readers, who have led stirring lives, have such men as Shakspeare with them always, in their very struggles and sufferings, and in the tragic spectacles of the world. Great crowds and great passions are Shakspeares; and we, for one (and such we take to be the case with many readers). are sometimes as willing to retire from their " infinite agitation of wit," as from strifes less exalted; and retreat into the placider corners of genius more humble. It is out of no disrespect to their greatness; neither, we may be allowed to say, is it from any fear of being unable to sustain it; for we have seen perhaps as many appalling faces of things in our time as they have, and we are always ready to confront more if duty demand it. But we do not choose to be always suffering over again in books what we have suffered in the world. We prefer, when in a state of repose, to renew what we have enjoyed—to possess wholly what we enjoy still—to discern in the least and gentlest things the greatest and sweetest intentions of Nature—and to cultivate those soothing, serene, and affectionate feelings, which leave us in peace with all the world, and in good hope of the world to come. The very greatest genius, after all, is not the greatest thing in the world, any more than the greatest city in the world is the country or the sky. It is a concentration of some of its greatest powers, but it is not the greatest diffusion of its might. It is not the habit of its success, the stability of its sereneness. And this is what readers like ourselves desire to feel and know. The greatest use of genius is but to subserve to that end; to further the means of enjoying it, and to freshen and keep it pure; as the winds and thunders, which come rarely, are purifiers of the sweet fields, which are abiding.

The book, therefore, as originally contemplated, was to consist principally, besides the pieces mentioned, of such others as Cowley's *Garden*, Wotton's *Happy Life*, the favourite passages about the country from Horace and Virgil, Claudian's *Old Man of Verona*, Pope's *Ode on Solitude*, a selection from the Coverley papers in the *Spectator*, Thomson's *Castle of Indolence, Letters* of Gray, Virgil's *Grat* out of Spenser; and, though we have several editions of the work constantly by us, we think we could not have denied ourselves the pleasure of having something out of the *Arabian Nights*. Our *Sequestered Book* (for such, in our mind, we called it) would hardly have seemed complete without a chapter or two about *Sindbad* or the *Forty Thieves*, or the retirement of the *Fairy Banou*. The book was to have been addressed entirely to lovers of sequestered pleasures, and chiefly to such as were in the decline of life, or poetically beginning it.

When the volume, however, came to be considered with a view to publication, objections were made to the smallness of its size, and the probable fewness of its readers. Had we been rich, we should have parried the objection, and sent forth a volume at any rate, with the contents of which the few would have been pleased. We consoled ourselves with reflecting that we had other favourite passages which could be included in a larger book; and an extension of the plan now struck us, which in the eyes of many readers, perhaps of most, would in all probability improve it. This was, to suppose our sequestered reader thinking, not merely of the pleasures of his childhood or of his old age, but of his whole life, past or to come, and thus calling to mind passages from favourite authors of all kinds in illustration of its successive phases. The spirit of the first conception was still, however, to be carefully retained. Life, without effeminately shutting one's eyes to its perplexities, was to be rogarded, not in spleen, or in sorrow, or in narrowness of any kind, but with a cheerfulness befitting childhood, a manliness befitting a man, and with that calm and loving wisdom in age which discerns so much beauty and goodness in the face of Nature, that it cannot doubt the benevolence of her soul.

Hence the inclusion in the present volume of knaveries and other half-witted activities out in the world, and of terrors and tragedies in solitude. Hence extracts from Le Sage and Fielding, from Steele, Smollett, Goldsmith, Mrs. Radcliffe, and others.

We have imagined a book-loving man, or man able to refresh himself with books, at every successive period of his life;—the child at his primer, the sanguine boy, the youth entering the world, the man in the thick of it, the man of alternate business and repose, the retired man calmly considering his birth and his death; and in this one human being we include, of course, the whole race and both sexes, mothers, wives, and daughters, and all which they do to animate and sweeten existence. Thus our invisible, or rather many-bodied hero (who is the reader himself), is in the first instance a baby; then a child under the *Schoolmistress* of Shenstone; then the schoolboy with Gray and Walpole, reading poetry and romance; then *Gil Blas* entering the world; then the sympathiser with the *John Buncles* who enjoy it, and the *Travellers* who fill it with enterprise; then the matured man beginning to talk of disappointments, and standing in need of admonition *Against*

Inconsistency in his Expectations; then the reassured man comforted by his honesty and his just hopes, and refreshing himself with his *Club* or his country-lodging, his pictures, or his theatre; then the retiring, or retired, or finally old man, looking back with tenderness on his enjoyments, with regret for his errors, with comfort in his virtues, and with a charity for all men, which gives him a right to the comfort; loving all the good things he ever loved, particularly the books which have been his companions and the childhood which he meets again in the fields; and neither wishing nor fearing to be gathered into that kindly bosom of Nature, which covers the fields with flowers, and is encircled with the heavens.

The reader, however, is not to suppose that any attention to this plan of the book is exacted of him. Such a demand would be a pedantry and a folly. It is only suggested to him in case he may like it, and for the purpose of showing that we set nothing before him which does not possess a principle of order. He may regard the book, if more convenient to do so, as a mere set of extracts with comments, or of extracts alone, not requiring comments Our sequestered book was to have been without comments; and we should have been well content, had none been desired for this. There is a pleasure, it is true, in expressing love and admiration, and in hoping that we contribute to the extension of such feelings in the world; but we can truly say, that we seldom quote a fine passage, and comment upon it at any length, without wishing that everybody had been as well acquainted with it as ourselves, and could dispense with the recommendation. All we expect of the reader is that he should like the extracts on which the comments are made. If he does not do that, he has no business to be a reader of the book, or perhaps to be a reader at all. At least he is no universalist; no sympathiser with the entire and genial round of existence; and it is for the reader who is, that these volumes are emphatically intended.

A universalist, in one high bibliographical respect, may be said to be the only true reader; for he is the only reader on whom no writing is lost. Too many people approve no books but such as are representatives of some opinion or passion of their own. They read, not to have human nature reflected on them, and so be taught to know and to love everything, but to be reflected themselves as in a pocket mirror, and so interchange admiring looks with their own narrow cast of countenance. The universalist alone puts up with difference of opinion, by reason of his own very difference; because his difference is a right claimed by him in the spirit of universal allowance, and not a privilege arrogated by conceit. He loves poetry and prose, fiction and matter of fact, seriousness and mirth, because he is a thorough human being, and contains portions of all the faculties to which they appeal. A man who can be nothing but serious, or nothing but merry, is but half a man. The lachrymal or the risible organs are wanting in him. He has no business to have eyes or muscles like other men. The universalist alone can put up with *him*, by reason of the very sympathy of his antipathy. He understands the defect enough to pity, while he dislikes it. The universalist is the only reader who can make something out of books for which he has no predilection. He sees differences in them to sharpen his reasoning; sciences which impress on him a sense of his ignorance; nay, languages which, if they can do nothing else, amuse his eye and set him thinking of other countries. He will detect old acquaintances in Arabic numerals, and puzzle over a sum or a problem, if only to try and taste the curiosity of it. He is the only man (except a soldier or a gardener) to whom an army list or an almanac would not be thoroughly disgusting on a rainy day in a country alehouse, when nothing else readable is at hand, and the coach has gone "just ten minutes." The zodiacal light of " Francis Moore, Physician," would not be lost on him. He would laugh at the Doctor's verses; wonder who St. Alphage or St. Hugh could have been, as affecting the red-letter days; and see what christian or surnames prevailed in the army, or what personages had authority in those days. The words "Royal Highness the Duke of York" would set him thinking on the good-natured though not astonishing prince, and imagining how hearty a dish of beef-steaks he would have dispatched in the room in which he was sitting.

Our compilation, therefore, though desirous to please all who are willing to be pleased, is ambitious to satisfy this sort of person most of all. It is of *his* childhood we were mostly thinking when we extracted the *Schoolmistress*. He will thoroughly understand the wisdom lurking beneath the playfulness of its author. He will know how wholesome as well as amusing it is to become acquainted with books like *Gil Blas* and *Joseph Andrews*. He will derive agreeable terror from *Sir Bertram* and the *Haunted Chamber;* will assent with delighted reason to every sentence in *Mrs. Barbauld's Essay;* will feel himself wandering into solitudes with *Gray;* shake honest hands with *Sir Roger de Coverley;* be ready to embrace *Parson Adams,* and to chuck *Pounce* out of window, instead of the hat; will travel with *Marco Polo* and *Mungo Park;* stay at home with *Thomson;* retire with *Cowley;* be industrious with *Hutton;* sympathizing with *Shenstone* and *Mrs. Inchbald;* laughing with (and at) *Buncle;* melancholy, and forlorn, and self-restored, with the shipwrecked mariner of *De Foe.* There are *Robinson Crusoes* in the moral as well as physical world, and even a universalist may be one of them; men, cast on desert islands of thought and speculation; without companionship; without worldly resources; forced to arm and clothe themselves out of the remains of shipwrecked hopes, and to make a home for their solitary hearts in the nooks and corners of imagination and reading. It is not the worst lot in the world Turned to account for others, and embraced with patient cheerfulness, it may, with few exceptions, even be one of the best. We hope our volume may light into the hands of such men. Every extract which is made in it, has something of a like second-purpose, beyond what appears on its face. There is amusement for those who require nothing more, and instruction in the shape of amusement for those who choose to find it. We only hope that the "knowing reader" will not think we have assisted inquiry too often. We hate, with our friends the little boys, nothing so much as the "Moral" that officiously treads the heels of the great Æsop, and which assumes that the sage has not done his work when he has told his story. It is bad enough to be forced to interpret wisdom of any kind; but to talk after such transparent lessons as those, is overweeningness horrible. The little boys will find nothing of the sort to frighten them in this book; and they need not look at the prefaces, if they have no mind for them. It is beautiful to think how ignorant our grown memories are of prefaces to books of amusement that were put into our hands when young, and how intensely we remember the best extracts. What grown up people in general know anything of good Dr. Enfield or didactic Dr. Knox, or even of Percy, the editor of *Ancient Reliques?* Yet who that has read the *Speaker* and *Elegant Extracts* ever forgot the soliloquy in *Hamlet*, Goldsmith's *Beau Tibbs* and *Contented Beggar*, or the story of *Robin Hood?*

Those exquisite humours of Goldsmith, and the story of Robin Hood, we have omitted, with a hundred others, partly because we had not room for an abundance of things which we admired, chiefly because they did not fall within a certain idea of our plan. The extremely familiar knowledge also which readers have of them might have been another objection, even in a work consisting chiefly of favourite passages;—things, which imply a certain amount of familiar knowledge, if not in the public at large, yet among readers in general. If any persons should object that some of these also are too familiar, the answer is, that they are of a nature which rendered it impossible for us. consistently with our plan, to omit them, and that readers in general would have missed them. We allude, in particular, to the *Elegy in a Country Church-Yard* and the *Ode on the Prospect of Eton College*. It is the privilege of fine writers, when happy in their treatment of a universal subject of thought or feeling, to leave such an impression of it in the reading world as almost to identify it with everybody's own reflections, or constitute it a sort of involuntary mental quotation. Of this kind are Gray's reflections in the church-yard, and his memories of school-boy happiness. Few people who know these passages by heart, ever think of a church-yard or a school-ground without calling them to mind.

The nature and the amount of the reader's familiarity with many other extracts are the reasons why we have extracted them. They constitute part of the object and essence of the book; for the familiarity is not a vulgar and repulsive one, but that of a noble and ever-fresh companion. whose society we can the less dispense with, the more we are accustomed to it. The book in this respect resembles a set of pictures which it delights us to live with, or a collection of favourite songs and pieces of music, which we bind up in volumes in order that we may always have them at hand, or know where to find them. Who, in such a room full of pictures, would object to his Raphael or Titian? Or in such a collection of music, to his Beethoven, Rossini, or Paisiello? Our book may have little novelty in the least sense of the word; but it has the best in the greatest sense; that is to say, *never-dying novelty ;*—antiquity hung with ivy-blossoms and rose-buds; old friends with the ever-new faces of wit, thought, and affection. Time has proved the genius with which it is filled. " Age cannot wither it," nor " custom stale its variety." We ourselves have read, and shall continue to read it to our dying day; and we should not say thus much, especially on such an occasion, if we did not know that hundreds and thousands would do the same, whether they read it in this collection or not

Letter to a New-born Child.

BY CATHERINE TALBOT.

This lady, whose posthumous "Essays" and "Reflections" were admired in their day, was niece of Thomson's friend, Lord Chancellor Talbot; and the "very young correspondent" to whom her pleasant letter is addressed, was daughter of the Chancellor's third son, John, afterwards a Welsh judge, ancestor of the present Earl Talbot. What became of the little lady is not mentioned. Miss Talbot had very delicate health, which she bore with great sweetness of temper. She led a maiden life, and died in the year 1770, aged forty-nine.

YOU are heartily welcome, my dear little cousin, into this unquiet world; long may you continue in it, in all the happiness it can give, and bestow enough on all your friends to answer fully the impatience with which you have been expected. May you grow up to have every accomplishment that your good friend, the Bishop of Derry,* can already imagine in you; and in the meantime, may you have a nurse with a tuneable voice, that may not talk an immoderate deal of nonsense to you. You are at present, my dear, in a very philosophical disposition; the gaieties and follies of life have no attraction for you; its sorrows you kindly commiserate! but, however, do not suffer them to

* Thomas Rundle, another friend of Thomson's and the Chancellor's. See the note ensuing.

disturb your slumbers, and find charms in nothing but harmony and repose. You have as yet contracted no partialities, are entirely ignorant of party distinctions, and look with a perfect indifference on all human splendour. You have an absolute dislike to the vanities of dress; and are likely, for many months, to observe the Bishop of Bristol's first rule of conversation, Silence, though tempted to transgress it by the novelty and strangeness of all objects round you.* As you advance further in life, this philosophical temper will by degrees wear off; the first object of your admiration will probably be the candle, and thence (as we all of us do) you will contract a taste for the gaudy and the glaring, without making one moral reflection upon the danger of such false admiration as leads people many a time to burn their fingers. You will then begin to show great partiality for some very good aunts, who will contribute all they can towards spoiling you; but you will be equally fond of an excellent mamma who will teach you, by her example, all sorts of good qualities; only let me warn you of one thing, my dear, and that is, not to learn of her to have such an immoderate love of home as is quite contrary to all the privileges of this polite age, and to give up so entirely all those pretty graces of whim, flutter, and affection, which so many charitable poets have declared to be the prerogative of our sex. Oh! my poor cousin, to what purpose will you boast this prerogative, when your nurse tells you (with a pious care to sow

---

* The Bishop of Bristol, afterwards Archbishop of Canterbury, was Secker. His "first rule of conversation" is very good. It was on these two prelates that Pope wrote his couplet—

E'en in a bishop I can spy desert;
Secker is decent, Rundle has a heart.

By "decent" we are to understand the word in its classical sense of *becoming*.

the seeds of jealousy and emulation as early as possible) that you have a fine little brother " come to put your nose out of joint?" There will be nothing to be done then but to be mighty good; and prove what, believe me, admits of very little dispute (though it has occasioned abundance), that we girls, however people give themselves airs of being disappointed, are by no means to be despised. The men un-envied shine in public; but it is we must make their homes delightful to them—and, if they provoke us, no less un-comfortable. I do not expect you to answer this letter yet awhile; but, as I dare say you have the greatest interest with your papa, will beg you to prevail upon him that we may know by a line (before his time is engrossed by another secret committee) that you and your mamma are well. In the meantime, I will only assure you that all here rejoice in your existence extremely; and that I am, my very young correspondent, most affectionately yours, &c

The Schoolmistress.

BY SHENSTONE.

The Schoolmistress is one of those poems (delightful, to our thinking) which are to be read with a smile on the face, and thoughtfulness at heart:—the smile, for the assumption of dignity in its tone; the thoughtfulness, for the human interest of the subject. It is Shenstone's masterpiece. Its playful imitation of the manner of Spenser saved him from that inferior artificial style of the day, which injured the natural feeling of most of his other poems; and the manliness at the heart of its gentle wisdom ought to have saved the writer from the fears which he condescended to entertain, lest undiscerning critics should take it for something as dull as themselves. The poem has the pungent sweetness and balminess of the herbs described in its cottage garden. We never think of it without seeming to inhale their fragrance.

The good dame, the heroine of the poem, was the schoolmistress of Shenstone's own infancy. He was the offspring of a race now almost extinct, the small uneducated country-gentleman, farming his own estate; and he was sent to the first nurse-like teacher that presented herself in the neighbourhood. Her name was Sarah Lloyd. Let this be known, for the glory and encouragement of all such educers of infant "bards sublime," or future "Chancellors in embryo." The birch-tree is not in so much request as it was in her days. The "little bench of heedless bishops" may now look at it without "shaping it into rods," "and tingling at the view." The change is better for all parties, considering that a proper amount of healthy vigour, reflection, and superiority to petty pains is to be secured by better means. It is not for its mode of infant training that the poem is here reprinted; but for its urchness, its humour, its agreeable description, and the writer's thoughtful humanity.

  Ah me! full sorely is my heart forlorn,
   To think how modest worth neglected lies,
  While partial Fame doth with her blasts adorn
  Such deeds alone, as pride and pomp disguise;
  Deeds of ill sort, and mischievous emprize:
  Lend me thy clarion, goddess! let me try
  To sound the praise of merit, ere it dies;
  Such as I oft have chaunced to espy,
Lost in the dreary shades of dull obscurity.

  In every village mark'd with little spire,
  Embower'd in trees, and hardly known to fame,
  There dwells, in lowly shed and mean attire,
  A matron old, whom we Schoolmistress name:
  Who boasts unruly brats with birch to tame;
  They grieven sore in piteous durance pent,
  Aw'd by the power of this relentless dame;
  And oft-times, on vagaries idly bent,
For unkempt hair, or task unconn'd, are sorely shent.

  And all in sight doth rise a birchen tree,
  Which Learning near her little dome did stowe;
  Whilom a twig of small regard to see,
  Though now so wide its waving branches flow
  And work the simple vassals mickle woe;
  For not a wind might curl the leaves that blew,
  But their limbs shudder'd, and their pulse beat low,
  And as they look'd, they found their horror grew,
And shap'd it into rods, and tingled at the view.

  So I have seen (who has not, may conceive)
  A lifeless phantom near a garden plac'd;

So doth it wanton birds of peace bereave,
Of sport, of song, of pleasure, of repast;
They start, they stare, they wheel, they look aghast;
Sad servitude! such comfortless annoy
May no bold Briton's riper age e'er taste!
No superstition clog his chance of joy,
No vision empty, vain, his native bliss destroy.

Near to this dome is found a patch so green,
On which the tribe their gambols do display;
And at the door imprisoning board is seen,
Lest weakly wights of smaller size should stray,
Eager, perdie, to bask in sunny day!
The noises intermix'd, which thence resound,
Do learning's little tenement betray;
Where sits the dame, disguis'd in look profound,
And eyes her fairy throng, and turns her wheel around.

Her cap, far whiter than the driven snow,
Emblem right meet of decency does yield:
Her apron, dy'd in grain, is blue, I trowe,
As is the harebell that adorns the field:
And in her hand, for sceptre, she does wield
Tway birchen sprays with anxious fear entwin'd,
With dark distrust, and sad repentance fill'd,
And stedfast hate, and sharp affliction join'd,
And fury uncontroul'd, and chastisement unkind.*

Few but have ken'd, in semblance meet pourtray'd,
The childish faces of old Eol's train,
Libs, Notus, Auster;† these in frowns array'd,

* A memorial of the tremendous ingredients that composed the thunderbolts of Jupiter.
† The winds, in the likeness of children, puffing and blowing in the corners of old maps.

How then would fare or earth, or sky, or main,
Were the stern god to give his flaws the rein?
And were not she rebellious breasts to quell,
And were not she her statutes to maintain,
The cot no more, I ween, were deem'd the cell,
Where comely peace of mind and decent order dwell.

A russet stole was o'er her shoulders thrown;
A russet kirtle fenc'd the nipping air;
'T was simple russet, but it was her own;
'T was her own country bred the flock so fair;
'T was her own labour did the fleece prepare;
And, sooth to say, her pupils, rang'd around,
Through pious awe did term it passing rare:
For they in gaping wonderment abound,
And think, no doubt, she been the greatest wight on ground.

Albeit ne flattery did corrupt her truth,
Ne pompous title did debauch her ear;
Goody, good-woman, gossip, n'aunt, forsooth,
Or dame, the sole additions she did hear;
Yet these she challeng'd, these she held right dear;
Ne would esteem him act as mought behove,
Who should not honour'd eld with these revere;
For never title yet so mean could prove,
But there was eke a mind which did that title love.

One ancient hen she took delight to feed,
The plodding pattern of the busy dame;
Which, ever and anon, impell'd by need,
Into her school, begirt with chickens, came;
Such favour did her past deportment claim;
And if neglect had lavish'd on the ground

Fragment of bread, she would collect the same;
For well she knew, and quaintly could expound,
What sin it were to waste the smallest crumb she found.

Herbs, too, she knew, and well of each could speak,
That in her garden sipp'd the silvery dew;
Where no vain flower disclos'd a gaudy streak;
But herbs for use and physic not a few,
Of grey renown, within those borders grew;
The tufted basil, pun-provoking thyme,
Fresh baum, and marygold of cheerful hue:
The lowly gill,* that never dares to climb;
And more I fain would sing, disdaining here to rhyme.

Yet euphrasy may not be left unsung,
That gives dim eyes to wander leagues around;
And pungent radish, biting infant's tongue;
And plaintain ribb'd, that heals the reaper's wound;
And marjoram sweet, in shepherd's posie found;
And lavender, whose spikes of azure bloom
Shall be ere-while in arid bundles bound,
To lurk amidst the labours of her loom,
And crown her kerchiefs clean with mickle rare perfume;

And here trim rosemarine, that whilom crown'd
The daintiest garden of the proudest peer,
Ere, driven from its envy'd site, it found
A sacred shelter for its branches here,
Where edg'd with gold its glittering skirts appear.
Oh wassel days! O customs meet and well,
Ere this was banish'd from its lofty sphere!

* Ground-ivy.

Simplicity then sought this humble cell,
Nor ever would she more with thane and lordling dwell.*

Here oft the dame, on Sabbath's decent eve,
Hymnèd such psalms as Sternhold forth did mete;
If winter 't were, she to her hearth did cleave,
But in her garden found a summer-seat:
Sweet melody! to hear her then repeat
How Israel's sons, beneath a foreign king,
While taunting foemen did a song entreat,
All for the nonce, untuning every string,
Uphung their useless lyres—small heart had they to sing.

For she was just, and friend to virtuous lore,
And pass'd much time in truly virtuous deed;
And in those elfins' ears would oft deplore
The times when Truth by Popish rage did bleed,
And tortuous death was true devotion's meed,
And simple faith in iron chains did mourn,
That nould on wooden image place her creed;
And lawny saints in smouldering flames did burn:
Ah! dearest lord, forefend, thilk days should e'er return.

In elbow chair, like that of Scottish stem
By the sharp tooth of cankering eld defac'd,
In which, when he receives his diadem,
Our sovereign prince and liefest liege is plac'd,
The matron sate; and some with rank she grac'd,
(The source of children's and of courtiers' pride!)
Redress'd affronts (for vile affronts there pass'd)

† Rosemary was in great request as a flavourer of wine and ale, and hence it is associated by the poet with the wassail-bowl of old times.

And warn'd them not the fretful to deride,
But love each other dear, whatever them betide.

Right well she knew each temper to descry,
To thwart the proud, and the submiss to raise;
Some with vile copper-prize exalt on high,
And some entice with pittance small of praise;
And other some with baleful sprig she frays;
Ev'n absent, she the reins of power doth hold,
While with quaint arts the giddy crowd she sways;
Forewarn'd if little bird their pranks behold,
T will whisper in her ear, and all the scene unfold.

Lo! now with state she utters the command;
Eftsoons the urchins to their tasks repair;
Their books of stature small they take in hand,
Which with pellucid horn securèd are,
To save from finger wet the letters fair;
The work so gay, that on their back is seen,
St. George's high atchievements does declare;
On which thilk wight that has y-gazing been,
Kens the forthcoming rod;—unpleasing sight, I ween.

Ah luckless he, and born beneath the beam
Of evil star! it irks me whilst I write!
As erst the bard by Mulla's silver stream,*
Oft as he told of deadly dolorous plight,
Sigh'd as he sung, and did in tears indite.
For, brandishing the rod, she doth begin
To loose the brogues, the stripling's late delight!
And down they drop. Appears his dainty skin,
Fair as the furry coat of whitest ermilin

* Spencer. Mulla (Mole) is the river by which he dwelt in Ireland.

O ruthful scene! when from a nook obscure
His little sister doth his peril see:
All playful as she sate, she grows demure:
She finds all soon her wonted spirits flee;
She meditates a prayer to set him free;
Nor gentle pardon could this dame deny
(If gentle pardon did with dames agree)
To her sad grief, which swells in either eye,
And wrings her so that all for pity she could die.

No longer can she now her shrieks command,
And hardly she forbears, through awful fear,
To rushen forth, and with presumptuous hand,
To stay harsh justice in his mid-career.
On thee she calls, on thee, her parent dear!
(Ah! too remote to ward the shameful blow!)
She sees no kind domestic visage near,
And soon a flood of tears begins to flow,
And gives a loose at last to unavailing woe.

But ah! what pen his piteous plight may trace?
Or what device his loud laments explain?
The form uncouth of his disguisèd face?
The pallid hue that dyes his looks amain?
The plenteous shower that does his cheek distain?
When he in abject wise implores the dame,
Ne hopeth aught of sweet reprieve to gain;
Or when from high she levels well her aim,
And through the thatch his cries each falling stroke pro-
    claim.

The other tribe, aghast, with sore dismay,
Attend and con their tasks with mickle care;

By turns, astonied, every twig survey,
And from their fellow's hateful wounds beware,
Knowing, I wis, how each the same may share,
Till fear has taught them a performance meet,
And to the well-known chest the dame repair,
Whence oft with sugar'd cates she doth them greet,
And ginger-bread y-rare; now, certes, doubly sweet.

See to their seats they hie with merry glee,
And in beseemly order sitten there;
All but the wight of flesh y-gallèd;—he
Abhorreth bench, and stool, and fourm, and chair;
(This hand in mouth y-fix'd, that rends his hair;)
And eke with snubs profound, and heaving breast,
Convulsions intermitting, doth declare
His grievous wrong, his dame's unjust behest;
And scorns her offer'd love, and shuns to be caress'd.

His face besprent with liquid crystal shines,
His blooming face, that seems a purple flower,
Which low to earth its drooping head declines,
All smear'd and sullied by a vernal shower.
O the hard bosoms of despotic Power!
All, all but she, the author of his shame,
All, all but she, regret this mournful hour;
Yet hence the youth, and hence the flower, shall claim,
If so I deem aright, transcending worth and fame.

Behind some door in melancholy thought,
Mindless of food, he, dreary caitiff! pines;
Ne for his fellows' joyance careth aught,
But to the wind all merriment resigns,
And deems it shame if he to peace inclines;

And many a sullen look askance is sent,
Which for his dame's annoyance he designs;
And still the more to pleasure him she's bent,
The more doth he, perverse, her 'haviour past resent.

Ah me! how much I fear lest pride it be!
But if that pride it be, which thus inspires,
Beware, ye dames, with nice discernment see
Ye quench not, too, the sparks of nobler fires:
Ah! better far than all the Muse's lyres,
All coward arts, is valour's generous heat;
The firm fixt breast, which fit and right requires
Like Vernon's patriot soul,* more justly great
Than craft that pimps for ill, or flowery false deceit.

Yet, nurs'd, with skill, what dazzling fruits appear!
Ev'n now sagacious foresight points to show
A little bench of heedless bishops here,
And there a chancellor in embryo,
Or bard sublime (if bard may e'er be so)
As Milton, Shakspeare, names that ne'er shall die,
Though now he crawl along the earth so low,
Nor, weeting how the Muse should soar on high,
Wisheth, poor starvling elf! his paper kite may fly.

And this perhaps, who, censuring the design,
Low lays the house which that of cards doth build,
Shall Dennis be,† if rigid fate incline,
And many an epic to his rage shall yield;
And many a poet quit the Aonian field;
And, sour'd by age, profound he shall appear

* Admiral Vernon, the conqueror of Porto Bello.
† The famous snarling critic.

As he who now, with 'sdainful fury thrill'd,
Surveys mine work, and levels many a sneer,
And furls his wrinkly front, and cries, "What stuff is here!

But now Don Phœbus gains the middle skie,
And liberty unbars her prison-door,
And like a rushing torrent out they fly,
And now the grassy cirque han covered o'er
With boisterous revel-rout and wild uproar;
A thousand ways in wanton rings they run;
Heaven shield their short-liv'd pastimes, I implore!
For well may Freedom, erst so dearly won,
Appear to British elf more gladsome than the sun.

Enjoy, poor imps! enjoy your sportive trade,
And chace gay flies, and cull the fairest flowers;
For when my bones in grass-green sods are laid,
Then never may ye taste more careless hours
In knightly castles or in ladies' bowers.
O vain to seek delight in earthly things!
But most in courts, where proud ambition towers.
Deluded wight! who weens fair peace can spring
Beneath the pompous dome of kesar or of king.

See in each sprite some various bent appear!
These rudely carol must incondite lay;
Those sauntering on the green with jocund leer,
Salute the stranger passing on his way;
Some to the standing lake their courses bend,
Some builden fragile tenements of clay;
With pebbles smooth at duck and drake to play;
Thilk to the huxter's savory cottage tend,
In pastry kings and queens th' allotted mite to spend.

Here as each season yields a different store,
Each season's stores in order rangèd been;
Apples with cabbage-net y-covered o'er,
Galling full sore th' unmoney'd wight are seen;
And gooseb'rie, clad in livery red and green;
And here, of lovely dye, the catherine pear;
Fine pear! as lovely for thy juice, I ween;
O may no wight e'er pennyless come there,
Lest smit with ardent love he pine with hopeless care.

See!—Cherries here, ere cherries yet abound,
With thread so white in tempting posies ty'd,
Scattering like blooming maid their glances round,
With pamper'd look draw little eyes aside,
And must be bought, though penury betide.
The plum all azure, and the nut all brown,
And here, each season, do those cakes abide,
Whose honour'd names th' inventive city own,
Rendering through Britain's isle Salopia's praises known.*

Admired Salopia! that with venial pride
Eyes her bright form in Severn's ambient wave,
Fam'd for her loyal cares in perils try'd,†
Her daughters lovely, and her striplings brave;
Ah! midst the rest, may flowers adorn his grave,
Whose art did first these dulcet cates display;
A motive fair to Learning's imps he gave,
Who cheerless o'er her darkling region stray,
Till Reason's morn arise, and light them on their way.

* Shrewsbury cakes.
† Shrewsbury, the capital of Shenstone's native county, was devoted to the cause of Charles the First.

Grown Schoolboys.

A LETTER FROM HORACE WALPOLE TO HIS FRIEND GEORGE MONTAGU.

GEORGE MONTAGU, one of Horace Walpole's schoolfellows at Eton, was of the Halifax branch of the family of that name. He became Member of Parliament for Northampton, and Private Secretary to Lord North while Chancellor of the Exchequer.

Walpole, who was now at Cambridge, in his nineteenth year, does not write so correctly as he did afterwards; yet the germ of his wit is very evident in this letter; also of his foppery or effeminacy; and some may think, of his alleged heartlessness. A wit he was of the first water; effeminate too, no doubt, though he prided himself on his open-breasted waistcoats in his old age, and possessed exquisite good sense and discernment, where party-feelings did not blind him. But of the charge of heartlessness, his zeal and painstaking in behalf of a hundred people, and his beautiful letter to his friend Conway in particular, offering, in a way not to be doubted, to share his fortune with him (see *Correspondence*, vol. i. p. 358), ought to acquit him by acclamation.

The letter, here presented to the reader, is (with some qualification as to prettiness of manner) a perfect exhibition of the thoughts and feelings that go through the mind of a romantic schoolboy. How good is his wishing to have had a kingdom, "only for the pleasure of *being driven from it*, and living disguised in an *humble vale!*"

KING'S COLLEGE, May 6th, 1736.

DEAR GEORGE,
I agree with you entirely in the pleasure you take in talking over old stories, but can't say but I meet every day with new circumstances, which will be still more pleasure

to me to recollect. I think at our age 't is excess of joy, to think, while we are running over past happiness, that it is still in our power to enjoy as great. Narrations of the greatest actions of other people are tedious in comparison of the serious trifles that every man can call to mind of himself while he was learning those histories. Youthful passages of life are the chippings of Pitt's diamond, set into little heart-rings with mottos; the stone itself more worth, the filings more gentle and agreeable. Alexander, at the head of the world, never tasted the true pleasure that boys of his own age have enjoyed at the head of a school. Little intrigues, little schemes, and policies engage their thoughts; and at the same time that they are laying the foundations for their middle age of life, the mimic republic they live in furnishes materials of conversation for their latter age; and old men cannot be said to be children a second time with greater truth from any one cause, than their living over again their childhood in imagination. To reflect on the season when first they felt the titillation of love, the budding passions, and the first dear object of their wishes! how unexperienced they gave credit to all the tales of romantic loves! Dear George, were not the playing fields at Eton food for all manner of flights? No old maid's gown, though it had been tormented into all the fashions from King James to King George, ever underwent so many transformations as those poor plains have in my idea. At first I was contented with tending a visionary flock, and sighing some pastoral name to the echo of the cascade under the bridge. How happy should I have been to have had a kingdom, only for the pleasure of being driven from it, and living disguised in an humble vale! As I got further into Virgil and Clelia,* I found myself transported from Arca-

* An old French romance, founded on Roman history.

dia to the garden of Italy; and saw Windsor Castle in no other view than the *Capitoli immobile saxum.** I wish a committee of the House of Commons may ever seem to be the senate; or a bill appear half so agreeable as a billet-doux. You see how deep you have carried me into old stories; I write of them with pleasure, but shall talk of them with more to you. I can't say I am sorry I was never quite a schoolboy: an expedition against bargemen, or a match at cricket, may be very pretty things to recollect; but thank my stars, I can remember things that are very near as pretty. The beginning of my Roman history was spent in the asylum,† or conversing in Egeria's hallowed grove; not in thumping and pummelling King Amulius's herdsmen. I was sometimes troubled with a rough creature or two from the plough; one that, one should have thought, had worked with his head, as well as his hands, they were both so callous. One of the most agreeable circumstances I can recollect is the Triumvirate, composed of yourself, Charles,‡ and Your sincere Friend.

* "The immovable rock of the Capitol."
† The infant city of Rome, when it was a refuge for offenders.
‡ Charles Montagu, brother of George, afterwards a general in the army. Another of these schoolboy coteries was called the Quadruple Alliance, and consisted of Walpole, Gray, West, and Ashton (afterwards a clergyman). Walpole's schoolfellows gave themselves names out of the classics and old romances, such as Tydeus, Plato, Oroondates, and Almanzor. Such things have always been going on in schools, and always will as long as schools continue to be worth anything at all, and cultivate a respect for generous and exalted sentiments.

Ode on Solitude.

WRITTEN BY POPE AT TWELVE YEARS OF AGE.

Pope never wrote more agreeable or well-tuned verses than this interesting effusion of his boyhood. Indeed there is an intimation of sweetness and variety in the versification, which was not borne out afterwards by his boasted smoothness: nor can we help thinking, that had the author of the *Ode on Solitude* arisen in less artificial times, he would have turned out to be a still finer poet than he was. But the reputation which he easily acquired for wit and criticism, the recent fame of Dryden, and perhaps even his little warped and fragile person, tempted him to accept such power over his contemporaries as he could soonest realize.

It is observable that Pope never repeated the form of verse in which this poem is written. It might have reminded him of a musical feeling he had lost. All the little concluding lines of the stanzas have a spirited yet touching modulation, very unusual with him afterwards:—

> In his own ground—
> In winter fire—
> Quiet by day, &c.

The closeness and straightforwardness of the style are remarkable in so young a writer, and singularly announce his future conciseness. The reader smiles to think of the unambitious wish expressed in the final stanza; yet it is pleasant to consider that the youthful poet remained true to his love of the country all his life; and still more pleasant, that he was rich enough to indulge it. The Ode was probably written at Binfield in Windsor Forest, when he was a happy child, living with his father and mother, and feeling the first delighted power of making verses, in scenery fitted to inspire them.

HAPPY the man whose wish and care
    A few paternal acres bound,
Content to breathe his native air
    In his own ground:

Whose herds with milk, whose fields with bread,
    Whose flocks supply him with attire,
Whose trees in summer yield him shade,
    In winter fire.

Blest who can unconcern'dly find
    Hours, days, and years slide soft away,
In health of body, peace of mind,
    Quiet by day,

Sound sleep by night; study and ease,
    Together mix'd; sweet recreation;
And innocence, which most doth please
    With meditation.

Thus let me live, unseen, unknown;
    Thus unlamented let me die;
Steal from the world, and not a stone
    Tell where I lie.

Sir Bertrand.—A Fragment.

BY DR. AIKIN.

If we may judge of others' impressions by our own, and have not been led to overrate the merit of this Fragment by early associations, there is nothing perused in boyhood which is of a nature to remain longer in the recollection, or to link itself more strongly with analogous ideas. The tolling bell, the bloody stump of the arm, the lady who addresses the knight "in these words" (not related), and above all, the "dreary moors" at the commencement, and the light seen at a distance, have recurred, we think, oftener to memory in the course of our life than any other passages in books, with the exception of some in Gray, Spenser, and the Arabian Nights. We cannot read them to this day without feeling a sort of thrilling and desolate evening gloom fall upon our mind; nor can we ever see a piece of moorland, or a distant light at the close of day, without thinking of them. The finest poetry has only added to their impression; not displaced it. The "woulds" that Sir Bertrand crosses, are precisely those in which the ear listens at evening to

> "Undescribed sounds,
> That come a-swooning over hollow grounds,
> And wither drearily on barren moors."

Dr. Aikin was a writer from whom this effusion was hardly to have been looked for. He was bred in a limited and somewhat formal school of taste, and was no very sensitive critic; but a good deal of enthusiasm was repressed in him by circumstances; and he was brother of an undoubted and fervid woman of genius, Mrs. Barbauld. There was more in the Aikin family than academical and sectarian connections suffered to come out of it.

SIR BERTRAND turned his steed towards the woulds, hoping to cross these dreary moors before the curfew. But ere he had proceeded half his journey, he was bewildered by the different tracks; and not being able, as far as the eye could reach, to espy any object but the brown heath surrounding him, he was at length quite uncertain which way he should direct his course. Night overtook him in this situation. It was one of those nights when the moon gives a faint glimmering of light through the thick black clouds of a louring sky. Now and then she emerged in full splendour from her veil, and then instantly retired behind it, having just served to give the forlorn Sir Bertrand a wide extended prospect over the desolate waste. Hope and native courage awhile urged him to push forwards, but at length the increasing darkness and fatigue of body and mind overcame him; he dreaded moving from the ground he stood on, for fear of unknown pits and bogs; and alighting from his horse in despair, he threw himself on the ground. He had not long continued in that posture when the sullen toll of a distant bell struck his ears—he started up, and turning towards the sound, discerned a dim twinkling light. Instantly he seized his horse's bridle, and with cautious steps advanced towards it. After a painful march he was stopt by a moated ditch surrounding the place from whence the light proceeded; and by a momentary glimpse of moon-light he had a full view of a large antique mansion, with turrets at the corners, and an ample porch in the centre. The injuries of time were strongly marked on everything about it. The roof in various places was fallen in, the battlements were half demolished, and the windows broken and dismantled. A draw-bridge, with a ruinous gate-way at each end, led to the court before the building. He entered; and instantly the light, which proceeded from a window in one of the turrets, glided along and vanished; at the same moment the moon sunk beneath a black cloud, and the night was darker than ever. All was silent.— Sir Bertrand fastened his steed under a shed, and approaching the house, traversed its whole front with light and slow footsteps.—All was still as death.—He looked in at the lower windows, but could not distinguish a single object through the impenetrable gloom. After a short parley with himself, he entered the porch, and seizing a massy iron knocker at the gate, lifted it up, and, hesitating, at length struck a loud stroke.—The noise resounded through the whole mansion with hollow echoes.—All was still again— he repeated the strokes more boldly and loudly—another interval ensued—a third time he knocked, and a third time all was still. He then fell back to some distance, that he might discern whether any light could be seen in the whole front. It again appeared in the same place, and quickly glided away as before—at the same instant a deep sullen toll sounded from the turret. Sir Bertrand's heart made a fearful stop—he was a while motionless; then terror impelled him to make some hasty steps towards his steed— but shame stopt his flight; and urged by honour and a resistless desire of finishing the adventure, he returned to the porch; and working up his soul to a full steadiness of resolution, he drew forth his sword with one hand, and with the other lifted up the latch of the gate. The heavy door, creaking upon its hinges, reluctantly yielded to his hand— he applied his shoulder to it, and forced it open—he quitted it, and stepped forward—the door instantly shut with a 'hundering clap. Sir Bertrand's blood was chilled—he turned back to find the door, and it was long ere his trembling hands could seize it: but his utmost strength could not open it again. After several ineffectual attempts, he looked behind him, and beheld, across a hall, upon a large staircase, a pale bluish flame, which cast a dismal gleam of light around. He again summoned forth his courage, and advanced towards it. It retired. He came to the foot of the stairs, and after a moment's deliberation ascended. He went slowly up, the flame retiring before him, till he came to a wide gallery. The flame proceeded along it, and he followed in silent horror, treading lightly, for the echoes of his footsteps startled him. It led him to the foot of another staircase, and then vanished. At the same instant another toll sounded from the turret—Sir Bertrand felt it strike upon his heart. He was now in total darkness, and with his arms extended, began to ascend the second staircase. A dead cold hand met his left hand, and firmly grasped it, drawing him forcibly forwards—he endeavored to disengage himself, but could not—he made a furious blow with his sword, and instantly a loud shriek pierced his ears, and the dead hand was left powerless with his—He dropt it, and rushed forward with a desperate valour. The stairs were narrow and winding, and interrupted by frequent breaches, and loose fragments of stone. The staircase grew narrower and narrower, and at length terminated in a low iron grate. Sir Bertrand pushed it open—it led to an intricate winding passage, just large enough to admit a person upon his hands and knees. A faint glimmering of light served to show the nature of the place. Sir Bertrand entered. A deep hollow groan resounded from a distance through the vault. He went forwards, and proceeding beyond the first turning, he discerned the same blue flame which had before conducted him. He followed it. The vault at length suddenly opened into a lofty gallery, in the midst of which a figure appeared, completely armed, thrusting forwards the bloody stump of an arm with a terrible frown and menacing gesture, and brandishing a sword in his hand. Sir Bertrand undauntedly sprung forwards, and aiming a fierce blow at the figure, it instantly vanished, letting fall a massy iron key. The flame now rested upon a pair of ample folding-doors at the end of the gallery. Sir Bertrand went up to it, and applied the key to a brazen lock—with difficulty he turned the bolt—instantly the doors flew open, and discovered a large apartment, at the end of which was a coffin rested upon a bier, with a taper burning upon each side of it. Along the room on both sides were gigantic statues of black marble, attired in the Moorish habit, and holding enormous sabres in their right hands. Each of them reared his arm, and advanced one leg forwards, as the knight entered; at the same moment the lid of the coffin flew open, and the bell tolled. The flame still glided forwards, and Sir Bertrand resolutely followed, till he arrived within six paces of the coffin. Suddenly, a lady in a shroud and black veil rose up in it, and stretched out her arms towards him; at the same time the statues clashed their sabres and advanced. Sir Bertrand flew to the lady and clasped her in his arms—she threw up her veil and kissed his lips; and instantly the whole building shook as with an earthquake, and fell asunder with a horrible crash. Sir Bertrand was thrown into a sudden trance, and on recovering, found himself seated on a velvet sofa, in the most magnificent room he had ever seen, lighted with innumerable tapers, in lustres of pure crystal. A sumptuous banquet was set in the middle. The doors opening to soft music, a lady of incomparable beauty, attired with amazing splendour, entered, surrounded by a troop of gay nymphs more fair than the Graces. She advanced to the knight, and falling on her knees thanked him as her deliverer. The nymphs placed a garland of laurel upon his head, and the lady led him by the hand to the banquet, and sat beside him. The nymphs placed themselves at the table, and a numerous train of servants entering, served up the feast, delicious music playing all the time. Sir Bertrand could not speak for astonishment—he could only return their honours by courteous looks and gestures. After the banquet was finished, all retired but the lady, who leading back the knight to the sofa, addressed him in these words:——

Robinson Crusoe.

THE FIVE POINTS IN HIS HISTORY.

THESE are Crusoe's loneliness, his contrivances how to live, his discovery of the footmark on the sea-shore, his first sight of the savages, and his obtainment of a companion and servant in Friday. The second, though the least surprising, is the one most habitually felt by the reader; the one he oftenest thinks of. It is indeed the main subject of the book. But, as its interest spreads over the greater part of it, and could only be duly represented by copious extracts (minuteness of detail being necessary to do justice to its ingenuity and perseverance) it would have occupied too large a share of these pages. The lesser quantity and more startling quality of the other points render them obviously fittest for selection. The loneliness, which is in itself a *one-ness*, can be well enough represented by one impressive extract; the footmark is essentially one (never was there a finer *unique*); the first sight of the savages is of the same brief and independent order of interest; and two "man Fridays" are not in the regions of possibility. Peter Wilkins's "man Friday" was obliged to be turned into a woman, and Philip Quarll's into a monkey.

Robinson Crusoe is understood to be founded on the real history of Alexander Selkirk, a summary of which, charmingly written, was given to the public by Steele. The greatest genius might have been proud to paint a picture after that sketch. Yet we are not sure that Selkirk's adventure was not an injury, instead of a benefit to De Foe. A benefit it undoubtedly was, to him and to all of us, if it was required in order to put the thought into De Foe's head; but what we mean is, that the world would probably have had the fiction, whether the fact had existed or not. Desert islands and cast-away mariners existed before Selkirk: children have played at hermits and house-building, even before they read Robinson Crusoe; and the whole inimitable romance would have required but a glance of De Foe's eye upon a child at play, or at a page in an old book of voyages, or even at his own restless and isolated thoughts. This is a conjecture, however, impossible to prove; and we only throw it out in justice to an original genius. After all, it would make little difference; for Selkirk was not Crusoe, nor did he see the ghost of a human footstep, nor obtain a man Friday. The inhabitant of the island was De Foe himself.

May we add, nevertheless, that when De Foe thought himself most himself, he was least clever and least pleasant? We were not so disappointed with the Second Part of Crusoe as we expected to be, when we read the book over again the other day, but still it is very inferior; not wanted; not even of a piece; for Crusoe's isolation is the charm. Who cares, after that, for a common settlement? We dread even the remaining of the savages on the island; not for fear they should eat Robinson, but lest they should become friends with him, and make up a dinner-party. Man Friday is quite enough. He is single and subordinate, and does but administer to the superiority of his master.

De Foe did better with one person than with many. He was a very honest man, and very good at conceiving matters of fact; but it is curious to see how impossible he finds it, even in a fiction, to present any thing to his imagination which does not come palpably home to a man's worldly or other-worldly interest and importance; and how fond he is, whether alone or in company, of being all in all; of playing the "monarch of all he surveys," and dictating people's religion and politics to them the moment he catches a listener. He was the prose half of as inventive a genius as ever existed: and his footstep on the sea-shore has left its mark within the borders of the greatest poetry; but it originated, so to speak, in the same intense spirit of self-reference. It was the one isolated Robinson Crusoe reflected by some one other tremendous individual, come to contest with him his safety and his independence. The abstract idea of a multitude followed it; but what would their presence have been in comparison? What would a thousand footsteps have been? The face of things would have been changed at once, and Crusoe's face have no longer matched it. All the savages

...rwards never tread out that footmark: nor does Crusoe allow them to remain, and run the chance of it.

It is observable, that De Foe never invented a hero to write about greater than himself; while, at the same time, he willingly recorded such as were inferior. No rogue or vagabond came amiss to him, any more than a mariner or a merchant. And it is curious to consider how heartily such a minute dealer in matter of fact could set about telling a lie;—at least what a deliberate and successful one he told about the *Ghost of Mrs. Veal;* a long-credited fiction which he invented at the request of a bookseller, in order to sell a devout publication. His *History of the Plague* was long considered equally true, and reaped a like success. But the fact is, it is a mistake to suppose De Foe a lover of truth in any other sense than that of a workman's love for his tools, or for any other purpose than that of a masterly use of it, and a consciousness of the mastery. We do not mean to dispute his veracity between man and man: though his peculiar genius may not have been without its recommendation of him to that secret government agency in which he was at one time employed under his hero, William the Third. But the singularly material and mechanical nature of that genius, great as it was, while it hindered him from missing no impressions which could be made personally on himself as a creature of flesh and blood, kept him unembarrassed with any of the more perplexing truths suggested by too much thought and by imaginations poetical; and hence it is, that defect itself conspired to perfect and keep clear his astonishing impress of matter of fact, and render him an object of admiration, great, but not of an exalted kind. De Foe was in one respect as unvulgar a man as can be conceived; nobody but Swift could have surpassed him in such a work as *Robinson Crusoe;* yet we cannot conceal from ourselves, that something vulgar adheres to our idea of the author of *Moll Flanders,* the *Complete English Tradesman,* and even of *Robinson* himself. He has no music, no thorough style, no accomplishments, no love; but he can make wonderful shift without them all; was great in the company of man Friday; and he has rendered his shipwrecked solitary immortal.

CRUSOE'S MEDITATIONS AND MODE OF LIFE.

EVIL.	GOOD.
I AM cast upon an horrible desolate island: void of all hope of recovery.	But I am alive, and not drowned, as all my ship's company was.
I am singled out and separated as it were from the world, to be miserable.	But I am singled out too from all the ship's crew, to be spared from death; and He that miraculously saved me from death, can deliver me from this condition.
I am divided from mankind, a solitary, one banished from human society.	But I am not starved and perishing on a barren place, affording no sustenance.
I have no clothes to cover me.	But I am in an hot climate, where, if I had clothes, I could hardly wear them.
I am without any defence or means to resist any violence of man or beast.	But I am cast upon an island where I see no wild beasts to hurt me, as I saw on the coast of Africa: and what if I had been shipwrecked there?
I have no soul to speak to or relieve me.	But God wonderfully sent the ship in, near enough to the shore, that I have gotten out so many necessary things, as will either supply my wants or enable me to supply myself, even as long as I live.

Upon the whole, here was an undoubted testimony that

there was scarce any condition in the world so miserable, but there was something negative, or something positive, to be thankful in it; and let this stand as a direction from the experience of the most miserable of all conditions in this world, that we may always find in it something to comfort ourselves from, and to set, in the description of good and evil, on the credit side of the account.

You are to understand that I now had, as I may call it, two plantations in the island: one, my little fortification or tent, with the wall about it, under the rock, with the cave behind me, which by this time I had enlarged into several apartments or caves, one within another. One of these, which was the driest and largest, and had a door out beyond my wall or fortification, that is to say, beyond where my wall joined to the rock, was all filled up with the large earthen pots, of which I have given an account, and with fourteen or fifteen great baskets, which would hold five or six bushels each, where I laid up my stores of provision, especially my corn; some in the ear, cut off short from the straw, and the other rubbed out with my hand.

As for my wall, made, as before, with long stakes or piles, those piles grew all like trees, and were by this time grown so big, and spread so very much, that there was not the least appearance, to any one's view, of any habitation behind them.

Near this dwelling of mine, but a little farther within the land, and upon lower ground, lay my two pieces of corn-ground; which I kept duly cultivated and sowed, and which duly yielded me their harvest in its season; and whenever I had occasion for more corn, I had more land adjoining as fit as that.

Besides this, I had my country seat, and I had now a tolerable plantation there also; for first, I had my little bower, as I called it, which I kept in repair; that is to say, I kept the hedge which circled it in constantly fitted up to its usual height, the ladder standing always in the inside; I kept the trees, which at first were no more than my stakes, but were now grown very firm and tall; I kept them always so cut, that they might spread and grow thick and wild, and make the more agreeable shade, which they did effectually to my mind. In the middle of this I had my tent always standing, being a piece of a sail spread over poles set up for that purpose, and which never wanted any repair or renewing; and under this I had made me a squab or couch, with the skins of the creatures I had killed, and with other soft things, and a blanket laid on them, such as belonged to our sea-bedding, which I had saved, and a great watch-coat to cover me; and here, whenever I had occasion to be absent from my chief seat, I took up my country habitation.

Adjoining to this I had my inclosures for my cattle, that is to say, my goats; and as I had taken an inconceivable deal of pains to fence and inclose this ground, I was so uneasy to see it kept entire, lest the goats should break through, that I never left off, till with infinite labour I had stuck the outside of the hedge so full of small stakes, and so near to one another, that it was rather a pale than a hedge, and there was scarce room to put a hand through between them; which, afterwards, when those stakes grew, as they all did in the next rainy season, made the inclosure strong, like a wall; indeed stronger than any wall.

This will testify for me that I was not idle, and that I spared no pains to bring to pass whatever appeared necessary for my comfortable support; for I considered, the keeping up a breed of tame creatures thus at my hand would be a living magazine of flesh, milk, butter, and cheese for me as long as I lived in the place, if it were to be forty years;

and that keeping them in my reach depended entirely upon my perfecting my inclosures to such a degree, that I might be sure of keeping them together: which, by this method, indeed, I so effectually secured, that when these little stakes began to grow, I had planted them so very thick, I was forced to pull some of them up again.

In this place also I had my grapes growing, which I principally depended on for my winter store of raisins, and which I never failed to preserve very carefully, as the best and most agreeable dainty of my whole diet: and, indeed, they were not agreeable only, but physical, wholesome, nourishing, and refreshing to the last degree.

As this was also about half way between my other habitation and the place where I had laid up my boat, I generally staid and lay here in my way thither; for I used frequently to visit my boat, and I kept all things about or belonging to her in very good order; sometimes I went out in her to divert myself, but no more hazardous voyages would I go, nor scarce ever above a stone's cast or two from the shore, I was so apprehensive of being hurried out of my knowledge again by the currents or winds, or any other accident. But now I come to a new scene of my life.

HE FINDS THE PRINT OF A MAN'S FOOT ON THE SEA-SHORE.

It happened one day about noon, going towards my boat, I was exceedingly surprised with the print of a man's naked foot on the shore, which was very plain to be seen in the sand: I stood like one thunderstruck, or as if I had seen an apparition; I listened, I looked round me, I could hear nothing, nor see anything; I went up to a rising ground to look farther; I went up the shore, and down the shore, but it was all one; I could see no other impression but that one. I went to it again to see if there were any more, and to observe if it might not be my fancy; but there was no room for that, for there was exactly the very print of a foot, toes, heel, and every part of a foot; how it came thither I knew not, nor could in the least imagine. But after innumerable fluttering thoughts, like a man perfectly confused and out of myself, I came home to my fortification, not feeling, as we say, the ground I went on, but terrified to the last degree, looking behind me at every two or three steps, mistaking every bush and tree, and fancying every stump at a distance to be a man; nor is it possible to describe how many various shapes an affrighted imagination represented things to me in; how many wild ideas were formed every moment in my fancy, and what strange unaccountable whimsies came into my thoughts by the way.

When I came to my castle, for so I think I called it ever after this, I fled into it like one pursued; whether I went over by the ladder, as first contrived, or went in at the hole in the rock, which I called a door, I cannot remember: for never frighted hare fled to cover, or fox to earth, with more terror of mind than I to this retreat.

I had no sleep that night; the farther I was from the occasion of my fright, the greater my apprehensions were; which is something contrary to the nature of such things, and especially to the usual practice of all creatures in fear. But I was so embarrassed with my own frightful ideas of the thing, that I formed nothing but dismal imaginations to myself, even though I was now a great way off it. Sometimes I fancied it must be the devil; and reason joined with me upon this supposition; for how should any other thing in human shape come into the place? Where was the vessel that brought them? What marks were there of any other footsteps? and how was it possible a man should come there? But then to think that Satan should take human shape upon him in such a place, where there could be no manner of occasion for it, but to leave the print of his foot behind him, and that even for no purpose too (for he could not be sure I should see it); this was an amazement the other way. I considered that the devil might have found out abundance of other ways to have terrified me, than this of the single print of a foot; that as I lived quite on the other side of the island, he would never have been so simple to leave a mark in a place where it was ten thousand to one whether I should ever see it or not; and in the sand too, which the first surge of the sea upon an high wind would have defaced entirely. All this seemed inconsistent with the thing itself, and with all notions we usually entertain of the subtlety of the devil.

Abundance of such things as these assisted to argue me out of all apprehensions of its being the devil; and I presently concluded then, that it must be some more dangerous creature, viz., that it must be some of the savages of the mainland over against me, who had wandered out to sea in their canoes; and, either driven by the currents, or by contrary winds, had made the island; and had been on shore, but were gone away again to sea, being as loath, perhaps, to have staid in this desolate island, as I would have been to have had them.

While these reflections were rolling upon my mind, I was very thankful in my thought, that I was so happy as not to be thereabouts at that time, or that they did not see my boat, by which they would have concluded that some inhabitants had been in the place, and, perhaps, have searched further for me. Then terrible thoughts racked my imaginations about their having found my boat, and that there were people here; and that, if so, I should certainly have them come again in greater numbers, and devour me; that, if it should happen so that they should not find me, yet they would find my inclosure, destroy all my corn, carry away all my stock of tame goats, and I should perish at last for mere want.

Thus my fear banished all my religious hope. All that former confidence in God, which was founded upon such wonderful experience, as I had had of his goodness, now vanished; as if he that had fed me by a miracle hitherto, could not preserve by his power the provision which he had made for me by his goodness. I reproached myself with my easiness, that would not sow any more corn one year than would just serve me until the next season, as if no accident could intervene to prevent my enjoying the crop that was upon the ground; and this I thought so just a reproof, that I resolved for the future to have two or three years' corn beforehand, so that whatever might come, I might not perish for want of bread.

How strange a chequer-work of Providence is the life of man! and by what secret differing springs are the affections hurried about, as differing circumstances present! To-day we love what to-morrow we hate; to-day we seek what to-morrow we shun; to-day we desire what to-morrow we fear, nay, even tremble at the apprehensions of. This was exemplified in me at this time in the most lively manner imaginable; for I, whose only affliction was, that I seemed banished from human society; that I was alone, circumscribed by the boundless ocean, cut off from mankind, and condemned to what I call a silent life; that I was as one whom Heaven thought not worthy to be numbered among the living, or to appear among the rest of his creatures; that to have seen one of my own species would have seemed to me a raising me from death to life, and the greatest blessing that Heaven itself, next to the supreme blessing of Salvation, could bestow; I say, that I should now tremble at the very apprehension of seeing a man, and was ready to sink into the ground at but the shadow or silent appearance of a man's having set his foot on the island.

HE SEES SAVAGES ON THE ISLAND, AND OBTAINS A SERVANT.

In the middle of these cogitations, apprehensions, and reflections, it came into my thoughts one day, that all this might be a mere chimera of my own, and that this foot might be the print of my own foot, when I came on shore from my boat. This cheered me up a little too, and I began to persuade myself it was all a delusion; that it was nothing else but my own foot; and why might not I come that way from the boat, as well as I was going that way to the boat? Again I considered also, that I could by no means tell for certain where I had trod, and where I had not; and that if at last this was only the print of my own foot, I had played the part of those fools who strive to make stories of spectres and apparitions, and then are themselves frighted at them more than anybody else.

Now I began to take courage, and to peep abroad again: for I had not stirred out of my castle for three days and nights, so that I began to starve for provision; for I had little or nothing within doors, but some barley-cakes and water. Then I knew that my goats wanted to be milked, too, which usually was my evening diversion; and the poor creatures were in great pain and inconvenience for want of it; and indeed it almost spoiled some of them, and almost dried up their milk.

Heartening myself therefore with the belief that this

was nothing but the print of one of my own feet (and so might be truly said to start at my own shadow), I began to go abroad again, and went to my country house to milk my flock. But to see with what fear I went forward, how often I looked behind me, how I was ready every now and then to lay down my basket and run for my life, it would have made any one have thought I was haunted with an evil conscience, or that I had been lately most terribly frighted; and so indeed I had.

However, as I went down thus two or three days, and having seen nothing, I began to be a little bolder, and to think there was really nothing in it but my own imagination; but I could not persuade myself fully of this, till I should go down to the shore again, and see this print of a foot, and measure it by my own, and see if there was any similitude or fitness, that I might be assured it was my own foot: but when I came to the place, first it appeared evidently to me that when I laid up my boat, I could not possibly be on shore any where thereabouts; secondly, when I came to measure the mark with my own foot, I found my foot not so long by a great deal. Both these things filled my head with new imaginations, and gave me the vapours again to the highest degree; so that I shook with cold, like one in an ague; and I went home again filled with a belief, that some man or men had been on shore there; or, in short, that the island was inhabited, and I might be surprised before I was aware; and what course to take for my security I knew not.

About a year and a half after I had entertained these notions, and by long musing had, as it were, resolved them all into nothing. I was surprised one morning early with seeing no less than five canoes all on shore together, on my side the island, and the people who belonged to them all landed and out of my sight. The number of them broke all my measures; for seeing so many, and knowing that they always came four or six or sometimes more in a boat, I could not tell what to think of it, or how to take my measures, to attack twenty or thirty men single-handed; so I lay still in my castle, perplexed and discomforted; however, I put myself into all the same postures for an attack that I had formerly provided, and was just ready for action, if anything had presented itself, having waited a good while listening to hear if they made any noise. At length, being very impatient, I set my guns at the foot of my ladder, and clambered up to the top of the hill by my two stages as usual; standing so, however, that my head did not appear above the hill: so that they could not perceive me by any means. Here I observed, by the help of my perspective glass, that there were no less than thirty in number, that they had a fire kindled, and that they had meat dressed; how they cooked it, that I knew not, or what it was; but they were all dancing in I know not how many barbarous gestures and figures, their own way, round the fire.

When I was thus looking on them, I perceived by my perspective two miserable wretches dragged from the boats, where it seems they were laid by, and were now brought out for the slaughter. I perceived one of them immediately fall, being knocked down, I suppose, with a club or wooden sword, for that was their way; and two or three others were at work immediately, cutting him open for their cookery, while the other victim was left standing by himself till they should be ready for him. In that very moment, this poor wretch seeing himself a little at liberty, nature inspired him with hopes of life, and he started away from them, and ran along the sands with incredible swiftness directly towards me; I mean towards that part of the coast where my habitation was.

I was dreadfully frighted (that I must acknowledge) when I perceived him to run my way; and especially when, as I thought, I saw him pursued by the whole body. There was between them and my castle the creek, which I mentioned often at the first part of my story, when I landed my cargoes out of the ship; and this I knew he must necessarily swim over, or the poor wretch would be taken there; but when the savage escaping came thither, he made nothing of it, though the tide was then up; but plunging in, swam through in about thirty strokes or thereabouts, landed, and ran on with exceeding strength and swiftness. When the three pursuers came to the creek, I found that two of them could swim, but the third could not, and that he, standing on the other side, looked at the others, but went no farther, and soon after went softly back again; which, as it happened, was very well for him in the main.

I observed that the two who swam were yet more than twice as long swimming over the creek than the fellow was that fled from them; it came now very warmly upon my thoughts, and indeed irresistibly, that now was my time to get me a servant, and perhaps a companion or assistant, and that I was called plainly by Providence to save this poor creature's life. I immediately got down the ladder with all possible expedition, fetched my two guns, for they were both at the foot of the ladder, as I observed above; and getting up again with the same haste to the top of the hill, I crossed towards the sea; and, having a very short cut, and all down hill, clapped myself in the way between the pursuers and the pursued, hallooing aloud to him that fled, who looking back, was at first perhaps as much frightened at me as at them; but I beckoned with my hand to him to come back; and in the meantime I slowly advanced towards the two that followed; then rushing at once upon the foremost, I knocked him down with the stock of my piece: I was loath to fire, because I would not have the rest hear; though at that distance it would not have been easily heard; and being out of sight of the smoke too, they would not have easily known what to make of it. Having knocked this fellow down, the other who pursued him stopped, as if he had been frightened, and I advanced a pace towards him; but as I came nearer, I perceived presently he had a bow and arrow, and was fitting it to shoot at me; so I was then necessitated to shoot at him first, which I did, and killed him at the first shot. The poor savage who fled but had stopped, though he saw both his enemies fallen and killed (as he thought), yet was so frighted with the fire and noise of my piece, that he stood stock-still, and neither came forward nor went backward, though he seemed rather inclined to fly still than to come on. I hallooed again to him and made signs to come forward, which he easily understood, and came a little way, then stopped again, and then a little farther, and then stopped again; and I could then perceive that he stood trembling, as if he had been taken prisoner, and had just been to be killed, as his two enemies were. I beckoned him again to come to me, and gave him all the signs of encouragement that I could think of; and he came nearer and nearer, kneeling down every ten or twelve steps, in token of acknowledgment for saving his life. I smiled at him and looked pleasantly, and beckoned to him to come still nearer. At length he came close to me, and then he kneeled down again, kissed the ground, and laid his head upon the ground, and taking me by the foot, set my foot upon his head: this, it seems, was in token of swearing to be my slave for ever. I took him up, and made much of him, and encouraged him all I could But there was more work to do yet; for I perceived the savage whom I knocked down was not killed, but stunned with the blow, and began to come to himself; so I pointed to him, and showed him the savage, that he was not dead; upon this he spoke some words to me, and though I could not understand them, yet I thought they were pleasant to hear, for they were the first sound of a man's voice that I had heard (my own excepted) for above five-and-twenty years: but there was no time for such reflections now : the savage who was knocked down recovered himself so far as to sit up upon the ground ; and I perceived that my savage began to be afraid; but when I saw that, I presented my other piece at the man, as if I would shoot him ; upon this my savage, for so I call him now, made a motion to me to lend him my sword, which hung naked in a belt by my side ; so I did : he no sooner had it but he runs to his enemy, and at one blow cut off his head so cleverly, no executioner in Germany could have done it sooner or better; which I thought it very strange for one who, I had reason to believe, never saw a sword in his life before, except their own wooden swords ; however, it seems, as I learned afterwards, they made their wooden swords so sharp, so heavy, and the wood is so hard, that they will cut off heads even with them, ay, and arms, and that at one blow too. When he had done this, he comes laughing to me in sign of triumph, and brought me the sword again ; and with abundance of gestures, which I did not understand, laid it down, with the head of the savage that he had killed just before me.

But that which astonished him most was, to know how I had killed the other Indian so far off: so pointing to him, he made signs to me to let him go to him : so I bade him go as well as I could. When he came to him he stood like one amazed, looking at him; turning him first on one side, then on the other; looked at the wound the bullet had made, which, it seems, was just in his breast, where it had made an hole, and no great quantity of blood had followed; but he had bled inwardly, for he was quite dead. Then he took up his bow and arrows, and came back; so I turned to go away, and beckoned to him to follow me, making signs to him, that more might come after them.

Upon this he signified to me, that he should bury them with sand, that they might not be seen by the rest, if they followed; and so I made signs again to him to do so. He fell to work, and in an instant he had scraped an hole in the sand with his hands big enough to bury the first in, and then dragged him into it, and covered him; and did so also by the other. I believe he had buried them both in a quarter of an hour. Then calling him away, I carried him, not to my castle, but quite away to my cave, on the farther part of the island.

Here I gave him bread, and a bunch of raisins to eat, and a draught of water, which I found he was indeed in great distress for by his running; and having refreshed himself, I made signs for him to go lie down and sleep, pointing to a place where I had laid a great parcel of rice straw, and a blanket upon it, which I used to sleep upon myself sometimes; so the poor creature lay down, and went to sleep.

He was a comely, handsome fellow, perfectly well-made, with straight long limbs, not too large. tall, and well-shaped; and, as I reckon, about twenty-six years of age. He had a very good countenance, not a fierce and surly aspect, but seemed to have something very manly in his face, and yet he had all the sweetness and softness of an European in his countenance too, especially when he smiled;

his hair was long and black, not curled like wool; his forehead very high and large, and a great vivacity and sparkling sharpness in his eyes. The colour of his skin was not quite black, but very tawny and yet not of an ugly, yellow, nauseous tawny, as the Brazilians, and Virginians, and other natives of America are, but of a bright kind of a dun olive colour, that had something in it very agreeable, though not very easy to describe. His face was round and plump, his nose small, not flat like the Negroes; a very good mouth, thin lips, and his teeth fine, well set, and white as ivory. After he had slumbered rather than slept, about half an hour, he waked again, and comes out of the cave to me, for I had been milking my goats, which I had in the inclosure just by. When he espied me, he came running to me, laying himself down again upon the ground, with all the possible signs of an humble thankful disposition, making many antick gestures to show it. At last he lays his head flat upon the ground, close to my foot, and sets my other foot upon his head, as he had done before; and after this, made all the signs to me of subjection, servitude, and submission imaginable, to let me know how much he would serve me as long as he lived. I understood him in many things, and let him know I was very well pleased with him. In a little time I began to speak to him, and teach him to speak to me; at first I made him know his name should be Friday, which was the day I saved his life, and I called him so in memory of the time. I likewise taught him to say, "Master," and then let him know that was to be my name; I likewise taught him to say Yes and No, and to know the meaning of them; I gave him some milk in an earthen pot, and let him see me drink it before him, and sop my bread in it, and I gave him a cake of bread to do the like, which he quickly complied with, and made signs that it was very good for him.

I kept there with him all that night, but as soon as it was day, I beckoned him to come with me, and let him know I would give him some clothes, at which he seemed very glad, for he was stark-naked. As he went by the place where he had buried the two men, he pointed exactly to the spot, and showed me the marks that he had made to find them again, making signs to me that he would dig them up again and eat them; at this I appeared very angry, expressed my abhorrence of it, made as if I would vomit at the thoughts of it, and beckoned with my hand to him to come away, which he did immediately with great submission. I then led him up to the top of the hill, to see if his enemies were gone; and pulling out my glass, I looked, and saw plainly the place where they had been, but no appearance of them or their canoes; so that it was plain that they were gone, and had left their two comrades behind them, without any search after them.

But I was not content with this discovery; but having now more courage, and consequently more curiosity, I took my man Friday with me, giving him the sword in his hand, with the bow and arrows at his back, which I found he could use very dexterously, making him carry one gun for me, and I two for myself, and away we marched to the place where these creatures had been; for I had a mind now to get some fuller intelligence of them. When I came to the place, my very blood ran chill in my veins, and my heart sunk within me at the horror of the spectacle. Indeed it was a dreadful sight; at least it was so to me, though Friday made nothing of it. The place was covered with human bones, the ground dyed with the blood, great pieces of flesh left here and there half eaten, mangled, and scorched; and in short, all the tokens of the triumphant feast they had been making there, after a victory over their enemies. I saw three skulls, five hands, and the bones of three or four legs and feet, and abundance of other parts of the bodies; and Friday, by his signs, made me understand, that they brought over four prisoners to feast upon; that three of them were eaten up, and that he (pointing to himself) was the fourth; that there had been a great battle between them and their next king, whose subjects, it seems, he had been one of; and that they had taken a great number of prisoners, all which were carried to several places by those that had taken them in the fight, in order to feast upon them, as was done here by these wretches upon those they brought hither.

I caused Friday to gather all the skulls, bones, flesh, and whatever remained, and lay them together on an heap, and make a great fire upon it and burn them all to ashes. I found Friday had still a hankering stomach after some of the flesh, and was still a cannibal in his nature; but I discovered so much abhorrence at the very thoughts of it, and at the least appearance of it, that he durst not discover it; for I had, by some means, let him know, that I would kill him if he offered it.

When we had done this, we came back to our castle and there I fell to work for my man Friday.

Peter Wilkins's Discovery of a Flying Woman

The *Life and Adventures of Peter Wilkins, a Cornish man*, is the only imitation of *Robinson Crusoe* that has stood its ground, with the exception of the inferior, but still not unmeritorious History of *Philip Quarll*. It is a Crusoe with the novelty of a Flying people; as Quarll is another, with the substitution of an affectionate ape, or Chimpanzee, for Man Friday. The modest author, who seems to have taken no steps to make either himself or his book known, has been but lately discovered; if indeed the receiver of the money for its copyright was the same person. And it is most likely he was, the initials by which the dedication of the work is signed being those of the receiver's name. The circumstances of the discovery is thus stated in the latest edition, published by Mr. Smith of Fleet Street.

"In the year 1835, Mr. Nicol, the printer, sold by auction a number of books and manuscripts in his possession, which had formerly belonged to the well-known publisher Dodsley; and in arranging them for sale, the original agreement for the sale of the manuscript of 'Peter Wilkins,' by the author, 'Robert Pultock of Clement's Inn,' to Dodsley, was discovered. From this document it appears, that Mr. Pultock received twenty pounds, twelve copies of the work, and 'cuts of the first impression,' *i. e.*, a set of proof impressions of the fanciful engravings that professed to illustrate the first edition, as the price of the entire copyright. This curious document was sold to John Wilks, Esq., M. P., on the 17th of December, 1835."

The reader will observe, that the words "by the author," in this extract, are not accompanied by marks of quotation. The fact, however, is stated as if he knew it for such, by the quoter of the document.

The Dedication is to Elizabeth, Countess of Northumberland, the lady to whom Percy addressed his *Reliques of Ancient English Poetry* She was a Wriothesley, descended of Shakspeare's Earl of Southampton, and appears to have been a very amiable woman. "R. P." professes himself to be under obligations to her; and says, that it was after the pattern of her virtues that he drew the "mind" of his Youwarkee.

It is interesting to fancy "R. P.," or "Mr. Robert Pultock of Clement's Inn," a gentle lover of books, not successful enough perhaps as a barrister to lead a public or profitable life, but eking out a little employment, or a bit of a patrimony, with literature congenial to him, and looking oftener to *Purchas's Pilgrims* on his shelves than to *Coke upon Littleton*. We picture him to ourselves, with *Robinson Crusoe* on one side of him, and *Gaudentio di Lucca* on the other, hearing the pen go over his paper in one of those quiet rooms in Clement's Inn, that look out of its old-fashioned buildings into the little garden with the dial in it, held by the negro; one of the prettiest corners in London, and extremely fit for a sequestered fancy that cannot get any farther. There he sits, the unknown, ingenious, and amiable Mr. Robert Pultock, thinking of an imaginary beauty for want of a better; and creating her for the delight of posterity, though his contemporaries were to know little or nothing of her. We shall never go through the place again, without regarding him as its crowning interest.

Peter Wilkins is no common production in any respect, though it is far inferior to Crusoe in contrivance and detail; and falls off, like all these imaginary works, in the latter part, when they begin laying down the law in politics and religion. It has been well observed too, that the author has not made his Flying People in general light and airy enough, or of sufficiently unvulgar materials, either in body or mind, to warrant the ethereal advantages of their wings. And it may be said on the other hand, that the kind of wing, the *graundee*, or elastic natural drapery, which opens and shuts at pleasure, however ingeniously and even beautifully contrived, would necessitate a creature, whose modifications of humanity, bodily and mental, though never so good after their kind, might have startled the inventor had he been more of a naturalist; might have developed a being very different from the feminine, sympathizing, and lovely Youwarkee. Muscles and nerves, not human, must have been associated with inhuman wants and feelings; probably have necessitated talons and a beak! At best, the woman would have been wilder; more elvish, capricious, and unaccountable. She would have ruffled her whalebones when angry; been horribly intimate perhaps with birds' nests, and fights with eagles; and frightened Wilkins out of his wits with dashing betwixt rocks, and pulling the noses of seals and gulls. So far the book is wanting in verisimilitude and imagination.

But then how willing we are to gain the fair winged creature at the expense of Zoonomy! and after all, how founded in nature itself is the human desire to fly! We do so in dreams: we all long for the power when children: we think of it in poetry and in sorrow. "Oh that I had the wings of a dove! then would I fly away and be at rest." Wilkins fled away into a beautiful twilight country, far from his unresting self and vulgar daylight; and not being able to give himself wings, he invented a wife that had them instead. Now a sweeter creature is not to be found in books; and she does him immortal honour. She is all tenderness and vivacity; all born good taste and blessed companionship. Her pleasure consists but in his: she prevents all his wishes; has neither prudery nor immodesty; sheds not a tear but from right feeling; is the good of his home, and the grace of his fancy. It is a pity the account of his bridal cannot be given; for never were love and purity better united; but to draw it forth from the general history, might give it in too many eyes a freedom which does not belong to it. We must content ourselves with extracting the account of the charmer's discovery, and of the way in which Peter first became acquainted with her powers of flight. The voices which he hears at night, the fall of some unknown weight at his door, the puzzle about the graundee that has been slit, and the first movements of the winged beauty over the lake, are all points particularly well-felt and interesting.

The reader is to understand, that Peter had by this time settled himself, à la Crusoe, in his solitary abode; which is in a cavern by the side of a lake, into which he had been drifted through a long subterraneous passage from the sea. It was a very beautiful place, but so far out of the ordinary course of the sun, that "the brightest daylight never exceeded that of half an hour after sunset in the summer-time in England, and little more than just reddened the sky." In consequence of this nature of her climate, Youwarkee was in all respects a very tender-eyed thing, and could not bear a strong light.

I HAD now well stored my grotto with all sorts of winter provisions; and feeling the weather grow very cold, I expected, and waited patiently for, the total darkness. I went little abroad, and employed myself within doors, endeavouring to fence against the approaching extremity of the cold. For this purpose I prepared a quantity of rushes, which being very dry, I spread them smoothly on the floor of my bed-chamber a good thickness, and over them I laid my mattress: then I made a double sheet of the boat's awning, or sail, that I had brought to cover my goods; and having skewered together several of the jackets and clothes I found in the chest, of them I made a coverlid; so that I lay very commodiously, and made very long nights of it, now the dark season was set in.

As I lay awake one night, or day, I know not whether, I very plainly heard the sound of several human voices, and sometimes very loud; but though I could easily distinguish the articulations, I could not understand the least word that was said; nor did the voices seem at all to me like such as I had anywhere heard before, but much softer and more musical. This startled me, and I rose immediately, slipping on my clothes and taking my gun in my hand (which I always kept charged, being my constant travelling companion), and my cutlass. Thus equipped, I walked into my antechamber, where I heard the voices much plainer; till, after some little time, they quite died away. After watching here, and hearkening a good while, hearing nothing, I walked back into the grotto, and laid me down again on my bed. I was inclined to open the door of my antechamber, but I own I was afraid; beside, I considered, that if I did, I could discover nothing at any distance, by reason of the thick and gloomy wood that enclosed me.

I had a thousand different surmises about the meaning of this odd incident; and could not conceive how any human creature should be in my kingdom (as I called it) but myself, and I never yet see them or any traces of their habitation. But then again I reflected, that though I had surrounded the whole lake, yet I had not traced the outbounds of the wood, next the rock, where there might be innumerable grottos like mine; nay, perhaps some as spacious as that I had sailed through to the lake; and that though I had not perceived it yet, this beautiful spot might be very well peopled. But, says I again, if there be any such beings as I am fancying here, surely they don't skulk in their dens, like savage beasts, by daylight, and only patrol for prey by night; if so, I shall probably become a delicious morsel for them ere long, if they meet with me. This kept me still more within doors than before, and I hardly ever stirred out but for water or firing. At length, hearing no more voices, or seeing any one, I began to be more composed in my mind, and at last grew persuaded it was all a mere delusion, and only a fancy of mine without any real foundation; and sometimes, though I was sure I was fully awake when I heard them, I persuaded myself I had rose in my sleep upon a dream of voices, and recollected with myself the various stories I had heard when a boy of walking in one's sleep, and the surprising effects of it; so the whole notion was now blown over.

I had not enjoyed my tranquillity above a week, before my fears were roused afresh, hearing the same sound of voices twice the same night, but not many minutes at a time. What gave me most pain was, that they were at such a distance, as I judged by the languor of the sound, that if I had opened my door I could not have seen the utterers through the trees, and I was resolved not to venture out, but then I determined, if they should come again, anything near my grotto, to open the door, see who they were, and stand upon my own defence, whatever came of it. For, says I, my entrance is so narrow and high, that more than one cannot come at a time; and I can with ease dispatch twenty of them, before they can secure me, if they should be savages; but if they prove sensible human creatures, it will be a great benefit to me to join myself to their society. Thus had I formed my scheme, but I heard no more of them for a great while; so that at length beginning to grow ashamed of my fears, I became tranquil again.

* * * * *

I passed the summer, though I had never yet seen the sun's body, very much to my satisfaction, partly in the work I have been describing [he had taken what he calls some "beast-fish" and got a great quantity of oil from them], partly in building me a chimney in my antechamber, of mud and earth burnt on my own hearth into a sort of brick; in making a window at one end of the above said chamber, to let in what little light would come through the trees, when I did not choose to open my door; in moulding an earthen lamp for my oil; and finally, in providing and laying in stores, fresh and salt; for I had now cured and dried many more fish against winter. These, I say, were my summer employments at home, intermixed with many agreeable summer excursions. But now the winter coming on, and the days growing very short, or indeed there being no day, properly speaking, but a kind of twilight, I kept mostly in my habitation (though not so much as I had done the winter before, when I had no light within doors) and slept, or at least lay still, great part of my time, for now my lamp was never out. I also turned two of my beast-fish skins into a rug to cover my bed, and the third into a cushion, which I always sat upon; and a very soft and warm cushion it made. All this together rendered my life very easy; yea, even comfortable.

An indifferent person would now be apt to ask, what would this man desire more than he had? To this I answer, that I was contented while my condition was such as I have been describing; but a little while after the darkness or twilight came on, I frequently heard the voices again, sometimes a few only at a time, as it seemed, and then again in great numbers. This threw me into new fears, and I became as uneasy as ever, even to the degree of growing quite melancholy; though otherwise I never received the least injury from anything. I foolishly attempted several times, by looking out of window, to discover what these odd sounds proceeded from, though I knew it was too dark to see anything there.

I was now fully convinced, by a more deliberate attention to them, that they could not be uttered by the beast-fish, as I had before conjectured, but only by beings capable of articulate speech. But then, what or where they were, it galled me to be ignorant of.

At length, one night or day, I cannot say which, hearing the voices very distinctly, and praying very earnestly to be either delivered from the uncertainty they had put me under, or to have them removed from me, I took courage, and arming myself with gun, pistols, and cutlass, I went out of my grotto, and crept down the wood. I then heard them plainer than before, and was able to judge from what point of the compass they proceeded. Hereupon I went forward towards the sound till I came to the verge of the wood, where I could see the lake very well by the dazzle of the water. Thereon, as I thought, I beheld a fleet of boats, covering a large compass, and not far from the bridge. I was shocked hereat beyond expression: I could not conceive where they came from, or whither they would go; but supposed there must be some other passage to the lake, than I had found in my voyage through the cavern, and that for certain they came that way, and from some place of which as yet I had no manner of knowledge.

Whilst I was entertaining myself with this speculation, I heard the people in the boats laughing and talking very merrily, though I was too distant to distinguish the words. I discerned soon after all the boats (as I still supposed them) draw up, and push for the bridge; presently after, though I was sure no boat entered the arch, I saw a multitude of people on the opposite shore, all marching towards the bridge; and what was the strangest of all, there was not the least sign of a boat left on the lake. I then was in a greater consternation than before; but was still much more so, when I saw the whole posse of people, that, as I have just said, were marching towards the bridge, coming over it to my side of the lake. At this my heart failed; and I was just going to run to my grotto for shelter, but taking one look more, I plainly discovered, that the people, leaping one after another from the top of the bridge, as if into the water, and then rising again, flew in a long train over the lake, the lengthways of it, quite out of sight, laughing, hallooing, and sporting together; so that, looking back again to the bridge and on the lake, I could neither see person, boat, or anything else, nor hear the least noise or stir afterwards for that time.

I returned to my grotto brim-full of this amazing adventure, bemoaning my misfortune in being at a place where I was likely to remain ignorant of what was doing about me. For, says I, if I am in a land of spirits, as now I have little room to doubt, there is no guarding against them. I am never safe, even in my grotto; for that can be no security against such beings as can sail on the water in no boats, and fly in the air on no wings (as the case now appears to me), who can be here and there, and wherever they please. What a miserable state, I say, am I fallen to! I should have been glad to have had human converse, and to have found inhabitants in this place; but there being none, as I supposed, hitherto, I contented myself with thinking I was at least safe from all those evils mankind in society are obnoxious to. But now, what may be the consequence of the next hour, I know not; nay, I am not able to say; but whilst I speak and show my discontent, they may at a distance conceive my thoughts, and be hatching revenge against me for my dislike of them.

The pressure of my spirits inclining me to repose, I laid me down, but could get no rest; nor could all my most serious thoughts, even of the Almighty Providence, give me relief under my present anxiety. And all this was only from my state of uncertainty concerning the reality of what I had heard and seen, and from the earnestness with which I coveted a satisfactory knowledge of those beings who had just taken their flight from me.

I really believe the fiercest wild beast, or the most savage of mankind that had met me, and put me upon my defence, would not have given me half the trouble that then lay upon me; and the more, for that I had no seeming possibility of ever being rid of my apprehensions. So finding I could not sleep, I got up again; but as I could not fly from myself, all the art I could use with myself was but in vain to obtain me any quiet.

In the height of my distress I had recourse to prayer, with no small benefit; begging, that if it pleased not the Almighty power to remove the object of my fears, at least to resolve my doubts about them, and to render them rather helpful than hurtful to me. I hereupon, as I always did on such occasions, found myself much more placid and easy, and began to hope the best, till I had almost persuaded myself that I was out of danger; and then laying myself down, I rested very sweetly, till I was awakened by the impulse of the following dream:

Methought I was in Cornwall, at my wife's aunt's; and inquiring after her and my children, the old gentlewoman informed me, both my wife and children had been dead some time, and that my wife, before her departure, desired her (that is her aunt), immediately upon my arrival, to tell me she was only gone to the lake, where I should be sure to see her, and be happy with her after. I then, as I fancied, ran to the lake to find her. In my passage, she stopped me, crying, Whither so fast, Peter? I am your wife, your Patty. Methought I did not know her, she was so altered; but observing her voice, I looked more wistfully at her, she appeared to me as the most beautiful creature I ever beheld. I then went to seize her in my arms, and the hurry of my spirits awakened me.

When I got up, I kept at home, not caring even to look out at my door. My dream ran strangely in my head, and I had now nothing but Patty in my mind. Oh! cries I, how happy could I be with her, though I had only her in this solitude. Oh! that this was but a reality, and not a dream. I could scarce refrain from running to the lake to meet my Patty. But then I checked my folly, and reasoned myself into some degree of temper again. However, I could not forbear crying out. What! nobody to converse with, nobody to assist, comfort, or counsel me! this is a melancholy situation indeed. Thus I ran on lamenting, till I was almost weary; when, on a sudden, I again heard the voices. Hark! says I, here they come again. Well, I am now resolved to face them; come life come death. It is not to be alone I thus dread; but to have company about me, and not know who or what, is death to me, worse than I can suffer from them, be they who or what they will.

During my soliloquy the voices increased, and then by degrees diminished as usual; but I had scarce got my gun in my hand, to pursue my resolution of showing myself to those who uttered them, when I felt such a thump upon the roof of my antechamber as shook the whole fabric, and set me all over into a tremor; I then heard a sort of shriek, and a rustle near the door of my apartment, all which together seemed very terrible. But I, having before determined to see what and who it was, resolutely opened my door and leaped out. I saw nobody; all was quite silent, and nothing, that I could perceive, but my own fears a-moving. I went then softly to the corner of the building, and there, looking down by the glimmer of my lamp, which stood in the window, I saw something in human shape lying at my feet. I gave the word, Who's there?—Still no one answered. My heart was ready to force a way through my side. I was for a while fixed to the earth like a statue. At length recovering, I stepped in, fetched my lamp, and returning, saw the very beautiful face my Patty appeared under in my dream; and not considering that it was only a dream, I verily thought that I had my Patty before me, but she seemed to be stone dead. Upon viewing her other parts—for I had never yet removed my eyes from her face—I found she had a sort of brown chaplet, like lace, round her head, under and about which her hair was tucked up and twined; and she seemed to me to be clothed in a thin hair-coloured silk garment which, upon trying to raise her

I found to be quite warm, and therefore hoped there was life in the body it contained. I then took her into my arms, and treading a step backwards with her, I put out my lamp; however, having her in my arms, I conveyed her through the doorway in the dark into my grotto; here I laid her upon my bed, and then ran out for my lamp.

This, thinks I, is an amazing adventure. How could Patty come here, and dressed in silk and whalebone, too! sure that is not the reigning fashion in England now. But my dream said she was dead. Why truly, says I, so she seems to be. But be it so, she is warm. Whether this is the place for persons to inhabit after death or not, I cannot tell (for I see there are people here, though I do not know them); but be it as it will, she feels as flesh and blood; and if I but bring her to stir and act again as my wife, what matters it to me what she is! It will be a great blessing and comfort to me, for she never would have come to this very spot but for my good.

Top-full of these thoughts, I re-entered my grotto, shut my door, and lighted my lamp; when going to my Patty, (as I delighted to fancy her), I thought I saw her eyes stir a little. I then set the lamp further off, for fear of offending them if she should look up; and warming the last glass I had reserved of my Madeira, I carried it to her, but she never stirred. I now supposed the fall had absolutely killed her, and was prodigiously grieved, when laying my hand on her breast I perceived the fountain of life had some motion. This gave me infinite pleasure; so not despairing, I dipped my finger in the wine, and moistened her lips with it two or three times, and I imagined they opened a little. Upon this methought me, and taking a teaspoon, gently poured a few drops of wine by that means into her mouth. Finding she swallowed it, I poured in another spoonful, and another, till I brought her to herself so well as to be able to sit up. All this I did by a glimmering light, which the lamp afforded from a distant part of the room where I had placed it, as I have said, out of her sight.

I then spoke to her and asked her divers questions, as if she had really been Patty, and understood me; in return of which she uttered a language I had no idea of, though in the most musical tone, and with the sweetest accent I had ever heard. It grieved me I could not understand her. However, thinking she might like to be upon her feet, I went to lift her off the bed, when she felt to my touch in the oddest manner possible; for while in one respect it was as though she had been cased in whalebone, it was as soft and warm as if she had been naked.*

I then took her in my arms and carried her into my antechamber again; where I would fain have entered into conversation with her, but found she and I could make nothing of it together, unless we could understand one another's speech. It is very strange my dream should have prepossessed me so much of Patty, and of the alteration of her countenance, that I could by no means persuade myself the person I had with me was not she; though, upon a deliberate comparison, Patty, as pleasing as she always was to my taste, would no more come up to this fair creature, than a coarse ale-wife would to Venus herself.

* The flying apparatus of Wilkins's newly discovered people was called a *graundee*, and consisted of a natural investment like delicate silk and whalebone, which flew open at pleasure, and thus furnished its possessor with wings or a dress, according to the requirement of the moment. Peter's future wife had been sporting in the air with some other young damsels, one of whom happening to brush too strongly against her, as they stooped among some trees, had occasioned the accident which was the cause of his good fortune.

You may imagine we stared heartily at each other, and I doubted not but she wondered as much as I by what means we came so near each other. I offered her everything in my grotto which I thought might please her, some of which she gratefully received, as appeared by her looks and behaviour. But she avoided my lamp, and always placed her back towards it. I observing that, and ascribing it to her modesty, in my company, let her have her will, and took care to set it in such a position myself as seemed agreeable to her, though it deprived me of a prospect I very much admired.

After we had sat a good while, now and then, I may say, chattering to one another, she got up and took a turn or two about the room. When I saw her in that attitude, her grace and motion perfectly charmed me, and her shape was incomparable; but the strangeness of her dress put me to my trumps, to conceive either what it was, or how it was put on.

Well, we supped together, and I set the best of everything I had before her, nor could either of us forbear speaking in our own tongue, though we were sensible neither of us understood the other. After supper I gave her some of my cordials, for which she showed great tokens of thankfulness, and often, in her way, by signs and gestures, which were very far from being insignificant, expressed her gratitude for my kindness. When supper had been some time over, I showed her my bed and made signs for her to go to it; but she seemed very shy of that, till I showed her where I meant to lie myself, by pointing to myself, then to that, and again pointing to her and to my bed. When at length I had made this matter intelligible to her, she lay down very composedly; and after I had taken care of my fire, and set the things we had been using for supper in their places,

I laid myself down too; for I could have no suspicious thoughts, or fear of danger from a form so excellent.

I treated her for some time with all the respect imaginable, and never suffered her to do the least part of my work. It was very inconvenient to both of us only to know each other's meaning by signs; but I could not be otherwise than pleased to see, that she endeavoured all in her power to learn to talk like me. Indeed I was not behindhand with her in that respect, striving all I could to imitate her. What I all the while wondered at was, she never showed the least disquiet at her confinement; for I kept my door shut at first, through fear of losing her, thinking she would have taken an opportunity to run away from me, for little did I then think she could fly.

After my new love had been with me a fortnight, finding my water ran low, I was greatly troubled at the thought of quitting her at any time to go for more; and having hinted it to her with seeming uneasiness, she could not for awhile fathom my meaning; but when she saw me much confused, she came at length, by the many signs I made, to imagine it was my concern for her which made me so; whereupon she expressively enough signified I might be easy, for she did not fear anything happening to her in my absence. On this, as well as I could declare my meaning, I entreated her not to go away before my return. As soon as she understood what I signified to her by actions, she sat down with her arms across, leaning her head against the wall to assure me she would not stir. However, as I had before nailed a cord to the outside of the door, I tied that for caution's sake to a tree, for fear of the worst; but I believe she had not the least design of removing.

I took my boat, net, and water-cask, as usual; desirous of bringing her home a fresh-fish dinner; and succeeded so well as to catch enough for several good meals, and to spare What remained I salted, and found she liked that better than the fresh, after a few days' salting: though she did not so well approve of that I had formerly pickled and dried. As my salt grew very low, though I had used it very sparingly, I now resolved to try making some; and the next summer I effected it.

Thus we spent the remainder of the winter together, till the days began to be light enough for me to walk abroad a little in the middle of them: for I was now under no apprehension of her leaving me; as she had before this time so many opportunities of doing so, but never once attempted it.

When the weather cleared up a little, by the lengthening of daylight, I took courage one afternoon to invite her to walk with me to the lake; but she sweetly excused herself from it whilst there was such a frightful glare of light, as she said; but, looking out of the door, told me if I would not go out of the wood she would accompany me: so we agreed to take a turn only there. I first went myself over the stile at the door, and thinking it rather too high for her, I took her in my arms and lifted her over. But even when I had her in this manner, I knew not what to make of her clothing, it sat so true and close; but seeing her by a steadier and truer light in the grove, though a heavy gloomy one, than my light had afforded, I begged she would let me know of what silk or other composition her garment was made. She smiled and asked me if mine was not the same under my jacket. "No, lady," says I, "I have nothing but my skin under my clothes." "Why what do you mean?" replies she, somewhat tartly; "but indeed I was afraid something was the matter, by that nasty covering you wear, that you might not be seen. Are not you a glumm?"* "Yes,'

* A man.

says I, "fair creature." (Here, though you may conceive she spoke part English, part her own country tongue, and I the same, as we best understood each other, yet I shall give you our discourse word for word in plain English.) "Then," says she, "I am afraid you must have been a very bad man, and have been crashee,* which I should be very sorry to hear." I told her I believed we were none of us so good as we might be, but I hoped my faults had not at most exceeded other men's; but I had suffered abundance of hardships in my time, and that at last Providence having settled me in this spot, from whence I had no prospect of ever departing, it was none of the least of its mercies to bring to my knowledge and company the most exquisite piece of all his works in her, which I should acknowledge as long as I lived. She was surprised at this discourse, and asked me (if I did not mean to impose upon her, and was indeed an ingcrashee glumm†), why I should tell her I had no prospect of departing from hence? "Have not you," says she, "the same prospect that I or any other person has of departing? Sir," added she, "you don't do well, and really I fear you are slit, or you would not wear this nasty cumbersome coat (taking hold of my jacket sleeve), if you were not afraid of showing the signs of a bad life upon your natural clothing."

I could not for my heart imagine what way there was to get out of my dominions; but certainly, thought I, there must be some way or other, or she would not be so peremptory. And as to my jacket, and showing myself in my natural clothing, I profess she made me blush; and, but for the shame, I would have stripped to the skin to have satisfied her. "But, madam," says I, "pray pardon me, for you really are mistaken; I have examined every nook and corner of

---

* Slit;—a punishment inflicted on the wings, or *graundee*, of criminals.
† A man whose wings had not been slit.

this new world in which we now are, and can find no possible outlet; nay, even by the same way I came in, I am sure it is impossible to get out again." "Why," says she," what outlets have you searched for, or what way can you expect out but the way you came in? and why is that impossible to return by again? If you are not slit, is not the air open to you? will not the sky admit you to patrol in it as well as other people? I tell you, sir, I fear you have been slit for your crimes; and though you have been so good to me that I cannot help loving of you heartily for it, yet, if I thought you had been slit, I would not, nay, could not, stay a moment longer with you; no, though it should break my heart to leave you!"

I found myself now in a strange quandary, longing to know what she meant by being slit, and had a hundred strange notions in my head whether I was slit or not; for though I knew what the word naturally signified well enough, yet in what manner, or by what figure of speech she applied it to me, I had no idea of. But seeing her look a little angrily upon me, "Pray, madam," says I, "do not be offended if I take the liberty to ask you what you mean by the word crashee, so often repeated by you, for I am an utter stranger to what you mean by it?" "Sir," says she, "pray answer me first how came you here?" "Madam," replied I, "will you please to take a walk to the verge of the wood, and I will show you the very passage?" "Sir," says she, "I perfectly know the range of the rocks all around, and by the least description, without going to see them, can tell from which you descended." "In truth," said I, "most charming lady, I descended from no rock at all; nor would I for a thousand worlds attempt what could not be accomplished but by my destruction." "Sir," says she, in some anger, "it is false, and you impose on me." "I declare to you," says I, "madam, what I tell you is strictly true; I never was near the summit of any of the surrounding rocks or anything like it; but as you are not far from the verge of the wood, be so good as to step a little further, and I will show you my entrance in hither." "Well," says she, "now this odious dazzle of light is lessened, I do not care if I do go with you."

When we came far enough to see the bridge, "There, madam," says I, "there is my entrance, where the sea pours into this lake from yonder cavern." "It is not possible," says she; "this is another untruth; and as I see you would deceive me and are not to be believed, farewell, I must be gone. But hold," says she, "let me ask you one thing more, that is, by what means did you come through that cavern? you could not have used to have come over the rock." "Bless me, madam," says I, "do you think I and my boat could fly? Come over the rock, did you say? No, madam, I sailed from the great sea, the main ocean, in my boat, through that cavern into this very lake here." "What do you mean by your boat?" says she; "you seem to make two things of your boat you say you sailed with, and yourself." "I do so," replied I, "for, madam, I take myself to be good flesh and blood, but my boat is made of wood and other materials." "Is it so?" says she; "and pray where is this boat that is made of wood and other materials? under your jacket?" "Lord, madam," says I, "you put me in fear that you were angry, but now I hope you only joke with me; what, put a boat under my jacket! no, madam, my boat is in the lake." "What! more untruths?" says she. "No, madam," I replied; "if you would be satisfied of what I say, every word of which is as true as that my boat now is in the lake, pray walk with me thither, and make your own eyes judges what sincerity I speak with." To this she agreed, it growing dusky; but assured me, if I did not give her good satisfaction, I should see her no more.

We arrived at the lake, and going to my wet dock, "Now, madam," says I, "pray satisfy yourself whether I spake true or not." She looked at my boat, but could not yet frame a proper notion of it. Says I, "Madam, in this very boat I sailed from the main sea through that very cavern into this lake; and shall at last think myself the happiest of all men, if you continue with me, love me, and credit me; and I promise you I will never deceive you, but think my life happily spent in your service." I found she was hardly content yet to believe what I told her of my boat to be true, until I stepped into it, and pushing from the shore, took my oars in my hand, and sailed along the lake by her as she walked on the shore. At last she seemed so well reconciled to me and my boat, that she desired I would take her in. I immediately did so, and we sailed a good way; and as we returned to my dock, I described to her how I procured the water we drank, and brought it to shore in that vessel.

"Well," says she, "I have sailed, as you call it, many a mile in my lifetime, but never in such a thing as this. I own it will serve very well where one has a great many things to carry from place to place; but to be labouring thus at an oar when one intends pleasure in sailing, is, in my mind, a most ridiculous piece of slavery." "Why, pray, madam, how would you have me sail; for getting into the boat only will not carry us this way or that, without using some force." "But," says she, "pray where did you get this boat, as you call it?" "Oh! madam," says I, "that is too long and fatal a story to begin upon now; this boat was made many thousand miles from hence, among a people coal black, a quite different sort from us; and when I first had it, I little thought of seeing this country; but I will make a faithful relation of all to you when we come home." Indeed I began to wish heartily we were there, for it grew into the night; and having strolled so far without my gun, I was afraid of what I had before seen and heard, and hinted our return; but I found my motion was disagreeable to her, and so I dropped it.

I now perceived, and wondered at it, that the later it grew, the more agreeable it seemed to her; and as I had now brought her into a good humour again by seeing and sailing in my boat, I was not willing to prevent its increase. I told her, if she pleased we would land, and when I had docked my boat, I would accompany her where and as long as she liked. As we talked and walked by the lake, she made a little run before me, and jumped into it. Perceiving this, I cried out; whereupon she merrily called on me to follow her. The light was then so dim as prevented my having more than a confused sight of her, when she jumped in; and looking earnestly after her, I could discern nothing more than a small boat on the water, which skimmed along at so great a rate that I almost lost sight of it presently; but running along the shore for fear of losing her, I met her gravely walking to meet me, and then had entirely lost sight of the boat on the lake. "This," says she, accosting me with a smile, "is my way of sailing, which I perceive by the fright you were in, you are altogether unacquainted with; and as you tell me you came from so many thousand miles off, it is possible you may be made differently from me; but surely we are the part of the creation which has had most care bestowed upon it; and I suspect from all your discourse, to which I have been very attentive, it is possible you may no more be able to fly than to sail as I do." "No, charming creature," says I, "that I cannot, I will assure you." She then, stepping to the edge of the lake, for the advantage of a descent before her, sprang up into the air, and away she went, further than my eyes could follow her.

I was quite astonished. So, says I, then all is over, all a delusion which I have so long been in, a mere phantom! better had it been for me never to have seen her, than thus to lose her again. But what could I expect had she staid? for it is plain she is no human composition. But, says I, she felt like flesh too, when I lifted her out at the door. I had but very little time for reflection; for in about ten minutes after she had left me in this mixture of grief and amazement, she alighted just by me on her feet.

Her return, as she plainly saw, filled me with a transport not to be concealed, and which, as she afterwards told me, was very agreeable to her. Indeed, I was some moments in such an agitation of mind, from these unparalleled incidents, that I was like one thunderstruck; but coming presently to myself, and clasping her in my arms with as much love and passion as I was capable of expressing. "Are you returned again, kind angel," said I. "to bless a wretch who can only be happy in adoring you? Can it be that you, who have so many advantages over me, should quit all the pleasures that nature has formed you for, and all your friends and relations, to take an asylum in my arms? But I here make you a tender of all I am able to bestow—my love and constancy." "Come, come," says she, "no more raptures. I find you are a worthier man than I thought I had reason to take you for; and I beg your pardon for my distrust, whilst I was ignorant of your perfections; but now I verily believe all you said is true; and I promise you, as you have seemed so much to delight in me, I will never quit you, till death or other as fatal accident shall part us. But we will now, if you choose, go home; for

I know you have been some time uneasy in this gloom, though agreeable to me. For, giving my eyes the pleasure of looking eagerly on you, it conceals my blushes from your sight."

In this manner, exchanging mutual endearments and soft speeches, hand in hand, we arrived at the grotto.

Gil Blas and the Parasite.

FROM LE SAGE.

GIL BLAS is a book which makes a great impression in youth with particular passages; becomes thoroughly appreciated only by the maturest knowledge; and remains one of the greatest of favourites, with old people who are wise and good-natured. Every body knows the Robbers' Cave, the Beggar who asks alms with a loaded musket, the Archbishop who invited a candour which he could not bear, the dramatic surprise and exquisite lesson of the story transcribed into the present volume; and perhaps we all have a general, entertaining recollection of authors, and actresses, and great men. But the hundreds of delicate strokes at every turn, the quiet, arch reference (never failing) to the most hidden sources of action and nicest evidences of character, require an experienced taste and discernment to do them justice. When they obtain this, they complete the charm of the reader by flattering his understanding. The hero (strange critical term for individuals the most unheroical!) is justly popular with all the world, because he resembles them in their mixture of sense and nonsense, craft and credulity, selfishness and good qualities. We have a sneaking regard for him on our weak side; while we flatter ourselves we should surpass him on the strong. Then how pleasant the hypocrisy of the false hermit Lamela, reconciled to us by his animal spirits; how consolatory (if extension of evil can console) the bile and melancholy of the great minister, the Count-Duke, who always sees a spectre before him; and how charming, as completing the round of its universality, the alternations from town to country, from solitudes to courts, and the settlement of the once simple Gil Blas, now Signior de Santillane, in his comfortable farm at Lirias, over the door of which was to be written a farewell to vicissitude:—

> Inveni portum. Spes et Fortuna, valete.
> Sat me lusisti: ludite nunc alios.
>
> My port is found. Farewell, ye freaks of chance;
> The dance ye led me, now let others dance.

Le Sage is accused, like Moliere, of having stolen all his good things from Spain. Do not believe it. Rest assured, that whatever he stole he turned to the choicest account with his own genius; otherwise the Spaniards would have got the fame for his works, and not he. Nobody stole Cervantes. Le Sage was a good, quiet man, very deaf, who lived in a small house at Boulogne with a bit of trellised garden at the back, in which he used to walk up and down while he composed. He had a son, a celebrated actor, who came to live with him; and these two were as fast friends, as they were honest and pleasant men.

But if every body knows the adventure of Gil Blas with the Parasite, why, it may be asked, repeat it? For the reason given in the Preface,—because there are passages in books which readers love to see repeated, for the very sake of their intimacy with them. It is with fine passages in books as with songs. Some we like, because they are good and new; and some, because they are very good indeed, and old acquaintances. Besides, there are hundreds of readers who only just recollect them well enough to desire to know them better.

It is to be borne in mind, that our hero has just set out in life; and that this is his first journey since he left school at Oviedo.

I ARRIVED in safety at Pennaflor, and halting at the gate of an inn that made a tolerable appearance, I no sooner alighted, than the landlord came out, and received me with great civility; he untied my portmanteau with his own hands, and throwing it on his shoulder, conducted me into a room, while one of his servants led my mule into the stable. This innkeeper, the greatest talker of the Asturias, and as ready to relate his own affairs without being asked, as to pry into those of another, told me his name was Andrew Corcuelo; that he had served many years in the king's army in quality of a serjeant; and had quitted the service fifteen months ago to marry a damsel of Castropol, who (though she was a little swarthy) knew very well how to turn the penny. He said a thousand other things, which I could have dispensed with the hearing of; but after having made me his confidant, he thought he had a right to exact the same condescension of me, and accordingly asked whence I came, whither I was going, and what I was. I was obliged to answer article by article; for he accompanied every question by a profound bow, and begged me to excuse his curiosity with such a respectful air, that I could not refuse to satisfy him in every particular. This engaged me in a long conversation with him, and gave me occasion to mention my design, and the reason I had for disposing of my mule, that I might take the opportunity of a carrier. He approved of my intention, though not in a very succinct manner; for he represented all the troublesome accidents that might befall me on the road; he recounted many dismal stories of travellers: and I began to be afraid he would never have done. He concluded at length however with telling me, that if I had a mind to sell my mule, he was acquainted with a very honest jockey who would buy her. I assured him he would oblige me in sending for him; upon which he went in quest of him immediately with great eagerness. It was not long before he returned with his man, whom he introduced to me as a person of exceeding honesty, and we went into the yard all together, where my mule was produced, and passed and repassed before the jockey, who examined her from head to foot, and did not fail to speak very disadvantageously of her. I own there was not much to be said in her praise; but, however, had it been the pope's mule, he would have found some defects in her. He assured me, that she had all the defects a mule could have; and to convince me of his veracity, appealed to the landlord, who, doubtless, had his reasons for supporting his friend's assertions. " Well,' said the dealer with an air of indifference, " how much money do you expect for this wretched animal?" After the eulogium he had bestowed on her, and the attestation of Signior Corcuelo, whom I believed to be a man of honesty and understanding, I would have given my mule for nothing; and therefore told him I would rely on his integrity; bidding him appraise the beast in his own conscience, and I would stand to the valuation. Upon this he assumed the man of honour; and replied, that in engaging his conscience I took him on the weak side. In good sooth, that did not seem to be his strong side; for instead of valuing her at ten or twelve pistoles, as my uncle had done, he fixed the price at three ducats; which I accepted with as much joy as if I had made an excellent bargain.

After having so advantageously disposed of my mule, the landlord conducted me to a carrier, who was to set out the next day for Astorga. This muleteer let me know that he should set out by day-break, and promised to awake me in time, after we had agreed upon the price, as well for the hire of a mule, as my board on the road; and when everything was settled between us, I returned to the inn with Corcuelo, who, by the way, began to recount the carrier's history. He told me every circumstance of his character in town; in short, was going to stupify me again with his intolerable loquacity, when, luckily for me, a man of pretty good appearance prevented my misfortune, by accosting him with great civility. I left them together, and went on, without suspecting that I had the least concern in their conversation.

When I arrived at the inn, I called for supper; and it being a meagre day, was fain to put up with eggs; which while they got ready, I made up to my landlady, whom I had not seen before. She appeared handsome enough ; and withal so sprightly and gay, that I should have concluded (even if her husband had not told me so) that her house was pretty well frequented. When the omelet I had bespoken was ready, I sat down to table by myself; and had not yet swallowed the first mouthful, when the landlord came in, followed by the man who had stopt him in the street. This cavalier, who wore a long sword, and seemed to be about thirty years of age, advanced towards me with an eager air, saying. "Mr. Student, I am informed that you are that Signior Gil Blas of Santillane, who is the link of philosophy, and ornament of Oviedo ! Is it possible that you are that mirror of learning, that sublime genius, whose reputation is so great in this country? You know not," continued he, addressing himself to the innkeeper and his wife, "you know not what you possess ! You have a treasure in your house! Behold in this young gentleman, the eighth wonder of the world!" Then turning to me, and throwing his arms about my neck. "Forgive," cried he, "my transports! I cannot contain the joy that your presence creates."

I could not answer for some time, because he locked me so close in his arms, that I was almost suffocated for want of breath ; and it was not till I had disengaged my head from his embrace, that I replied "Signior Cavalier. I did not think my name was known at Penaflor." "How! known !" resumed he in his former strain. "we keep a register of all the celebrated names within twenty leagues of us. You in particular are looked upon as a prodigy ; and I don't at all doubt, that Spain will one day be as proud of you, as Greece was of her Seven Sages." These words were followed by a fresh hug, which I was forced to endure, though at the risk of strangulation. With the little experience I had, I ought not to have been the dupe of his professions and hyperbolical compliments. I ought to have known, by his extravagant flattery, that he was one of those parasites which abound in every town, and who, when a stranger arrives, introduce themselves to him, in order to fill their bellies at his expense. But my youth and vanity made me judge otherwise. My admirer appeared to me so much of a gentleman, that I invited him to take a share of my supper. "Ah, with all my soul," cried he; "I am too much obliged to my kind stars for having thrown me in the way of the illustrious Gil Blas, not to enjoy my good fortune as long as I can! I have no great appetite," pursued he, "but I will sit down to bear you company, and eat a mouthful purely out of complaisance."

So saying, my panegyrist took his place right over against me; and a cover being laid for him, attacked the omelet as voraciously as if he had fasted three whole days. By his complaisant beginning I foresaw that our dish would not last long; and therefore ordered a second; which they dressed with such dispatch, that it was served just as we—or rather he—had made an end of the first. He proceeded on this with the same vigour; and found means, without losing one stroke of his teeth, to overwhelm me with praises during the whole repast, which made me very well pleased with my sweet self. He drank in proportion to his eating; sometimes to my health, sometimes to that of my father and mother, whose happiness in having such a son as me he could not enough admire. All the while he plied me with wine, and insisted upon my doing him justice, while I toasted health for health; a circumstance which, together with his intoxicating flattery, put me into such good humour, that seeing our second omelet half devoured, I asked the landlord if he had no fish in the house. Signior Corcuelo, who in all likelihood had a fellow-feeling with the parasite, replied, "I have a delicate trout; but those who eat it must pay for the sauce;—'tis a bit too dainty for your palate, I doubt." "What do you call too dainty?" said the sycophant, raising his voice; "you're a wiseacre, indeed! Know, that there is nothing in this house too good for Signior Gil Blas de Santillane, who deserves to be entertained like a prince."

I was pleased at his laying hold of the landlord's last words, in which he prevented me; who finding myself offended, said with an air of disdain, "Produce this trout of yours, Gaffer Corcuelo, and give yourself no trouble about the consequence." This was what the innkeeper wanted. He got it ready, and served it up in a trice. At sight of this new dish, I could perceive the parasite's eye sparkle with joy; and he renewed that complaisance — I mean for the fish — which he had already shown for the eggs. At last, however, he was obliged to give out, for fear of accident, being crammed to the very throat. Having, therefore, eaten and drank his bellyfull, he thought proper to conclude the farce, by rising from table, and accosting me in these words:—"Signior Gil Blas, I am too well satisfied with your good cheer, to leave you without offering an important advice, which you seem to have great occasion for. Henceforth beware of praise, and be upon your guard against everybody you do not know. You may meet with other people inclined to divert themselves with your credulity, and perhaps to push things still further; but don't be duped again, nor believe yourself (though they should swear it) the eighth wonder of the world." So saying, he laughed in my face, and stalked away.

I was as much affected by this bite as I have since been by misfortunes of far greater consequence. I could not forgive myself for having been so grossly imposed upon; or

.ather, I was shocked to find my pride so humbled. "How! (said I to myself) has the traitor, then, made a jest of me? His design in accosting my landlord in the street was only to pump him; or perhaps they understand one another. Ah! simple Gil Blas! Go hang thyself for shame, for having given such rascals an opportunity of turning thee into ridicule! I suppose they'll trump up a fine story of this affair, which will reach Oviedo, and doubtless do thee a great deal of honour, and make thy parents repent their having thrown away so much good counsel on an ass. Instead of exhorting me not to wrong anybody, they ought to have cautioned me against the knavery of the world."

Chagrined with these mortifying reflections, and inflamed with resentment, I locked myself in my chamber and went to bed, where, however, I did not sleep; for before I could close my eyes, the carrier came to let me know he was ready to set out, and only waited for me. I got up instantly; and while I put on my clothes, Corcuelo brought me a bill, in which, I assure you, the trout was not forgotten; and I was not only obliged to gratify his exorbitance, but I had also the mortification to perceive, while I counted the money, that the sarcastic knave remembered my adventure. After having paid sauce for a supper which I had so ill digested, I went to the muleteer with my bags, wishing the parasite, the innkeeper, and his inn, at the

Ludovico in the Haunted Chamber.

FROM THE MYSTERIES OF UDOLPHO.

Mrs. Radcliffe, a beautiful little woman of delicate constitution and sequestered habits, as fond, as her own heroines, of lonely sea-shores, picturesque mountains, and poetical meditations, perfected that discovery of the capabilities of *an old house* or *castle* for exciting a romantic interest, which lay ready to be made in the mind of every child and poet, but which (if Gray did not put it into his head) first suggested itself to the feudal dilletanteism of Horace Walpole. Horace had more genius in him than his contemporaries gave him credit for; but the reputation which his wit obtained him, the material philosophy of the day, and the pursuit of fashionable amusement, did it no good. He lost sight of the line to be drawn between the imposing and the incredible; and though there is real merit in the *Castle of Otranto*, and even grandeur of imagination, yet the conversion of dreams into gross daylight palpabilities, which nothing short of iron-founders could create—swords that take a hundred men to lift them, and supernatural yet substantial helmets, big as houses and actually serving for prisons—turns the sublime into the ridiculous, and has completely spoilt an otherwise interesting narrative. Mrs. Radcliffe, frightened perhaps by Walpole's failure (for this great mistress of Fear was too often a servant of it), went to another extreme; and except in what she quoted from other story-tellers, resolved all her supernatural effects into commonplace causes. Those effects, however, while they lasted, and every thing else capable of frightening people out of their wits—old haunted houses and corridors, mysterious music, faces behind curtains, cowled and guilty monks, inquisitors, nuns, places to commit murders in, and the murders themselves—she understood to perfection. To dress these in appropriate circumstances, she possessed also the eye of a painter as well as the feeling of a poetess. She conceived to a nicety the effect of a storm on a landscape, the playing of a meteor on the point of a spear, and the sudden appearance of some old castle to which travellers have been long coming, and which they have reasons to fear living in. It has been objected to her that she is too much of a melodramatic writer, and that her characters are inferior to her circumstances; the background (as Hazlitt says) of more importance than the figures. This in a great measure is true; but she has painted characters also, chiefly weak ones, as in the querulous duped aunt in *Udolpho*, and the victim of error, St. Pierre, in the *Romance of the Forest*. It must be considered, however, that her effects, however produced, are successful, and greatly successful; and that Nature herself deals in precisely such effects, leaving men to be operated upon by them passively, and not to play the chief parts in the process by means of their characters. Mrs. Radcliffe brings on the scene Fear and Terror themselves, the grandeurs of the known world, and the awes of the unknown; and if human beings become puppets in her hands, it is as people in storm and earthquake are puppets in the hands of Nature.

The following passage, from the *Mysteries of Udolpho*, is one of the most favourite in her writings. Mr. Hazlitt thinks the Provençal tale in it "the greatest treat which Mrs. Radcliffe's pen has provided for the lovers of the marvellous and terrible." Sir Walter Scott says, "The best and most admired specimen of her art is the mysterious disappearance of Ludovico, after having undertaken to watch for a night in a haunted apartment; and the mind of the reader is finely wound up for some strange catastrophe, by the admirable ghost-story which he is represented as perusing to amuse his solitude, as the scene closes upon him. Neither can it be denied, that the explanation afforded of this mysterious accident is as probable as romance requires, and in itself completely satisfactory."

What that explanation is, the reader will find at the close of the extract.

THE count gave orders for the north apartments to be opened and prepared for the reception of Ludovico; but Dorothée, remembering what she had lately witnessed there, feared to obey; and not one of the other servants daring to venture thither, the rooms remained shut up till the time when Ludovico was to retire thither for the night, an hour for which the whole household waited with the greatest impatience.

After supper, Ludovico, by the order of the count, attended him in his closet, where they remained alone for near half an hour, and on leaving which his lord delivered to him a sword.

"It has seen service in mortal quarrels," said the count, jocosely, "you will use it honourably no doubt in a spiritual one. To-morrow let me hear that there is not one ghost remaining in the château."

Ludovico received it with a respectful bow. "You shall be obeyed, my lord," said he; "I will engage that no spectre shall disturb the peace of the château after this night."

They now returned to the supper-room, where the count's guests awaited to accompany him and Ludovico to the north apartments; and Dorothée, being summoned for the keys, delivered them to Ludovico, who then led the way, followed by most of the inhabitants of the château. Having reached the back staircase, several of the servants shrunk back and refused to go further, but the rest followed him to the top of the staircase, where a broad landing-place allowed them to flock round him, while he applied the key to the door, during which they watched him with as much eager curiosity as if he had been performing some magical rite.

Ludovico, unaccustomed to the lock, could not turn it, and Dorothée, who had lingered far behind, was called forward, under whose hand the door opened slowly, and her eye glancing within the dusky chamber, she uttered a sudden shriek and retreated. At this signal of alarm the greater part of the crowd hurried down, and the count, Henri, and Ludovico were left alone to pursue the inquiry, who instantly rushed into the apartment. Ludovico with a drawn sword, which he had just time to draw from the scabbard, the count with a lamp in his hand, and Henry carrying a basket containing provision for the courageous adventurer.

Having looked hastily round the first room, where nothing appeared to justify alarm, they passed on to the second; and here too all being quiet, they proceeded to a third in a more tempered step. The count had now leisure to smile at the discomposure into which he had been surprised, and to ask Ludovico in which room he designed to pass the night.

"There are several chambers beyond these, your excellenza," said Ludovico, pointing to a door, "and in one of them is a bed, they say. I will pass the night there; and when I am weary of watching, I can lie down."

"Good," said the count; "let us go on. You see, these rooms show nothing but damp walls and decaying furniture. I have been so much occupied since I came to the château, that I have not looked into them till now. Remember, Ludovico, to tell the housekeeper to-morrow to throw open these windows. The damask hangings are dropping to pieces; I will have them taken down, and this antique furniture removed."

"Dear sir," said Henri, "here is an arm-chair so massy with gilding, that it resembles one of the state chairs in the Louvre more than anything else."

"Yes," said the count, stopping a moment to survey it, "there is a history belonging to that chair, but I have not time to tell it; let us pass on. This suite runs to a greater extent than I imagined; it is many years since I was in them. But where is the bed-room you speak of, Ludovico? these are only ante-chambers to the great drawing-room. I remember them in their splendour."

"The bed, my lord," replied Ludovico, "they told me was in a room that opens beyond the saloon and terminates the suite."

"O, here is the saloon," said the count, as they entered the spacious apartment in which Emily and Dorothée had rested. He here stood for a moment, surveying the reliques of faded grandeur which it exhibited, the sumptuous tapestry, the long and low sofas of velvet with frames heavily carved and gilded, the floor inlaid with small squares of fine marble, and covered in the centre with a piece of rich tapestry work, the casements of painted glass, and the large Venetian mirrors of a size and quality such as at that period France could not make, which reflected on every side the spacious apartment. These had also formerly reflected a gay and brilliant scene, for this had been the state room of the château, and here the marchioness had held the assemblies that made part of the festivities of her nuptials. If the wand of a magician could have recalled the vanished groups—many of them vanished even from the earth!—that once had passed over these polished mirrors, what a varied and contrasted picture would they have exhibited with the present! Now, instead of a blaze of lights, and a splendid and busy crowd, they reflected only the rays of the one glimmering lamp which the count held up, and which scarcely served to show the three forlorn figures that stood surveying the room, and the spacious and dusky walls around them.

"Ah!" said the count to Henri, awaking from his deep reverie, "how the scene is changed since last I saw it! I was a young man then, and the marchioness was alive and in her bloom; many other persons were here too, who are now no more. There stood the orchestra, here we tripped in many a sprightly maze—the walls echoing to the dance. Now they resound only one feeble voice, and even that will, ere long, be heard no more. My son, remember that I was once as young as yourself, and that you must pass away like those who have preceded you—like those who, as they sung and danced in this most gay apartment, forgot that years are made up of moments, and that every step they took carried them nearer to their graves. But such reflections are useless—I had almost said criminal—unless they teach us to prepare for eternity, since otherwise they cloud our present happiness without guiding us to a future one. But enough of this—let us go on."

Ludovico now opened the door of the bed-room, and the count, as he entered, was struck with the funeral appearance which the dark arras gave to it. He approached the bed with an emotion of solemnity, and, perceiving it to be covered with a pall of black velvet, paused. "What can this mean?" said he, as he gazed upon it.

"I have heard, my lord," said Ludovico, as he stood at the feet, looking within the canopied curtains, "that the Lady Marchioness de Villeroi died in this chamber, and remained here till she was removed to be buried; and this, perhaps, signor, may account for the pall."

The count made no reply, but stood for a few moments engaged in thought, and evidently much affected. Then, turning to Ludovico, he asked him with a serious air, whether he thought his courage would support him through the night. "If you doubt this," added the count, "do not be ashamed to own it; I will release you from your engagement without exposing you to the triumphs of your fellow-servants." Ludovico paused; pride and something very like fear seemed struggling in his breast: pride, however, was victorious;—he blushed, and his hesitation ceased.

"No, my lord," said he, "I will go through with what

I have begun; and I am grateful for your consideration. On that hearth I will make a fire; and with the good cheer in this basket, I doubt not I shall do well."

"Be it so," said the count; "but how will you beguile the tediousness of the night, if you do not sleep?"

"When I am weary, my lord," replied Ludovico, "I shall not fear to sleep; in the meanwhile, I have a book that will entertain me."

"Well," said the count, "I hope nothing will disturb you; but if you should be seriously alarmed in the night, come to my apartment. I have too much confidence in your good sense and courage to believe you will be alarmed on slight grounds, or suffer the gloom of this chamber, or its remote situation, to overcome you with ideal terrors. To-morrow I shall have to thank you for an important service; these rooms shall then be thrown open, and my people will then be convinced of their error. Good-night, Ludovico; let me see you early in the morning, and remember what I lately said to you."

"I will, my lord. Good-night to your excellenza—let me attend you with the light."

He lighted the count and Henri through the chambers to the outer door. On the landing-place stood a lamp, which one of the affrighted servants had left; and Henri, as he took it up, again bade Ludovico "good-night," who, having respectfully returned the wish, closed the door upon them and fastened it. Then, as he retired to the bed-chamber, he examined the rooms through which he passed with more minuteness than he had done before; for he apprehended that some person might have concealed himself in them for the purpose of frightening him. No one, however, but himself was in these chambers; and leaving open the doors through which he passed, he came again to the great drawing-room, whose spaciousness and silent gloom somewhat startled him. For a moment he stood looking back through the long suite of rooms he had just quitted; and as he turned, perceiving a light and his own figure reflected in one of the large mirrors, he started. Other objects, too were seen obscurely on its dark surface, but he paused not to examine them, and returned hastily into the bed-room, as he surveyed which, he observed the door of the Oriel, and opened it. All within was still. On looking round, his eye was caught by the portrait of the deceased marchioness, upon which he gazed for a considerable time with great attention and some surprise; and then, having examined the closet he returned into the bed-room, where he kindled a wood fire, the bright blaze of which revived his spirits, which had begun to yield to the gloom and silence of the place; for gusts of wind alone broke at intervals this silence. He now drew a small table and a chair near the fire, took a bottle of wine and some cold provision out of his basket, and regaled himself. When he had finished his repast he laid his sword upon the table, and not feeling disposed to sleep, drew from his pocket the book he had spoken of. It was a volume of old Provençal tales. Having stirred the fire into a brighter blaze, trimmed his lamp, and drawn his chair upon the hearth, he began to read; and his attention was soon wholly occupied by the scenes which the page disclosed.

The count, meanwhile, had returned to the supper-room, whither those of the party who had attended him to the north apartment had retreated upon hearing Dorothée's scream, and who were now earnest in their inquiries concerning those chambers. The count rallied his guests on their precipitate retreat, and on the superstitious inclinations which had occasioned it; and this led to the question whether the spirit, after it has quitted the body, is ever permitted to revisit the earth ; and if it is, whether it was possible for spirits to become visible to the sense? The baron was of opinion, that the first was probable, and the last was possible ; and he endeavoured to justify this opinion by respectable authorities, both ancient and modern, which he quoted. The count, however, was decidedly against him : and a long conversation ensued, in which the usual arguments on these subjects were on both sides brought forward with skill and discussed with candour, but without converting either party to the opinion of his opponent. The effect of their conversation on their auditors was various. Though the count had much the superiority of the baron in point of argument, he had fewer adherents ; for that love, so natural to the human mind, of whatever is able to distend its faculties with wonder and astonishment, attached the majority of the company to the side of the baron ; and though many of the count's propositions were unanswerable, his opponents were inclined to believe this the consequence of their own want of knowledge on so abstracted a subject, rather than that arguments did not exist which were forcible enough to conquer him.

Blanche was pale with attention, till the ridicule in her father's glance called a blush upon her countenance, and she then endeavoured to forget the superstitious tales she had been told in the convent. Meanwhile, Emily had been listening with deep attention to the discussion of what was to her a very interesting question ; and remembering the appearance she had seen in the apartment of the late marchioness, she was frequently chilled with awe. Several times she was on the point of mentioning what she had seen, but the fear of giving pain to the count, and the dread of his ridicule, restrained her ; and awaiting in anxious expectation the event of Ludovico's intrepidity, she determined that her future silence should depend upon it.

When the party had separated for the night, and the count retired to his dressing-room, the remembrance of the desolate scenes he had so lately witnessed in his own mansion deeply affected him, but at length he was aroused from his reverie and his silence. "What music is that I hear?" said he suddenly to his valet. "Who plays at this late hour?"

The man made no reply; and the count continued to listen, and then added, "That is no common musician; he touches the instrument with a delicate hand. Who is it, Pierre?"

"My lord!" said the man, hesitatingly.

"Who plays that instrument?" repeated the count.

"Does not your lordship know, then?" said the valet.

"What mean you?" said the count somewhat sternly.

"Nothing, my lord, I mean nothing," rejoined the man submissively; "only—that music—goes about the house at midnight often, and I thought your lordship might have heard it before."

"Music goes about the house at midnight! Poor fellow! Does nobody dance to the music, too?"

"It is not in the château, I believe, my lord. The sounds come from the woods, they say, though they seem so very near; but then a spirit can do anything."

"Ah, poor fellow!" said the count, "I perceive you are as silly as the rest of them; to-morrow you will be convinced of your ridiculous error. But, hark! what noise is that?"

"Oh, my lord! that is the voice we often hear with the music."

"Often!" said the count; "how often, pray? It is a very fine one."

"Why, my lord, I myself have not heard it more than two or three times; but there are those who have lived here longer, that have heard it often enough."

"What a swell was that!" exclaimed the count, as he still listened; "and now, what a dying cadence! This is surely something more than mortal."

"That is what they say, my lord," said the valet; "they say it is nothing mortal that utters it; and if I might say my thoughts——"

"Peace!" said the count; and he listened till the strain died away.

"This is strange," said he, as he returned from the window. "Close the casements, Pierre."

Pierre obeyed, and the count soon after dismissed him but did not so soon lose the remembrance of the music, which long vibrated in his fancy in tones of melting sweetness, while surprise and perplexity engaged his thoughts.

Ludovico, meanwhile in his remote chamber, heard now and then the faint echo of a closing door as the family retired to rest; and then the hall-clock, at a great distance, struck twelve. "It is midnight," said he, and he looked suspiciously round the spacious chamber. The fire on the hearth was now nearly expiring, for his attention having been engaged by the book before him, he had forgotten everything besides; but he soon added fresh wood, not because he was cold, though the night was stormy, but because he was cheerless; and having again trimmed the lamp, he poured out a glass of wine, drew his chair nearer to the crackling blaze, tried to be deaf to the wind that howled mournfully at the casements, endeavoured to abstract his mind from the melancholy that was stealing upon him, and again took up his book. It had been lent to him by Dorothee, who had formerly picked it up in an obscure corner of the marquis's library; and who, having opened it, and perceived some of the marvels it related, had carefully preserved it for her own entertainment, its condition giving her some excuse for detaining it from its proper station. The damp corner into which it had fallen, had caused the cover to be disfigured and mouldy, and the leaves to be so discoloured with spots, that it was not without difficulty the letters could be traced. The fictions of the Provençal writers, whether drawn from the Arabian legends brought by the Saracens into Spain, or recounting the chivalric exploits performed by crusaders whom the troubadours accompanied to the East, were generally splendid, and always marvellous both in scenery and incident; and it is not wonderful that Dorothée and Ludovico should be fascinated by inventions which had captivated the careless imagination in every rank of society in a former age. Some of the tales, however, in the book now before Ludovico were of simple structure, and exhibited nothing of the magnificent machinery and heroic manners which usually characterized the fables of the twelfth century, and of this description was the one he now happened to open; which in its original style was of great length, but may be thus shortly related. The reader will perceive it is strongly tinctured with the superstition of the times.

THE PROVENÇAL TALE.

There lived, in the province of Bretagne, a noble baron, famous for his magnificence and courtly hospitalities. His castle was graced with ladies of exquisite beauty, and thronged with illustrious knights; for the honour he paid to feats of chivalry invited the brave of distant countries to enter his lists, and his court was more splendid than those of many princes. Eight minstrels were retained in his ser vice, who used to sing to their harps romantic fictions taken from the Arabians, or adventures of chivalry that befell knights during the crusades, or the martial deeds of the baron, their lord; while he, surrounded by his knights and ladies, banqueted in the great hall of the castle, where the costly tapestry that adorned the walls with pictured exploits of his ancestors, the casements of painted glass enriched with armorial bearings, the gorgeous banners that waved along the roof, the sumptuous canopies, the profusion of gold and silver that glittered on the sideboards, the numerous dishes that covered the tables, the number and gay liveries of the attendants, with the chivalric and splendid attire of the guests, united to form a scene of magnificence such as we may not hope to see in these degenerate days.

Of the baron the following adventure is related:—One night, having retired late from the banquet to his chamber, and dismissed his attendants, he was surprised by the appearance of a stranger of a noble air, but of a sorrowful and dejected countenance. Believing that this person had been secreted in the apartment, since it appeared impossible he could have lately passed the ante-room unobserved by the pages in waiting, who would have prevented this intrusion on their lord, the baron, calling loudly for his people, drew his sword, which he had not yet taken from his side, and stood upon his defence. The stranger, slowly advancing, told him that there was nothing to fear; that he came with no hostile intent, but to communicate to him a terrible secret, which it was necessary for him to know.

The baron, appeased by the courteous manner of the stranger after surveying him for some time in silence, returned his sword into the scabbard, and desired him to explain the means by which he had obtained access to the chamber, and the purpose of this extraordinary visit.

Without answering either of these inquiries, the stranger said that he could not then explain himself, but that, if the baron would follow him to the edge of the forest, at a short distance from the castle walls, he would there convince him that he had something of importance to disclose.

This proposal again alarmed the baron, who would scarcely believe that the stranger meant to draw him to so solitary a spot at this hour of the night without harbouring a design against his life, and he refused to go; observing at the same time, that if the stranger's purpose was an honourable one, he would not persist in refusing to reveal the occasion of his visit in the apartment where they stood.

While he spoke this, he viewed the stranger still more attentively than before, but observed no change in his countenance, or any symptom that might intimate a consciousness of evil design. He was habited like a knight, was of a tall and majestic stature, and of dignified and courteous manners. Still, however, he refused to communicate the substance of his errand in any place but that he had mentioned; and at the same time gave hints concerning the secret he would disclose, that awakened a degree of solemn curiosity in the baron, which at length induced him to consent to the stranger on certain conditions.

"Sir knight," said he, "I will attend you to the forest, and will take with me only four of my people, who shall witness our conference."

To this, however, the knight objected.

"What I would disclose," said he with solemnity, "is to you alone. There are only three living persons to whom the circumstance is known; it is of more consequence to you and your house than I shall now explain. In future years you will look back to this night with satisfaction or re pentance, accordingly as you now determine. As you would hereafter prosper, follow me; I pledge you the honour of a knight that no evil shall befall you. If you are contented to dare futurity, remain in your chamber, and I will depart as I came."

"Sir knight," replied the baron; "how is it possible that my future peace can depend upon my present determination?"

"That is not now to be told," said the stranger; "I have explained myself to the utmost. It is late; if you follow me it must be quickly; you will do well to consider the alternative."

The baron mused, and, as he looked upon the knight, he perceived his countenance assume a singular solemnity.

(Here Ludovico thought he heard a noise, and he threw a glance round the chamber, and then held up the lamp to assist his observation; but not perceiving anything to confirm his alarm, he took up the book again, and pursued the story.)

The baron paced his apartment for some time in silence, impressed by the words of the stranger, whose extraordinary request he feared to grant, and feared also to refuse. At length he said, "Sir knight, you are utterly unknown to me; tell me, yourself, is it reasonable that I should trust myself alone with a stranger, at this hour, in the solitary forest? Tell me, at least, who you are, and who assisted to secrete you in this chamber?"

The knight frowned at these words, and was a moment silent; then, with a countenance somewhat stern, he said, "I am an English knight; I am called Sir Bevys of Lancaster, and my deeds are not unknown at the holy city, whence I was returning to my native land, when I was benighted in the forest."

"Your name is not unknown to fame," said the baron; "I have heard of it." (The knight looked haughtily.) "But why, since my castle is known to entertain all true knights, did not your herald announce you? Why did you not appear at the banquet, where your presence would have been welcomed, instead of hiding yourself in my castle, and stealing to my chamber at midnight?"

The stranger frowned, and turned away in silence; but the baron repeated the questions.

"I come not," said the knight, "to answer inquiries, but to reveal facts. If you would know more, follow me; and again I pledge the honour of a knight that you shall return in safety. Be quick in your determination—I must be gone."

After some farther hesitation, the baron determined to follow the stranger, and to see the result of his extraordinary request; he therefore again drew forth his sword, and, taking up a lamp, bade the knight lead on. The latter obeyed; and opening the door of the chamber, they passed into the ante-room, where the baron, surprised to find all his pages asleep, stopped, and with hasty violence was going to reprimand them for their carelessness, when the knight waved his hand, and looked so expressively at the baron, that the latter restrained his resentment, and passed on.

The knight, having descended a staircase, opened a secret door, which the baron had believed was only known to himself; and proceeding through several narrow and winding passages, came at length to a small gate that opened beyond the walls of the castle. Meanwhile, the baron followed in silence and amazement, on perceiving that these secret passages were so well known to a stranger, and felt inclined to turn back from an adventure that appeared to partake of treachery as well as danger. Then, considering that he was armed, and observing the courteous and noble air of his conductor, his courage returned, he blushed that it had failed him for a moment, and he resolved to trace the mystery to its source.

He now found himself on the heathy platform, before the great gates of his castle, where, on looking up, he perceived lights glimmering in the different casements of the guests, who were retiring to sleep; and while he shivered in the blast, and looked on the dark and desolate scene around him, he thought of the comforts of his warm chamber, rendered cheerful by the blaze of wood, and felt, for a moment, the full contrast of his present situation.

(Here Ludovico paused a moment, and, looking at his own fire, gave it a brightening stir.)

The wind was strong, and the baron watched his lamp with anxiety, expecting every moment to see it extinguished; but though the flame wavered, it did not expire, and he still followed the stranger, who often sighed as he went, but did not speak.

When they reached the borders of the forest, the knight turned and raised his head, as if he meant to address the baron, but then closing his lips, in silence he walked on.

As they entered beneath the dark and spreading boughs, the baron, affected by the solemnity of the scene, hesitated whether to proceed, and demanded how much farther they were to go. The knight replied only by a gesture, and the baron, with hesitating steps and a suspicious eye, followed through an obscure and intricate path, till, having proceeded a considerable way, he again demanded whither they were going, and refused to proceed unless he was informed.

As he said this, he looked at his own sword and at the knight alternately, who shook his head, and whose dejected countenance disarmed the baron, for a moment, of suspicion.

"A little farther is the place whither I would lead you," said the stranger; "no evil shall befall you—I have sworn it on the honour of a knight."

The baron, reassured, again followed in silence, and they soon arrived at a deep recess of the forest, where the dark and lofty chestnuts entirely excluded the sky, and which was so overgrown with underwood that they proceeded with difficulty. The knight sighed deeply as he passed, and sometimes paused; and having at length reached a spot where the trees crowded into a knot, he turned, and with a terrific look, pointing to the ground, the baron saw there the body of a man, stretched at its length, and weltering in blood; a ghastly wound was on the forehead, and death appeared already to have contracted the features.

The baron, on perceiving the spectacle, started in horror, looked at the knight for explanation, and was then going to raise the body, and examine if there were any remains of life; but the stranger, waving his hand, fixed upon him a look so earnest and mournful, as not only much surprised him, but made him desist.

But what were the baron's emotions when, on holding the lamp near the features of the corpse, he discovered the exact resemblance of the stranger his conductor, to whom he now looked up in astonishment and inquiry! As he gazed he perceived the countenance of the knight change and begin to fade, till his whole form gradually vanished from his astonished sense! While the baron stood, fixed to the spot, a voice was heard to utter these words:—

(Ludovico started, and laid down the book, for he thought he heard a voice in the chamber, and he looked toward the bed, where, however, he saw only the dark curtain and the pall. He listened, scarcely daring to draw his breath, but heard only the distant roaring of the sea in the storm, and the blast that rushed by the casements; when, concluding that he had been deceived by its sighings, he took up his book to finish his story.)

While the baron stood, fixed to the spot, a voice was heard to utter these words:—

"The body of Sir Bevys of Lancaster, a noble knight of England, lies before you. He was this night waylaid and murdered, as he journeyed from the holy city towards his native land. Respect the honour of knighthood, and the law of humanity; inter the body in christian ground, and cause his murderers to be punished. As ye observe or neglect this, shall peace and happiness, or war and misery, light upon you and your house for ever!"

The baron, when he recovered from the awe and astonishment into which this adventure had thrown him, returned to his castle, whither he caused the body of Sir Bevys to be removed; and on the following day it was interred with the honours of knighthood, in the chapel of the castle, attended by all the noble knights and ladies who graced the court of Baron de Brunne.

Ludovico, having finished this story, laid aside the book, for he felt drowsy; and after putting more wood on the fire, and taking another glass of wine, he reposed himself in the arm-chair on the hearth. In his dream he still beheld the chamber where he really was, and once or twice started from imperfect slumbers, imagining he saw a man's face looking over the high back of his arm-chair. This idea had so strongly impressed him, that, when he raised his eyes, he almost expected to meet other eyes fixed upon his own; and he quitted his seat, and looked behind the chair before he felt perfectly convinced that no person was there.

Thus closed the hour.

The count, who had slept little during the night, rose early, and, anxious to speak with Ludovico, went to the north apartment; but the outer door having been fastened on the preceding night, he was obliged to knock loudly for admittance. Neither the knocking nor his voice was heard: he renewed his calls more loudly than before; after which a total silence ensued; and the count, finding all his efforts to be heard ineffectual, at length began to fear that some accident had befallen Ludovico, whom terror of an imaginary being might have deprived of his senses. He therefore left the door with an intention of summoning his servants to force it open, some of whom he now heard moving in the lower part of the château.

To the count's inquiries whether they had seen or heard any thing of Ludovico, they replied, in affright, that not one of them had ventured on the north side of the château since the preceding night.

"He sleeps soundly, then," said the count, "and is at such a distance from the outer door, which is fastened, that to gain admittance to the chambers it will be necessary to force it. Bring an instrument, and follow me."

The servants stood mute and dejected, and it was not till nearly all the household were assembled, that the count's orders were obeyed. In the meantime, Dorothée was telling of a door that opened from a gallery leading from the great staircase into the last ante-room of the saloon, and this being much nearer to the bed-chamber, it appeared probable that Ludovico might be easily awakened by an attempt to open it. Thither, therefore, the count went; but his voice was as ineffectual at this door as it had proved at the remoter one; and now, seriously interested for Ludovico, he was himself going to strike upon the door with the instrument, when he observed its singular beauty, and withheld the blow. It appeared on the first glance to be of ebony, so dark and close was its grain, and so high its polish; but it proved to be only of larch-wood, of the growth of Provence, then famous for its forests of larch. The beauty of its polished hue, and of its delicate carvings, determined the count to spare this door, and he returned to that leading from the back staircase, which being at length forced, he entered the first ante-room, followed by Henri and a few of the most courageous of his servants, the rest waiting the event of the inquiry on the stairs and landing-place.

All was silence in the chambers through which the count passed, and having reached the saloon, he called loudly upon Ludovico; after which, still receiving no answer, he threw open the door of the bed-room, and entered.

The profound stillness within confirmed his apprehensions for Ludovico, for not even the breathings of a person in sleep were heard; and his uncertainty was not soon terminated, since the shutters being all closed, the chamber was too dark for any object to be distinguished in it.

The count bade a servant open them, who, as he crossed the room to do so, stumbled over something. and fell to the floor, when his cry occasioned such a panic among the few of his fellows who had ventured thus far. that they instantly fled, and the count and Henri were left to finish the adventure.

Henri then sprang across the room, and, opening a window-shutter, they perceived that the man had fallen over a chair near the hearth, in which Ludovico had been sitting;—for he sat there no longer, nor could anywhere be seen by the imperfect light that was admitted into the apartment. The count, seriously alarmed, now opened other shutters, that he might be enabled to examine farther; and Ludovico not yet appearing, he stood for a moment suspended in astonishment, and scarcely trusting his senses, till his eyes glancing on the bed, he advanced to examine whether he was there asleep. No person, however, was in it; and he proceeded to the Oriel, where every thing remained as on the preceding night; but Ludovico was nowhere to be found.

The count now checked his amazement, considering that Ludovico might have left the chamber during the night, overcome by the terrors which their lonely desolation and the recollected reports concerning them had inspired. Yet, if this had been the fact, the man would naturally have sought society, and his fellow-servants had all declared they had not seen him; the door of the outer room also had been found fastened, with the key on the inside; it was impossible, therefore, for him to have passed through that; and all the outer doors of this suite were found, on examination, to be bolted and locked, with the keys also within them. The count, being then compelled to believe that the lad had escaped through the casements, next examined them: but such as opened wide enough to admit the body of a man were found to be carefully secured either by iron bars or by shutters, and no vestige appeared of any person having attempted to pass them; neither was it probable that Ludovico would have incurred the risk of breaking his neck by leaping from a window, when he might have walked safely through a door.

The count's amazement did not admit of words; but he returned once more to examine the bed-room, where was no appearance of disorder, except that occasioned by the late overthrow of the chair, near which had stood a small table; and on this Ludovico's sword, his lamp, the book he had been reading, and the remains of a flask of wine, still remained. At the foot of the table, too, was the basket, with some fragments of provision and wood.

Henri and the servant now uttered their astonishment without reserve, and though the count said little, there was a seriousness in his manner that expressed much. It appeared that Ludovico must have quitted these rooms by some concealed passage, for the count could not believe that any supernatural means had occasioned this event; yet, if there was any such passage, it seemed inexplicable why he should retreat through it; and it was equally surprising that not even the smallest vestige should appear by which his progress could be traced. In the rooms, everything remained as much in order as if he had just walked out by the common way.

The count himself assisted in lifting the arras with which the bed-chamber, saloon, and one of the ante-rooms were hung, that he might discover if any door had been concealed behind it; but after a laborious search, none was found; and he at length quitted the apartments, having secured the door of the last ante-chamber, the key of which he took into his own possession. He then gave orders that strict search should be made for Ludovico, not only in the château, but in the neighbourhood, and retiring with Henri to his closet, they remained there in conversation for a considerable time; and whatever was the subject of it, Henri from this hour lost much of his vivacity; and his manners were particularly grave and reserved, whenever the topic which now agitated the count's family with wonder and alarm, was introduced.*

* The château had been inhabited before the count came into its possession. He was not aware that the apparently outward walls contained

a series of passages and staircases, which led to unknown vaults underground; and, therefore, he never thought of looking for a door in those parts of the chamber which he supposed to be next to the air. In these was a communication with the room. The château (for we are not here in Udolpho) was on the sea-shore in Languedoc; its vaults had become the store-house of pirates, who did their best to keep up the supernatural delusions that hindered people from searching the premises; and these pirates had carried Ludovico away.

The Warning.

FROM THE NOVEL OF "NATURE AND ART," BY MRS. INCHBALD.

ELIZABETH INCHBALD, an amusing dramatist, a writer of stories of the highest order for sentiment and passion, and a beautiful woman, admirable for attractiveness of almost every kind, especially candour and self-denial, was daughter of a farmer in Suffolk, of the name of Simpson. She married an actor, a very worthy man, who died not long after their union. She performed on the stage herself for some years, in spite of an impediment in her speech, which seems to have been generally under control; and then settled down into a successful authoress, courted by high and low, often with a view to marriage. In one or two instances offers would evidently have been accepted had they been made, but she was superior to all that were unconnected with the heart. She maintained some relatives at the expense of personal sacrifices that sometimes left her without a fire in winter; and she died at a respectable lodging-house in Kensington, where she was buried in the churchyard. She wrote the dramas of *The Midnight Hour, The Mogul Tale, Such Things Are,* &c.; and, besides the novel from which the following incident is taken, was authoress of *The Simple Story,* one of the deepest-felt and best-written tales in the language. We had not the honor of knowing Mrs. Inchbald; but we love her memory for many reasons—one of which is, that a mother who possessed similar virtues was fond of those novels, particularly *Nature and Art,* and recommended it strongly to us in our boyhood. Passages more beautiful and pathetic than those which we have selected are not to be found in the whole circle of English prose.

The reader will observe that the warning is not aimed at lawyers in particular. The writer would have done nothing so unjust. A lawyer is only selected for the more striking illustration of it; and as the profession, generally speaking, has been as free in its way of life as most others, however admirable for the final wisdom and virtue in which its many-thoughted experience tends to settle it, the dreadful circumstances imagined in this story are but too possible—perhaps have often occurred in spirit, though not in letter. The exclamation "Oh, not from you!" may rank with the finest bursts of emotion in the tragic poets; and it comes more dreadfully home to the bosom of society.

THE day at length is come on which Agnes shall have a sight of her beloved William! She who has watched for hours near his door, to procure a glimpse of him going out or returning home; who has walked miles to see his chariot pass; she now will behold him, and he will see her, by command of the laws of his country. Those laws, which will deal with rigour towards her, are in this one instance still indulgent.

The time of the assizes at the county town in which she is imprisoned, is arrived—the prisoners are demanded at the shire-hall—the jail doors are opened—they go in sad procession. The trumpet sounds—it speaks the arrival of the judge—and that judge is William.

The day previous to her trial, Agnes had read, in the printed calendar of the prisoners, his name as the learned judge before whom she was to appear. For a moment she forgot her perilous state in the excess of joy which the still unconquerable love she bore to him permitted her to taste, even on the brink of the grave! After reflection made her check these worldly transports, as unfit for the present solemn occasion. But, alas! to her, earth and William were so closely united, that, till she forsook the one, she could never cease to think, without the contending passions of hope, of fear, of love, of shame, and of despair, on the other.

Now fear took place of her first immoderate joy; she feared that, although much changed in person since he had seen her, and her real name now added to many an *alias*— yet she feared that some well-known glance of the eye, turn of the action, or accent of speech, might recall her to his remembrance; and at that idea, shame overcame all her other sensations—for still she retained pride, in respect to his opinion, to wish him not to know Agnes was that wretch she felt she was! Once a ray of hope beamed on her, that if he knew her—if he recognised her—he might possibly befriend her cause; and life, bestowed through William's friendship, seemed a precious object! But, again, that rigorous honour she had often heard him boast, that firmness to his word, of which she had fatal experience, taught her to know he would not, for any improper compassion, any unmanly weakness, forfeit his oath of impartial justice.

In meditations such as these she passed the sleepless night.

When, in the morning, she was brought to the bar, and her guilty hand held up before the righteous judgment-seat of William, imagination could not form two figures, or two situations more incompatible with the existence of former familiarity than the judge and the culprit; and yet, these very persons had passed together the most blissful moments that either ever tasted! Those hours of tender dalliance were now present to her mind—his thoughts were more nobly employed in his high office; nor could the haggard face, hollow eye, desponding countenance, and meagre person of the poor prisoner, once call to his memory, though her name was uttered among a list of others which she had assumed, his former youthful, lovely Agnes!

She heard herself arraigned, with trembling limbs and downcast looks, and many witnesses had appeared against her, before she ventured to lift her eyes up to her awful judge; she then gave one fearful glance, and discovered William, unpitying but beloved William, in every feature! It was a face she had been used to look on with delight, and a kind of absent smile of gladness now beamed on her poor wan visage.

When every witness on the part of the prosecutor had been examined, the judge addressed himself to her—

"What defence have you to make?"

It was William spoke to Agnes! The sound was sweet; the voice was mild, was soft, compassionate, encouraging. It almost charmed her to a love of life! Not such a voice as when William last addressed her; when he left her undone and pregnant, vowing never to see or speak to her more.

She would have hung upon the present word for ever. She did not call to mind that this gentleness was the effect of practice, the art of his occupation; which, at times, is but a copy, by the unfeeling, of the benevolent brethren of the bench. In the present judge, tenderness was not designed for consolation of the culprit, but for the approbation of the auditors.

There were no spectators, Agnes, by your side when last he parted from you;—if there had, the awful William would have been awed to marks of pity.

Stunned with the enchantment of that well-known tongue directed to her, she stood like one just petrified—all vital power seemed suspended.

Again he put the question, and with these additional sentences, tenderly and emphatically delivered:—"Recollect yourself; have you no witnesses? no proof on your behalf?"

A dead silence followed these questions.

He then mildly but forcibly added—" What have you to say ?"

Here a flood of tears burst from her eyes, which she fixed earnestly upon him, as if pleading for mercy, while she faintly articulated—

" Nothing, my lord."

After a short pause, he asked her in the same forcible, but benevolent tone—

" Have you no one to speak to your character ?"

The prisoner answered—

" No."

A second gush of tears followed this reply, for she called to mind by whom her character had first been blasted.

He summed up the evidence, and every time he was obliged to press hard upon the proofs against her, she shrunk, and seemed to stagger with the deadly blow—writhed under the weight of his minute justice, more than from the prospect of a shameful death.

The jury consulted but a few minutes, the verdict was—" Guilty."

She heard it with composure.

But when William placed the fatal velvet on his head, and rose to pronounce the fatal sentence, she started with a kind of convulsive motion, retreated a step or two back, and lifting up her hands, with a scream exclaimed—

" Oh, not from you !"

The piercing shriek which accompanied these words, prevented their being heard by part of the audience ; and those who heard them thought little of their meaning, more than that they expressed her fear of dying.

Serene and dignified, as if no such exclamation had been uttered, William delivered the final speech ending with—" Dead, dead, dead."

She fainted as he closed the period, and was carried back to prison in a swoon; while he adjourned the court to go to dinner.

If, unaffected by the scene he had witnessed, William sat down to dinner with an appetite, let not the reader conceive that the most distant suspicion had struck his mind of his ever having seen, much less familiarly known, the poor offender whom he had just condemned. Still this forgetfulness did not proceed from the want of memory for Agnes. In every peevish or heavy hour passed with his wife, he was sure to think of her; yet it was self-love, rather than love of her, that gave rise to these thoughts. He felt the lack of female sympathy and tenderness to soften the fatigue of studious labour, to soothe a sullen, a morose disposition—he felt he wanted comfort for himself, but never once considered what were the wants of Agnes.

In the chagrin of a barren bed he sometimes thought, too, even on the child that Agnes bore him; but whether it were male or female, whether a beggar in the streets or dead, various and important public occupation forbade him to inquire. Yet the poor, the widow, and the orphan frequently shared William's ostentatious bounty. He was the president of many excellent charities, gave largely, and sometimes instituted benevolent societies for the unhappy; for he delighted to load the poor with obligation, and the rich with praise.

There are persons like him who love to do every thing good but that which their immediate duty requires. There are servants that will serve every one more cheerfully than their masters; there are men who will distribute money liberally to all except their creditors; and there are wives who will love all mankind better than their own husbands. *Duty* is a familiar word which has little effect upon an ordinary mind, and as ordinary minds make a vast majority, we have acts of generosity, self-denial, and honesty, where smaller pains would constitute greater virtues. Had William followed the common dictates of charity, had he adopted private pity instead of public munificence, had he cast an eye at home before he sought abroad for objects of compassion, Agnes had been preserved from an ignominious death, and he had been preserved from—*remorse*, the tortures of which he for the first time proved on reading a printed sheet of paper, accidentally thrown in his way a few days after he had left the town in which he had condemned her to die.

"March 10th, 179—.

"The last dying words, speech, and confession, birth, parentage, and education, life, character, and behaviour, of Agnes Primrose, who was executed this morning between the hours of ten and twelve, pursuant to the sentence passed upon her by the Honourable Justice Norwynne.

"Agnes Primrose was born of honest parents, in the village of Anfield, in the county of ——" (William started at the name of the village and county); "but being led astray by the arts and flattery of seducing man, she fell from the paths of virtue, and took to bad company, which instilled into her young heart all their evil ways, and at length brought her to this untimely end. So she hopes her death will be a warning to all young persons of her own sex, how they listen to the praises and courtship of young men, especially of those who are their betters; for they only court to deceive. But the said Agnes freely forgives all persons who have done her injury or given her sorrow, from the young man who first won her heart, to the jury who found her guilty, and the judge who condemned her to death.

"And she acknowledges the justice of her sentence, not only in respect of her crime for which she suffers, but in regard to many other heinous sins of which she has been guilty, more especially that of once attempting to commit a murder upon her own helpless child; for which guilt she now considers the vengeance of God has overtaken her, to which she is patiently resigned, and departs in peace and charity with all the world, praying the Lord to have mercy on her parting soul."

POSTSCRIPT TO THE CONFESSION.

"So great was this unhappy woman's terror of death and the awful judgment that was to follow, that when sentence was pronounced upon her she fell into a swoon, from that into convulsions, from which she never entirely recovered, but was delirious to the time of her execution, except that short interval in which she made her confession to the clergyman who attended her. She has left one child, a youth almost sixteen, who has never forsaken his mother during all the time of her imprisonment, but waited on her with true filial duty; and no sooner was her final sentence passed than he began to droop, and now lies dangerously ill near the prison from which she is released by death. During the loss of her senses, the said Agnes Primrose raved continually of her child; and, asking for pen, ink, and paper, wrote an incoherent petition to the judge, recommending the youth to his protection and mercy. But notwithstanding this insanity, she behaved with composure and resignation when the fatal morning arrived in which she was to be launched into eternity. She prayed devoutly during the last hour, and seemed to have her whole mind fixed on the world to which she was going. A crowd of spectators followed her to the fatal spot, most of whom returned weeping at the recollection of the fervency with which she prayed, and the impression which her dreadful state seemed to make upon her."

* * * * * *

No sooner had the name of "Anfield" struck William, than a thousand reflections and remembrances flashed on his mind to give him full conviction who it was he had judged and sentenced. He recollected the sad remains of Agnes, such as he once had known her; and now he wondered how his thoughts could have been absent from an object so pitiable, so worthy of his attention, as not to give him even suspicion who she was, either from her name or from her person, during the whole trial.

But wonder, astonishment, horror, and every other sensation was absorbed by—*remorse.* It wounded, it stabbed, it rent his hard heart as it would do a tender one; it havocked on his firm inflexible mind as it would on a weak and pliant brain! Spirit of Agnes! look down, and behold all your wrongs revenged! William feels—*remorse.*

John Buncle.

THE *Life of John Buncle, Esq.; containing various Observations and Reflections made in several parts of the World, and many Extraordinary Relations,* is a book unlike any other in the language, perhaps in the world; and the introduction of passages from it into the present volume must be considered as being, like itself, an exception to rules; for it will resemble rather a notice in a review, than our selections in general. John's Life is not a classic: it contains no passage which is a general favourite: no extract could be made from it of any length, to which readers of good taste would not find objections. Yet there is so curious an interest in all its absurdities; its jumble of the gayest and gravest considerations is so founded in the actual state of things; it draws now and then such excellent portraits from life; and above all, its animal spirits are at once so excessive and so real, that we defy the best readers not to be entertained with it, and having had one or two specimens, not to desire more. Buncle would say, that there is "cut and come again" in him, like one of his luncheons of cold beef and a foaming tankard.

John Buncle, Esq., is the representative of his author, Thomas Amory; of whom little is known, except that he was a gentleman of singular habits and appearance, who led a retired life, was married, was a vehement Unitarian, wrote another extraordinary book professing to be "*Lives of Several Ladies*" (in which there is a link with John), and died, to the glory of animal spirits, and of rounds of bread and butter (into which his good cheer seems latterly to have merged), at the ripe old age of ninety-seven. He is supposed to have been bred a physician. His father was a barrister, and is understood to have acquired considerable property in Ireland, in consequence of becoming secretary to the forfeited estates.

John Bunele is evidently Amory himself. This is apparent from the bits of real autobiography which are mixed with the fictitious, and which constitute one of the strange jumbles in his book. Hazlitt has called him the "English Rabelais;" and in point of animal spirits, love of good cheer, and something of a mixture of scholarship, theology, and profane reading, he may be held to deserve the title; but he has no claim to the Frenchman's greatness of genius, freedom from bigotry, and profoundness of wit and humour. He might have done very well for a clerk to Rabelais; and his master would have laughed quite as much at, as with him. John is a kind of innocent Henry the Eighth "of private life," without the other's fat, fury, and solemnity. He is a prodigious hand at matrimony, at divinity, at a song, at a loud "hem," and at a turkey and chine. He breaks with the Trinitarians as confidently and with as much scorn as Henry did with the Pope; and he marries seven wives, whom he disposes of by the lawful process of fever and small-pox. His book is made up of natural history, mathematics (literally), songs, polemics, landscapes, eating and drinking, and characters of singular men, all bound together by his introductions to and marriages with these seven successive ladies, every one of whom is a charmer, a Unitarian, and cut off in the flower of her youth. Bunele does not know how to endure her loss; he shuts his eyes "for three days;" is stupified; is in despair; till suddenly he recollects that Heaven does not like such conduct; that it is a mourner's business to bow to its decrees; to be devout; to be philosophic: in short, to be jolly, and look out for another dear, bewitching partner, "on Christian principles." This is, literally, a fair account of his book; and our readers are now qualified to understand the passages we proceed to extract.

The "*Lives of Several Ladies*," which preceded Bunele's autobiography, professed to be genuine lives, and were equally manifest fictions, mixed with a portion of truth. The ladies, like the wives, were all Unitarians, and all charming; and the writer, after a certain spiritual mode, fell in love with them. They partook of his zest for all the pleasures of life; had a great objection to ugly, as well as to Athanasian husbands, and none in the world to a good supper. The lives are addressed to a friend of the name of Jewks—a name which is often apostrophized with an abrupt joviality of the most amusing kind, in the midst of theological disquisitions. As the opening of this work is no unfavourable specimen of the author, and furnishes a pretty thorough foretaste of his spirit, the reader is presented with a few pages of it.

"Your letter, dear Jewks, I had the pleasure of receiving; and, that you should not suspect me of neglecting you, I postpone my journey to Chadson, to answer your questions. To the best of my power I will give you a monument of my friendship, though at present my condition is such, that I cannot subtract too much from the organs of the intellect, to give to those of motion. You shall have all I know relating to the lady you inquire after. You shall have, by the way, a few occasional observations.

"In the year 1739, I travelled many hundred miles to visit ancient monuments, and discover curious things; and as I wandered, to this purpose, among the vast hills of Northumberland, fortune conducted me one evening, in the month of June, when I knew not where to rest, to the sweetest retirement my eyes have ever beheld. This is Hali-farm. It is a beautiful vale surrounded with rocks, forest, and water. I found at the upper end of it the prettiest thatched house in the world, and a garden of the most artful confusion I had ever seen. The little mansion was covered on every side with the finest flowery greens. The streams, all round, were murmuring and falling a thousand ways. All the kinds of singing birds were here collected, and in high harmony on the sprays. The ruins of an abbey enhance the beauties of this place; they appear at the distance of four hundred yards from the house; and as some great trees are now grown up among the remains, and a river winds between the broken walls, the view is solemn, the picture fine.

"When I came up to the house, the first figure I saw was the lady whose story I am going to relate. She had the charms of an angel, but her dress was quite plain and clean like a country maid. Her person appeared faultless, and of the middle size, between the disagreeable extremes; her face a sweet oval, and her complexion the brunette of the bright rich kind; her mouth, like a rose-bud that is just beginning to blow; and a fugitive dimple, by fits, would lighten and disappear. The finest passions were always passing in her face; and in her long, even, chestnut eyes, there was a fluid fire sufficient for half-a-dozen pair.

"She had a volume of Shakspeare in her hand as I came softly towards her, having left my horse at a distance with my servant; and her attention was so much engaged with the extremely poetical and fine lines which Titania speaks in the third act of the *Midsummer Night's Dream*, that she did not see me till I was quite near her. She seemed then in great amazement. She could not be much more surprised if I had dropped from the clouds. But this was soon over, upon my asking her if she was not the daughter of Mr. John Bruce, as I supposed from a similitude of faces, and informing her that her father, if I was right, was my near friend, and would be glad to see his chum in that part of the world. Marinda replied, 'You are not wrong;' and immediately asked me in. She conducted me to a parlour that was quite beautiful in the rural way, and welcomed me to Hali-farm, as her father would have done, she said, had I arrived before his removal to a better world. She then left me for a while, and I had time to look over the room I was in. The floor was covered with rushes wrought into the prettiest mat, and the walls decorated all round with the finest flowers and shells. Robins and nightingales, the finch and the linnet, were in the neatest red cages of her own making; and at the upper end of the chamber, in a charming little open grotto, was the finest *strix capite aurito, corpore rufo*, that I have seen, that is, the *great eagle owl*. This beautiful bird, in a niche like a ruin, looked vastly fine. As to the flowers which adorned this room, I thought they were all natural at my first coming in, but on inspection it appeared that several baskets of the finest kinds were inimitably painted on the walls by Marinda's hand.

"These things afforded me a pleasing entertainment for about half an hour, and then Miss Bruce returned. One of the maids brought in a supper—such fare, she said, as her little cottage afforded; and the table was covered with green peas and pigeons, cream cheese, new bread and butter. Everything was excellent in its kind. The cider and ale were admirable. Discretion and dignity appeared in Marinda's behaviour; she talked with judgment; and, under the decencies of ignorance, was concealed a valuable knowledge."—Vol. I., p. 1.

This is the way in which Buncle meets with most of his ladies. They are discovered in lovely places reading books, and are always prepared for nice little suppers. Their fathers or other companions are generally people to match. Jack Bruce, Marinda's father, was an excellent good fellow, disinherited by his own father for refusing to sign the thirty-nine articles. He disappears in a solitude, marries a farmer's daughter ("an extraordinary beauty" with an "uncommon understanding"), and becomes a farmer himself.

"'Religion,' would Jack Bruce say, as we passed an evening over a little bowl of nectar—for he never taught in the dry, sober method—'religion,' &c."

Then follows a picture of philosophic Unitarianism.

"This was a glorious faith, Jewks." People, he says, "may substitute inventive pieces in the place of true religion, and multiply their fancies into endless volumes; such as, *Revelation examined with Candour*, the most uncandid thing that ever was written; the *Life of David*, &c., by the same author; Rogers's *Discourse of the Visible and Invisible Church*; Waterland's *Importance*, and other writings; the execrable dialogues called *Ophiomaches*; *Trapp, Webster,* and *Vernon;* the miserable *Answers* to the *Bishop of Clogher;* Dodwell, *Church*, and *Brooks*, against *Middleton;* Knowles against the *Argument à Priori;* and cartloads of such *religious lumber*" (these italics are the author's); "but, my dear Jewks, true Christianity lies in repentance and amendment."

Miss Bruce wins a husband by painting pictures of "Arcadia" and the "Crucifixion," and "playing on the fiddle." Divers charming young ladies come to her house by accident, and form extempore never-dying friendships, in the manner of the people in the *Rovers*—

"Come to my arms, my slight acquaintance."

Among others are Mrs. Schomberg and Miss West.

"They were riding to Crawford Dyke, near Dunglass, the place I intended for, and by a wrong turn in the road came to Mrs. Benlow's house, instead of going to Robin's Toad, where they designed to bait. It was between eight and nine at night when they got to her door; and as they appeared, by the richness of their riding-dress, their servants, and the beautiful horses they rid, to be women of distinction, Mrs. Benlow invited them in, and requested they would lie at her house that night, as the inn they were looking for was very bad. Nothing could be more grateful to the ladies than this proposal. They were on the ground in a moment; and we all sat down soon after, with the greatest cheerfulness, to a fine dish of trouts, roasted chickens, tarts, and sparragrass. The strangers were quite charmed with everything they saw. The sweet rural room they were in, and the wild beauties of the garden in view, they could not enough admire; and they were so struck with Mrs. Benlow's goodness, and the lively happy manner she has of showing it, that they conceived immediately the greatest affection for her. Felicity could not rise higher than it did at this table. *For a couple of hours we laughed most immoderately.*"—Id., p. 92.

But to quit the lives of ladies who married other men, and come to John Buncle and his own. John quits his father, as Jack Bruce did, on account of a religious difference, and goes about the world, seeking whom he may marry. His first wife is a Miss Melmoth. He had known her some time, when having been led one day into some particularly serious reflections on life and death by the sight of a skeleton, he considered that it would be a good thing to "commence a matrimonial relation with some sensible, good-humoured, dear, delightful girl of the mountains, and persuade her to be the cheerful partner of his still life." He thought that "nature and reason" would then "create the highest scenes of felicity, and that he should live, as it were, in the suburbs of heaven."

" This is fine," concludes he, in an ecstacy. " For once in my life I am fortunate. And suppose this partner I want in my solitude could be Miss Melmoth, one of the wisest and most discreet of women, thinking a bloom and good-humour itself in a human figure, then, indeed, I must be happy in this silent, romantic station. This spot of earth would then have all the felicities.—Resolved. *Conclusum est contra Manichæos*, said the great St. Austin; *and with a thump of his fist, he* (*St. Austin*) *cracked the table.*"—Vol. II., Edit. 1770, p. 62.

Miss Melmoth, being one of the wisest as well as loveliest of women, accepts of course the hand that draws so convincing a conclusion from the fist of St. Austin. For two years they lead a life of bliss; but at the end of that time she dies of a fever, and John quits a solitude which he could not bear.

His second wife is the lovely Miss Statia Henley, "bright and charming as Aurora," daughter of John Henley, Esquire, of the Groves of Basil. She had some fugitive notions of celibacy, which our hero refutes on Christian principles; and, as in the former instance, they lead a life of bliss for two years. The "illustrious Statia" then dies of the small-pox, and is laid by Charlotte's side.

"Thus did I again become a mourner. I sat with my eyes shut for three days; but at last called for my horse, to try what air, exercise, and variety of objects could do."— Vol. III., p. 57.

Air, exercise, and a variety of objects did very well; for Mr. Buncle misses his way into the house and grounds of the exquisite Miss Antonia Cramer, "a heaven-born maid" and "innocent beauty," whom he marries of course. But her, also, alas! he loses of the small-pox, at the end of two—no, three years. "Four" days, too, he sits with his eyes shut, which is a day more than he gave to Statia; and then he left the lodge once more, "to live, if he could, since his religion ordered him so to do, and see what he was next to meet with in the world."

"Nota bene," says our author at this place. "As I mention nothing of any children by so many wives, some readers may perhaps wonder at this; and therefore, to give a general answer, once for all, I think it sufficient to observe, that I had a great many to carry on the *succession*; but as they never were concerned in any extraordinary affairs, nor ever did any remarkable things, that I ever heard of;—only rise and breakfast, read and saunter, drink and eat, it would not be fair, in my opinion, to make any one pay for their history."—P. 151.

This kind of progeny, by the way, hardly does credit to our hero's very exquisite marriages. But as extremes meet, and fair play must be seen to the mass of the community, we suppose the young Buncles were dull, in consideration of the vivacity of the parents.

Mr. Buncle having laid his beloved Antonia by the side of his Charlotte and his Statia, now goes to Harrogate; and while there, "it .s his fortune to dance with a lady who had the head of an Aristotle, the heart of a primitive Christian, and the form of a Venus de Medicis."

"This was Miss Spence, of Westmoreland. I was not many hours in her company," says he, "before I became most passionately in love with her. I did all I could to win her heart, and at last asked her the question. But before I inform my readers what the consequence of this was, I must take some notice of what I expect from the Critical Reviewers. These gentlemen will attempt to raise the laugh. Our moralist (they will say) has buried three wives running, and they are hardly cold in their graves before he is dancing like a buck at the Wells, and plighting vows to a fourth girl, the beauty Miss Spence. *An honest fellow*, this Suarez, as Pascal says of that Jesuit, in his Provincial Letters.

"To this I reply, that I think it unreasonable and impious to grieve immoderately for the dead. A decent and proper tribute of tears and sorrow humanity requires; but when that duty has been paid, we must remember, that *to lament a dead woman is not to lament a wife!* A wife must be a living woman."—Vol. III., p. 180.

He argues furthermore, that it would be sinful to behave on such occasions as if Providence had been unjust. The lady has been lent but for a term; and we must bow to the limitation. Besides, she is in Heaven; and therefore it would be senseless to continue murmuring, and not make the most of the world that remains to us, while she is "breathing the balmy air of Paradise," and being "beyond description happy."

Miss Spence, however, is a little coy. She is a very learned as well as charming young lady. She quotes Virgil, discourses with her lover on fluxions and the Differential Calculus, and is not to be won quite so fast as he wishes. Nevertheless, he wins her at last; loses her in six months of a malignant fever and four doctors; and in less than three months afterwards, marries the divine Miss Emilia Turner, of Skelsmore Vale—alas! for six weeks only. A chariot and four runs away with them, and his "charmer is killed." She lives about an hour, repeats some consolatory verses to him out of a Latin epitaph, and bids him adieu with "the spirit of an old Roman."

John's next "intended" (for the marriage did not take place in due order) was the enchanting Miss Dunk, famous for "exact regularity of beauty, and elegant softness of propriety." This elegant softness of propriety does not hinder the fair Agnes from running away with him from her father's house; but she has scarcely arrived at the village where they are to be married, when she falls sick, is laid out for dead, and is buried in the next churchyard. Not long afterwards the unhappy lover meets her, alive, laughing, *and taking no notice*, in the character of the wife of Dr. Stanvil, an amiable *anatomist*. The word will explain the accident that brought the charmer into the doctor's hands. Buncle, vexed as he owns himself to lose her, could not but see the reasonableness of the result and the folly of making an "uproar;" so he gallantly imitates the lady's behaviour, and rides off to fall in with that "fine creature" Julia Fitzgibbons, as charming for a bewitching negligence, as Miss Dunk was for a divine self-possession. John studies physic under her father; marries her in the course of two years; and at the end of ten months loses her in a river while they are fishing. He sits with his eyes shut *ten* days (so highly do his wives increase in value); and then calls his man "to bring out the horses," and is off, on Christian principles, for wife the seventh.

Who should this be but Miss Dunk? His friend, Dr. Stanvil, her husband, drops down dead of an apoplexy on purpose to oblige him. The widow lets him know that her reserve had not proceeded a bit from dislike; quite the contrary. She marries him; they lead a blissful life for a year and a half, during which he is reconciled with his father, who has become a convert to Unitarianism; and then the lady goes the way of all Buncle's wives, dying of his favourite uxoricide, the small-pox; and John, after diverting himself at sea, retires to a "little flowery retreat," in the neighbourhood of London, to hear purling streams on the one hand, and news on the other, and write verses about going to Heaven.

The reader is to bear in mind, that all these marriages are interspersed with descriptions, characters, adventures of other sorts, natural nistory, and, above all, with polemics full of the most ridiculous beggings of the question, and the most bigoted invectives against bigotry. A few specimens of the table of contents will show him what sort of reading he has missed:—

" The History of Miss Noel.

" A Conversation in relation to the Primævity of the Hebrew Tongue.

" Of Mrs. O'Hara's and Mrs. Grafton's Grottoes.

" Miss Noel's Notion of Hutchinson's Cherubim.

" The Origin of Earthquakes—of the Abyss, &c.

" An Account of Muscular Motion.

" An Account of Ten Extraordinary Country Girls.

" A Rule to Determine the Tangents of Curved Lines.

" What a Moral Shekinah is.

" Of Mr. Macknight's Harmony (of the Gospels).

" Description of a Society of Protestant Married Friars.

" The Author removes to Oldfield Spaw, on account of Indisposition occasioned by Hard Drinking; and his Reflections on Hard Drinking.

" A Discourse on Fluxions between Miss Spence and the Author.

" Of the Athanasian Creed.

" What Phlogiston is.

" Picture and Character of Curll, the Bookseller." (He says he was " very tall, thin, ungainly, goggle-eyed, white-faced, splay-footed, and baker-kneed; very profligate, but not ill-natured.")

It is impossible to be serious with John Buncle, Esquire, jolly dog, Unitarian, and Blue Beard; otherwise, if we were to take him at his word, we should pronounce him, besides being a jolly dog, to be one of a very selfish description, with too good a constitution to correct him, a prodigious vanity, no feeling whatever, and a provoking contempt for everything unfortunate, or opposed to his whims. He quarrels with bigotry, and is a bigot; with abuse, and riots in it. He hates the cruel opinions held by Athanasius, and sends people to the devil as an Arian. He kills off seven wives out of pure incontinence and love of change, yet cannot abide a rake or even the poorest victim of the rake, unless both happen to be his acquaintances. The way in which he tramples n the miserable wretches in the streets, is the very rage and triumph of hard-heartedness, furious at seeing its own vices reflected on it, unredeemed by the privileges of law, divinity, and success. But the truth is, John is no more responsible for his opinions than health itself, or a high-mettled racer. He only "thinks he's thinking." He does, in reality, nothing at all but eat, drink, talk, and enjoy himself. Amory, Buncle's creator, was in all probability an honest man, or he would hardly have been innocent enough to put such extravagances on paper. What Mrs. Amory thought of the seven wives does not appear. Probably he invented them before he knew her; perhaps was not anxious to be reminded of them afterwards. When he was in the zenith of his health and spirits, he must have been a prodigious fellow over a bottle and beefsteak.

It is hardly necessary to say, that by the insertion of passages from this fantastical book no disrespect is intended to the respectable sect of Unitarians; who, probably, care as little for Buncle's friendship as the Trinitarians do for his enmity. There is apt to be too little real Christianity in polemics of any kind; and John is no exception to the remark. He contrives to be so absurd, even when most reasonable, that the charms of Nature herself and of animal spirits would suffer under his admiration and example, if readers could not easily discern the difference; and even the youngest need scarcely be warned against overlooking it. Our volumes are intended to include all the phases of humanity that can be set before them without injury; and among these were not to be omitted the eccentric.

Delights of Books of Travel.

FROM WILLIAM DE RUBRUQUIS, MARCO POLO, LEDYARD, AND MUNGO PARK.

In an old house, or new house, or any house, but particularly in a house in the country, where there are storms at night, and the wind is thundering in the trees, and the rain comes dashing against the windows in the gusts of it, who does not think of men at sea, of disasters by shipwreck, of husbands and sons far away, struggling perhaps in breakers on the shore, or clinging to icy shrouds, while we are lying in the safe and warm bed? It seems as if none of us ought to be comfortable on such occasions; and yet, provided we do our duty to the unfortunate, we ought to be as much so as we can; for, in the first place, none of our friends may be in danger; and, secondly, Nature, in the course of her harshest but always beneficent operations, never desires more suffering to be inflicted than can be helped.

Now, homes have always a tendency to make us think of remote places; comfortable beds remind us of travellers by night; and comfortable books, of travellers at all hours who cannot get any; but of all books, those which are written by travellers themselves give us a quintessence of all these feelings: and the older the books are, and the remoter the countries they treat of, the completer becomes our satisfaction, because the antiquity itself has become a sort of reverend novelty, and danger is over with all parties except in the happy shuddering sense of it on the part of the reader.

"With many a tempest had his beard been shaken,"

says Chaucer of his seaman. It *had* been shaken, observe. So have all the beards of travellers of old; and the older or more ancient they were, the more bearded one fancies them. An old folio book of ro mantic yet credible voyages and travels to read, an old bearded traveller for its hero, a fireside in an old country-house to read it by, curtains drawn, and just wind enough stirring out of doors to make an accompaniment to the billows or forests we are reading of, this surely is one of the perfect moments of existence.

English reading of this kind, we mean the reading of books of travels in the English language, may be said to commence with the travels of good old William de Rubruquis and accomplished Marco Polo. See how instinctively our good friend Dr. John Harris, thorough disinterested bookworm, and one of the fathers of these collections of knowledge, intimates their superiority over their precursors, in the Table of Contents prefixed to his huge folio volumes, one of which is now before us:—

"An account of the Several Passages to the Indies, both by sea and land, that have been attempted, discovered, or practised by the Ancients.

"An account of the Travels of two Mahommedans through India and China in the ninth century.

"The Travels of Rabbi Benjamin, the son of Jonas of Tudela, through Europe, Asia, and Africa, from Spain to China, from the year of our Lord 1160 to 1173; from the Latin versions of Benedict Arias Montanus, and Constantine l'Empereur, compared with other Translations into different languages."

"The *remarkable* Travels of William de Rubruquis, a monk, sent by Louis IX., king of France, commonly styled St. Louis, ambassador into different parts of the East, particularly into Tartary and China, A.D. 1253, containing abundance of curious Particulars relating to those Countries, written by the Ambassador, and addressed to his Royal Master King Louis.

"The *curious* and *remarkable* Voyages and Travels of Marco Polo, a gentleman of Venice, who, in the middle of the thirteenth century, passed through a great part of Asia, all the dominions of the Tartars, and returned home by sea through the Islands of the East Indies; taken chiefly from the accurate edition of Ramusio, compared with an original manuscript in His Prussian Majesty's library, and with most of the translations hitherto published."

The very tables of contents in these good folio writers, who give "full measure, pressed down and running over," are a kind of books in themselves, and save us the trouble of stating who their heroes were. Only, for the pleasure of the thing, we may add, that these two fine old voyagers, from whom we are about to make some extracts, were, the one as simple, honest, truth-telling, and intelligent a soul withal as ever took monkery for a good thing; and the other, a man of as proved a credibility in his way, a noble, trading, and accomplished Venetian, though he may have leant his ear a little too much to reports. He dealt in such very large and prosperous matters, both of jewellery and government, and saw such heaps of countries, and cities, and populations, and revenues, that although he fairly overbore the incredulity of his astounded countrymen with the bushels of diamonds and precious stones which he poured forth before their eyes (in a scene which our readers will meet with), he left behind him the nickname of Marco Milione; and a worthy epitomiser of his book informs us, that the Venetians in their carnival entertainments long had a character of that name, whose "chief jest lay in describing cities with a million of bridges, husbands with a million of wives, birds with a million of wings, beasts with a million of legs," &c.* But if Marco had come to life again, he might have retorted by personifying a buffoon populace possessed of a million of ignorances. Marco, like Bruce, has outlived misconception. Every fresh traveller has tended to confirm the relations both of him and Rubruquis; and as those relations chiefly concern one of the largest, most curious, and most unchanging countries and people on the face of the earth, they present a singular combination of modern with ancient interest. The Tartars are still nomade rovers in one part of their vast possessions, and Chinese rulers in the other. Their dresses are the same as of old, their faces the same; they still exhibit the same mixture of great and civilized, yet clumsy, undertakings; and if in their joint character of Tartar and Chinese, their philosopher, Confucius, has rendered them a far wiser and more thinking people than is supposed even by the thinking

* *Vide* Mr. MacFarlane, himself a traveller, and very shrewd and entertaining observer, in a publication entitled the *Romance of Travel*, vol. i., p. 239 (*Knight's Weekly Volumes*). We have read Mr. MacFarlane's first two little books with the greatest pleasure; but though not wanting in curious extract as well as abridgment, he is too summary for the purpose of the present book. Our extracts from Marco Polo and Rubruquis are taken from the revised republication of Harris;—*Navigantium atque Itinerantium Bibliotheca; or, a Complete Collection of Voyages and Travels, consisting of above six hundred of the most authentic writers, &c.,* two volumes folio, 1764. Harris includes Hackluyt and Purchas, and translations from the best authorities in other languages

European (himself not so free from prejudice and foolish custom as he fancies), their jealousy of innovation is a remnant of the old Tartar pride, as well as an instinct of security. The greatest innovation in China, next to philosophy, was tea; which, however, appears to be of older date than the times of Polo and Rubruquis, though Mr. MacFarlane has observed the curious fact of their making no mention of it. There are no three ideas which we associate more strongly with the two great portions of the East, than tea with the Chinese, and coffee and smoking with the Turks and Persians; yet tea is not alluded to by the oldest Chinese writers, and the use of coffee and tobacco by mankind dates no further back than a few centuries. There is no mention of smoking in the *Arabian Nights;* nor was there of coffee, till Mr. Lane found it in one of his additional stories. The Mussulman's drink was sherbet; and instead of smoke, he chewed dates and tarts.

This honesty on the part of our two good old travellers is, in fact, a virtue belonging emphatically to the best travellers, ancient and modern. Herodotus, the first authentic traveller, was an honest man. Nearchus, Alexander's admiral, the first authentic voyager, was an honest man. The great Columbus was one; Drake was one; Dampier, Bernier, Cook, Bell of Antimony, Niebuhr, Pocock, Park, Ledyard, the other explorers of Africa, and the heroical men who adorn our own days, the Franklins, Richardsons, and Backs. Bruce's fault was not dishonesty, but ostentation. It is impossible indeed to conceive men of this kind unpossessed of great virtues. Nothing less could animate or support them. Hence, in reading the best books of travels, we have the double pleasure of feeling ourselves to be in the company of the brave and the good.

In selecting the following extracts from some of the most interesting of these writers, we have gone upon the principle of exemplifying the chief points of attraction in books of voyages and travels; to wit, remoteness and obscurity of place, difference of custom, marvellousness of hearsay, surprising but conceivable truth, barbaric or civilized splendour, savage or simple contentment, personal danger, courage, and suffering, and moral enthusiasm.

WILLIAM DE RUBRUQUIS.

And first for a taste of William de Rubruquis. It is to be borne in mind, that he was sent into the East by the French king and crusader Louis IX., in the middle of the thirteenth century. The crusades had opened up a new Christian interest all over that quarter of the world. Enterprising monks, and remnants of Christian churches in Turkey and Armenia, had occasioned exaggerated notions of the state of the faith in various parts of it; and Louis had heard of the famous *Prester John*, or imaginary Christian *presbyter* and king, reigning somewhere over Christian subjects, who is supposed to have meant the king of Abyssinia. Louis had sent some monks to look out for this royal brother in vain; and now he sent three more, to find him in the person of a Tartar king of the name of Sartach. One of these was our good monk William, who seems to have been a Brabanter, and who had Latinized his name, after the fashion of those times, from Ruysbrock or Rysbruck into De Rubruquis. The servant of the church militant went rejoicing on his perilous mission, armed with a Bible and prayer-book, with a few lowly presents of wine, dried fruit, and biscuits, which the Tartars plundered and laughed at, and with a heap of bad arguments in divinity, which Sartach appears to have laughed at still more. As to Prester John, William could hear not a word about him, except from a few Nestorian Christians, who had nothing to show for the existence of such a personage. Prester John was eternally sitting on his throne somewhere; but it was always in some other place.

Of Sartach the reader will find little in our extracts, the glory of the sight of him having been prejudiced by that of his brother chief and vagabond, Zagatai, whom Rubruquis saw first, and of whose state and presence he gives a more particular account. All the statements of Rubruquis are full of the life of truth. The appearance of Zagatai's carts with their houses on them, moving towards the traveller as if "a great city came to him," is particularly striking; and Zagatai's consort, with her lovely noseless face, has a virtue of repulsion in her, beyond all the foreign beauties we ever read of.

7*

WANDERING TARTARS AND THEIR CHIEF ZAGATAI, IN THE THIRTEENTH CENTURY.

FROM THE TRAVELS OF WILLIAM DE RUBRUQUIS.

THE third day after we were departed out of these precincts of Soldaia, we found the Tartars, amongst whom being entered, methought I was come into a new world, whose life and manners I will describe unto your highness as well as I can.

They have no settled habitation, neither know they to-day where they shall lodge to-morrow.

They have all Scythia to themselves, which stretcheth from the River Danube to the utmost extent of the East. Each of their captains, according to the number of his people, knows the bounds of his pastures, and where he ought to feed his cattle winter and summer, spring and autumn; for in the winter they remove into warm regions southward, and in the summer they go up into the cold regions northward. In winter, when snow lies upon the ground, they feed their cattle in pastures where there is no water, because then they use snow instead of water. Their houses in which they sleep they raise upon a round foundation of wickers artificially wrought and compacted together, the roof consisting of wickers also meeting above in one little roundell, out of which there rises upwards a neck like a chimney, which they cover with white felt; and often they lay mortar or white earth upon the felt with the powder of bones, that it may shine and look white: sometimes also they cover their houses with black felt. This cupola of their house they adorn with variety of pictures.

Before the door they hang a felt curiously painted over, for they spend all their coloured felt in painting vines, trees, birds, and beasts thereupon. These houses they make so large that they contain thirty feet in breadth; for measuring once the breadth between the wheel-ruts of one of their carts or wains, I found it to be twenty feet over, and when the house was upon the cart it stretched over the wheels on each side five feet at least. I told two-and-twenty oxen in one draught, drawing an house upon a cart, eleven in one row according to the breadth of the cart, and eleven more on the other side. The axle-tree of the cart was of an huge bigness like the mast of a ship, and a fellow stood in the door of the house upon the forestall of the cart, driving the oxen. They likewise make certain four-square baskets of slender twigs, as big as great chests; and afterwards from one side to another they frame an hollow lid or cover of such-like twigs, and make a door in it before. Then they cover the said chest or house with black felt, rubbed over with tallow or sheep's milk, to keep the rain from soaking through, which they likewise adorn with painting or white feathers. Into these chests they put their whole household stuff, or treasure, and bind them upon other carts which are drawn by camels, that they may pass through rivers; neither do they ever take down these chests from their carts.

When they take down their dwelling-houses, they turn the doors always to the south, and next they place the carts laden with chests here and there within a stone's cast of the house, insomuch that the house standeth between two ranks of carts, as it were between two walls.

The women make themselves (adorn?) beautiful carts, which I am not able to describe to your majesty but by pictures only. I would willingly have painted all things for you, had my skill being great enough in that art. A rich Tartar hath a hundred or two such carts with chests. Baatu hath sixteen wives, every one of which hath one great house besides other little houses, which they place behind the great one, being as it were chambers for their women to dwell, and to each of the houses belong two hundred carts. When they take their houses off their carts, the principal wife placeth her court on the west, and so all the rest in order; so that the last wife's house is on the east frontier, and the court of each wife is distant from another about a stone's cast.

Hence it is that the court of a rich Tartar will appear like a very large village, few men being to be seen therein. One woman will guide twenty or thirty carts at once, for their country is very flat, and they fasten the carts with camels or oxen one behind another. A wench sits in the foremost cart driving the oxen, and all the rest of themselves follow at a like pace. When they come to a place which is a bad passage, they loose them, and guide them one by one, for they go at a slow pace, and not much faster than an ox can walk.

On my arrival among these barbarous people I thought, as I before observed, that I was come into a new world; for they came flocking about us on horseback, after they had made us wait for them in the shade under the black carts. The first question they asked was, whether we had ever been with them heretofore or not; and on our answering that we had not, they began impudently to beg our victuals from us. We gave them some of our biscuit and wine, which we had brought with us from the town of Soldai; and having drunk off one flaggon of our wine, they demanded another, telling us that a man does not go into a house with one foot. We gave them no more, however, excusing ourselves that we had but little. Then they asked us whence we came, and whither we were bound. I answered them in these words, That we had heard concerning their Prince Sartach, that he was become a Christian, and that unto him our determination was to travel, having your majesty's letter to deliver unto him. They were very inquisitive to know if I came of mine own accord, or whether I was sent. I answered that no man compelled me to come, neither had I come unless I had been willing; and that there I was come, according to my own will and that of my superior. I took the utmost care never to say I was your majesty's ambassador. Then they asked what we had in our carts, whether it were gold, silver, or rich garments to take to Sartach. I answered that Sartach should see what we had brought when we were come unto him; that they had nothing to do to ask such questions, but rather ought to conduct me unto their captain; and that he, if he thought proper, should cause me to be directed to Sartach—if not, that I would return; for there was in the same province one of Baatu's kinsmen, called Zagatai, to whom the Emperor of Constantinople had written letters to suffer me to pass through his territories.

With this answer of ours they were satisfied, giving us horses and oxen and two men to conduct us. But before they would allow us these necessaries, they made us wait a long while, begging our bread for their brats, wondering at all things they saw about our servants, as their knives, gloves, purses, and points, and desiring to have them. I excused myself, saying we had a long way to travel, and we could not deprive ourselves of things necessary to finish so long a journey. They said I was a niggardly scoundrel. It is true they took nothing by force from me, but they will beg all they see very importunately; and if a man bestows anything upon them, it is but lost; for they are thankless wretches. They esteem themselves *lords*, and think that nothing should be denied them by any man. If a man gives them nothing, and afterwards stands in need of their assistance, they will do nothing for him. They gave us of their cows' milk to drink after their butter was churned out of it, which was very sour, which they call Apram; so we departed from them; and indeed it seemed to me that we were escaped out of the hands of devils. The next day we were introduced to their captain. From the time wherein we departed from Soldai till we arrived at the court of Sartach, which was the space of two months, we never lay in house or tent, but always under the canopy of heaven, and in the open air, or under our carts; neither saw we any village, or heard of any building where any village had been; but the graves of the Comanians we saw in great abundance.

We met the day following with the carts of Zagatai, laden with houses, and I really thought that a great city came to meet me. I wondered at the multitudes of droves of oxen and of horses, and droves of sheep; I could see but few men that guided all these, upon which I inquired how many men he had under him, and they told me that he had not above five hundred in all, and that one-half of this number never lay in another lodging. Then the servant, which was our guide, told me that I must present somewhat to Zagatai, and so he caused us to stay, going themselves before to give notice of our coming. By this time it was past three, and they unladed their houses near a river, and there came unto us his interpreter, who, being informed by us that we were never there before, demanded some of our victuals, and we granted his request. He also required of us some garment as a reward, because he was to interpret our message to his master. We excused ourselves as well as we could. Then he asked us what we would prefer to his lord, and we took a flaggon of wine, and filled a basket with biscuit, and a salver with apples and other fruits; but ne was not contented therewith, because we brought him not some rich garment.

We were however admitted into his presence with fear and bashfulness. He sat on his bed, holding a musical instrument in his hand, and his wife sat by him, who, in my opinion, had cut and pared her nose between the eyes that she might seem to be more flat-nosed; for she had left herself no nose at all in that place, having anointed the very scar with black ointment, as she also did her eyebrows, which sight seemed to us most ugly. Then I repeated to him the same words which I had done in other places; for we were directed in this circumstance by some that had been amongst the Tartars, that we should never vary in our tale. I besought him that he would accept this small gift at our hands, excusing myself that I was a monk, and that it was against our profession to possess gold, silver, or precious garments, and therefore that I had not any such thing to give him, unless he would receive some part of our victuals instead of a blessing. He caused thereupon our present to be received, and immediately distributed the same amongst his men, who were met together for that purpose, to drink and make merry. I delivered also to him the Emperor of Constantinople's letters, eight days after the feast of Ascension, and he sent them to Soldai to have them interpreted there; for they were written in Greek, and he had none about him that was skilled in the Greek tongue.

He asked us if we could drink any Cosmos—that is to say, mare's milk, for those that are Christians among them, as the Russians, Grecians, and Alans, who keep their own laws very strictly, will not drink thereof, for they account themselves no Christians after they have once drank of it; and their priests reconcile them to the church, as if they had renounced the Christian faith. I answered, that as yet we had sufficient of our own to drink, and that when it failed us we should be constrained to drink such as should be given us. He inquired also what was contained in the letters your majesty sent to Sartach. I answered they were sealed up, and nothing contained in them but friendly words. And he asked what words we would deliver unto Sartach. I answered the words of Christian Faith. He asked again what those words were, for he was very desirous to hear them. Then I expounded to him, as well as I could by my interpreter, who was a very sorry one, the Apostle's Creed, which after he had heard he shook his head.

Here endeth (as far as our pages are concerned) good William de Rubruquis; and here beginneth the good Signor Jeweller and noble Venetian, Messer Marco Polo.

MARCO POLO.

Harris suffered his pen to slip in his table of contents when he described Marco Polo travelling in the middle of the twelfth century That was the date of the father and uncle of Marco, who went into China and Tartary before him. Marco, however, includes the history of their travels in his own, so that Harris's date does not violate the spirit of the truth. The father and uncle, Niccolo and Maffeo Polo, had had better luck than Rubruquis. They saw not only the wild and roving Tartars, but the civilized; those who lived in great cities, not of houses on carts, but of magnificent palaces, descendants of the conquerors under Genghis Khan, lord of India, Persia, and Northern China, whose descendant Kubla (Coleridge's Kubla) was now reigning

"In Cambalu, seat of Cathaian Khan."
PARADISE LOST.

Milton had seen him before Coleridge, in the pages of Marco Polo. The great poet had also seen the Tartars of William de Rubruquis, and the subsequent Chinese improvements on their carts:—

> "As when a vulture on Imaus bred,
> Whose snowy ridge the roving Tartar bounds,
> Dislodging from a region scarce of prey
> To gorge the flesh of lambs or yeanling kids
> On hills where flocks are fed, flies tow'rds the springs
> Of Ganges or Hydaspes, Indian streams,
> But in his way lights on the barren plains
> Of Sericana, where Chineses drive
> With sails and wind their cany waggons light;
> So on this windy sea of land the Fiend
> Walk'd up and down alone, bent on his prey."
>
> ID., Book III.

The reader will also find Milton presently with Marco Polo in the desert. He was fond of the East and South, from Tartary down to Morocco, from the red and white complexions of the conical-hatted sons of Hologou down to the

> "Dusk faces with white silken turbans wreath'd."

But what poet is not? Chaucer got his *Squire's Tale*, nobody knows how, from

> ——"Sarra, in the land of Tartary."

Other old English poets confounded, or chose to confound,

> ——"the loathly lakes of Tartary"

with those of Tartarus; at least, one word with the other. They thought both the places so grim and remote, as to deserve to have the same appellation.

Niccolo and Maffeo Polo went into the East to trade in jewels. They entered the service of Kubla, assisted him in his wars with their knowledge of engineering, and became agents for religious affairs between the Pope and their master, who (with a liberality which is apt to be more honourable to the person who is willing to hear, than to the zealots who assume that they are qualified to teach him) was desirous to understand what a people so clever in the affairs of this world had to tell him respecting the world unknown. On their return to the Khan (which terminated in nothing to that end), they brought with them the younger Polo Marco, who also entered the Khan's service and who subsequently became the most enterprising traveller of al. three, and the relater of their adventures. He told the history to a friend, who took it from his mouth; and hence it is, that he is always spoken of in the third person.

The reader must conceive Marco in full progress for the court of the Great Khan, and about to pass over the terrible desert of Lop or Kobi, where he (or Dr. Harris) has omitted, however, what we could swear we once beheld in it, by favour of some other account; to wit, a dreadful unendurable *face*, that used to stare at people as they went by. Polo's account, deprived of this rich bit of horror, is comparatively tame; but still the sounds, and the invisible host of passengers, are much; and the poetic reader will trace the footsteps of Milton, who has clearly been listening, in this same desert of Lop, to the ghastly calling of people's names—to

> "Voices calling in the dead of night,
> And airy tongues that syllable men's names
> On sands and shores and desert wildernesses."

He has another line in the same passage about "ghastly fury's apparition," which we cannot but think was suggested by our friend, the dreadful face.

MARCO POLO PASSES THE DESERT OF LOP.

CASCIAN is subject to the Tartars; the name of the province and chief city is the same; it hath many cities and castles, many precious stones are found there in the rivers, especially jasper and chalcedons, which merchants carry quite to Ouaback to sell and make great gain; from Piem to this province, and quite through it also, is a sandy soil with many bad waters and few good. When an army passes through the province, all the inhabitants thereof, with their wives, children, cattle, and all their house stuff fly two days' journey into the sands, where they know that great waters are, and stay there, and carry their corn thither, also to hide it in the sand after harvests from the like fears.

The wind doth so deface their steps in the sand, that their enemies cannot find their way.

Departing from this province, you are to travel five days' journey through the sands, where no other water almost than that which is bitter is anywhere to be found, until you come to the city called Lop, which is a great city from which is the entrance of a great desert, called also the wilderness of Lop, seated between the east and the north-east. The inhabitants are Mahommedans, subject to the Great Khan.

In the city of Lop, merchants who desire to pass over the desert, cause all necessaries to be provided for them, and when victuals begin to fail in the desert, they kill their asses and camels, and eat them. They make it mostly their choice to use camels, because they are sustained with little meat, and bear great burthens. They must provide victuals for a month to cross it only, for to go through it lengthways would require a year's time. They go through the sands and barren mountains, and daily find water; yet it is sometimes so little that it will hardly suffice fifty or a hundred men with their beasts: and in three or four places the water is salt and bitter. The rest of the road, for eight-and-twenty days, is very good. In it there are not either beast, or birds; they say that there dwell many spirits in this wilderness, which cause great and marvellous illusions to travellers, and make them perish; for if any stay behind, and cannot see his company, he shall be called by his name, and so going out of the way, is lost. In the night they hear as it were the noise of a company, which taking to be theirs they perish likewise. Concerts of music-instruments are sometimes heard in the air, likewise drums and noise of armies. They go therefore close together, hang bells on their beasts' necks, and set marks if any stray.

We must now suppose our traveller arrived at the dwelling of

KUBLA KHAN.

This magnificent Tartar prince has always been an object of interest with readers of the old travellers. A fine poet has noticed him, and rendered him a hundred times more so. Coleridge was reading an account of one of his structures in Purchas's *Pilgrimage*, when he fell into a sleep occasioned by opium, during which, he tells us, he poured forth some hundreds of lines, of which an accident deprived us of more than the divine fragment known under the title of *Kubla Khan, or a Vision in a Dream*. Opium takers are said to have such visions; but only such an opium taker as Coleridge ever had one, we suspect, so thoroughly fit and poetical, or related it in such exquisite music. It is impossible to refer to it, and not repeat it. The reader shall first have not only the words which the poet quotes from Purchas as having occasioned it, but the original of Purchas from Marco Polo. He will then see what a poet can do, even for a book of old travels and a king of kings.

Coleridge says he fell asleep while reading "the following sentence, or words of the same substance," from Purchas's book:—"Here the Khan Kubla commanded a palace to be built, and a stately garden thereunto; and thus ten miles of fertile ground were enclosed with a wall." "The author," he proceeds, "continued for about three hours in a profound sleep, at least of the external senses, during which he has the most vivid confidence that he could not have composed less than from two to three hundred lines; if that indeed can be called composition in which all the images rose up before him as things, with a parallel production of the corresponding expressions, without any sensation, or a consciousness of effort. On awaking, he appeared to himself to have a distinct recollection of the whole; and taking his pen, ink, and paper, instantly and eagerly wrote down the lines that are here preserved. At this moment he was unfortunately called out by a person on business from Porlock, and detained by him above an hour; and on his return to his room, found to his no small surprise and mortification, that though he still retained some vague and dim recollection of the general purport of the vision, yet, with the exception of some eight or ten scattered lines and images, all the rest had passed away like the images on the surface of a stream into which a stone had been cast; but, alas! without the after restoration of the latter."

The veracity of this statement has been called in question; by what right of superior knowledge to the poet's own, we cannot say. For our parts, we devoutly believe it. We know very little of opium; but perhaps every writer of verse has experienced what it is to pour forth poetry in dreams, though he may have been as unable to call his production to mind, as Scarlatti was his famous "Devil's Sonata." Coleridge, by some process perhaps of the mysterious herb which had set him to sleep, had the ability given him; perhaps he had not been asleep at all in the ordinary sense of the word, but in some state of what is called *coma vigil*. At all events, the poem, exquisite as it is, is no finer than he could have written awake; and what he could have written awake, he might have conceived asleep, especially under the preternatural kind of excitement to which opiates give rise.

The following is Marco Polo's account of the structure alluded to. We give it, however, not from Harris, but from the later and better pages of Mr. Murray, who published not long ago the completest version of the travels of Marco Polo. The "Shandu" of Mr. Murray is the "Xanadu" of Coleridge.

KUBLA KHAN'S PALACE AT XANADU.

At Shandu in Tartary, near the western frontier of China, he has built a very large palace of marble and other valuable stones. The halls are gilded all over, and wonderfully beautiful, and a space sixteen miles in circuit is surrounded by a wall within which are fountains, rivers, and meadows. He finds stags, deer, and wild-goats, to give for food to the falcons and ger-falcons, which he keeps in cages, and goes out once a week to sport with them. Frequently he rides through that enclosure, having a leopard on the crupper of his horse, which, whenever he is inclined, he lets go, and it catches a stag, deer, or wild-goat, which is given to the ger-falcons in the cage. In this park, too, the monarch has a large palace framed of cane, in interior gilded all over, having pictures of beasts and birds most skilfully worked on it. The roof is of the same material, and so richly varnished that no water can penetrate. I assure you that these canes are more than three palms thick, and from ten to fifteen paces long. They are cut lengthways, from one knot to the other, and then arranged so as to form the roof. The whole structure is so disposed that the Khan, when he pleases, can order it to be taken down, for it is supported by more than two hundred cords of silk. His majesty remains there three months of the year, June, July, and August, the situation being cool and agreeable; and during this period his palace of cane is set up, while all the rest of the year it is down. On the 28th of August, he departs thence, and for the following purpose:—there are a race of mares white as snow, with no mixture of any other colour, and in number 10,000, whose milk must not be drunk by any one who is not of imperial lineage. Only one other race of men can drink it, called Boriat, because they gained a victory for Gengis Khan. When one of these white animals is passing, the Tartars pay respect to it as a great lord, standing by to make way for it.

Now for the architecture and landscape gardening of the po:—

    In Xanadu did Kubla Khan
    A stately pleasure-dome decree,
    Where Alph, the sacred river, ran
    Through caverns measureless to man
    Down to a sunless sea.
So twice five miles of fertile ground
With walls and towers were girded round:
And here were gardens bright with sinuous rills,
Where blossomed many an incense-bearing tree;
And here were forests ancient as the hills,
Enfolding sunny spots of greenery.

But, oh! that deep romantic chasm which slanted
Down the green hill athwart a cedarn cover!
A savage place! as holy and enchanted
As e'er beneath a waning moon was haunted
By woman wailing for her demon lover!
And from this chasm with ceaseless turmoil seething,
As if this earth in fast thick pants were breathing,
A mighty fountain momently was forced:
Amid whose swift half-intermitted burst
Huge fragments vaulted like rebounding hail,
Or chaffy grain beneath the thresher's flail:
And 'mid these dancing rocks at once and ever
It flung up momently the sacred river.
Five miles, meandering with a mazy motion,
Through wood and dale the sacred river ran,
Then reached the caverns measureless to man,
And sank in tumult to a lifeless ocean:
And 'mid this tumult Kubla heard from far
Ancestral voices prophesying war!

  The shadow of the dome of pleasure
  Floated midway on the waves;
  Where was heard the mingled measure
  From the fountain and the caves.
It was a miracle or rare device,
A sunny pleasure-dome with caves of ice!
  A damsel with a dulcimer
  In a vision once I saw;
  It was an Abyssinian maid,
  And on her dulcimer she play'd,
  Singing of Mount Abora.
  Could I revive within me

  Her symphony and song,
   To such a deep delight 't would win me
That with music loud and long
I would build that dome in air,
That sunny dome! those caves of ice!
And all who heard should see them there,
And all should cry—beware! beware!
His flashing eyes, his floating hair!
Weave a circle round him thrice,
And close your lips with holy dread,
For he on honey dew hath fed,
And drank the milk of Paradise.

  Neither Marco Polo, nor Rubruquis, no, nor Raleigh himself, nor any traveller that existed, ever saw a vision like that!
  But we must hasten out of its divine company. Marco resumes with an account of

KUBLA KHAN'S PERSON AND STATE.

  The Great Khan, lord of lords, named Kublai, is of a fine middle size, neither too tall nor too short; he has a beautiful fresh complexion, and well-proportioned limbs. His colour is fair and vermeil like the rose, his eyes dark and fine, his nose well formed and placed. He has four ladies, who always rank as his wives; and the eldest son, born to him by one of them, succeeds as the rightful heir of the empire. They are named empresses; each bears his name, and holds a court of her own; there is not one who has not three hundred beautiful maidens, with eunuchs, and many other male and female attendants, so that some of the courts of these ladies contain 10,000 persons.
  Kubla resides in the vast city of Kambalu, three months in the year, December, January, and February, and has here his great palace, which I will now describe.

The floor rises ten palms above the ground, and the roof is exceedingly lofty. The walls of the chambers and stairs are all covered with gold and silver, and adorned with pictures of dragons, horses, and other races of animals. The hall is so spacious that 6000 can sit down to banquet; and the number of apartments is incredible. The roof is externally painted with red, blue, green, and other colours, and is so varnished that it shines like crystal, and is seen to a great distance around.

The Tartars celebrate a festival on the day of their nativity. The birthday of the Khan is on the 28th of September, and is the greatest of all, except that at the beginning of the year. On this occasion he clothes himself in robes of beaten gold, and his twelve barons and 12,000 soldiers wear, like him, dresses of a uniform color and shape; not that they are so costly, but similarly made of silk, gilded, and bound by a cincture of gold. Many have their robes adorned with precious stones and pearls, so as to be worth 10,000 golden bezants. The Great Khan, twelve times in the year, presents to those barons and knights robes of the same colour with his own; and this is what no lord in the world can do.

And now I will relate a most wonderful thing, namely, that a large lion is led into his presence, which as soon as it sees him, drops down, and makes a sign of deep humility, owning him for its lord, and moving about without any chain.

Chaucer had certainly read of Kubla. He has described him sitting, as above, at his table,

"Harking his minstrellès their thingès play
Before him at his board, deliciously."

And so, leaving him in this proper imperial attitude with his minstrelsy, his lords, and his lion, we take leave of Marco and his mighty Khan. Nations in those times appear to have tried what they could do to aggravate the welfare and importance of a single man. It was a very absurd though a very amusing endeavour. The single man, at his peril, at least in Europe, must now try what he can do to aggravate the welfare and importance of the people.

We must not quit, however, the old times of travels, and the most authentic of their illustrators, without quoting some passages in the narratives of Mandeville, Oderico, and others, whose names, though not worthy to stand beside the former, are associated with those regions of wild and preternatural interest which lie between truth and fiction; places, of which more is truly related than the narrators have been given credit for, but with such colouring from the reports of others, and from their own excited imagination, as give us leave to doubt or to believe just as much as may be suitable to the frame of mind in which we read them. The dreadful or delightful sounds, for instance, which these old travellers heard in deserts, have been reasonably attributed to winds and other natural causes; and the terrible "faces" which they saw, to robbers or gigantic sculpture. But what care we for "pure reason," when we desire romance? There is enough mystery in everything, however commonplace, to leave its causes inexplicable; and if we choose to have our mysterious music or our terrible face without the alloy of explanation, "neat as imported," we have all the right in the world, whether as boys or sages, to have the wish indulged.

FRIAR ODERIC'S RICH MAN WHO WAS FED BY FIFTY VIRGINS.

While in the province of Mangi, or Southern China, I passed by the palace of a rich man, who is continually attended upon by fifty young virgins, who feed him at every meal as a bird feeds her young; and all the time they are so employed, they sing to him most sweetly. The revenues of this man are thirty tomans of tagars of rice, each toman being 10,000 tagars, and one tagar is the burthen of an ass. His palace is two miles in circuit, and is paved with alternate layers of gold and silver. Near the wall of his palace there is an artificial mould of gold and silver, having turrets and steeples and other magnificent ornaments, contrived for the solace and recreation of this great man.

The personal title of the following tremendous old gentleman (called "Senex" by the first translator of Oderico) means nothing more, with the "reasonable," than Sheik, or Elder. He is a kind of dreadful Alderman. But who would part with the words "Old Man of the Mountain,"—their wrinkled old vigour and reverend infamy? He is first cousin of the shocking old fellow in Sinbad, the Old Man of the Sea, who rode upon the shoulders of that voyager like a nightmare, and stuck his knees in his sides. It is proper to retain the "Of" in the old heading of the story. "*Of* the old man," &c., is much more ancient and mysterious than the modern custom of beginning with "*The.*"

OF THE OLD MAN OF THE MOUNTAIN.

Proceeding on my travels towards the south, I arrived at a certain pleasant and fertile country, called Melistorte, in which dwells a certain aged person called the Old Man of the Mountain. This person had surrounded two mountains by a high wall, within which he had the finest gardens and finest fountains in the world, inhabited by great numbers of most beautiful virgins. It was likewise supplied with fine horses, and every article that could contribute to luxury and delightful solace; on which account it was called by the people of the country, the terrestrial paradise. Into this delightful residence the old man used to entice all the young and valiant men he could procure, where they were initiated into all the delights of the earthly paradise, in which milk and wine flowed in abundance, through certain hidden conduits. When desirous of assassinating any prince or nobleman, who had offended him, the old man would order the governor of his paradise to entice into that place some acquaintance or servant of the prince or baron whom he wished to slay. Allowing this person to take a full taste of the delights of the place, we was cast into a deep sleep by means of a strong potion, in which state he was removed from paradise; on recovering from his sleep, and finding himself excluded from the pleasures of paradise, he was brought before the old man, whom he entreated to restore him to the place from whence he had been taken. He was then told, that if he would slay such or such a person, he should not only be permitted to return into paradise, but should remain there for ever.

By these means the old man used to get all those murdered against whom he had conceived any displeasure; on which account all the kings and princes of the east stood in awe of him and paid him tribute.

When the Tartars had subdued a large portion of the earth, they came into the country of the old man, and took from him his paradise. Being greatly incensed at this, he sent out many of his resolute and desperate dependents, by whom numbers of the Tartar nobles were slain. Upon this the Tartars besieged the city of the old man of the mountain; and making him prisoner, they put him to a cruel and ignoble death.

The famous Prester John must by no means be omitted in the list of these remote personages who sit "throned" in old books. Prester, that is to say, Presbyter, or Priest John, has generally been thought in later times to mean the Christian King of Abyssinia; but the most recent investigators are inclined to restore him his old locality, and consider him as a Tartar king, probably a Mongol of the name of Whang, who was supposed to have been converted to the Christian faith by Nestorian missionaries. *Whang* is almost identical with the pronunciation of the Spanish form of John—*Juan;* which is very unlike what we call it in England. The imagination is to consider Prester John as a compound of priest and sovereign, an eastern pope or Christian Grand Lama, sitting clothed in white, and holding a cross instead of a sceptre. He is a Christian Tartar, subjugating the nations around him, till he is conquered by the more famous Zinghis Khan. Little, however, is known of him beyond his name. The most wonderful anecdote we can find of him is one that is related by Friar John de Carpini, who was sent ambassador to the Tartars by Pope Innocent IV., in the middle of the thirteenth century. It seems to anticipate the appearance of artillery in Europe.

HOW PRESTER JOHN BURNT UP HIS ENEMY'S MEN AND HORSES.

When Zinghis and his people had rested some time after their conquest of Cathay, he divided his army, and sent one of his sons, named Thosut Khan, against the Comainans, whom he vanquished in many battles, and then returned into his own country. Another of his sons was sent with an army against the Indians, who subdued the Lesser India. These Indians are the Black Saracens, who are also named Ethiopians. From thence the Mongol army marched to fight against the Christians dwelling in the greater part of India; and the king of that country, known by the name of Prester John, came forth with his army against them. This prince caused a number of hollow copper figures to be made, resembling men, which were stuffed with combustibles and set upon horses, each having a man behind on the horse, with a pair of bellows to stir up the fire. When approaching to give battle, these mounted images were first sent forwards against the enemy, and the men who rode behind set fire by some means to the combustibles, and blew strongly with their bellows; and the Mongol men and horses were burnt with wild-fire, and the air was darkened with smoke. Then the Indians charged the Mongols, many of whom were wounded and slain, and they were expelled from the country in great confusion, and we have not heard that they ever ventured to return.

It is a pity we cannot give a hundred other romantic particulars out of these old travellers, from the times of Herodotus downwards; but our limits will not permit us. We must pass, with a due amount of delight or horror, his semi-annual sleepers and pious cannibals; the isle of Nearchus, from which no one returned; the accounts of Gog and Magog, and the wall of Doolkarnien; the one-eyed and one-legged people of Mandeville, the latter of whom make an umbrella of their foot; isles of giants and rivers of gems; goblets of wine that came to the drinker of their own accord; and the Region of Darkness where there never appeared sun, moon, or star, &c. Sindbad or Ulysses could not beat them; sometimes had the same identical experiences, as in valleys of diamonds and raw-men-eating giants. We must escape from old fictions founded on truth, to modern narratives full of truth and more touching than fiction. And first for honest, admirable

LEDYARD.

LEDYARD's touching praise of women and of the kindness which he ever experienced at their hands, has been repeated in many a book of selections; but who shall be the first person to leave it out? Certainly not the compiler of this. Ledyard was a man who possessed every qualification for a traveller of the highest order, except a little more composure of purpose. He had health, strength, observation, reflection, integrity, undauntedness, enthusiasm, but was somewhat too restless and impatient; and this single flaw in his perfections probably tended to shorten his career and leave him without a great practical name. He was an American, and intended for a missionary; but he could not bear to remain at school. He became a sailor, a marine, circumnavigated the world with Cook (who respected and made use of him), and finally went to Africa under the auspices of the association for making discoveries, but died prematurely in Egypt, in the year 1788. When he presented himself at the Institute as a candidate for discovery, he was asked when he would be ready to set out. He answered, "To-morrow morning."

The following passage from a letter which he wrote before embarking for Africa, will show the natural dignity and purity of his character.

"I was last evening in company with Mr. Jarvis, of New-York, whom I accidentally met in the city, and invited to my lodgings. When I was in Paris in distress, he behaved very generously to me, and, as I do not want money at present, I had a double satisfaction in our meeting, being equally happy to see him, and to pay him one hundred livres, which I never expected to be able to do, and I suppose he did not think I should. If he goes to New-York as soon as he mentioned, I shall trouble him with this letter to you, and with some others to your address for my other friends. I wrote you last from this place, nearly two years ago, but I suppose you heard from me at Petersburg, by Mr. Franklin of New-York. I promised to write you from the remote parts of Siberia. I promise everything to those I love; and so does fortune to me sometimes, but we reciprocally prevent each other from fulfilling our engagements. She left me so poor in Siberia, that I could not write you, because I could not frank the letter."

Ledyard's honest biographer, though a great and intelligent admirer of his hero, finds fault with his style for its incorrectness. The fault, if it existed, must be confined to passages in his journal, not given by Mr. Sparks, for we cannot discover it in those which he has. To us it appears admirable; quite correct and pure; indeed the best we ever saw for sheer, unaffected eloquence from an American pen. The one before us is a positive masterpiece, in style as well as feeling.

LEDYARD'S PRAISE OF WOMEN.

FROM "MEMOIRS OF HIS LIFE AND TRAVELS, BY JARED SPARKS."

I HAVE observed among all nations that the women ornament themselves more than the men; that wherever found, they are the same civil, kind, obliging, humane tender beings; that they are ever inclined to be gay and cheerful, timorous and modest. They do not hesitate, like man, to perform a hospitable or generous action; not haughty, nor arrogant, nor supercilious, but full of courtesy, and fond of society; industrious, economical, ingenuous, more liable, in general, to err than man, but in general, also, more virtuous, and performing more good actions than he. I never addressed myself, in the language of decency and friendship, to a woman, whether civilized or savage, without receiving a decent and friendly answer. With man it has often been otherwise. In wandering over the barren plains of inhospitable Denmark, through honest Sweden, frozen Lapland, rude and churlish Finland, unprincipled Russia, and the wide spread regions of the wandering Tartar, if hungry, dry, cold, wet, or sick, woman has ever been friendly to me, and uniformly so; and to add to this virtue, so worthy of the appellation of benevolence, these actions have been performed in so free and so kind a manner, that, if I was dry, I drank the sweet draught, and if hungry, ate the coarse morsel, with a double relish.

MUNGO PARK.

What Ledyard wanted to complete his character, the famous Mungo Park eminently possessed. He had not so large a grasp of mind as Ledyard, but he was in no need of it. He had quite enough for his purpose, and not any of a doubtful sort to distract it. But who needs to be told what a thorough man for his purpose he was, what sufferings he went through with the simplest and most touching courage, what successes he achieved, and what a provoking, mortal mischance befell him after all? It was not so mortifying a one as Bruce's, who broke his neck down his own staircase; but it was sadder by a great deal, so far from home and on the threshold of the greatest of his adventures.

The reader of the following passages (which are like fine tunes in the history of men, and bear endless repetition), will bear in mind, that one of the objects of Park's journey was to discover the real course of the River Niger, which had been a subject of dispute for ages.

What a passage is the first one to read, when we are going to bed And what a climax of suffering, fortitude, and piety is the last!

MUNGO PARK'S BED IN THE DESERT.

FROM HIS "TRAVELS IN AFRICA."

I SADDLED my horse, and continued my journey. I travelled over a level but more fertile country than I had seen for some time, until sunset, when coming to a path that took a southerly direction, I followed it until midnight, at which time I arrived at a small pool of rain water; and the wood being open, I determined to rest by it for the night. Having given my horse the remainder of the corn, I made my bed as formerly; but the musquitoes and flies from the pool prevented sleep for some time, and I was twice disturbed in the night by wild beasts, which came very near, and whose howling kept the horse in continual terror.

July 4th.—At daybreak, I pursued my course through the woods as formerly; saw numbers of antelopes, wild hogs, and ostriches; but the soil was more hilly, and not so fertile as I had found it the preceding day. About eleven o'clock, I ascended an eminence, where I climbed a tree and discovered, at about eight miles' distance, an open part of the country, with several red spots, which I concluded were cultivated land; and, directing my course that way, came to the precincts of a watering-place about one o'clock. From the appearance of the place, I judged it to belong to the Foulahs, and was hopeful that I should meet a better reception thad I had experienced at Shrilla. In this I was not deceived; for one of the shepherds invited me to come into his tent, and partake of some dates. This was one of those low Foulah tents in which is just room sufficient to sit upright, and in which the family, the furniture, &c., seem huddled together like so many articles in a chest. When I had crept upon my hands and knees into this humble habitation, I found that it contained a woman and three children; who, together with the shepherd and myself, completely occupied the floor. A dish of boiled corn and dates was produced, and the master of the family, as is customary in this part of the country, first tasted it himself, and then desired me to follow his example. Whilst I was eating, the children kept their eyes fixed upon me; and no sooner did the shepherd pronounce the word Nazarani, than they began to cry, and their mother crept slowly towards the door, out of which she sprang like a greyhound, and was instantly followed by her children. So frightened were they at the very name of Christian, that no entreaties could induce them to approach the tent. Here I purchased some corn for my horse, in exchange for some brass buttons; and having thanked the shepherd for his hospitality, struck again into the woods. At sunset I came to a road that took the direction for Bambarra, and resolved to follow it for the night; but about eight o'clock, hearing some people coming from the southward, I thought it prudent to hide myself among some thick bushes near the road. As these thickets are generally full of wild beasts, I found my situation rather unpleasant; sitting in the dark, holding my horse by the nose with both hands to prevent him from neighing, and equally afraid of the natives without and the wild beasts within. My fears, however, were soon dissipated; for the people, after looking round the thicket and perceiving nothing, went away, and I hastened to the more open parts of the wood, where I pursued my journey E.S.E. until midnight, when the joyful cry of frogs induced me once more to deviate a little from my route, in order to quench my thirst. Having accomplished this from a large pool of rain water, I sought for an open spot with a single tree in the midst, under which I made my bed for the night. I was disturbed by some wolves towards morning, which induced me to set forward a little before day; and having passed a small village called Wassalita, I came about ten o'clock (July 5th) to a negro town.

THE FIRST SIGHT OF THE NIGER.

Hearing that two negroes were going to Sego, I was happy to have their company, and we set out immediately. I was constantly taken for a Moor, and became the subject of much merriment to the Bambarrans, who seeing me drive my horse before me, laughed heartily at my appearance. "He has been at Mecca," says one; "you may see that by his clothes;" another asked if my horse was sick; a third wished to purchase it, &c.; so that I believe the very slaves were ashamed to be seen in my company. Just before it was dark, we took up our lodgings for the night at a small village, where I procured some victuals for myself and some corn for my horse, at the moderate price of a button, and was told that I should see the Niger (which the negroes call Joliba, or the great water). early the next day. The lions are here very numerous; the gates are shut a little after sunset, and nobody allowed to go out. The thoughts of seeing the Niger in the morning, and the troublesome buzzing of musquitoes, prevented me from shutting my eyes during the night, and I had saddled my horse, and was in readiness before daylight; but on account of the wild beasts we were obliged to wait until the people were stirring and the gates opened. This happened to be a market day at Sego, and the roads were every where filled with people carrying different articles to sell. We passed four large villages, and at eight o'clock saw the smoke over Sego.

As we approached the town, I was fortunate enough to overtake the fugitive Kaartans, to whose kindness I had been so much indebted in my journey through Bambarra. They readily agreed to introduce me to their king; and we rode together through the marshy ground, where, as I was looking anxiously around for the river, one of them called out *geo affilli* (see the water); and looking forwards, I saw with infinite pleasure the great object of my mission, the long-sought for majestic Niger, glittering to the morning sun, as broad as the Thames at Westminster, and flowing slowly *to the eastward.* I hastened to the brink, and having drank of the water, lifted up my fervent thanks in prayer to the Great Ruler of all things, for having thus far crowned my endeavours with success.

KINDNESS OF A WOMAN TO HIM, AND A SONG OVER HIS DISTRESS.

I waited more than two hours without having an opportunity of crossing the river; during which time, the people who had crossed carried information to Mansong the king, that a white man was waiting for a passage, and was coming to see him. He immediately sent over one of his chief men, who informed me that the king could not possibly see me until he knew what had brought me into this country; and that I must not presume to cross the river without the king's permission. He therefore advised me to lodge at a distant village, to which he pointed, for the night; and said, that in the morning he would give me further instructions how to conduct myself. This was very discouraging. However, as there was no remedy, I set off for the village, where I found, to my great mortification, that no person would admit me into his house. I was regarded with astonishment and fear, and was obliged to sit all day without victuals in the shade of a tree; and the night threatened to be very uncomfortable, for the wind rose, and there was great appearance of a heavy rain; and the wild beasts are so very numerous in the neighbourhood, that I should have been under the necessity of climbing up the tree and resting among the branches. About sunset, however, as I was preparing to pass the night in this manner, and had turned my horse loose that he might graze at liberty, a woman, returning from the labours of the field, stopped to observe me, and perceiving that I was weary and dejected, inquired into my situation, which I briefly explained to her; whereupon, with looks of great compassion, she took up my saddle and bridle, and told me to follow her. Having conducted me into her hut, she lighted up a lamp, spread a mat on the floor, and told me I might remain there for the night. Finding that I was very hungry, she said she would procure me something to eat. She accordingly went out and returned in a short time with a very fine fish, which, having caused to be half broiled upon some embers, she gave me for supper. The rites of hospitality being thus performed towards a stranger in distress, my worthy benefactress (pointing to the mat, and telling me that I might sleep there without apprehension) called to the female part of the family, who had stood gazing on me all the while in fixed astonishment, to resume their task of spinning cotton, in which they continued to employ themselves great part of the night. They lightened their labour by songs, one of which was composed extempore, for I was myself the subject of it. It was sung by one of the young women, the rest joining in a sort of chorus. The air was sweet and plaintive, and the words, literally translated, were these:—"The winds roared and the rains fell. The poor white man, faint and weary, came and sat under our tree. He has no mother to bring him milk; no wife to grind his corn. *Chorus.*—Let us pity the white man; no mother has he, &c. &c. &c." Trifling as this recital may appear to the reader, to a person in my situation the circumstance was affecting in the highest degree; I was oppressed by such unexpected kindness, and sleep fled from my eyes. In the morning I presented my landlady with two of the four brass buttons which remained on my waistcoat, the only recompense I could make her.

HE PASSES A LION.

July 28th.—I departed from Nyara, and reached Nyamee about noon. This town is inhabited chiefly by Foulahs, from the kingdom of Masina. The dooty (the head man of the place), I know not why, would not receive me, but civilly sent his son on horseback to conduct me to Modiboo; which, he assured me, was at no great distance.

We rode nearly in a direct line through the woods, but in general went forwards with great circumspection. I observed that my guide frequently stopped and looked under the bushes. On inquiring the reason of this caution, he told me that lions were very numerous in that part of the country, and frequently attacked—travelling through the woods. While he was speaking my horse started; looking round, I observed a large animal, of the cameleopard kind, standing at a little distance. The neck and fore-legs were very long; the head was furnished with two short black horns, turning backwards; the tail, which reached down to the ham joint, had a tuft of hair at the end. The animal was of a mouse colour, and it trotted away from us in a very sluggish manner, moving its head from side to side to see if we were pursuing it. Shortly after this, as we were crossing a large open plain, where there were a few scattered bushes, my guide, who was a little way before me, wheeled his horse round in a moment, calling out something in the Foulah language which I did not understand. I inquired in Mandingo what he meant. *Warra billi billi*, a very large lion, said he; and made signs for me to ride away. But my horse was too much fatigued; so we rode slowly past the bush from which the animal had given us the alarm. Not seeing anything myself, however, I thought my guide had been mistaken, when the Foulah suddenly put his hand to his mouth, exclaiming, *Soubah an alluhi* (God preserve us!) and to my great surprise I then perceived a large red lion, at a short distance from the bush, with his head couched between his fore paws. I expected he would instantly spring upon me, and instinctively pulled my feet from the stirrups to throw myself on the ground, that my horse might become the victim rather than myself. But it is probable that the lion was not hungry, for he quietly suffered us to pass, though we were fairly within his reach. My eyes were so rivetted upon this sovereign of the beasts, that I found it impossible to remove them until we were at a considerable distance. We now took a circuitous route through some swampy ground, to avoid any more of these disagreeable rencounters.

NARROW ESCAPE FROM ANOTHER LION.

In the evening I arrived at a small village called Song, the surly inhabitants of which would not receive me, nor so much as permit me to enter the gate; but as lions were very numerous in this neighbourhood, and I had frequently, in the course of the day, seen the impression of their feet on the road, I resolved to stay in the vicinity of the village. Having collected some grass for my horse, I accordingly lay down under a tree by the gate. About ten o'clock I heard the hollow roar of a lion at no great distance, and attempted to open the gate; but the people from within told me, that no person must attempt to enter the gate without the dooty's permission. I begged them to inform the dooty that a lion was approaching the village, and I hoped he would allow me to come within the gate. I waited for an answer to this message with great anxiety; for the lion kept prowling round the village, and once advanced so very near me, that I heard him rustling among the grass, and climbed the tree for safety. About midnight the dooty with some of his people opened the gate and desired me to come in. They were convinced, they said, that I was not a Moor; for no Moor ever waited any time at the gate of a village without cursing the inhabitants.

THE MOSS IN THE DESERT.

Aug. 25th.—I departed from Kooma, accompanied by two shepherds, who were going towards Sibidooloo. The road was very steep and rocky, and as my horse had hurt his feet much in coming from Bammakoo, he travelled slowly and with great difficulty; for in many places the ascent was so sharp, and the declivities so great, that if he had made one false step, he must inevitably have been dashed to pieces. The shepherds being anxious to proceed, gave themselves little trouble about me or my horse, and kept walking on at a considerable distance. It was about eleven o'clock, as I stopped to drink a little water at a rivulet (my companions being near a quarter of a mile before me), that I heard some people calling to each other, and presently a loud screaming as from a person in great distress. I immediately conjectured that a lion had taken one of the shepherds, and mounted my horse to have a better view of what had happened. The noise, however, ceased; and I rode slowly towards the place from whence I thought it proceeded, calling out, but without receiving any answer. In a little time, however, I perceived one of the shepherds lying among the long grass near the road; and though I could see no blood upon him, concluded he was dead. But when I came close to him, he whispered to me to stop, telling me that a party of armed men had seized upon his companion, and shot two arrows at himself as he was making his escape. I stopped to consider what course to take, and looking round, saw at a little distance a man sitting upon the stump of a tree; I distinguished also the heads of six or seven more, sitting amongst the grass with muskets in their hands. I had now no hopes of escaping, and therefore determined to ride forward amongst them. As I approached them, I was in hopes they were elephant-hunters, and, by way of opening the conversation, inquired if they had shot anything; but, without returning an answer, one of them ordered me to dismount; and then, as if recollecting himself, waved with his hand for me to proceed. I accordingly rode past, and had with some difficulty crossed a deep rivulet, when I heard somebody holloa; and looking back, saw those I took for elephant-hunters now running after me, and calling out to me to turn back. I stopped until they were all come up, when they informed me that the king of the Foulahs had sent them on purpose to bring me, my horse, and everything that belonged to me, to Fooladoo, and that therefore I must turn back, and go along with them. Without hesitating a moment, I turned round and followed them, and we travelled together near a quarter of a mile without exchanging a word. When coming to a dark place of the wood, one of them said, in the Mandingo language, " This place will do," and immediately snatched my hat from my head. Though I was by no means free of apprehension, yet I resolved to show as few signs of fear as possible, and therefore told them, unless my hat was returned to me, I should go no farther. But before I had time to receive an answer, another drew his knife, and seizing upon a metal button which remained upon my waistcoat, cut it off, and put it in his pocket. Their intentions were now obvious, and I thought that the easier they were permitted to rob me of everything, the less I had to fear. I therefore allowed them to search my pockets without resistance, and examine every part of my apparel, which they did with scrupulous exactness. But observing that I had one waistcoat under another, they insisted that I should cast them both off; and at last, to make sure work, stripped me quite naked. Even my half-boots (though the sole of one of them was tied to my foot with a broken bridle-rein) were narrowly inspected. Whilst they were examining the plunder, I begged them with great earnestness to return my pocket compass; but when I pointed it out to them, as it was lying on the ground, one of the banditti, thinking I was about to take it up, cocked his musket, and swore that he would lay me dead on the spot if I presumed to lay my hand on it. After this some of them went away with my horse, and the remainder stood considering whether they should leave me quite naked, or allow me something to shelter me from the sun. Humanity at last prevailed; they returned me the worst of the two shirts and a pair of trousers; and, as they went away, one of them threw back my hat, in the crown of which I kept my memorandums; and this was probably the reason they did not wish to keep it. After they were gone, I sat for some time looking around me with amazement and terror; whichever way I turned, nothing appeared but danger and difficulty. I saw myself in the midst of a vast wilderness in the depth of the rainy season, naked and alone, surrounded by savage animals, and men still more savage. I was five hundred miles from the nearest European settlement. All these circumstances crowded at once on my recollection; and I confess, that my spirits began to fail me. I considered my fate as certain, and that I had no alternative but to lie down and perish. The influence of religion, however, aided and supported me. I reflected, that no human prudence or foresight could possibly have averted my present sufferings. I was indeed a stranger in a strange land, yet I was still under the protecting eye of that Providence who has condescended to call himself the stranger's friend. At this moment, painful as my reflections were, the extraordinary beauty of a small moss in fructification irresistibly caught my eye. I mention this, to show from what trifling circumstances the mind will sometimes derive consolation; for though the whole plant was not larger than the tip of one of my fingers, I could not contemplate the delicate conformation of its roots, leaves, and capsule without admiration. Can that Being (thought I) who planted, watered, and brought to perfection, in this obscure part of the world, a thing which appears of so small importance, look with unconcern upon the situation and sufferings of creatures formed after his own image?—surely not! Reflections like these would not allow me to despair; I started up, and disregarding both hunger and fatigue, travelled forwards, assured that relief was at hand; and I was not disappointed. In a short time I came to a small village, at the entrance of which I overtook the two shepherds who had come with me from Kooma. They were much surprised to see me, for they said they never doubted that the Foulahs, when they had robbed, had murdered me. Departing from this village, we travelled over several rocky ridges, and at sunset arrived at Sibidooloo, the frontier town of the kingdom of Manding.

A Shipwreck, a Sea Voyage, and an Adventure by the Way.

VOYAGES, for the most part, are not so entertaining as travels. They are less diversified in subject, and less conversant with flesh and blood. When they are otherwise, no reading is more attractive. Voyages among icebergs, and to newly discovered lands, combine the charms of romance with the greatest personal interest; and few things affect us more strongly than a well-told and disastrous shipwreck. Such catastrophes, however, are in general too painful to warrant isolated extract into a book of entertainment. The compiler seems almost cruel in making it. It furnishes too great a contrast to the reader's comfort, without possessing the excuse of utility.

The almost universal defect of Voyages is, that they take little notice of the element on which they are made. Most people who journey by sea, have no wish but to get over it as fast as possible. The "wonders of the deep" are, for them, as if they did not exist; and even those who are more curious, are content to see little. Geology has not yet been accompanied by its proper amount of *Hydrology*. The ocean, physically and intellectually speaking, is comparatively an unploughed field, even by the English; yet what it may produce, let the reader judge who is acquainted with the narratives of the Cooks, the Scoresbys, and the Humboldts.

That the perils of shipwreck, however, may not be wanting to the pleasures of this our Book for a Corner, and that our inland habits may be refreshed by their due contrast with a sense of being "out at sea," we have selected, in the first instance, the following brief but comprehensive account of the loss of a Spanish vessel from the pages of Mr. Redding's *Shipwrecks and Disasters at Sea;* and in the second, with due omissions, an abstract of Cook's first voyage to Otaheite, because it keeps the reader longer and more pleasantly on the water than most such narratives, besides furnishing a singular peril by the way, and calling to mind some of the most interesting reading of one's childhood.

The Spanish vessel was bound from Panama to Caldera, a port in New Spain; and both before and after the following mishap, the crew and passengers encountered much suffering; but the present is the most interesting point of the narrative. It is remarkable for answering more completely than usual to what a landsman's imagination conceives of such horrors; that is to say, the suddenness of the danger, the noise of the waters, the darkness of the night, the cutting away of masts, and the frightened awakening of guilty consciences. The loud, confessing voices, heard even above the loudness of the thunder, is particularly dreadful.

SHIPWRECK OF A SPANISH VESSEL.

ABOUT seven, one evening, the crew of a Spanish vessel of burden, with various goods, bound for Caldera, beheld the desired port. All was joy in the ship. The captain presented the sailors with a cask of wine, and a Genoese merchant on board gave them another. The men were in too good a temper to postpone tasting the wine until the next day.

They attacked the cask at once, headed by the pilot, and it was soon emptied, but not without materially affecting their heads.

The Genoese merchant, fearing the ill effects that must arise from such a state of things when so near the shore, posted himself, in his excess of caution, between the man at the helm and the pilot, from having remarked that the pilot, sitting on his seat quite drunk, worked the ship from recollection alone, as he was close to a port perfectly well known to him. The merchant placed himself in the situation already mentioned, to repeat with more precision the words of the pilot to the timoneer (man at the helm), and this act caused the loss of the ship. The pilot gave the word " northwest, to the north-west," *Al norueste;*" the merchant, who stammered and spoke bad Spanish, repeated the words " *Al nornorueste,*" to the north-*north*-west, which is a different point of the compass. The timoneer, thinking it was his master's orders, did as he was told—kept away from the port and yet approached the coast.

In the meanwhile night was approaching fast. The passengers and the captain were in their beds wrapped in slumber. About two in the morning, the captain was surprised by hearing the waves breaking upon the rocks. He cried out to the pilot, " What is this, pilot? are we entering the port already?" The pilot, on the question being reiterated, roused from his lethargy, and saw with astonishment and terror that the vessel was steering right upon a rock which could scarcely be seen for the obscurity. Above all a high mountain towered in shadow, covered apparently with trees. The pilot called out to come about, but there was now no time, the vessel was close on the shore, and struck with such force that one of her sides opened.

A huge wave recoiled from the rock against which it had dashed, swept over the vessel, and filled her with water.

Then there was nothing heard throughout the ship but clamorous cries and shrieks of horror. Lamentations succeeded to sounds of mirth and revelry, which had been heard so short a time before. Some awaked suddenly from their sleep, and cried in astonishment as they heard the others do who were aware of the danger, though they knew not yet any reason wherefore.

The noise of the vast waves of the Pacific thundering around and over the ship, the darkness of the night, the dashing of the sea on the rocks, increased the terror of the scene.

What was still more extraordinary, the vessel was lost none could tell how or where. This reverse of fortune was terrible to them. They had imagined themselves close to the entrance of the port. In the terror which came upon the crew, some fell on their knees in prayer, making vows to heaven for their safety; others with uplifted hands demanded God's mercy; while many in a loud voice, heard even amid the louder thundering of the waves around, revealed their most secret sins.

The captain preserved his presence of mind. Seeing that all must perish if something were not attempted speedily for the safety of those on board, he encouraged the sailors to cut away the masts, and to provide themselves with planks, or any loose timber upon which there was a chance of gaining the shore. Everything above deck contributing to the breaking up of the ship by its weight, was cut away or flung overboard.

In this state morning broke upon them. The captain, when the vessel had opened her planks and was settling in the water, seeing that the sailors would endeavour to gain the shore upon anything they could seize that would swim, advised several of them to fasten themselves to the ends of a long rope, one at each end, so that whoever got on shore first might draw after him a second, who might not be so fortunate in his attempt at reaching it. In this manner the captain got the pilot safe to land, although he did not deserve it. Nearly all the crew escaped. Five or six only, who were dashed by the waves with great force against the ship or the rocks head foremost, were lost.

A SEA VOYAGE, AND AN ADVENTURE BY THE WAY.

[The narrative of Cook's voyages was drawn up by Hawkesworth, author of *The Adventurer*. The Mr. Banks mentioned in it was afterwards the well known Sir Joseph, President of the Royal Society; and Dr. Solander became a distinguished botanist.]

HAVING received my commission, which was dated the 25th of May, 1768, I went on board on the 27th, hoisted the pennant, and took charge of the ship, which then lay in the basin in Deptford yard. She was fitted for sea with all expedition; and stores and provisions being taken on board, sailed down the river on the 30th of July, and on the 13th of August anchored in Plymouth Sound.

On Friday the 26th of August, the wind becoming fair, we got under sail, and put to sea. On the 31st we saw several of the birds which the sailors call Mother Carey's chickens, and which they suppose to be the forerunners of a storm; and on the next day we had a very hard gale, which brought us under our courses, washed overboard a small boat belonging to the boatswain, and drowned three or four dozen of our poultry, which we regretted still more.

On Friday the 2d of September we saw land between Cape Finisterre and Cape Ortegal, on the coast of Gallicia, in Spain; and on the 5th, by an observation of the sun and moon, we found the latitude of Cape Finisterre to be 42° 53′ north, and its longitude 8° 46′ west, our first meridian being always supposed to pass through Greenwich; variation of the needle 21° 4′ west.

During this course, Mr. Banks and Dr. Solander had an opportunity of observing many marine animals, of which no naturalist has hitherto taken notice; particularly a new species of the *oniscus*, which was found adhering to the *medusa pelagica;* and an animal of an angular figure, about three inches long, and one thick, with a hollow passing quite through it, and a brown spot on one end, which they conjectured might be its stomach; four of these adhered together by their sides when they were taken, so that at first they were thought to be one animal; but upon being put into a glass of water they soon separated, and swam about very briskly. These animals are of a new genus, to which Mr. Banks and Dr. Solander gave the name of *Dagysa*, from the likeness of one species of them to a gem. Several specimens of them were taken adhering together sometimes to the length of a yard or more, and shining in the water with very beautiful colours. Another animal of a new genus they also discovered, which shone in the water with colours still more beautiful and vivid, and which indeed exceeded in variety and brightness anything that we had ever seen. The colouring and splendour of these animals were equal to those of an opal, and from their resemblance to that gem, the genus was called *Carcinium Opalinum*. One of them lived several hours in a glass of salt water, swimming about with great agility, and at every motion displaying a change of colours almost infinitely various. We caught also among the rigging of the ship, when we were at the distance of about ten leagues from Cape Finisterre. several birds which have not been described by Linnæus; they were supposed to have come from Spain, and our gentlemen called the species *Motacilla velificans* (sail-making), as they said none but sailors would venture themselves on board a ship that was going round the world. One of them was so exhausted that it died in Mr. Banks's hand almost as soon as it was brought to him.

It was thought extraordinary that no naturalist had hitherto taken notice of the Dagysa, as the sea abounds with them not twenty leagues from the coast of Spain; but, unfortunately for the cause of science, there are but very few of those who traverse the sea, that are either desposed or qualified to remark the curiosities of which nature has made it the repository.

On the 12th we discovered the islands of Porto Santo and Madeira, and on the next day anchored in Funchiale road, and moored with the stream-anchor: but in the night the bend of the hawser of the stream-anchor slipped, owing to the negligence of the person who had been employed to make it fast. In the morning the anchor was heaved up into the boat, and carried out to the southward; but in heaving it again, Mr. Weir, the master's mate, was carried overboard by the buoy-rope, and went to the bottom with the anchor; the people in the ship saw the accident, and got the anchor up with all possible expedition, it was, however, too late, the body came up entangled in the buoy-rope, but it was dead.

When the island of Madeira is first approached from the sea, it has a very beautiful appearance; the sides of the hills being entirely covered with vines almost as high as the eye can distinguish; and the vines are green when every kind of herbage, except where they shade the ground, and here and there, by the sides of a rill, is entirely burnt up, which was the case at this time.

The refreshments to be had here, are water, wine, fruit of several sorts, onions in plenty, and some sweetmeats; fresh meat and poultry are not to be had without leave from the governor, and the payment of a very high price.

We took in 270 lbs. of fresh beef, and a live bullock, charged at 613 lbs., 3,032 gallons of water, and ten tons of wine; and in the night, between Sunday the 18th and Monday the 19th September, we set sail in prosecution of our voyage.

On Friday, the 23rd of September, we saw the Peak of Teneriffe bearing W. by S. ½ S. Its appearance at sunset was very striking; when the sun was below the horizon, and the rest of the island appeared of a deep black, the mountain still reflected his rays, and glowed with a warmth of colour which no painting can express.

On the next day, Saturday the 24th, we came into the north-east trade-wind, and on Friday, the 30th, saw Bona Vista, one of the Cape de Verd Islands: we ranged the east side if it, at the distance of three or four miles from the shore, till we were obliged to haul off to avoid a ledge of rocks which stretch out S. W. by W. from the body, or S. E. point of the island, to the extent of a league and a half.

During our course from Teneriffe to Bona Vista, we saw great numbers of flying fish, which from the cabin-windows appear beautiful beyond imagination, their sides having the colour and brightness of burnished silver; when they are seen from the deck, they do not appear to so much advantage, because their backs are of a dark colour. We also took a shark, which proved to be the *Squalus Carcharias* of Linnæus.

Having lost the trade-wind on the 3rd, in latitude 12° 14', and longitude 22° 10', the wind became somewhat variable, and we had light airs and calms by turns.

On the 7th, Mr. Banks went out in the boat, and took what the seamen call a Portuguese man-of-war; it is the *Holuthuria Physalis* of Linnæus, and a species of the *Mollusca*. It consisted of a small bladder about seven inches long, and very much resembling the air-bladder of fishes, from the bottom of which descended a number of strings of a bright blue and red, some of them three or four feet in length, which, upon being touched, sting like a nettle, but with much more force. On the top of the bladder is a membrane which is used as a sail, and turned so as to receive the wind which way soever it blows. This membrane is marked in fine pink-coloured veins, and the animal is in every respect an object exquisitely curious and beautiful.

We also took several of the shell fishes, or testaceous animals, which are always found floating upon the water, particularly the *Helix Ianthina* and *Violacea*: they are about the size of a snail, and are supported upon the surface of the water by a small cluster of bubbles, which are filled with air, and consist of a tenacious slimy substance that will not easily part with its contents; the animal is oviparous, and these bubbles serve also as a *nidus* for its eggs. It is probable that it never goes down to the bottom, nor willingly approaches any shore; for the shell is exceedingly brittle, and that of few fresh-water snails is so thin. Every shell contains about a tea-spoonful of liquor, which it easily discharges upon being touched, and which is of the most beautiful red-purple that can be conceived. It dyes linen cloth, and it may perhaps be worth inquiry (as the shell is certainly found in the Mediterranean), whether it be not the *Purpura* of the ancients.*

* It is quite impossible to discuss this subject here. But it may be worth while to refer the learned reader for some curious information about it, to the illustrious Bochart's work entitled *Hierozoicon*, part ii. book v., ch. ii. There are several sorts of sea shells, that yield the purple-dye so much esteemed among the ancients. Pliny, who has written on the subject, divides them into two classes, the *buccinum* and *purpura*, of which the latter was most in request. According to him, the best kinds were found in the vicinity of Tyre. That city was famous for the manufacture of purple. To be *Tyrio conspectus in ostro*, seemed, in the estimation of the Mantuan poet, essential to his due appearance in honour of

In the evening of the 29th of October, we observed that luminous appearance of the sea, which has been so often mentioned by navigators, and of which such various causes have been assigned; some supposing it to be occasioned by fish, which agitated the water by darting on their prey, some by the putrefaction of fish and other marine animals, some by electricity, and others referring it to a great variety of different causes. It appeared to emit flashes of light exactly resembling those of lightning, only not so considerable; but they were so frequent that sometimes eight or ten were visible almost at the same moment. We were of opinion that they proceeded from some luminous animal, and upon throwing out the casting-net our opinion was confirmed. It brought up a species of the *Medusa*, which when it came on board had the appearance of metal violently heated, and emitted a white light. With these animals were taken some very small crabs, of three different species, each of which gave as much light as a glow-worm, though the creature was not so large by nine-tenths. Upon examination of these animals, Mr. Banks had the satisfaction to find that they were all entirely new.*

Augustus, Geor. 3-17. But several other places in the Mediterranean afforded this precious article. Thus Horace speaks of Spartan purple,

" Nec *Laconicas* mihi
Trahunt honestæ *purpuras* clientæ."
Od. lib. ii. 18.

The English reader will be much pleased with several interesting remarks as to the purple and other colours known to the ancients, given in President Goguet's valuable work on the origin of laws, arts, &c. &c., of which a translation by Dr. Henry was published at Edinburgh in 1761 *Hawksworth*.

* The reader is referred to the account of Captain Krusenstern's circumnavigation, for a very satisfactory relation of an experiment on this subject, which clearly proves the truth of the opinion above stated, as to the cause of the shining appearance so often noticed at sea. It is too long for quotation in this place.—*Kerr*.

On the 6th of November, being in latitude 19° 3' south, longitude 35° 50' west, the colour of the water was observed to change, upon which we sounded, and found ground at the depth of thirty-two fathoms; the lead was cast three times within about four hours, without a foot difference in the depth or quality of the bottom, which was coral rock, fine sand, and shells; we therefore supposed that we had passed over the tail of the great shoal which is laid down in all our charts by the name of Abrolhos, on which Lord Anson struck soundings in his passage outwards. At four the next morning we had no ground with 100 fathom.

As several articles of our stock and provisions now began to fall short, I determined to put into Rio de Janeiro, rather than at any port in Brazil or Falkland's Islands, knowing that it could better supply us with what we wanted.

It is remarkable, that, during the last three or four days of our staying in the harbour, the air was loaded with butterflies. They were chiefly of one sort, but in such numbers that thousands were in view in every direction, and the greatest part of them above our mast-head.

The country, at a small distance round the town, which is all that any of us saw, is beautiful in the highest degree; the wildest spots being varied with a greater luxuriance of flowers, both as to number and beauty, than the best gardens in England.

Upon the trees and bushes sat an almost endless variety of birds, especially small ones, many of them covered with the most elegant plumage; among which were the humming-bird. Of insects too there was a great variety, and some of them very beautiful; but they were much more nimble than those of Europe, especially the butterflies, most of which flew near the tops of the trees, and were therefore very difficult to be caught, except when the sea breeze blew fresh, which kept them nearer to the ground.

When the boat which had been sent on shore returned, we hoisted her on board, and stood out to sea.

On the 9th of December, we observed the sea to be covered with broad streaks of a yellowish colour, several of them a mile long, and three or four hundred yards wide. Some of the water thus coloured was taken up, and found to be full of innumerable atoms pointed at the end, of a yellowish colour, and none more than a quarter of a line, or the fortieth part of an inch long In the microscope they appeared to be *fascicula* of small fibres interwoven with each other, not unlike the nidus of some of the *phygancas*, called caddices ; but whether they were animal or vegetable substances, whence they came, or for what they were designed, neither Mr. Banks nor Dr. Solander could guess. The same appearance had been observed before, when we first discovered the continent of South America.

On the 3d of January, 1769, being in latitude 47o 17' S. and longitude 61° 29' 45" W., we were all looking out for Pepy's island, and for some time an appearance was seen in the east which so much resembled land, that we bore away for it ; and it was more than two hours and a half before we were convinced that it was nothing but what sailors call a fog-bank.

The people now beginning to complain of cold, each of them received what is called a Magellanic jacket, and a pair of trowsers. The jacket is made of a thick woollen stuff, called *Fearnought*, which is provided by the government. We saw, from time to time, a great number of penguins, albatrosses, and sheer-waters, seals, whales, and porpoises ; and on the 11th, having passed Falkland's Islands, we discovered the coast of Terra del Fuego, at the distance of about four leagues, extending from the W. to S.E. by S. We had here five-and-thirty fathom, the ground soft, small slate stones. As we ranged along the shore to the S. E. at the distance of two or three leagues, we perceived smoke in several places, which was made by the natives, probably as a signal, for they did not continue it after we had passed by.

At two o'clock on the 15th of January, we anchored in the bay of Good Success; and after dinner I went on shore, accompanied by Mr. Banks and Dr. Solander, to look for a watering-place, and speak to the Indians, several of whom had come in sight. We landed on the starboard side of the bay near some rocks, which made smooth water and good landing; thirty or forty of the Indians soon made their appearance at the end of a sandy beach on the other side of the bay, but seeing our number, which was ten or twelve, they retreated. Mr. Banks and Dr. Solander then advanced about one hundred yards before us, upon which two of the Indians returned, and, having advanced some paces towards them, sat down; as soon as they came up, the Indians rose, and each of them having a small stick in his hand threw it away, in a direction both from themselves and the strangers, which was considered as the renunciation of weapons in token of peace. They then walked briskly towards their companions, who had halted at about fifty yards behind them, and beckoned the gentlemen to follow, which they did. They were received with many uncouth signs of friendship; and, in return, they distributed among them some beads and ribbons, which had been brought on shore for that purpose, and with which they were greatly delighted. A mutual confidence and good-will being thus produced, our parties joined; the conversation, such as it was, became general; and three of them accompanied us back to the ship. When they came on board, one of them whom we took to be a priest, performed much the same ceremonies which M. Bougainville describes, and supposes to be an exorcism. When he was introduced into a new part of the ship, or when anything that he had not seen before caught his attention, he shouted with all his force for some minutes, without directing his voice either to us or his companions.*

*The incident related by Bougainville, to which the allusion is made, is somewhat affecting. An interesting boy, one of the savages' children, had unwarily, and from ignorance of its dangerous nature, put some bits of glass into his mouth which the sailors gave him. His lips and palate, &c., were cut in several places, and he soon began to spit blood, and to be violently convulsed. This excited the most distressing alarm and suspicion among the savages. One of them, whom Bougainville denominates a juggler, immediately had recourse to very strange and unlikely means in order to relieve the poor child. He first laid him on his back, then kneeling down between his legs, and bending himself, he pressed the child's belly as much as he could with his head and hands, crying out continually, but with inarticulate sounds. From time to time he raised himself, and seeming to hold the disease in his joined hands, opened them at once into the air, blowing, as if he drove away some evil spirit. During those rites, an old woman in tears howled with great violence in the child's ears. These ceremonies, however, not proving effectual, but rather, indeed, as might have been expected, doing mischief, the juggler disappeared for a little in order, as should seem, to procure a peculiar dress, in which he might practise his exorcism with greater confidence of success, and to bring a brother in the trade, similarly apparalled, to aid him in his labours. But so much the worse for the wretched patient, who was now pummelled and squeezed all over, till his body was completely bruised. Such treatment, it is almost unnecessary to say, aggravated his sufferings, but accomplished no cure. The jugglers at last consented to allow the interference of the French surgeon, but appeared to be very jealous of his skill. The child became somewhat easier towards night; however, from his continual sickness, there was much room to apprehend that he had swallowed some of the glass, and died in consequence; for "about two o'clock in the morning," says Bougainville, "we on board heard repeated howls, and at break of day, though the weather was very dreadful, the savages went off. They doubtless fled from a place defiled by death, and by unlucky strangers, who, they thought, were come merely to destroy them." It is very probable that the person whom Cook supposed a priest,

They ate some bread and some beef, but not apparently with much pleasure, though such part of what was given them as they did not eat, they took away with them; but they would not swallow a drop either of wine or spirits; they put the glass to their lips, but, having tasted the liquor, they returned it with strong expressions of disgust. Curiosity seems to be one of the few passions which distinguish men from brutes; and of this our guests appeared to have very little. They went from one part of the ship to another, and looked at the vast variety of new objects that every moment presented themselves, without any expression either of wonder or pleasure, for the vociferation of our exorcist seemed to be neither.

After having been on board about two hours, they expressed a desire to go ashore. A boat was immediately ordered, and Mr. Banks thought fit to accompany them. He landed them in safety, and conducted them to their companions, among whom he remarked the same vacant indifference as in those who had been on board; for as on one side there appeared no eagerness to relate, so on the other side there seemed to be no curiosity to hear, how they had been received, or what they had seen. In about half an hour Mr. Banks returned to the ship, and the Indians retired from the shore.

On the 16th, early in the morning, Mr. Banks and Dr. Solander, with their astendants and servants, and two seamen, to assist in carrying the baggage, accompanied by Mr. Monkhouse the surgeon, and Mr. Green the astronomer, set out from the ship with a view to penetrate as far as they

practised the charms spoken of, in order to destroy any ill luck, and to prevent the occurrence of such like misfortunes in his intercourse with the wonderful strangers. There is an allusion to this incident in a following section.—*Krer.*

could into the country, and return at night. The hills, when viewed at a distance, seemed to be partly a wood, partly a plain, and above them a bare rock. Mr. Banks hoped to get through the wood, and made no doubt but that, beyond it, he should, in a country which no botanist had ever yet visited, find alpine plants which would abundantly compensate his labour. They entered the wood at a small sandy beach, a little to the westward of the watering place, and continued to ascend the hill, through the pathless wilderness, till three o'clock, before they got a near view of the places which they intended to visit. Soon after they reached what they had taken for a plain; but, to their great disappointment, found it a swamp, covered with low bushes of birch, about three feet high, interwoven with each other, and so stubborn that they could not be bent out of the way: it was therefore necessary to lift the leg over them, which at every step was buried ankle deep in the soil. To aggravate the pain and difficulty of such travelling, the weather, which had hitherto been very fine, much like one of our bright days in May, became gloomy and cold, with sudden blasts of a most piercing wind, accompanied with snow. They pushed forward, however, in good spirits, notwithstanding their fatigue, hoping the worst of the way was past, and that the bare rock which they had seen from the tops of the lower hills was not more than a mile before them; but when they had got about two-thirds over this woody swamp, Mr. Buchan, one of Mr. Banks's draughtsmen, was unhappily seized with a fit. This made it necessary for the whole company to halt, and as it was impossible that he should go any farther, a fire was kindled, and those who were most fatigued were left behind to take care of him. Mr. Banks, Dr. Solander, Mr. Green, and Mr. Monkhouse, went on, and in a short time reached the summit. As botanists, their expectations were here abundantly gratified; for they found a great variety of plants, which, with respect to the alpine plants in Europe, are exactly what those plants are with respect to such as grow in the plain.

The cold was now become more severe, and the snow-blasts more frequent; the day also was so far spent, that it was found impossible to get back to the ship, before the next morning. To pass the night upon such a mountain, in such a climate, was not only comfortless but dreadful; it was impossible, however, to be avoided, and they were to provide for it as well as they could.

Mr. Banks and Dr. Solander, while they were improving an opportunity which they had, with so much danger and difficulty, procured, by gathering the plants which they found upon the mountain, sent Mr. Green and Mr. Monkhouse back to Mr. Buchan and the people that were with him, with directions to bring them to a hill, which they thought lay in a better route for returning to the wood, and which was therefore appointed as a general rendezvous. It was proposed, that from this hill they should push through the swamp, which seemed by the new route not to be more than half a mile over, into the shelter of the wood, and there build their wigwam, and make a fire. This, as their way was all down hill, it seemed easy to accomplish. Their whole company assembled at the rendezvous, and, though pinched with the cold, were in health and spirits. Mr. Buchan himself having recovered his strength in a much greater degree than could have been expected. It was now near eight o'clock in the evening, but still good day-light, and they set forward for the nearest valley, Mr. Banks himself undertaking to bring up the rear, and see that no straggler was left behind. This may perhaps be thought a superfluous caution, but it will soon appear to be otherwise. Dr. Solander, who had more than once crossed the mountains which divide Sweden from Norway, well knew that extreme cold, especially when joined with fatigue, produces a torpor and sleepiness that are almost irresistible. He therefore conjured the company to keep moving, whatever pain it might cost them, and whatever relief they might be promised by an inclination to rest. Whoever sits down, says he, will sleep; and whoever sleeps, will wake no more. Thus, at once admonished and alarmed, they set forward; but while they were still upon the naked rock, and before they had got among the bushes, the cold became suddenly so intense, as to produce the effects that had been most dreaded. Dr. Solander himself was the first who found the inclination, against which he had warned others, irresistible; and insisted upon being suffered to lie down. Mr. Banks entreated and remonstrated in vain, down he lay upon the ground, though it was covered with snow; and it was with great difficulty that his friend kept him from sleeping. Richmond also, one of the black servants, began to linger, having suffered from the cold in the same manner as the doctor. Mr. Banks, therefore, sent five of the company, among whom was Mr. Buchan, forward to get a fire ready at the first convenient place they could find; and himself, with four others, remained with the doctor and Richmond, whom, partly by persuasion and entreaty, and partly by force, they brought on; but when they had got through the greatest part of the birch and swamp, they both declared they could go no farther. Mr. Banks had recourse again to entreaty and expostulation, but they produced no effect. When Richmond was told, that if he did not go on he would in a short time be frozen to death, he answered, that he desired nothing but to lie down and die. The doctor did not so explicitly renounce his life; he said he was willing to go on, but that he must first take some sleep, though he had before told the company that to sleep was to perish. Mr. Banks and the rest found it impossible to carry them, and there being no remedy, they were both suffered to sit down, being partly supported by the bushes, and in a few minutes they fell into a profound sleep. Soon after, some of the people who had been sent forward returned, with the welcome news that a fire was kindled about a quarter of a mile farther on the way. Mr. Banks then endeavoured to wake Dr. Solander, and happily succeeded. But, though he had not slept five minutes, he had almost lost the use of his limbs, and the muscles were so shrunk that his shoes fell from his feet; he consented to go forward with such assistance as could be given him, but no attempts to relieve poor Richmond were successful. It being found impossible to make him stir, after some time had been lost in the attempt, Mr. Banks left his other black servant and a seaman, who seemed to have suffered least by the cold, to look after him; promising that as soon as two others should be sufficiently warmed, they should be relieved. Mr. Banks, with much difficulty, at length got the doctor to the fire; and soon after sent two of the people who had been refreshed, in hopes that, with the assistance of those who had been left behind, they would be able to bring Richmond, even though it should still be found impossible to wake him. In about half an hour, however, they had the mortification to see these two men return alone; they said, that they had been all around the place to which they had been directed, but could neither find Richmond nor those who had been left with him; and that, though they had shouted many times, no voice had replied. This was matter of equal surprise and concern, particularly to Mr. Banks, who, while he was wondering how it could happen, missed a bottle of rum, the company's whole stock, which they now concluded to be in the knapsack of one of the absentees. It was conjectured, that with this Richmond had been roused by the two persons who had been left with him, and that, having perhaps drank too freely of it themselves, they had all rambled from the place where they had been left, in search of the fire, instead of waiting for those who should have been their assistants and guides. Another fall of snow now came on, and continued incessantly for two hours, so that all hopes of seeing them again, at least alive, were given up; but about twelve o'clock, to the great joy of those at the fire, a shouting was heard at some distance. Mr. Banks, with four men, immediately went out, and found the seaman with just strength enough left to stagger along, and call out for assistance. Mr. Banks sent him immediately to the fire, and, by his direction, proceeded in search of the other two, whom he soon after found. Richmond was upon his legs, but not able to put one before the other; his companion was lying upon the ground, as insensible as a stone. All hands were now called from the fire, and an attempt was made to carry them to it; but this, notwithstanding the united efforts of the whole company, was found to be impossible. The night was extremely dark, the snow was now very deep, and, under these additional disadvantages, they found it very difficult to make way through the bushes and the bog for themselves, all of them getting many falls in the attempt. The only alternative was to make a fire upon the spot; but the snow which had fallen, and was still falling, besides what was every moment shaken in flakes from the trees, rendered it equally impracticable to kindle one there, and to bring any part of that which had been kindled in the wood thither. They were, therefore, reduced to the sad necessity of leaving the unhappy wretches to their fate;

having first made them a bed of boughs from the trees, and spread a covering of the same kind over them to a considerable height.

Having now been exposed to the cold and the snow near an hour and a half, some of the rest began to lose their sensibility; and one Briscoe, another of Mr. Banks's servants, was so ill, that it was thought he must die before he could be got to the fire.

At the fire, however, at length they arrived; and passed the night in a situation which, however dreadful in itself, was rendered more afflicting by the remembrance of what was past, and the uncertainty of what was to come. Of twelve, the number that set out together in health and spirits, two were supposed to be already dead; a third was so ill, that it was very doubtful whether he would be able to go forward in the morning; and a fourth, Mr. Buchan, was in danger of a return of his fits, by fresh fatigue, after so uncomfortable a night. They were distant from the ship a long day's journey, through pathless woods, in which it was too probable they might be bewildered till they were overtaken by the next night; and, not having prepared for a journey of more than eight or ten hours, they were wholly destitute of provisions, except a vulture, which they happened to shoot while they were out, and which, if equally divided, would not afford each of them half a meal; and they knew not how much more they might suffer from the cold, as the snow still continued to fall,—a dreadful testimony of the severity of the climate, as it was now the midst of summer in this part of the world, the 21st of December being here the longest day; and everything might justly be dreaded from a phenomenon which, in the corresponding season, is unknown even in Norway and Lapland.

When the morning dawned, they saw nothing round them

as far as the eye could reach, but snow, which seemed to lie as thick upon the trees as upon the ground; and the blasts returned so frequently, and with such violence, that they found it impossible for them to set out. How long this might last they knew not, and they had but too much reason to apprehend that it would confine them in that desolate forest till they perished with hunger and cold.

After having suffered the misery and terror of this situation till six o'clock in the morning, they conceived some hope of deliverance by discovering the place of the sun through the clouds, which were become thinner, and began to break away. Their first care was to see whether the poor wretches whom they had been obliged to leave among the bushes were yet alive; three of the company were dispatched for that purpose, and very soon afterwards returned with the melancholy news that they were dead.

Notwithstanding the flattering appearance of the sky, the snow still continued to fall so thick that they could not venture out on their journey to the ship; but about eight o'clock a small regular breeze sprung up, which, with the prevailing influence of the sun, at length cleared the air; and they soon after, with great joy, saw the snow fall in large flakes from the trees, a certain sign of an approaching thaw. They now examined more critically the state of their invalids. Briscoe was still very ill, but said, that he thought himself able to walk; and Mr. Buchan was much better than either he or his friends had any reason to expect. They were now, however, pressed by the calls of hunger, to which, after long fasting, every consideration of future good or evil immediately gives way. Before they set forward, therefore, it was unanimously agreed that they should eat their vulture; the bird was accordingly skinned, and, it being thought best to divide it before it was fit to be eaten, it was cut into ten portions, and every man cooked his own as he thought fit. After this repast, which furnished each of them with about three mouthfuls, they prepared to set out; but it was ten o'clock before the snow was sufficiently gone off, to render a march practicable. After a walk of about three hours, they were agreeably surprised to find themselves upon the beach, and much nearer to the ship than they had any reason to expect. Upon reviewing their track from the vessel, they perceived that, instead of ascending the hill in a line, so as to penetrate into the country, they had made almost a circle round it. When they came on board, they congratulated each other upon their safety, with a joy that no man can feel who has not been exposed to equal danger; and as I had suffered great anxiety at their not returning in the evening of the day on which they set out, I was not wholly without my share.

On the 1st of March, we were in latitude 38° 44′ S. and longitude 110° 33′ W. Many birds, as usual, were constantly about the ship, so that Mr. Banks killed no less than sixty-two in one day; and what is more remarkable, he caught two forest flies, both of them of the same species, but different from any that have hitherto been described; these probably belonged to the birds, and came with them from the land, which we judged to be at a great distance. Mr. Banks, also, about this time, found a large cuttle-fish, which had just been killed by the birds, floating in a mangled condition upon the water; it is very different from the cuttle-fishes that are found in the European seas; for its arms, instead of suckers, were furnished with a double row of very sharp talons, which resemble those of a cat, and, like them, were retractable into a sheath of skin, from which they might be thrust at pleasure. Of this cuttle-fish we made one of the best soups we had ever tasted.

The albatrosses now began to leave us, and after the 8th there was not one to be seen. We continued our course without any memorable event till the 24th, when some of the people who were upon the watch in the night reported that they saw a log of wood pass by the ship; and that the sea, which was rather rough, became suddenly as smooth as a mill-pond. It was a general opinion that there was land to windward; but I did not think myself at liberty to search for what I was not sure to find; though I judged we were not far from the islands that were discovered by Quiros in 1606. Our latitude was 22° 11′ S. and longitude 127° 55′ W.

On the 25th, about noon, one of the marines, a young fellow about twenty, was placed as sentry at the cabin door; while he was upon this duty, one of my servants was at the same place preparing to cut a piece of seal-skin into tobacco-pouches. He had promised one to several of the men, but had refused one to this young fellow, though he had asked him several times; upon which he jocularly threatened to steal one, if it should be in his power. It happened that the servant, being called hastily away, gave the skin in charge to the sentinel, without regarding what had passed between them. The sentinel immediately secured a piece of the skin, which the other missing at his return, grew angry; but, after some altercation, contented himself with taking it away, declaring that, for so trifling an affair, he would not complain of him to the officers. But it happened that one of his fellow-soldiers, overhearing the dispute, came to the knowledge of what had happened, and told it to the rest; who, taking it into their heads to stand up for the honour of their corps, reproached the offender with great bitterness, and reviled him in the most opprobrious terms; they exaggerated his offence into a crime of the deepest dye; they said it was a theft by a sentry when he was upon duty, and of a thing that had been committed to his trust; they declared it a disgrace to associate with him; and the sergeant, in particular, said, that if the person from whom the skin had been stolen would not complain, he would complain himself; for that his honour would suffer if the offender was not punished. From the scoffs and reproaches of these men of honour, the poor young fellow retired to his hammock in an agony of confusion and shame. The sergeant soon after went to him, and ordered him to follow him to the deck. He obeyed without reply; but it being in the dusk of the evening, he slipped from the sergeant and went forward. He was seen by some of the people, who thought he was gone to the head; but a search being made for him afterwards, it was found that he had thrown himself overboard; and I was then first made acquainted with the theft and its circumstances. The loss of this man was the more regretted, as he was remarkably quiet and industrious.*

About one o'clock, on Monday the 10th of April, some of the people who were looking out for the island to which we were bound, said they saw land ahead, in that part of the horizon where it was expected to appear; but it was so faint, that, whether there was land in sight or not, remained a matter of dispute till sunset. The next morning, however, at six o'clock, we were convinced that those who said they had discovered land were not mistaken; it appeared to be very high and mountainous, extending from W. by S. ½ S. to W. by N. ½ N.; and we knew it to be the same that Captain Wallis had called King George the Third's Island.

---

* This poor lad was probably one of the most conscientious persons among the crew, and had been envied for his good conduct. But his quiet may have been accompanied with reserve, an unpopular and indeed suspicious quality.

We were delayed in our approach to it by light airs and calms, so that in the morning of the 12th we were but little nearer than we had been the night before; but about seven a breeze sprung up, and before eleven several canoes were seen making towards the ship. There were but few of them, however, that would come near; and the people in those that did, could not be persuaded to come on board. In every canoe there were young plantains, and branches of a tree which the Indians call *E'Midho;* these, as we afterwards learned, were brought as tokens of peace and amity; and the people in one of the canoes handed them up the ship's side, making signals at the same time with great earnestness which we did not immediately understand; at length we guessed that they wished these symbols should be placed in some conspicuous part of the ship; we, therefore, immediately stuck them among the rigging, at which they expressed the greatest satisfaction. We then purchased their cargoes, consisting of cocoa-nuts, and various kinds of fruit, which, after our long voyage, were very acceptable.

We stood on with an easy sail all night, with soundings from twenty-two fathoms to twelve; and about seven o'clock in the morning we came to an anchor in thirteen fathoms in Port Royal Bay, called by the natives Matavai. We were immediately surrounded by the natives in their canoes, who gave us cocoa-nuts, fruit resembling apples, bread-fruit, and some small fishes, in exchange for beads and other trifles. They had with them a pig, which they would not part with for anything but a hatchet, and therefore we refused to purchase it; because, if we gave them a hatchet for a pig now, we knew they would never afterwards sell one for less, and we could not afford to buy as many as it was probable we should want at that price. The bread-fruit grows on a tree that is about the size of a middling oak : its leaves are frequently a foot and a half long, of an oblong shape, deeply sinuated like those of the fig-tree, which they resemble in consistence and colour, and in the exuding of a white milky juice upon being broken. The fruit is about the size and shape of a child's head, and the surface is reticulated not much unlike a truffle ; it is covered with a thin skin, and has a core about as big as the handle of a small knife ; the eatable part lies between the skin and the core ; it is as white as snow, and somewhat of the consistence of new bread. It must be roasted before it is eaten, being first divided into three or four parts. Its taste is insipid, with a slight sweetness somewhat resembling that of the crumb of wheaten bread mixed with a Jerusalem artichoke.

Among others who came off to the ship was an elderly man, whose name, as we learned afterwards, was *Owhaw*, and who was immediately known to Mr. Gore and several others who had been here with Captain Wallis. As I was informed that he had been very useful to them, I took him on board the ship with some others, and was particularly attentive to gratify him, as I hoped he might also be useful to us.

As soon as the ship was properly secured, I went on shore with Mr. Banks and Dr. Solander, a party of men under arms, and our friend Owhaw. We were received from the boat by some hundreds of the inhabitants, whose looks at least gave us welcome, though they were struck with such awe, that the first who approached us crouched so low that he almost crept upon his hands and knees. It is remarkable, that he, like the people in the canoes, presented to us the same symbol of peace that is known to have been in use among the ancient and mighty nations of the northern hemisphere—the green branch of a tree. We re ceived it with looks and gestures of kindness and satisfaction; and observing that each of them held one in his hand, we immediately gathered every one a bough, and carried it in our hands in the same manner.

They marched with us about half a mile towards the place where the Dolphin had watered, conducted by Owhaw; then they made a full stop, and having laid the ground bare, by clearing away all the plants that grew upon it, the principal persons among them threw their green branches upon the naked spot, and made signs that we should do the same. We immediately showed our readiness to comply, and to give a greater solemnity to the rite, the marines were drawn up, and marching in order, each dropped his bough upon those of the Indians, and we followed their example. We then proceeded, and when we came to the watering-place it was intimated to us by signs, that we might occupy that ground, but it happened not to be fit for our purpose. During our walk they had shaken off their first timid sense of our superiority, and were become familiar; they went with us from the watering-place, and took a circuit through the woods. As we went along, we distributed beads and other small presents among them, and had the satisfaction to see that they were much gratified. Our circuit was not less than four or five miles, through groves of trees, which were loaded with cocoa-nuts and bread-fruit, and afforded the most grateful shade. Under these trees were the habitations of the people, most of them being only a roof without walls, and the whole scene realized the poetical fables of Arcadia.

Business, Books, and Amusement.

It is a common thing for men of business to say that they are "fond of books, but have no time for reading." In some instances this may really be the case; but, for the most part, they had better acknowledge that they care little for what they can find no time to do. In these, as in most other circumstances, "where there is a will there is a way;" and it is the design of the following extracts from the life of William Hutton to show it. They may be of service both to employers and the employed. The best workman is he who can do his work with cheerfulness; he is the man whose nature is the best and completest, who has his faculties most about him, and in the most fitting abundance; and the way to turn our faculties to the best account, is to give them fair play—to see that the senses of the mind (if we may so call them) have as much reasonable fruition as those that contribute to the nourishment and refreshment of the body. Hutton of Birmingham (as he is familiarly called) combined, in a remarkable manner, prudence with enterprise, industry with amusement, and the love of books with devotion to business, and all because he was a thorough human being of his class, probably from causes anterior to his birth. Not that his father was a person of any very edifying description. His son gives the following amusing account of him:—"Though my father was neither young, being forty-two, nor handsome, having lost an eye, nor sober, for he spent all he could get in liquor, nor clean, for his trade was oily, nor without shackles, for he had five children, yet women of various descriptions courted his smiles, and were much inclined to pull caps for him." But this squalid Lothario probably supplied him with wit and address, and his mother with thought and a good constitution.

William Hutton was the son of a poor wool-worker. He was brought up as a poor weaver, had not a penny in the world, became a bookbinder under the poorest auspices, and ended with being a rich man, and living in wealth and honour to the age of ninety-two. The passages selected are from a life of him written by himself, and in the original are accompanied with a great deal of additional matter, all worth reading, and in the course of which he gives an account of the rise and progress of his courtship of Mrs. Hutton, here only intimated. He was one of the sufferers from the Riots of Birmingham (which he has recorded), and author of amusing Histories of that town and of Derby. The Robert Bage whom he mentions as his friend and benefactor, and who was another man of his sort, though in every respect of a higher class, is better known by his writings than his name, being no other than the author of *Hermsprong, Man as he Is*, and other novels well known to the readers of circulating libraries, and admired by Walter Scott. Two such men of business as Hutton and Robert Bage have seldom come together, at least not in the eyes of the world; and as they came in the shapes of bookseller and paper-maker, we have special pleasure in thus bringing them before the reader.

PASSAGES FROM THE AUTOBIOGRAPHY OF WILLIAM HUTTON.

1741. WHAT the mind is bent upon obtaining, the hand seldom fails in accomplishing. I detested the frame, as totally unsuitable to my temper; therefore I produced no more profit than necessity demanded. I made shift, however, with a little overwork and a little credit, to raise a genteel suit of clothes, fully adequate to the sphere in which I moved. The girls eyed me with some attention; nay I eyed myself as much as any of them.

1743. At Whitsuntide I went to see my father, and was favourably received by my acquaintance. One of them played upon the bell-harp. I was charmed with the sound, and agreed for the price, when I could raise the sum, half a-crown.

At Michaelmas I went to Derby, to pay for and bring back my bell-harp, whose sound I thought seraphic. This opened a scene of pleasure which continued many years. Music was my daily study and delight. But, perhaps, I laboured under greater difficulties than any one had done before me. I could not afford an instructor. I had no books, nor could I borrow, or buy; neither had I a friend to give me the least hint, or put my instrument in tune.

Thus I was in the situation of a first inventor, left to grope in the dark to find something. I had first my ear to bring into tune, before I could tune the instrument; for the ear is the foundation of all music. That is the best tune which best pleases the ear, and he keeps the best time who draws the most music from his tune.

For six months did I use every effort to bring a tune out of an instrument which was so dreadfully out, it had no tune in it. Assiduity never forsook me. I was encouraged by a couplet I had seen in Dyce's Spelling-book:

> "Despair of nothing that you would attain,
> Unwearied diligence your point will gain!"

When I was able to lay a foundation, the improvement and the pleasure were progressive. Wishing to rise, I borrowed a dulcimer, made one by it, then learned to play upon it. But in the fabrication of this instrument, I had neither timber to work upon, tools to work with, nor money to purchase either. It is said "necessity is the mother of invention." I pulled a large trunk to pieces, one of the relics of my family but formerly the property of Thomas Parker, the first Earl of Macclesfield. And as to tools, I considered that the hammer-key and the plyers belonging to the stocking-frame, would supply the place of hammer and pincers. My pocket-knife was all the edge-tools I could raise; a fork, with one limb, was made to act in the double capacity of spring-awl and gimlet.

I quickly was master of this piece of music; for if a man can play upon one instrument he can soon learn upon any.

A young man, apprentice to a baker, happening to see the dulcimer, asked if I could perform upon it. Struck with the sound, and with seeing me play with what he thought great case, he asked if I would part with the instrument, and at what price? I answered in the affirmative, and, for sixteen shillings. He gave it. I told him, "If he wanted advice, or his instrument wanted tuning, I would assist him." "Oh no, there's not a doubt but I shall do." I bought a coat with the money, and constructed a better instrument. . . . .

1746. An inclination for books began to expand; but here, as in music and dress, money was wanting. The first article of purchase was three volumes of the Gentleman's Magazine, 1742, 3, and 4. As I could not afford to pay for binding, I fastened them together in a most cobbled style. These afforded me a treat.

I could only raise books of small value, and these in worn-out bindings. I learned to patch, procured paste, varnish, &c., and brought them into tolerable order; erected shelves, and arranged them in the best manner I was able.

If I purchased shabby books, it is no wonder that I dealt with a shabby bookseller who kept his working apparatus in his shop. It is no wonder, too, if by repeated visits I became acquainted with this shabby bookseller, and often saw him at work; but it is a wonder and a fact, that I never saw him perform one act but I could perform it myself; so strong was the desire to attain the art.

I made no secret of my progress, and the bookseller rather encouraged me, and for two reasons: I bought such rubbish as nobody else would; and he had often an opportunity of selling me a cast-off tool for a shilling, not worth a penny. As I was below every degree of opposition, a rivalship was out of the question.

The first book I bound was a very small one, Shakspeare's *Venus and Adonis*. I showed it to the bookseller. He seemed surprised. I could see jealousy in his eye. However, he recovered in a moment. He had no doubt but I should break.

He offered me a worn-down press for two shillings, which no man could use, and which was laid by for the fire. I considered the nature of its construction, bought it, and paid the two shillings. I then asked him to favour me with a hammer and a pin, which he brought with half a conquering smile, and half a sneer. I drove out the garter-pin, which, being galled, prevented the press from working, and turned another square, which perfectly cured the press. He said in anger, "If I had known, you should not have had it." However, I could see he consoled himself with the idea that all must return in the end. This proved for forty-two years my best binding press.

I now purchased a tolerably genteel suit of clothes, and was so careful of them, lest I should not be able to procure another, that they continued my best for five years.

The stocking-frame being my own, and trade being dead, the hosiers would not employ me; they could scarcely employ their own frames. I was advised to try Leicester, and took with me half-a-dozen pair of stockings to sell. I visited several warehouses; but, alas! all proved blank. They would neither employ me, nor give for my goods anything near prime cost. As I stood like a culprit before a gentleman of the name of Bennet, I was so affected, that I burst into tears, to think that I should have served seven years to a trade at which I could not get bread.

My sister took a house, and to soften the rent, my brother and I lodged with her.

1747. It had been the pride of my life, ever since pride commenced, to wear a watch. I bought a silver one for thirty-five shillings. It went ill. I kept it for four years, then gave *that* and a guinea for another, which went as ill. I afterwards exchanged this for a brass one, which going no better, I sold it for five shillings; and to complete the watch farce, I gave the five shillings away, and went without a watch thirty years.

I had promised to visit my father on Whitsun eve, at Derby. Business detained me till it was eleven at night before I arrived. Expectation had for some time been on the stretch, and was now giving way. My father being elevated with liquor, and by my arrival, rose in ecstasy, and gave me the first kiss, and, I believe, the last he ever gave me.

This year I began to dip into rhyme. The stream was pleasant, though I doubt whether it flowed from Helicon. Many little pieces were the produce of my pen, which, perhaps, pleased; however, they gave no offence, for they slept on my shelf till the rioters burnt them in 1791.

1748. Every soul who knew me scoffed at the idea of my book-binding, except my sister, who encouraged and aided me; otherwise I must have sunk under it. I considered that I was naturally of a frugal temper; that I could watch every penny, live upon a little; that I hated stocking-making, but not book-binding; that if I continued at the frame, I was certain to be poor; and if I ventured to leave it, I could not be so. My only fear was lest I should draw in my friends; for I had nothing of my own.

I had frequently heard that every man had, some time or other in his life, an opportunity of rising. As this was a received opinion, I would not contradict it. I had, however, watched many years for the high tide of my affairs, but thought it never yet had reached me.

I still pursued the two trades. Hurt to see my three volumes of magazines in so degraded a state, I took them to pieces, and clothed them in a superior dress.

1749. It was now time to look out for a future place of residence. A large town must be the mark, or there would be no room for exertion. London was thought of, between my sister and me, for I had no soul else to consult. This was rejected for two reasons. I could not venture into such a place without a capital, and my work was not likely to pass among a crowd of judges.

My plan was to fix upon some market town, within a stage of Nottingham, and open shop there on the market day, till I should be better prepared to begin the world at Birmingham.

I fixed upon Southwell, as the first step of elevation. It was fourteen miles distant, and the town as despicable as the road to it. I went over at Michaelmas, took a shop at the rate of twenty shillings a-year, sent a few boards for shelves, a few tools, and about two hundredweight of *trash*, which might be dignified with the name of *books*, and worth, perhaps, a year's rent of my shop. I was my own joiner, put up the shelves and their furniture, and in one day became the most eminent bookseller in the place.

During this rainy winter, I set out at five every Saturday morning, carried a burden of from three pounds weight to thirty, opened shop at ten, starved in it all day upon bread, cheese, and half a pint of ale, took from one to six shillings, shut up at four, and by trudging through the solitary night and the deep roads five hours more, I arrived at Nottingham by nine; where I always found a mess of milk porridge by the fire, prepared by my valuable sister.

Nothing short of a surprising resolution and rigid economy could have carried me through this scene.

1750. Returning to Nottingham, I gave warning to quit at Southwell, and prepared for a total change of life.

On the 10th of April, I entered Birmingham, for the third time, to try if I could be accommodated with a small shop. If I could procure any situation, I should be in the way of procuring a better. On the 11th I travelled the streets of Birmingham, agreed with Mrs. Dix for the lesser half of her shop, No. 6 in Bull Street, at one shilling a-week; and slept at Lichfield in my way back to Nottingham.

On May 13th, Mr. Rudsdall, a dissenting minister of Gainsborough, with whom my sister had lived as a servant, travelling from Nottingham to Stamford, requested my company, and offered to pay my expenses, and give me eighteenpence a day for my time. The afternoon was wet in the extreme. He asked why I did not bring my greatcoat? Shame forbade an answer, or I could have said I had none. The water completely soaked through my clothes, but not being able to penetrate the skin, it filled my boots. Arriving at the inn, every traveller, I found, was wet; and every one produced a change of apparel but me. I was left out because the house could produce no more. I was obliged to sit the whole evening in my drenched garments, and to put them on nearly as wet on my return the next morning! What could I expect but destruction? Fortunately I sustained no injury.

It happened that Mr. Rudsdall, now declined housekeeping, his wife being dead. He told my sister that he should part with the refuse of his library, and would sell it to me. She replied, "He has no money." "We will not differ about that. Let him come to Gainsborough; he shall have the books at his own price." I walked to Gainsborough on the 15th of May, stayed there the 16th, and came back on the 17th.

The books were about two hundred pounds' weight. Mr. Rudsdall gave me his corn chest for their deposit; and for payment, drew the following note, which I signed:—

"I promise to pay to Ambrose Rudsdall, one pound seven shillings, when I am able." Mr. Rudsdall observed, "You never need pay this note if you only say you are not able." The books made a better show, and were more valuable than all I possessed beside.

I had now a most severe trial to undergo; parting with my friends, and residing wholly among strangers. May 23rd, I left Nottingham, and I arrived at Birmingham on the 25th. Having little to do but look into the street, it seemed singular to see thousands of faces pass, and not one that I knew. I had entered a new world, in which I led a melancholy life, a life of silence and tears. Though a young man, and of rather a cheerful turn, it was remarked "that I was never seen to smile."

The rude family into which I was cast added to the load of melancholy.

My brother came to see me about six weeks after my arrival, to whom I observed, that the trade had fully supported me. Five shillings a-week covered every expense; as food, rent, washing, lodging, &c. Thus a solitary year rolled round, when a few young men of elevated character and sense took notice of me. I had saved about twenty pounds, and was become more reconciled to my situation. The first who took a fancy to me was Samuel Salte, a mercer's apprentice, who five years after, resided in London, where he acquired £100,000. He died in 1797. Our intimacy lasted his life.

In this first opening of prosperity, an unfortunate circumstance occurred which gave me great uneasiness, as it threatened totally to eclipse the small prospect before me. The overseers, fearful I should become chargeable to the parish, examined me with regard to my settlement; and, with the voice of authority, ordered me to procure a certificate, or they would remove me. Terrified, I wrote to my father, who returned for answer, " That All Saints, in Derby, never granted certificates."

I was hunted by ill-nature two years. I repeatedly offered to pay the levies, which was refused. A succeeding overseer, a draper, of whom I had purchased two suits of clothes, value £10, consented to take them. The scruple exhibited a short sight, a narrow principle, and the exultations of power over the defenceless.

Among others who wished to serve me, I had two friends, Mr. Dowler, a surgeon, who resided opposite me, and Mr. Grace, a hosier at the Gateway, in the High-street. Great consequences often arise from small things. The house adjoining that of Mr. Grace's, was to be let. My friends both urged me to take it. I was frightened at the rent, eight pounds. However, one drew, and the other pushed, till they placed me there. A small house is too large for a man without furniture, and a small rent may be too large for an income which has nothing certain in it but the smallness Having felt the extreme of poverty, I dreaded nothing so much; but I believed I had seized the tide, and I was unwilling to stop.

Here I pursued business in a more elevated style, and with more success.

No event in a man's life is more consequential than marriage; nor is any more uncertain. Upon this die his sum of happiness depends. Pleasing views arise, which vanish as the cloud; because, like that, they have no foundation. Circumstances change, and tempers with them. Let a man's prior judgment be ever so sound, he cannot foresee a change; therefore he is liable to deception. I was deceived myself, but, thanks to my kind fate, it was on the right side. I found in my wife more than I ever expected to find in woman. Just in proportion as I loved her, I must regret her loss. If my father, with whom I only lived fourteen years, who loved me less, and has been gone forty, never is a day out of my thoughts, what must be my thoughts towards her, who loved me as herself, and with whom I resided an age!

1756.—My dear wife brought me a little daughter, who has been the pleasure of my life to this day. We had now a delightful plaything for both.

Robert Bage, an old and intimate friend, and a papermaker, took me to his inn, where we spent the evening. He proposed that I should sell paper for him, which I might either buy on my own account, or sell on his by commission. As I could spare one or two hundred pounds, I chose to purchase; therefore appropriated a room for the reception of goods, and hung out a sign—*The Paper Warehouse.* From this small hint I followed the stroke forty years, and acquired an ample fortune.

1763.—We took several pleasurable journeys; among others, one at Aston, and in a superior style to what we had done before. This is the peculiar privilege of us Birmingham men: if ever we acquire five pounds extraordinary, w. take care to show it.

1764.—Every man has his hobby-horse and it is no disgrace prudently to ride him. He is the prudent man who can introduce cheap pleasures without impeding business.

About ten of us, intimate friends, amused ourselves with playing at tennis. Entertained with the diversion, we erected a tennis-court and met on fine evenings for amusement, without expense. I was constituted steward of our little fraternity.

My family continued their journeys, and were in a prosperous state.

THE END.

CONTENTS OF THE SECOND SERIES.

	PAGE
AGAINST INCONSISTENCY IN OUR EXPECTATIONS . *Mrs. Barbauld.*	7
THE ENCHANTMENTS OF THE WIZARD INDOLENCE, AND EXPLOITS OF THE KNIGHT SIR INDUSTRY. From the "Castle of Indolence" *Thomson.*	14
STORIES, NOW FIRST COLLECTED, FROM THE "TATLER," "SPECTATOR," AND "GUARDIAN" . . . . *Sir Richard Steele.*	39
Valentine and Unnion	42
The Fire	43
The Wedding Day	46
The Shipwreck	48
The Alchemists	50
The Violent Husband	54
Inkle and Yarico	55
The Fits	58
CLUBS OF STEELE AND GOLDSMITH	61
The Spectator's Club . . . . *Steele.*	65
The Club of the Tatler . . . . "	71
Clubs—Choice Spirits—Muzzy Club—Harmonical Society . . . . *Goldsmith.*	77
COUNT FATHOM'S ADVENTURE IN THE LONE COTTAGE . *Smollett.*	84
THE HERMIT . . . . *Parnell.*	93
PETER POUNCE'S DIALOGUE WITH PARSON ADAMS. From "Joseph Andrews" . . . . *Fielding.*	104
VERSES WRITTEN AT AN INN AT HENLEY . . . . . *Shenstone.*	111
FIVE LETTERS . . . . *Gray.*	115
To HORACE WALPOLE—A Fox-hunter—A Poet's Solitude—Southern the Dramatist	116
To RICHARD WEST—Bad Spirits—Recollections of Husbands and Statesmen at School	118

CONTENTS

	PAGE
To the Reverend Norton Nicholls—Banter of Formal Excuses and Fine Exordiums—Southampton—An Abbot—Sunrise	119
To the Same—A Mother—Scenery of Kent	121
To the Same—Having a Garden of One's Own—Shenstone—Second Banter of Formal Apologies	123
Advantages of Cultivating a Taste for Pictures *Jon. Richardson.*	126
Ode on a Distant Prospect of Eton College .... *Gray.*	136
A Long Story .... "	140
Sir Roger de Coverley. From the "Spectator" . . *Addison.*	148
Sir Roger's Household Establishment	148
His Behavior in Church on a Sunday	152
Sir Roger and the Gipsies	155
His Visit to the Tombs in Westminster Abbey	159
Manners of the French .... *Colonel Pinckney.*	164
A House and Grounds	173
Thoughts on a Garden. From a Letter to Evelyn. *Cowley.*	178
Thoughts on Retirement. From one of his Letters *Sir W. Temple.*	183
Old English Garden of the Seventeenth Century "	185
Petition for an Absolute Retreat . . *Lady Winchilsea.*	188
An Old Country House and an Old Lady. From the "Lounger" . . . . *Mackenzie.*	192
Love of the Country in the Decline of Life. From the same	198
Two Sonnets, and an Inscription on a Spring. *Thomas Warton.*	204
Inscription over a Calm and Clear Spring	205
Written in a Blank Leaf of Dugdale's "Monasticon"	205
Written after seeing Wilton House	205
Descriptions of Night. From the Notes to Ossian . *Macpherson.*	207
Retirement and Death of a Statesman. From "Memoirs of The Right Honorable Charles James Fox" .... *Trotter.*	214
Elegy in a Country Churchyard .... *Gray.*	222

Against Inconsistency in our Expectations.

FROM AN ESSAY BY MRS. BARBAULD.

Better writing or reasoning than the following it would not be easy to find. There are some additional remarks in the original, which, though not without merit, we cannot help thinking by an inferior hand, and have, therefore, omitted. Every sentence here set down is admirable; nor is there anything, however vigorous in the tone, which a noble-minded woman might not utter, without committing the delicacy of her sex. All is conformable to kindness as well as zeal, and to the beauty of right thinking.

In reading this excellent piece of advice one feels astonished to think how so many could have stood in need of it, ourselves perhaps among the number. But so it is. We feel it to have been necessary, while we are surprised at its having been so; and we become anxious that all the world should be acquainted with it. The good it is calculated to do is evident, and of the greatest importance. We have heard of reflecting men who are proud to acknowledge their obligations to it; who say it has influenced the greater part of their lives; and we know of others who have spoken of it with admiration; Mr. Hazlitt for one.

At the same time, good as the spirit of the admonition is for everybody, the line drawn between the seekers of wealth and the cultivators of wisdom appears to us to be a little too strong; or at least to have become so in our days, whatever the case may have been in those in which it was written. The recognition of the beauty and even the utility of mental accomplishments has latterly been keeping better pace with commercial industry; men in trade have influenced the opinions of the world on the most unexpected and important points, by means of their share of them; and in the passages extracted from the biography of Hutton, the reader has seen an account of a man who, in Mrs. Barbauld's own time, rose to wealth from the humblest beginnings, and whose career was accompanied, nevertheless, by a love of books and by liberal feelings, by the regard and assistance of men of genius, and by the warmest affections of his family. The instance of his distinguished friend Bage, the novelist and paper-maker, is still more striking on the side of independence. But we have noticed them both more at large in the place referred to, as well as the exceptions to sordid rules that have occurred in all ages and nations. Still the essay remains necessary to many, useful and a good caution to all.

Our gratitude must not forget, that the chief honor of the admonition remains with the good old Stoic philosopher, the following passage out of whose writings Mrs. Barbauld made the text of her sermon:—

"What is more reasonable than that they who take pains for anything, should get most in that particular for which they take pains? They have taken pains for power, you for right principles; they for riches, you for a proper use of the appearance of things. See whether they have the advantage of you in that for which you have taken pains, and which they neglect. If they are in power, and you not, why will not you speak the truth to yourself, that you do nothing for the sake of power, but that they do everything? No: but since I take care to have right principles, it is more reasonable that I should have power. Yes, in respect to what you take care about, your principles; but give up to others the things in which they have taken more care than you; else it is just as if, because you have right principles, you should think it fit that when you shoot an arrow you should hit the mark better than an archer, or that you should forge better than a smith."—CARTER's *Epictetus*.

AS most of the unhappiness in the world arises rather from disappointed desires than from positive evil, it is of the utmost consequence to attain just notions of the laws and order of the universe, that we may not vex ourselves with fruitless wishes, or give way to groundless and unreasonable discontent. The laws of natural philosophy, indeed, are tolerably understood and attended to; and, though we may suffer inconveniences, we are seldom disappointed in consequence of them. No man expects to preserve oranges through an English winter; or when he has planted an acorn, to see it become a large oak in a few months. The mind of man naturally yields to necessity, and our wishes soon subside when we see the impossibility of their being gratified. Now, upon an accurate inspection, we shall find in the moral government of the world, and the order of the intellectual system, laws as determinate, fixed, and invariable as any in Newton's *Principia.* The progress of vegetation is not more certain than the growth of habit; nor is the power of attraction more clearly proved, than the force of affection, or the influence of example. The man, therefore, who has well studied the operations of nature in mind as well as matter, will acquire a certain moderation and equity in his claims upon Providence; he will never be disappointed either in himself or others; he will act with precision, and expect that effect, and that alone, from his efforts, which they are naturally adapted to produce. For want of this, men of merit and integrity often censure the dispositions of Providence for suffering the characters they despise to run away with advantages which, they yet know, are purchased by such means as a high and noble spirit could never submit to. If you refuse to pay the price, why expect the purchase? We should consider this world as a great mart of commerce, where Fortune exposes to our view various commodities,—riches, ease, tranquillity, fame, integrity, knowledge. Everything is marked at a settled price. Our time, our labor, our ingenuity, is so much ready money we are to lay out to the best advantage. Examine, compare, choose, reject, but stand to your own judgment, and do not, like children, when you have purchased one thing, repine that you do not possess another which you did not purchase. Such is the force of well-regulated industry, that a steady and vigorous exertion of our faculties, directed to one end, will generally insure success. Would you, for instance, be rich? Do you think that single point worth sacrificing everything else to? You may then be rich. Thousands have become so from the lowest beginnings, by toil and patient diligence, and attention to the minutest articles of expense and profit; but you must give up the pleasures of leisure, of a vacant mind, of a free, unsuspicious temper. If you preserve your integrity, it must be a coarse-spun and vulgar honesty. Those high and lofty notions of morals which you brought with you from schools must be considerably lowered, and mixed with a baser alloy of a jealous and worldly-minded prudence. You must learn to do hard, if not unjust things; and as for the nice embarrassments of a delicate and ingenuous spirit, it is necessary for you to get rid of them as fast as possible. You must shut your heart against the Muses, and be content to feed your understanding with plain household truths. In short, you must not attempt to enlarge your ideas, or polish your taste, or refine your sentiments; but keep on in one beaten track, without turning aside either to the right or to the left. "But I cannot submit to drudgery like this—I feel a spirit above it." 'Tis well: be above it then; only do not repine that you are not rich.

Is knowledge the pearl of price? That, too, may be purchased by steady application and long solitary hours of study and reflection. Bestow these, and you shall be wise. "But," says the man of letters, "what a hardship is it, that many an illiterate fellow, who cannot construe the motto of the arms on his coach, shall raise a fortune and make a figure, while I have little more than the common conveniences of life." *Et tibi magna satis!*—Was it in order to raise a fortune that you consumed the sprightly hours of youth in study and re-

.irement? Was it to be rich that you grew pale over the midnight lamp, and distilled the sweetness from the Greek and Roman spring? You have, then, mistaken your path, and ill employed your industry. "What reward have I then for all my labors?" What reward! A large comprehensive soul, well purged from vulgar fears, and perturbations, and prejudices, able to comprehend and interpret the works of man—of God; a rich, flourishing, cultivated mind, pregnant with inexhaustible stores of entertainment and reflection; a perpetual spring of fresh ideas; and the conscious dignity of superior intelligence. Good heaven!—and what reward can you ask besides?

"But is it not some reproach upon the economy of Providence that such a one, who is a mean, dirty fellow, should have amassed wealth enough to buy a nation?" Not in the least. He made himself a mean dirty fellow for that very end. He has paid his health, his conscience, his liberty for it; and will you envy him his bargain? Will you hang your head and blush in his presence, because he outshines you in equipage and show? Lift up your brow with a noble confidence, and say to yourself, "I have not these things, it is true; but it is because I have not sought, because I have not desired them. It is because I possess something better. I have chosen my lot. I am content and satisfied."

You are a modest man—you love quiet and independence, and have a delicacy and reserve in your temper which renders it impossible for you to elbow your way in the world, and be the herald of your own merits. Be content, then, with a modest retirement, with the esteem of your intimate friends, with the praises of a blameless heart, and a delicate ingenuous spirit; but resign the splendid distinctions of the world to those who can better scramble for them.

The man whose tender sensibility of conscience, and strict

regard to the rules of morality, makes him scrupulous and fearful of offending, is often heard to complain of the disadvantages he lies under in every path of honor and profit. "Could I but get over some nice points, and conform to the practice and opinion of those about me, I might stand as fair a chance as others for dignities and preferment." And why can you not? What hinders you from discarding this troublesome scrupulosity of yours which stands so grievously in your way? If it be a small thing to enjoy a healthful mind, sound at the very core, that does not shrink from the keenest inspection, inward freedom from remorse and perturbation, unsullied whiteness and simplicity of manners, a genuine integrity, "pure in the last recesses of the mind,"— if you think these advantages an inadequate recompense for what you resign, dismiss your scruples this instant, and be a slave-merchant, a director, or—what you please. If these be motives too weak, break off by times; and as you have not spirit to assert the dignity of virtue, be wise enough not to forego the emoluments of vice.

I much admire the spirit of the ancient philosophers, in that they never attempted, as our moralists often do, to lower the tone of philosophy, and make it consistent with all the indulgences of indolence and sensuality. They never thought of having the bulk of mankind for their disciples, but kept themselves as distinct as possible from a worldly life; they plainly told men what sacrifices were required, and what advantages they were which might be expected.

> Si virtus hoc una potest dare, fortis omissis
> Hoc age deliciis.

If you would be a philosopher, these are the terms. You must do thus and thus. There is no other way. If not, go and be one of the vulgar.

There is no one quality gives so much dignity to a character as consistency of conduct. Even if a man's pursuits be wrong and unjustifiable, yet if they are prosecuted with steadiness and vigor, we cannot withhold our admiration. The most characteristic mark of a great mind is to choose some one important object and pursue it through life. It was this made Cæsar a great man. His object was ambition; he pursued it steadily, and was always ready to sacrifice to it every interfering passion or inclination.

There is a pretty passage in one of Lucian's dialogues, where Jupiter complains to Cupid that though he has had so many intrigues, he was never sincerely beloved. "In order to be loved," says Cupid, " you must lay aside your ægis and your thunderbolts, and you must curl your hair and place a garland on your head, and walk with a soft step, and assume a winning obsequious deportment." "But," replied Jupiter, " I am not willing to resign so much of my dignity." " Then," returns Cupid, "leave off desiring to be loved."—He wanted to be Jupiter and Adonis at the same time.

The Enchantments of the Wizard Indolence, and Exploits of the Knight Sir Industry.

FROM THE "CASTLE OF INDOLENCE," BY THOMSON.

The sequestered mansion in which, either in reality or in imagination, we may be reading this poem, must not itself be a Castle of Indolence; yet everybody delights occasionally in being indolent, or in fancying that he shall have a right to be so some day or other. We please ourselves with pictures of perfect rest, even when we can neither enjoy them, nor mean to do so. We would fain have the luxury without the harm or the expense; there is a corner in every one's mind in which we nestle to it; and hence the enjoyment of such poems as this by Thomson, in which every delight of the kind is set before us. The second part is not so good as the first. Thomson found himself more inspired by the vice than by its consequences. And we secretly feel as he and his fellow-idlers did, when Sir Industry first interrupted them. We resent the termination of our pleasures, and look upon the reforming knight as a dull and meddling fellow. Why should he wake us from such a pleasant dream? On reflection, however, we see that the fault is not his, but our own; that we should wake up in a far worse manner, if Sir Industry did not rouse us. There is beautiful poetry in the second part, even exquisite *indolent* bits, or places at least in which we *might* be indolent; in fine, we congratulate ourselves on our virtue, and begin, like the knight, to abuse the old rascally wizard who had pretended to make us his victims. We have retained the best passages in both parts, and the best only; not without linking them in such a manner as the stanzas luckily enabled us to do, with no violation to a syllable, except the occasional loss of connection with a rhyme. Alteration was out of the question; every word retained is the poet's, and no other is admitted.

Thomson, who was once seen eating a peach off a tree with his hands in his waistcoat pockets, was fourteen or fifteen years writing the *Castle of Indolence;*—a fitting period! We are not to suppose he did nothing between whiles. He was both very indolent and very industrious, for his mind was always at work on his enjoyments, as the world has good reason to know in possessing his *Seasons*. And he wrote tragedies besides, not so good, but full of humane and generous sentiments, with passages worth picking out. He had the luck to be made easy in his circumstances by men in power before it was too late for him to enjoy what he made others enjoy; so he lived at Richmond, singing like one of the birds whom he so justly describes as singing the better, the better they are fed; that is to say, if the genius of singing be in them; for this implies the necessity of giving vent to it.

"What you observe concerning the pursuit of poetry," says he, in a letter to a friend, "so far engaged in it as I am, is certainly just. Besides, let him quit it who can, and 'erit mihi magnus Apollo,' or something as great. A true genius, like light, must be beaming forth, as a false one is an incurable disease. One would not, however, climb Parnassus, any more than your mortal hills, to fix forever on the barren top. No; it is some little dear retirement in the vale below that gives the right relish to the prospect, which, without that, is nothing but enchantment; and though pleasing for some time, at last leaves us in a desert. The great fat doctor of Bath* told me that poets should be kept poor, the more to animate their genius. This is like the cruel custom of putting a bird's eye out that it may sing the sweeter; but, surely, they sing sweetest amid the luxuriant woods, while the full spring blossoms around them."

Beautifully said is this, and well reasoned too. It is a final answer to all the grudgers of a poet's comfort. Singing, it is true, might and does console him under any circumstances; but why should we

---

* Supposed to be Dr. Cheyne, who got fat and melancholy with good living, whereas Thomson got fat and merry; for Cheyne was an owl, not a singing bird.

wish him to be consoled, when he can be made happy? as happy as he would make ourselves?

Thomson is a greater poet than the style of the *Seasons* would lead us to suppose. He was too modest to approach Nature in the garb of his natural simplicity, so he put on a sort of court suit of classicality, stuffed out with "taffeta phrases" and "silken terms precise." But the true genius is underneath. Perhaps there was something in it of a heavy temperament, and of the "indolence" to which it inclined him. He had a warm heart in a gross body. The *Castle of Indolence* has been thought his best poem, because the style was imitated from that of Spenser. It certainly contains as good poetry as any he wrote; and the tone of Spenser is charmingly imitated, with an arch but delighted reverence.

CANTO I.

*The castle hight of Indolence,
And its false luxury;
Where for a little time, alas!
We liv'd right jollily.*

O MORTAL man, who livest here by toil,
 Do not complain of this thy hard estate;
That, like an emmet, thou must ever moil,
Is a sad sentence of an ancient date;
And, certes, there is for it reason great;
For though sometimes it makes thee weep and wail,
And curse thy star, and early drudge and late,
Withouten that would come a heavier bale,
Loose life, unruly passions, and diseases pale.

In lowly dale, fast by a river's side,
With woody hill o'er hill encompass'd round,
A most enchanting wizard did abide,
Than whom a fiend more fell is nowhere found.
It was, I ween, a lovely spot of ground:
And there, a season atween June and May,

Half prankt with spring, with summer half embrown'd,
A listless climate made; where, sooth to say,
No living wight could work, ne cared ev'n for play.

Was naught around but images of rest,
Sleep-soothing groves, and quiet lawns between,
And flowery beds that slumberous influence kest,
From poppies breath'd, and beds of pleasant green,
Where never yet was creeping creature seen.
Meantime unnumber'd glittering streamlets play'd,
And hurlèd everywhere their waters sheen;
That, as they bicker'd through the sunny glade,
Though restless still themselves, a lulling murmur made.

Join'd to the prattle of the purling rills,
Were heard the lowing herds along the vale,
And flocks loud-bleating from the distant hills,
And vacant shepherds piping in the dale:
And now and then sweet Philomel would wail,
Or stock-doves plain amid the forest deep,
That drowsy rustled to the sighing gale;
And still a coil the grasshopper did keep;
Yet all these sounds yblent inclinèd all to sleep.

Full in the passage of the vale, above,
A sable, silent, solemn forest stood;
Where naught but shadowy forms was seen to move,
As Idless fancy'd in her dreaming mood;
And up the hills, on either side, a wood
Of blackening pines, ay waving to and fro,
Sent forth a sleepy horror through the blood;
And where this valley winded out, below,
The murmuring main was heard, and scarcely heard, to flow.

A pleasing land of drowsy-head it was,
Of dreams that wave before the half-shut eye,
And of gay castles in the clouds that pass,
Forever flushing round a summer sky;
There eke the soft delights, that witchingly
Instil a wanton sweetness through the breast,
And the calm pleasures always hover'd nigh;
But whate'er smack'd of noyance and unrest
Was far, far off expell'd from this delicious nest.

The landskip such, inspiring perfect ease,
Where Indolence (for so the wizard hight)
Close hid his castle 'mid embowering trees,
That half shut out the beams of Phœbus bright,
And made a kind of chequer'd day and night.
* * * * * *
While solitude and perfect silence reign'd,
So that to think you dreamt you almost was constrain'd.

As when a shepherd of the Hebrid Isles,
Plac'd far amid the melancholy main,
(Whether it be lone fancy him beguiles,
Or that aërial beings sometimes deign
To stand embodied to our senses plain)
Sees on the naked hill or valley low,
The whilst in ocean Phœbus dips his wain,
A vast assembly moving to and fro,
Then all at once in air dissolves the wondrous show.

The doors that knew no shrill alarming bell,
No cursed knocker ply'd by villain's hand,
Self-opened into halls, where who can tell
What elegance and grandeur wide expand,
The pride of Turkey and of Persia land?
Soft quilts on quilts, on carpets carpets spread,

And couches stretch'd around in seemly band,
And endless pillows rise to prop the head;
So that each spacious room was one full swelling bed.

And everywhere huge cover'd tables stood,
With wines high-flavor'd and rich viands crown'd;
Whatever sprightly juice or tasteful food
On the green bosom of this earth are found,
And all old ocean genders in his round:
Some hand unseen these silently display'd,
E'en undemanded by a sight or sound;
You need but wish, and, instantly obey'd,
Fair rang'd the dishes rose, and thick the glasses play'd.

The rooms with costly tapestry were hung,
Where was inwoven many a gentle tale,
Such as of old the rural poets sung,
Or of Arcadian or Sicilian vale;
Reclining lovers in the lonely dale
Pour'd forth at large the sweetly tortur'd heart,
Or, sighing tender passion, swell'd the gale,
And taught charm'd Echo to resound their smart,
While flocks, woods, streams, around, repose and peace impart.

Each sound, too, here to languishment inclin'd,
Lull'd the weak bosom, and induc'd to ease;
Aërial music in the warbling wind,
At distance rising oft, by small degrees
Nearer and nearer came, till o'er the trees
It hung, and breath'd such soul-dissolving airs
As did, alas! with soft perdition please:
Entangled deep in its enchanting snares,
The listening heart forgot all duties and all cares

A certain music, never known before,*
Here lull'd the pensive melancholy mind;
Full easily obtain'd. Behooves no more,
But sidelong to the gently-waving wind,
To lay the well-tun'd instrument reclin'd,
From which, with airy-flying fingers light,
Beyond each mortal touch the most refin'd,
The god of winds drew sounds of deep delight,
Whence, with just cause, the harp of Æolus it hight.

Ah me! what hand can touch the string so fine?
Who up the lofty diapason roll
Such sweet, such sad, such solemn airs divine,
Then let them down again into the soul?
Now, rising love they fann'd; now, pleasing dole
They breath'd in tender musings through the heart;
And now a graver sacred strain they stole,
As when seraphic hands an hymn impart;
Wild-warbling Nature all, above the reach of art!

Such the gay splendor, the luxurious state
Of Caliphs old, who, on the Tigris shore,
In mighty Bagdat, populous and great,
Held their bright court, where was of ladies store,
And verse, love, music, still the garland wore.
When sleep was coy, the bard, in waiting there,
Cheer'd the lone midnight with the Muses' lore:
Composing music bade his dreams be fair,
And music lent new gladness to the morning air.

Near the pavilions where we slept still ran
Soft tinkling streams, and dashing waters fell,
And sobbing waters sigh'd, and oft began
(So work'd the wizard) wintry storms to swell,

* The Æolian harp, just then invented

As heaven and earth they would together mell;
At doors and windows threatening seem'd to call
The demons of the tempest growling fell;
Yet the least entrance found they none at all,
Where sweeter grew our sleep, secure in mossy hall.

One great amusement of our household was,
In a huge crystal magic globe to spy,
Still as you turn'd it, all things that do pass
Upon this ant-hill earth; where constantly
Of idly-busy men the restless fry
Run bustling to and fro with foolish haste
In search of pleasures vain that from them fly,
Or which obtain'd the caitiffs dare not taste:
When nothing is enjoy'd, can there be greater waste?

Of vanity the mirror this was call'd.
Here you a muckworm of the town might see
At his dull desk, amid his ledgers stall'd,
Ate up with carking care and penurie,
Most like to carcase parch'd on gallows tree.
"A penny savèd is a penny got;"
Firm to this scoundrel-maxim keepeth he,
Ne of its rigor will he bate a jot,
Till it has quench'd his fire and banishéd his pot.

Strait from the filth of this low grub, behold!
Comes fluttering forth a gaudy spendthrift heir,
All glossy gay, enamell'd all with gold,
The silly tenant of the summer air.
In folly lost, of nothing takes he care;
Pimps, lawyers, stewards, harlots, flatterers vile,
And thieving tradesmen him among them share;
His father's ghost from Limbo Lake the while
Sees this, which more damnation doth upon him pile.

Of all the gentle tenants of the place,
There was a man of special grave remark;*
A certain tender gloom o'erspread his face,
Pensive, not sad; in thought involv'd, not dark;
As soot this man would sing as morning lark,
And teach the noblest morals of the heart;
But these his talents were yburied stark;
Of the fine stores he nothing would impart,
Which or boon Nature gave, or nature-painting Art.

To noontide shades incontinent he ran,
Where purls the brook with sleep-inviting sound,
Or when Dan Sol to slope his wheels began,
Amid the broom he bask'd him on the ground,
Where the wild thyme and camomil are found;
There would he linger, till the latest ray
Of light sate trembling on the welkin's bound;
Then homeward through the twilight shadows stray
Sauntering and slow: so had he passèd many a day.

Yet not in thoughtless slumber were they past;
For oft the heavenly fire, that lay conceal'd
Beneath the sleeping embers, mounted fast,
And all its native light anew reveal'd.
Oft as he travers'd the cerulean field,
And mark'd the clouds that drove before the wind
Ten thousand glorious systems would he build,
Ten thousand great ideas fill'd his mind;
But with the clouds they fled, and left no trace behind

With him was sometimes join'd in silent walk,
(Profoundly silent, for they never spoke,)

---

* Who this person was, does not appear to have been discover.ed.

One shier still,* who quite detested talk ;
Oft stung by spleen, at once away he broke
To groves of pine and broad o'ershadowing oak ;
There, inly thrill'd, he wander'd all alone,
And on himself his pensive fury wroke,
Ne never utter'd word save when first shone
The glittering star of eve—" Thank Heaven, the day is done !"

Here lurk'd a wretch who had not crept abroad
For forty years, ne face of mortal seen ;
In chamber brooding like a loathly toad,
And sure his linen was not very clean ;
Through secret loop-holes that had practis'd been
Near to his bed, his dinner vile he took ;
Unkempt and rough, of squalid face amd mien,
Our Castle's shame ; whence, from his filthy nook,
We drove the villain out, for fitter lair to look.

One day there channe'd into these hills to rove
A joyous youth,† who took you at first sight ;
Him the wild wave of pleasure hither drove
Before the sprightly tempest tossing light ;
Certes, he was a most engaging wight,
Of social glee, and wit humane tho' keen,
Turning the night to day and day to night ;
For him the merry bells had rung I ween,
If in this nook of quiet bells had ever been.

But not e'en pleasure to excess is good ;
What most elates, then sinks the soul as low :

---

* Supposed to be Armstrong.
† Probably the author's friend Patterson, his deputy in the office of Surveyor-General of the Leeward Islands.

When spring-tide joy pours in with copious flood,
The higher still th' exulting billows flow,
The farther back again they flagging go,
And leave us grovelling on the dreary shore.
Taught by this son of Joy, we found it so,
Who, whilst he staid, kept in a gay uproar
Our madden'd Castle all, the abode of Sleep no more.

As when in prime of June a burnish'd fly,
Sprung from the meads, o'er which he sweeps along,
Cheer'd by the breathing bloom and vital sky,
Tunes up amid these airy halls his song,
Soothing at first the gay reposing throng;
And oft he sips their bowl; or, nearly drown'd,
He, thence recovering, drives their beds among,
And scares their tender sleep with trump profound,
Then out again he flies to wing his mazy round.

Another guest there was of sense refin'd,*
Who felt each worth, for every worth he had;
Serene, yet warm; humane, yet firm his mind;
As little touch'd as any man's with bad:
Him through their inmost walks the Muses lad,
To him the sacred love of Nature lent,
And sometimes would he make our valley glad;
When as we found he would not here be pent,
To him the better sort this friendly message sent—

"Come, dwell with us, true son of Virtue! come;
But if, alas! we cannot thee persuade
To lie content beneath our peaceful dome
Ne ever more to quit our quiet glade,

* Lord Lyttleton.

Yet when at last thy toils, but ill apaid,
Shall dead thy fire, and damp its heavenly spark,
Thou wilt be glad to seek the rural shade,
There to indulge the Muse, and Nature mark;
We then a lodge for thee will rear in Hagley Park."

Here whilom ligg'd th' Esopus of the age,*
But call'd by Fame, in soul yprickèd deep,
A noble pride restor'd him to the stage,
And rous'd him like a giant from his sleep.
E'en from his slumbers we advantage reap:
With double force th' enliven'd scene he wakes,
Yet quits not Nature's bounds. He knows to keep
Each due decorum. Now the heart he shakes,
And now with well-urged sense th' enlightened judgment takes.

A bard here dwelt, more fat than bard beseems,†
Who void of envy, guile, or lust of gain,
On Virtue still, and Nature's pleasing themes,
Pour'd forth his unpremeditated strain;
The world forsaking with a calm disdain,
Here laugh'd he careless in his easy seat;
Here quaff'd encircled by the joyous train,
Oft moralizing sage; his ditty sweet
He loathèd much to write, ne carèd to repeat.

Full oft by holy feet our ground was trod;
Of clerks good plenty here you mote espy;
A little, round, fat, oily man of God,‡
Was one I chiefly mark'd among the fry:
He had a roguish twinkle in his eye,

---

* Quin, the actor.
† Thomson himself. All but the first line of this stanza is understood to have been written by a friend.
‡ The Rev. Mr. Murdoch, the poet's first biographer.

And shone all glittering with ungodly dew,
If a tight damsel chanc'd to trippen by;
Which when observ'd, he shrunk into his mew,
And strait would recollect his piety anew.

Nor be forgot a tribe who minded naught
(Old inmates of the place) but state affairs;
They look'd, perdie, as if they deeply thought,
And on their brow sat every nation's cares.
The world by them is parcel'd out in shares.
When in the Hall of Smoke they congress hold,
And the sage berry sun-burnt Mocha bears
Has clear'd their inward eye, then smoke-enroll'd,
Their oracles break forth, mysterious as of old.

Here languid beauty kept her pale-fac'd court:
Bevies of dainty dames of high degree
From every quarter hither made resort,
Where, from gross mortal care and business free,
They lay pour'd out, in ease and luxury:
Or should they a vain show of work assume,
Alas! and well a-day! what can it be?
To knot, to twist, to range the vernal bloom;
But far is cast the distaff, spinning-wheel, and loom.

Their only labor was to kill the time;
And labor dire it is, and weary woe:
They sit, they loll, turn o'er some idle rhyme,
Then, rising sudden, to the glass they go,
Or saunter forth with tottering step and slow:
This soon too rude an exercise they find;
Strait on the couch their limbs again they throw;
Where hours and hours they sighing lie reclin'd,
And court the vapory god, soft breathing in the wind.

Now must I mark the villany we found;
But ah! too late, as shall eftsoons be shown.
A place here was, deep, dreary, underground,
Where still our inmates, when unpleasing grown,
Diseas'd and loathsome, privily were thrown.
Far from the light of heaven, they languish'd there
Unpitied, uttering many a bitter groan:
For of these wretches taken was no care;
Fierce fiends and hags of hell their only nurses were.

*Alas! the change! from scenes of joy and rest,
To this dark den, where sickness toss'd alway.
Here Lethargy, with deadly sleep opprest,
Stretch'd on his back, a mighty lubbard, lay,
Heaving his sides, and snorèd night and day.
To stir him from his traunce it was not eath;
And his half-open'd eyne he shut straitway;
He led, I wot, the softest way to death,
And taught withouten pain and strife to yield the breath.

Of limbs enormous, but withal unsound,
Soft-swol'n and pale, here lay the Hydropsy:
Unwieldy man! with belly monstrous round,
Forever fed with watery supply:
For still he drank, and yet he still was dry.
And moping here did Hypochondria sit,
Mother of Spleen, in robes of various dye,
Who vexèd was full oft with ugly fit;
And some her frantic deem'd, and some her deem'd a wit.

A lady proud she was, of ancient blood,
Yet oft her fear her pride made crouchen low;

---

* These four concluding stanzas of Canto I. were written by Armstrong.

She felt, or fancied, in her fluttering mood,
All the diseases which the spittles know,
And sought all physic which the shops bestow,
And still new leeches and new drugs would try,
Her humor ever wavering to and fro;
For sometimes she would laugh, and sometimes cry,
Then sudden waxèd wroth, and all she knew not why.

Fast by her side a listless maiden pin'd,
With aching head, and squeamish heart-burnings;
Pale, bloated, cold, she seem'd to hate mankind,
Yet lov'd in secret all forbidden things.
And here the Tertian shakes his chilling wings:
The sleepless Gout here counts the crowing cocks;
A wolf now gnaws him, now a serpent stings:
Whilst Apoplexy cramm'd Intemperance knocks
Down to the ground at once, as butcher felleth ox.

CANTO II.

*The Knight of Arts and Industry,
And his achievements fair,
That by his Castle's overthrow
Secur'd and crownèd were.*

ESCAP'D the Castle of the Sire of Sin,
    Ah! where shall I so sweet a dwelling find?
For all around without, and all within,
Nothing save what delightful was and kind,
Of goodness savoring and a tender mind,
E'er rose to view: but now another strain
Of doleful note, alas! remains behind;
I now must sing of pleasure turn'd to pain,
And of the false enchanter Indolence complain.

Is there no patron to protect the Muse,
And fence for her Parnassus' barren soil?
To every labor its reward accrues,
And they are sure of bread who swink and moil;
But a fell tribe th' Aonian hive despoil,
As ruthless wasps oft rob the painful bee:
Thus while the laws not guard that noblest toil,
Ne for the Muses other meed decree,
They praisèd are alone, and starve right merrily.

I care not, Fortune, what you me deny;
You cannot rob me of free Nature's grace;
You cannot shut the windows of the sky,
Through which Aurora shows her brightening face;
You cannot bar my constant feet to trace
The woods and lawns, by living stream, at eve:
Let health my nerves and finer fibres brace,
And I their toys to the great children leave:
Of fancy, reason, virtue, naught can me bereave.

Come then, my Muse! and raise a bolder song;
Come, lig no more upon the bed of sloth,
Dragging the lazy languid line along,
Fond to begin, but still to finish loath,
Thy half-wit scrolls all eaten by the moth;
Arise, and sing that generous imp of fame,
Who with the sons of Softness nobly wroth,
To sweep away this human lumber came,
Or in a chosen few to rouse the slumbering flame.

The tidings reach'd to where, in quiet hall,
The good old knight enjoy'd well-earnt repose.
" Come, come, Sir Knight, thy children on thee call:
Come save us yet, ere ruin round us close,

The demon Indolence thy toil o'erthrows."
On this the noble color stain'd his cheeks,
Indignant, glowing thro' the whitening snows
Of venerable eld; his eye full-speaks
His ardent soul, and from his couch at once he breaks.

I will (he cried) so help me, God! destroy
That villain Archimage.—His page then strait
He to him called, a fiery-footed boy,
Benempt Dispatch. "My steed be at the gate;
My bard attend; quick, bring the net of Fate."
This net was twisted by the Sisters three,
Which when once cast o'er hardened wretch, too late
Repentance comes; replevy cannot be
From the strong iron grasp of vengeful Destiny.

He came, the bard, a little Druid-wight,
Of wither'd aspect; but his eye was keen,
With sweetness mix'd. In russet gown bedight,
As is his sister of the copses green,
He crept along, unpromising of mien.
Gross he who judges so. His soul was fair,
Bright as the children of yon azure sheen.
True comeliness, which nothing can impair,
Dwells in the mind; all else is vanity and glare.

"Come" (quoth the knight), "a voice has reach'd mine ear;
The demon Indolence threats overthrow
To all that to mankind is good and dear:
Come, Philomelus! let us instant go,
O'erturn his bowers, and lay his Castle low
Those men, those wretched men! who will be slaves
Must drink a bitter wrathful cup of woe;
But some there be thy song, as from their graves,
Shall raise. Thrice happy he! who without rigor saves."

Thus holding high discourse, they came to where
The cursed carle was at his wonted trade,
Still tempting heedless men into his snare,
In witching wise, as I before have said;
But when he saw, in goodly gear array'd,
The grave majestic knight approaching nigh,
And by his side the bard so sage and staid,
His countenance fell; yet oft his anxious eye
Mark'd them, like wily fox who roosted cock doth spy.

Nathless, with feign'd respect he bade give back
The rabble rout, and welcom'd them full kind;
Struck with the noble twain, they were not slack
His orders to obey, and fall behind.
Then he resum'd his song, and, unconfin'd,
Pour'd all his music, ran thro' all his strings;
With magic dust their eyne he tries to blind,
And virtue's tender airs o'er weakness flings.
What pity base his song, who so divinely sings!

Elate in thought he counted them his own,
They listen'd so intent with fix'd delight;
But they, instead, as if transmew'd to stone,
Marvell'd he could with such sweet art unite
The lights and shades of manners wrong and right.
Meantime the silly crowd the charm devour,
Wide pressing to the gate. Swift on the knight
He darted fierce to drag him to his bower,
Who back'ning shunn'd his touch, for well he knew his power

As in throng'd amphitheatre, of old,
The wary Retiarius trapp'd his foe,
E'en so the knight, returning on him bold,
At once involv'd him in the net of woe,

Whereof I mention made not long ago.
Enrag'd at first, he scorn'd so weak a jail,
And leapt, and flew, and flouncèd to and fro;
But when he found that nothing could avail,
He sat him felly down, and gnaw'd his bitter nail.

Alarm'd, th' inferior demons of the place
Rais'd rueful shrieks and hideous yells around;
Black stormy clouds deform'd the welkin's face,
And from beneath was heard a wailing sound,
As of infernal sprights in cavern bound;
A solemn sadness every creature strook
And lightnings flash'd, and horror rock'd the ground;
Huge crowds on crowds outpour'd with blemish'd look,
As if on time's last verge this frame of things had shook.

Soon as the short-liv'd tempest was yspent,
Steam'd from the jaws of vext Avernus' hole,
And hush'd the hubbub of the rabblement,
Sir Industry the first calm moment stole.
"There must" (he cried), "amid so vast a shoal,
Be some who are not tainted at the heart,
Not poison'd quite by this same villain's bowl;
Come then, my Bard! thy heavenly fire impart;
Touch soul with soul, till forth the latent spirit start."

The bard obey'd; and taking from his side,
Where it in seemly sort depending hung,
His British harp, its speaking strings he try'd,
The which with skilful touch he deftly strung,
Till tinkling in clear symphony they rung:
Then, as he felt the Muses come along,
Light o'er the chords his raptured hand he flung,
And play'd a prelude to his rising song;
The whilst, like midnight mute, ten thousands round him throng.

Thus ardent burst his strain—" Ye hapless race !
Dire-laboring here to smother Reason's ray,
That lights our Maker's image in our face,
And gives us wide o'er earth unquestion'd sway,
What is th' ador'd Supreme Perfection, say ?
What, but eternal never-resting soul,
Almighty power, and all-directing day,
By whom each atom stirs, the planets roll ;
Who fills, surrounds, informs, and agitates the whole.

" Is not the field, with lively culture green,
A sight more joyous than the dead morass?
Do not the skies with active ether clean
And fann'd by sprightly Zephyrs, far surpass
The foul November fogs, and slumb'rous mass
With which sad Nature veils her drooping face ?
Does not the mountain-stream, as clear as glass,
Gay-dancing on, the putrid pool disgrace ?
The same in all holds true, but chief in human race.

" Had unambitious mortals minded naught
But in loose joy their time to wear away,
Had they alone the lap of Dalliance sought,
Pleas'd on their pillow their dull heads to lay,
Rude Nature's state had been our state to-day;
No cities e'er their towery fronts had rais'd,
No arts had made us opulent and gay ;
With brother-brutes the human race had graz'd ;
None e'er had soar'd to fame, none honor'd been, none prais'd.

" Great Homer's song had never fir'd the breast
To thirst of glory and heroic deeds ;
Sweet Maro's muse, sunk in inglorious rest,
Had silent slept amid the Mincian reeds:

The wits of modern time had told their beads,
And monkish legends been their only strains;
Our Milton's Eden had lain wrapped in weeds,
Our Shakspeare stroll'd and laugh'd with Warwick swains,
Ne had my master Spenser charm'd his Mulla's plains.

"But should to fame your hearts unfeeling be,
If right I read, you pleasure all require;
Then hear how best may be obtain'd this fee,
How best enjoy'd this Nature's wide desire.
Toil, and be glad; let industry inspire
Into your quicken'd limbs her buoyant breath;
Who does not act, is dead: absorpt entire
In miry sloth, no pride, no joy he hath;
O leaden-hearted Men, to be in love with death!

" O who can speak the vigorous joys of health;
Unclogg'd the body, unobscur'd the mind;
The morning rises gay, with pleasing stealth,
The temperate evening falls serene and kind;
In health the wiser brutes true gladness find;
See! how the younglings frisk along the meads,
As May comes on, and wakes the balmy wind;
Rampant with life, their joy all joy exceeds;
Yet what but high-strung health this dancing pleasaunce
    breeds?

" There are, I see, who listen to my lay,
Who wretched sigh for virtue, but despair.
All may be done, (methinks I hear them say,)
E'en death despis'd, by generous actions fair;
All but for those who to these bowers repair;
Their every power dissolv'd in luxury,
To quit of torpid Sluggishness the lair,

And from the powerful arms of Sloth get free
'Tis rising from the dead—alas!—it cannot be!

'Would you then learn to dissipate the band
 Of these huge threat'ning difficulties dire,
 That in the weak man's way like lions stand,
 His soul appall, and damp his rising fire?
 Resolve, resolve, and to be men aspire.
 Exert that noble privilege, alone,
 Here to mankind indulg'd; control desire;
 Let godlike Reason, from her sovereign throne,
Speak the commanding word, I will!—and it is done.

"Heavens! can you then thus waste, in shameful wise,
 Your few important days of trial here?
 Heirs of eternity! yborn to rise
 Through endless states of being, still more near
 To bliss approaching, and perfection clear?
 Can you renounce a fortune so sublime?
 Such glorious hopes, your backward steps to steer,
 And roll, with vilest brutes, through mud and slime?
No! no! your heaven-touch'd hearts disdain the sordid
  crime!"

"Enough! enough!" they cried. Strait from the crowd
 The better sort on wings of transport fly;
 As when amid the lifeless summits proud
 Of Alpine cliffs, where to the gelid sky
 Snows pil'd on snows in wintry torpor lie,
 The rays divine of vernal Phœbus play,
 Th' awaken'd heaps, in streamlets from on high,
 Rous'd into action, lively leap away,
Glad warbling through the vales, in their new being gay.

But far the greater part with rage inflam'd,
Dire-mutter'd curses, and blasphem'd high Jove.
"Ye sons of Hate!" (they bitterly exclaim'd),
"What brought you to this seat of peace and love?
While with kind Nature, here amid the grove,
We passed the harmless sabbath of our time,
What to disturb it could, fell men, emove
Your barbarous hearts? Is happiness a crime?
Then do the fiends of hell rule in you heaven sublime.'

"Ye impious wretches!" (quoth the knight in wrath),
"Your happiness behold!"—then strait a wand
He wav'd, an anti-magic power that hath
Truth from illusive falsehood to command.
Sudden the landscape sinks on every hand;
The pure quick streams are marshy puddles found;
On baleful heaths the groves all blacken'd stand;
And o'er the weedy, foul, abhorrèd ground,
Snakes, adders, toads, each loathsome creature crawls around.

And here and there, on trees by lightning scath'd,
Unhappy wights, who loathèd life, yhung;
Or in fresh gore and recent murder bath'd,
They weltering lay; or else, infuriate flung
Into the gloomy flood, while ravens sung
The funeral dirge, they down the torrent roll'd:
These by distemper'd blood to madness stung,
Had doom'd themselves; whence oft, when night controll'd
The world, returning hither their sad spirits howl'd.

Attended by a glad acclaiming train
Of those he rescued had from gaping hell,

Then turn'd the knight, and to his hall again
Soft pacing, sought of Peace the mossy cell;
Yet down his cheeks the gems of pity fell,
To see the helpless wretches that remain'd,
There left through delves and deserts dire to yell;
Amaz'd, their looks with pale dismay were stain'd,
And spreading wide their hands, they meek repentance feign'd

But, ah! their scornèd day of grace was past;
For (horrible to tell) a desert wild
Before them stretch'd, bare, comfortless, and vast,
With gibbets, bones, and carcases defil'd.
There nor trim field nor lively culture smil'd,
Nor waving shade was seen, nor mountain fair;
But sands abrupt on sands lay loosely pil'd,
Thro' which they floundering toil'd with painful care,
Whilst Phœbus smote them sore, and fir'd the cloudless air.

Then, varying to a joyless land of bogs,
The sadden'd country a gray waste appear'd,
Where naught but putrid streams and noisome fogs
Forever hung on drizzly Auster's beard;
Or else the ground by piercing Caurus scar'd,
Was jagg'd with frost, or heap'd with glazèd snow:
Thro' these extremes a ceaseless round they steer'd,
By cruel fiends still hurried to and fro,
Gaunt Beggary, and Scorn, with many hell-hounds moe.

The first was with base dunghill rags yclad,
Tainting the gale in which they flutter'd light;
Of morbid hue, his features sunk and sad;
His hollow eyne shook forth a sickly light;
And o'er his lank jaw-bone, in piteous plight,
His black rough beard was matted rank and vile;

Direful to see! an heart-appalling sight!
Meantime foul scurf and blotches him defile,
And dogs, where'er he went, still barkèd all the while.

The other was a fell despightful fiend:
Hell holds none worse in baleful bower below;
By pride, and wit, and rage, and rancor, keen'd;
Of man alike, if good or bad, the foe;
With nose upturn'd, he always made a show,
As if he smelt some nauseous scent; his eye
Was cold and keen, like blast from boreal snow,
And taunts he casten forth most bitterly.
Such were the twain that off drove this ungodly fry.

E'en so thro' Brentford town, a town of mud,
An herd of bristly swine is prick'd along;
The filthy beasts, that never chew the cud,
Still grunt, and squeak, and sing their troublous song
And oft they plunge themselves the mire among;
But aye the ruthless driver goads them on,
And aye, of barking dogs the biter throng
Makes them renew their unmelodious moan;
Ne ever find they rest from their unresting fone.

Stories by Sir Richard Steele.

NOW FIRST COLLECTED.

These stories, with the exception of two, compose the entire set contributed by this great master of character and sentiment to the Tatler, Spectator, and Guardian. They are remarkable for going to the heart of their subjects with a comprehensive brevity; and are just such stories as a man might tell over his wine to a party of friends. Addison's stories are of a more fanciful sort, and more elegant in the style; some of them are charming; but they are pieces of writing—these are relations. They have all the warmth as well as brevity of unpremeditated accounts, given as occasion called them forth. Steele, indeed, may be said to have always talked, rather than written; and hence the beauties as well as defects of his style, which is apt to be too carelessly colloquial.

Steele, like Fielding, Smollett, Goldsmith—in fact, like almost all our most entertaining wits and novelists, not excepting (on a great scale) Sir Walter Scott himself—was an impulsive and imprudent man, not attentive enough to his outlays, and too sanguine about his income. He warranted, perhaps, the remonstrances of his staider friend Addison; and was more touched than comforted by them, from feeling that they were useless. The remonstrances (if they were of the harsh and practical nature they are said to have been), would have come with less ungraciousness from a more genial and generous man; that is to say, supposing such a man would have thought them advisable. Objections to men like Steele come indeed with grace from none but generous persons, liable to his temptations, and superior to them. Such persons have made such objections, though not unaccompanied with assumptions that might have been spared; probably in consequence of the re-action in Steele's favor in the writings of Hazlitt and others. The objections, however, deserve to be respectfully replied to; and the just reply, we think, is, that you must consider every writer and every man as the result of all the circumstances that have made him what he is, bodily and mental, and then judge whether that result is a gain and pleasure to the world, and a compensation for the less allowable of those circumstances. For a man cannot be one man and another too; cannot be Steele and Addison both; at least we are not aware that any such person has been met with, however modified the varieties of their like may be. Would you have had no such thing as Steele's imprudence, and been content to lose the *Tatler* and the *Guardian?* as Fielding's, and been without *Tom Jones* and *Amelia?* as Smollett's, and had no *Roderick Random* or *Humphrey Clinker?* Or, if you say that Addison could have written, and did write, as good and humorous things as those, will you say that the others did not write with a difference from Addison; and with such a difference as the world strongly feels and highly delights in? You will grant this of course. What constitutes, then, the difference of Steele, of Fielding, and of Smollet, from such a writer as Addison? and could that difference have delighted us as it does, had it not resulted from the entire natures and circumstances of the men? Very foolish and very presumptuous, we grant, would it be in any given imprudent person to quote their example in his defence, even though he should turn out some day to have had warrant for it, or be regarded with indulgence meantime by such as think he has. Those who have nothing in them to justify such an exceptional consideration, come under another category altogether, whatever may be said in their excuse; and those who have something, must be content modestly to await the chance of its recognition, and to pay in the meantime the penalty of its drawbacks.

If there were no worse men in the world than Steele, what a planet we should have of it? Steele knew his own foibles as well as any man. He regretted, and made amends for them, and left posterity a name for which they have reason to thank and love him. Posterity thanks Addison too; but it can hardly be said to love him, even by the help of the good old knight Sir Roger, whom Steele invented for him.

Perhaps they would have loved him more, had he too confessed his faults; or even had he told them in what the only one consisted, at which he hinted when he sent for Gay on his death-bed, and asked his pardon for having done him some wrong. Steele asked pardon for wrong, long before he died. The last thing we hear of him is neither a solitary acknowledgment nor a Christian vaunt, but his sitting out of doors in his retirement, giving the village maidens prizes to contend for. He said modestly of his life—(far too modestly, for he was a loving husband and father, and a disinterested patriot), that it " was but pardonable;" and in his beautiful effusion to the memory of his friend Estcourt the comedian, he expressed his gratitude to that honest mimic for having made him sensible of his defects, and taught him to care for nothing but the subjection of his will.

The reader will find the passage below.*

Truly curious was it, and lucky for the world that Dick Steele and Joseph Addison should have grown up together from childhood, and become the Beaumont and Fletcher of social ethics. But they had

---

* " What was peculiarly excellent in this memorable companion was, that in the accounts he gave of persons and sentiments he did not only hit the figure of their faces and manner of their gestures, but he would, in his narrations, fall into their way of thinking, and this when he recounted passages wherein men of the best wits were concerned, as well as such wherein were represented men of the lowest rank of understanding. It is certain as great an instance of self-love to a weakness, to be impatient of being mimicked, as any can be imagined. There were none but the vain, the formal, the proud, or those who were incapable of amending their faults, dreaded him; to others he was in the highest degree pleasing: and I do not know any satisfaction of any different kind I ever tasted so much, as having got over an impatience of seeing myself in the air he could put me when I had displeased him. It is indeed owing to his exquisite talent this way, more than any philosophy I could read on the subject, that my person is very little of my care; and it is indefferent to me what is said of my shape, my air, my manner, my speech, or my address. It is to poor Estcourt I chiefly owe, that I am arrived at the happiness of thinking nothing a diminution to me, but what argues a depravity of my will.

* * * * * * * *

" I have been present with him among men of the most delicate taste the whole night, and have known him (for he saw it was desired) keep the discourse to himself tho most part of it, and maintain his good-humor with a countenance and in a language so delightful, without offence to any person or thing upon earth, still preserving the distance his circumstances obliged him to; I say, I have seen him do all this in such a charming manner, that I am sure none of those I hint at will read this, without giving some sorrow for their abundant mirth, and one gush of tears for so many bursts of laughter. I wish it were any honor to the pleasant creature's memory, that my eyes are too much suffused to let me go on———"

tastes in common, and admirable was the result; a music more charming for the counter-point; Addison's hand the staider and the calmer, the more artful, the more informed, yet playful withal, though never losing its self-possession;—Steele's the more wandering and capricious, the lighter, the less solemn, yet now and then touching forth notes of a more tender sweetness, and such as fill the eyes with tears. Addison knew nothing of those.

The reader will find evidences of this pathos in most of the following stories. Those of *Valentine and Unnion*, and *Inkle and Yarico*, he has probably been acquainted with from childhood; but they are repeated for that reason. Both are master-pieces; the latter would be not unworthy of perusal after one of Chaucer's. The *Dream* is lovely; and the *Fire*, and the *Wedding Day*, heart-rending. It is remarkable, considering the gaiety of most of Steele's writings, that there should be only one comic story out of the eight. The husband's *flopping* down by the side of his wife, and whispering in her insensible ear, is very ludicrous.

VALENTINE AND UNNION.

AT the siege of Namur by the allies, there were in the ranks of the company commanded by Captain Pincent, in Colonel Frederick Hamilton's regiment, one Unnion a corporal, and one Valentine a private sentinel; there happened between these two men a dispute about a matter of love, which upon some aggravations grew to an irreconcilable hatred. Unnion, being the officer of Valentine, took all opportunities even to strike his rival, and profess the spite and revenge which moved him to it. The sentinel bore it without resistance, but frequently said he would die to be revenged of that tyrant. They had spent whole months thus, one injuring, the other complaining, when in the midst of this rage towards each other they were commanded upon the attack of the castle, where the corporal received a shot in the thigh, and fell; the French pressing on, and he expecting to be trampled to death, called out to his enemy, " Ah, Valentine! can you leave me here?" Valentine immediately ran back, and in the midst of a thick fire of the French took the corporal upon his back and brought him through all that danger as far as the Abbey of Salsine, where a cannon ball took off his head: his body fell under his enemy, whom he was carrying off. Unnion immediately forgot his wound, rose up, tearing his hair, and then threw himself upon the bleeding carcase, crying, " Ah, Valentine! was it for me who have so barbarously used thee, that thou hast died? I will not live after thee." He was not by any means to be forced from the body, but was removed with it bleeding in his arms, and attended with tears by all their comrades who knew their enmity. When he was brought to a tent his wounds were dressed by force; but the next day, still calling upon Valentine, and lamenting his cruelties to him, he died in the pangs of remorse and despair.

THE FIRE.

CLARINDA and Chloe, two very fine women, were bred up as sisters in the family of Romeo, who was the father of Chloe and guardian of Clarinda. Philander, a young gentleman of a good person and charming conversation, being a friend of old Romeo, frequented his house, and by that means was much in conversation with the young ladies, though still in the presence of the father and the guardian. The ladies both entertained a secret passion for him, and could see well enough, notwithstanding the delight which he really took in Romeo's conversation, that there was something more in his heart which made him so assiduous a visitant. Each of them thought herself the happy woman, but the person beloved was Chloe. It happened that both of them were at a play on a carnival evening, when it is the fashion there,* as well as in most countries of Europe, both for men and women, to appear in masks and disguises. It was in that memorable night in the year 1679, when the playhouse by some unhappy accident was set on fire. Philander, in the first hurry of the disaster, immediately ran where his treasure was, burst open the door of the box, snatched the lady up in his arms, and with unspeakable resolution and good fortune carried her off safe. He was no sooner out of the crowd but he set her down, and grasping her in his arms with all the raptures of a deserving lover, " How happy am I," says he, " in an opportunity to tell you I love you more than all things, and of showing you the sincerity of my passion at the very first declaration of it." " My dear, dear Philander," says the lady, pulling off her mask, " this is not the time for art ; you are much dearer to me than the life you have preserved, and the joy of my present deliverance does not transport me so much as the passion which occasioned it." Who can tell the grief, the astonishment, the terror, that appeared in the face of Philander when he saw the person he spoke to was Clarinda ! After a short pause, " Madam," says he, with the looks of a dead man, " we are both mistaken ;" and immediately flew away, without hearing the distressed Clarinda, who had just strength enough to cry out, " Cruel Philander ! why did you not leave me in the theatre ?" Crowds of people immediately gathered about her, and after having brought

---

* In Denmark. Philander, Chloe, &c. sound very absurd as Danish people, but this application of ancient names to modern persons was the taste of the age. Romeo, however, was an innovation still more fantastical. Steele, I suppose, in despair for some fresh name, had it suggested to him by the theatrical ground of this most affecting story.

her to herself, conveyed her to the house of the good old unhappy Romeo. Philander was now pressing against a whole tide of people at the doors of the theatre, and striving to enter with more earnestness, than any there endeavored to get out. He did it at last, and with much difficulty forced his way to the box where his beloved Chloe stood, expecting her fate, amidst this scene of terror and distraction. She revived at the sight of Philander, who fell about her neck with a tenderness not to be expressed, and amidst a thousand sobs and sighs told her his love and his dreadful mistake. The stage was now in flames, and the whole house full of smoke; the entrance was quite barred up with heaps of people who had fallen upon one another as they endeavored to get out. Swords were drawn, shrieks heard on all sides, and in short there was no possibility of an escape for Philander himself, had he been capable of making it without his Chloe. But his mind was above such a thought, and wholly employed in weeping, condoling, and comforting. He catches her in his arms—the fire surrounds them, while . . . . I cannot go on . . . .

Were I an infidel, misfortunes like this would convince me that there must be an hereafter; for who can believe that so much virtue could meet with so great distress without a following reward? For my part, I am so old-fashioned as firmly to believe, that all who perish in such generous enterprises are relieved from the further exercise of life; and Providence, which sees their virtue consummate and manifest, takes them to an immediate reward, in a being more suitable to the grandeur of their spirits.

THE WEDDING DAY.

A GENTLEMAN who had courted a most agreeable young woman and won her heart, obtained also the consent of her father, to whom she was an only child. The old man had a fancy that they should be married in the same church where he himself was, in a village in Westmoreland, and made them set out while he was laid up with the gout in London. The bridegroom took only his man, the bride her maid: they had the most agreeable journey imaginable to the place of marriage, from whence the bridegroom writ the following letter to his wife's father:—

"*March* 18, 1672.

"SIR,—After a very pleasant journey hither, we are preparing for the happy hour in which I am to be your son. I assure you that the bride carries it, in the eye of the vicar who married you, much beyond her mother; though, he says, your open sleeves, pantaloons, and shoulder-knot, made a much better show than the finical dress I am in. However, I am contented to be the second fine man this village ever saw, and shall make it very merry before night, because I shall write myself from thence

"Your most dutiful son,

"T. D.

"The bride gives her duty, and is as handsome as an angel.—I am the happiest man breathing."

The villagers were assembling about the church, and the happy couple took a walk in a private garden. The bridegroom's man knew his master would leave the place on a sudden after the wedding, and seeing him draw his pistols the night before, took this opportunity to go into his chamber and charge them. Upon their return from the garden, they went into that room; and after a little fond raillery on the subject of their courtship, the lover took up a pistol, which he knew he had unloaded the night before, and, presenting it to her, said, with the most graceful air, whilst she looked pleased at his agreeable flattery: " Now, madam, repent of all those cruelties you have been guilty of to me; consider, before you die, how often you have made a poor wretch freeze under your casement; you shall die, you tyrant, you shall die, with all those instruments of death and destruction about you, with that enchanting smile, those killing ringlets of your hair." " Give fire!" said she, laughing. He did so, and shot her dead. Who can speak his condition? but he bore it so patiently as to call upon his man. The poor wretch entered, and his master locked the door upon him. " Will," said he, " did you charge these pistols?" He answered " Yes." Upon which he shot him dead with that remaining. After this, amidst a thousand broken sobs, piercing groans, and distracted motions, he writ the following letter to the father of his dead mistress:—

" Sir,—I, who two hours ago, told you truly I was the happiest man alive, am now the most miserable. Your daughter lies dead at my feet, killed by my hand, through a mistake of my man's charging my pistols unknown to me. Him have I murdered for it. Such is my wedding-day. I will immediately follow my wife to her grave; but before I throw myself on my sword, I command my distraction so far as to explain my story to you. I fear my heart will not keep together until I have stabbed it. Poor, good old man! Remember he that killed your daughter, died for it. In the article of death, I give you my thanks, and pray for you, though I dare not for myself. If it be possible, do not curse me."

THE SHIPWRECK.

A YOUNG gentleman and lady, of ancient and honorable houses in Cornwall, had from their childhood entertained for each other a generous and noble passion, which had been long opposed by their friends, by reason of the inequality of their fortunes; but their constancy to each other, and obedience to those on whom they depended, wrought so much upon their relations, that these celebrated lovers were at length joined in marriage. Soon after their nuptials, the bridegroom was obliged to go into a foreign country to take care of a considerable fortune that had been left him by a relation, and came very opportunely to improve their moderate circumstances. They received the congratulations of all the country on the occasion; and I remember it was a common sentence in every one's mouth, "You see how faithful love is rewarded."

He took this agreeable voyage, and sent home, every post, fresh accounts of his success in his affairs abroad; but at last, though he designed to return with the next ship, he lamented, in his letters, that "business would detain him some time longer from home," because he would give himself the pleasure of an unexpected arrival.

The young lady, after the heat of the day, walked every evening on the sea-shore, near which she lived, with a familiar friend, her husband's kinswoman; and diverted herself with what objects they met there, or upon discourses of the future methods of life, in the happy change in their circumstances. They stood one evening on the shore together in a perfect tranquillity, observing the setting of the sun, the calm face of the deep, and the silent heaving of the waves which gently rolled towards them, and broke at their feet;

when, at a distance, her kinswoman saw something float on the waters, which she fancied was a chest, and with a smile told her, " she saw it first, and if it came ashore full of jewels, she had a right to it." They both fixed their eyes upon it, and entertained themselves with the subject of the wreck, the cousin still asserting her right; but promising, "if it was a prize, to give her a very rich coral for the child of which she was then big, provided she might be god-mother." Their mirth soon abated, when they observed, upon the nearer approach, that it was a human body. The young lady, who had a heart naturally filled with pity and compassion, made many melancholy reflections on the occasion. "Who knows," said she, "but this man may be the only hope and heir of a wealthy house, the darling of indulgent parents, who are now in impertinent mirth, and pleasing themselves with the thoughts of offering him a bride they have got ready for him? or may he not be the master of a family that wholly depended upon his life? There may, for aught we know, be half-a-dozen fatherless children, and a tender wife, now exposed to poverty by his death. What pleasure might he have promised himself in the different welcome he was to have from her and them? But let us go away; it is a dreadful sight! The best office we can do, is to take care that the poor man, whoever he is, is decently buried." She turned away, when a wave threw the carcase on the shore. The kinswoman immediately shrieked out, "Oh my cousin!" and fell upon the ground. The unhappy wife went to help her friend, when she saw her own husband at her feet, and dropped in a swoon upon the body. An old woman, who had been the gentleman's nurse, came out about this time to call the ladies in to supper, and found her child, as she always called him, dead on the shore, her mistress and kinswoman both lying dead by him. Her loud lamentations, and calling her young master to life, soon awaked the friend from her trance; but the wife was gone forever.

When the family and neighborhood got together round the bodies, no one asked any questions, but the objects before them told the story.

THE ALCHEMISTS.

BASILIUS Valentinus was a person who had arrived at the utmost perfection in the hermetic art, and initiated his son Alexandrinus in the same mysteries; but, as they are not to be attained but by the painful, the pious, the chaste, and the pure of heart, Basilius did not open to him, because of his youth and the deviations too natural to it, the greatest secrets of which he was master, as well knowing that the operation would fail in the hands of a man so liable to errors in life as Alexandrinus. But believing, from a certain indisposition of mind as well as body, his dissolution was drawing nigh, he called Alexandrinus to him, and as he lay on a couch over against which his son was seated, and prepared by sending out servants one after another, and admonition to examine that no one overheard them, he revealed the most important of his secrets with the solemnity and language of an adept. " My son," said he, " many have been the watchings, long the lucubrations, constant the labors of thy father, not only to gain a great and plentiful estate to his posterity, but also to take care that he should have no posterity. Be not amazed, my child; I do not mean that thou shalt be taken from me, but that I will never leave thee, and consequently cannot be said to have posterity. Observe this small phial and this gallipot; in this an unguent, in the other a liquor. In these, my child, are collected such powers as shall revive the springs of life when they are yet but just ceased, and give new strength, new spirits, and in a word wholly restore all the organs and senses of the human body, to as great a duration as it had before enjoyed from its birth to the day of the application of these my medicines. But, my beloved son, care must be taken to apply them within ten hours after the breath is out of the body, while yet the clay is warm with its late life, and yet capable of resuscitation. I find my frame grown crazy with perpetual toil and meditation, and I conjure you, as soon as I am dead, to anoint me with this unguent; and when you see me begin to move, pour into my lips this inestimable liquor, else the force of the ointment will be ineffectual. By this means you will give me life, as I have you, and we will from that hour mutually lay aside the authority of having bestowed life on each other, but live as brethren, and prepare new medicines against such another period of time as will demand another application of the same restoratives." In a few days after these wonderful ingredients were delivered to Alexandrinus, Basilius departed this life; but such was the pious sorrow of the son at the loss of so excellent a father, and the first transports of grief had so disabled him from all manner of business, that he never thought of the medicines till the time to which his father had limited their efficacy was expired. To tell the truth, Alexandrinus was a man of wit and pleasure, and considered his father had lived out his natural time—his life was long and uniform—suitable to the regularity of it—but that he himself, poor sinner, wanted a new life, to repent of a very bad one hitherto; and in the examination of his heart resolved to go on as he did with this natural being of his, but repent very faithfully, and spend very piously, the life to which he should be reduced by application of these rarities when time should come, to his own person.

It has been observed, that Providence frequently punishes the self-love of men who would do immoderately for their offspring, with children very much below their characters and qualifications; insomuch that they only transmit their names to be borne by those who give daily proofs of the vanity of the labor and ambition of their progenitors.

It happened thus in the family of Basilius; for Alexandrinus began to enjoy his ample fortune in all the extremities of household expenses, furniture, and insolent equipage; and this he pursued, till the departure began, as he grew sensible, to approach. As Basilius was punished with a son very unlike him, Alexandrinus, besides that jealousy, had proofs of the vicious disposition of his son Kenatus, for that was his name.

Alexandrinus, as I observed, having very good reasons for thinking it unsafe to trust the real secret of his phial and gallipot to any man living, projected to make sure work, and hope for his success depending from the avarice, not the bounty, of his benefactor.

With this thought he called Kenatus to his bedside, and bespoke him in the most pathetic gesture and accent. "As much, my son, as you have been addicted to vanity and pleasure, as I also have been before you, you nor I could escape the fame or the good effects of the profound knowledge of our progenitor, the renowned Basilius. His symbol is very well known in the philosophic world, and I shall never forget the venerable air of his countenance when he let me into the profound mysteries of the table of Hermes. 'It is true,' said he, ' and far removed from all color of deceit, that which is inferior is like that which is superior, by which are acquired and perfected all the miracles of a certain work; the father is the sun, the mother is the moon, the wind is the womb, the earth is the nurse of it, and the mother of all per fection.' All this must be received with modesty and wisdom. The chemical people carry in all their jargon a whimsical sort of piety which is ordinary with great lovers of money, and is no more but deceiving themselves, that their regularity and strictness of manners, for the ends of the world, has some affinity to the innocence of heart which must recommend them to the next." Kenatus wondered to hear his father talk so like an adept, and with such a mixture of piety, while Alexandrinus observing his attention fixed, proceeded. "This phial, child, and this little earthen pot, will add to thy estate so much as to make thee the richest man in the German empire. I am going to my long home, but shall not return to common dust." Then he resumed a countenance of alacrity, and told him that if within an hour after his death he anointed his whole body, and poured down his throat that liquor which he had from old Basilius, the corpse would be converted into pure gold. I will not attempt to express to you the unfeigned tenderness that passed between these two extraordinary persons; but if the father recommended the care of his remains with vehemence and affection, the son was not behindhand in professing that he would not cut off the least bit of him but upon the utmost extremity, or to provide for his younger brothers and sisters.

Well, Alexandrinus died, and the heir of his body, as our term is, could not forbear in the wantonness of his heart to measure the length and breadth of his beloved father, and cast up the ensuing value of him before he proceeded to operation. When he knew the immense reward of his pains, he began the work: but lo! when he had anointed the corpse all over, and began to apply the liquor the body stirred, and Kenatus, in a fright, broke the phial.

THE VIOLENT HUSBAND.

Mr. EUSTACE, a young gentleman of good estate near Dublin, in Ireland. married a lady of youth, beauty, and modesty, and lived with her, in general, with much ease and tranquillity; but was in his secret temper impatient of rebuke. She was apt to fall into little sallies of passion; yet as suddenly recalled by her own reflection on her fault, and the consideration of her husband's temper. It happened, as he, his wife, and her sister, were at supper together about two months ago, that in the midst of a careless and familiar conversation the sisters fell into a little warmth and contradiction. He, who was one of that sort of men who are never unconcerned at what passes before them, fell into an outrageous passion on the side of the sister. The person about whom they disputed was so near, that they were under no restraint from running into vain repetitions of past heats; on which occasion all the aggravations of anger and distaste boiled up, and were repeated with the bitterness of exasperated lovers. The wife, observing her husband extremely moved, began to turn it off, and rally him for interposing between two people, who from their infancy had been angry and pleased with each other every half-hour. But it descended deeper into his thoughts, and they broke up with a sullen silence. The wife immediately retired to her chamber, whither her husband soon after followed. When they were in bed he soon dissembled a sleep; and she, pleased that his thoughts were composed, fell into a real one. Their apartment was very distant from the rest of their family in a lonely country house. He now saw his opportunity, and with a dagger he had brought to bed with him, stabbed his wife in the side. She awaked in the highest terror; but immediately imagining it was a blow designed for her husband by ruffians, began to grasp him, and strove to awake and rouse him to defend himself. He still pretended himself sleeping, and gave her a second wound.

She now drew open the curtain, and, by the help of moonlight, saw his hand lifted up to stab her. The horror disarmed her from further struggling; and he, enraged anew at being discovered, fixed his poniard in her bosom. As soon as he believed he had despatched her, he attempted to escape out of the window; but she, still alive, called to him not to hurt himself, for she might live. He was so stung with the insupportable reflection upon her goodness, and his own villany, that he jumped to the bed, and wounded her all over with as much rage as if every blow was provoked by new aggravations. In this fury of mind he fled away. His wife had still strength to go to her sister's apartment, and give an account of this wonderful tragedy; but died the next day. Some weeks after, an officer of justice, in attempting to seize the criminal, fired upon him, as did the criminal upon the officer. Both their balls took place, and both immediately expired.

INKLE AND YARICO.

MR. THOMAS INKLE, of London, aged twenty years, embarked in the Downs on the good ship called the Achilles, bound for the West Indies, on the 16th of June, 1674, in order to improve his fortune by trade and merchandise. Our adventurer was the third son of an eminent citizen, who had taken particular care to instil into his mind an early love of gain by making him a perfect master of numbers, and consequently giving him a quick view of loss and advantage, and preventing the natural impulse of his passions, by prepossession towards his interests. With a mind thus turned, young Inkle had a person every way agreeable, a ruddy vigor in his countenance, strength in his limbs, with ringlets of fair hair loosely flowing on his shoulders. It happened, in the course of the voyage, that the Achilles in some distress put into a creek on the main of America, in search of provisions. The youth, who is the hero of my story, among others, went ashore on this occasion. From their first landing they were observed by a party of Indians, who hid themselves in the woods for that purpose. The English unadvisedly marched a great distance from the shore into the country, and were intercepted by the natives, who slew the greatest number of them. Our adventurer escaped among others by flying into a forest. Upon his coming into a remote and pathless part of the wood, he threw himself, tired and breathless, on a little hillock, when an Indian maid rushed from a thicket behind him. After the first surprise, they appeared mutually agreeable to each other. If the European was highly charmed with the limbs, features, and wild graces of the naked American, the American was no less taken with the dress, complexion, and shape of an European, covered from head to foot. The Indian grew immediately enamored of him, and consequently desirous for his preservation. She therefore conveyed him to a cave, where she gave him a delicious repast of fruits, and led him to a stream to slake his thirst. In the midst of these good offices, she would sometimes play with his hair, and delight in the opposition of its color to that of her fingers. Then open his bosom, then laugh at him for covering it. She was, it seems, a person of distinction, for she every day came to him in a different dress, of the most beautiful bugles, shells, and bredes. She likewise brought him a great many spoils, which her other lovers had presented to her, so that his cave was richly adorned with all the spotted skins of beasts, and most fancy-colored feathers of fowls, which that world afforded. To make his confinement more tolerable, she would carry him in the dusk of the evening. or by the favor of moonlight, to unfrequented groves and solitudes, and show him where to lie down in safety, and sleep amidst the falls of waters, and melody of nightingales. Her part was to watch and hold him awake in her arms, for fear of her countrymen, and awake him on occasion to consult his safety. In this manner did the lovers pass away their time, till they had learned a language of their own, in which the voyager communicated to his mistress how happy he should be to have her in his country. where she should be clothed in such silks as his waistcoat was made of, and be carried in houses drawn by horses without being exposed to wind or weather. All this he promised her the enjoyment of, without such fears and alarms as they were tormented with. In this tender correspondence these lovers lived for many months, when Yarico, instructed by her lover, discovered a vessel on the coast, to which she made signal; and in the night with the utmost joy and satisfaction accompanied him to a ship's crew of his countrymen bound for Barbadoes. When a vessel from the main arrives in that island, it seems the planters come down to the shore, where there is an immediate market of the Indians and other slaves, as with us of horses and oxen.

To be short, Mr. Thomas Inkle, now coming into English territories, began seriously to reflect upon his loss of time, and to weigh with himself how many days' interest of his money he had lost during his stay with Yarico. This thought made the young man very pensive, and careful what account he should be able to give his friends of his voyage. Upon which consideration, the prudent and frugal young man sold Yarico to a Barbadian merchant, notwithstanding that the poor girl, to incline him to commiserate her condition, told him she was with child by him; but he only make use of the information to rise in his demands upon the purchaser.

THE FITS.

A FINE town-lady was married to a country gentleman of ancient descent in one of the counties of Great Britain, who had good-humor to a weakness, and was that sort of person, of whom it is said, he is no man's enemy but his own; one, who had too much tenderness of soul to have any authority with his wife; and she too little sense to give him any authority, for that reason. His kind wife observed this temper in him, and made proper use of it. But knowing it was beneath a gentlewoman to wrangle, she resolved upon an expedient to save decorum, and wean her dear to her point at the same time. She therefore took upon her to govern him, by falling into fits whenever she was repulsed in a request, or contradicted in a discourse. It was a fish-day, when, in the midst of her husband's good-humor at table, she bethought herself to try her project. She made signs that she had swallowed a bone. The man grew pale as ashes, and ran to her assistance, calling for drink. "No, my dear," said she, recovering, "it is down, do not be frightened." This accident betrayed his fondness enough. The next day she complained, a lady's chariot, whose husband had not half his estate, had a crane-neck, and hung with twice the air that hers did. He answered, "Madam, you know my income: you know I have lost two coach-horses this spring,"—down she fell. "Hartshorn! Betty, Susan, Alice, throw water in her face." With much care and pains, she was at last brought to herself, and the vehicle in which she visited was amended in the nicest manner to prevent relapses; but they frequently happened during that husband's whole life, which he had the good fortune to end in a few years after. The disconsolate widow soon pitched upon a very agreeable successor, whom she very prudently designed to govern by the same method. This man knew her little arts, and resolved to break through all tenderness, and be absolute master as soon as occasion offered. One day it happened that a discourse arose about furniture; he was very glad of the occasion, and fell into an invective against china, protesting, that he "would never let five pounds more of his money be laid out that way as long as he breathed." She immediately fainted. He starts up as amazed, and calls for help. The maids run to the closet. He chafes her face, bends her forward, and beats the palms of her hands; her convulsions increase; and down she stumbles on the floor, where she lies quite dead, in spite of what the whole family, from the nursery to the kitchen, could do for her relief.

While every servant was there helping or lamenting their mistress, he, fixing his cheek to hers, seemed to be following in a trance of sorrow; but secretly whispers her, "My dear, this will never do: what is within my power and fortune you may always command; but none of your artifices; you are quite in other hands than those you passed these pretty passions upon." This made her almost in the condition she pretended; her convulsions now came thicker, nor was she to be held down. The kind man doubles his care, helps the servants to throw water in her face by full quarts; and when the sinking part of the fit came again, "Well, my dear," said he, "I applaud your actions; but I must take my leave of you till you are more sincere with me; farewell forever; you shall always know where to hear of me, and want for nothing." With that he ordered her maids to keep plying her with hartshorn, while he went for a physician; he was scarce at the stair-head when she followed, and pulling him into a closet, thanked him for her cure; which was so absolute, that she gave me this relation herself, to be communicated for the benefit of all the voluntary invalids of her sex.

Clubs of Steele and Goldsmith.

The primary signification of the word Club, in its sense of a meeting of companions, appears to be derived from the same root as that of the massy stick, and means a consolidated body of persons large enough to amount to something substantial; something more than accidental and of no account.

A club appears formerly to have meant any such body organized for a common object. It may now be defined to be a set of persons associated for companionable enjoyment, at stated times and with a division of expenses.

Clubs of this kind are thought to be of very modern origin. We suspect they are as old as flourishing communities. Traces of them are discernible in the literature of Greece and Rome, and the East, especially in bacchanalian poetry. Indeed it would be strange if such had not been the case, considering in how many respects men are alike in all ages, and that where good cheer is to be found, they naturally flock together. We are not aware, however, of any ascertained instance of a club, earlier than the famous one at the Devil Tavern, for which Ben Jonson wrote his Latin rules; and perhaps the name, in the modern sense, is hardly appropriate even to this. It is not certain that the rules applied to an organized body of contributors to the expense, in contradistinction to a permitted range of payers. Clubs thickened in the time of the Commonwealth, and exhibited their undoubted modern character in that of Steele and Addison. The meeting of wits in Dryden's time appears to have taken place in the open coffee-room. It is in the clubs of the *Tatler* and *Spectator*, that we first meet with all the characteristics of the modern club—its closed doors, regular members, and " creature comforts."

"Supper and friends expect me at the Rose."

Addison, whose home was not happy, and whose blood required a stimulus to set his wit flowing, found his greatest enjoyment in the tavern-room; Steele was born for one; and except wit, ladies, gallants, and good morals, there is nothing you hear more of in their periodicals, than clubs. The circumstances which brought people together in this kind of society, were often of so fantastic a nature, that it is not easy to distinguish the real from the imaginary sort in the pages of these writers; but some of the names are historical. There is, in the first place, the Spectator's own club, with immortal Sir Roger de Coverley, and Will Honeycomb. Then come the Fat Club, the Thin Club, the Club of Kings (that is to say, of people of the name of King); the St. George's Club, who swore " Before George" (which would seem to be Jacobitical, if they had not met on St. George's day); Street Clubs (composed of members residing in the same street); the Hum-Drum and Mum Clubs (who ingeniously smoked and held their tongues); the Duellists (famous for being killed and " hung"); the Kit-Cat (the great Whig Club, whose name originated in tarts made by Christopher Katt); the Beef-Steak (founded by Estcourt the comedian); the October (a club of Tory country-gentlemen and beer-drinkers); the Ugly Club; the Sighing or Amorous Club; the Fringe-Glove Club (a set of fops); the Hebdomadal (a set of quidnuncs); the Everlasting (some of whom were always sitting); the Club of She-Romps, who once a month " demolished a prude" (this looks like a foundation of Steele's acquaintance, Lady Mary Wortley Montague); the Mohocks, who demolished windows and watchmen, and ran their swords through sedan-chairs (really); the Little or Short Club (an invention of Pope's); the Tall (an invention of Addison's); the Terrible (Steele's); the Silent, who had loud wives, and whose motto was, " Talking spoils company" (an invention of Zachary Pearce's, bishop of Rochester); and last not least, the Club at the Trumpet, in Shire Lane, of which more anon. These, we believe, are all the Clubs mentioned in the *Tatler*, *Spectator*, and *Guardian*. Brookes's, and (we think) White's, which are still places of meeting for the wits, politicians, and gamblers of high life, arose before the dissolution of some of them. Then there is the second Beef-Steak Club (founded by Rich the harlequin); the famous Literary Club (originating with Dr. Johnson); the Club of Monks at Medmenham Abbey (a profligate mistake); the King of Clubs (Bobus Smith's, "himself a club," brother of Sydney); and the high quality club entitled *Nulli Secundus*, or Second to None (which a metaphysical wag might translate, Worse than Nothing). Endless would be the enumeration, even if they could be discovered, of the Freemason and other clubs, which have attained a minor celebrity, and imitations of which branch off through all the gradations of tavern and public-house, and are to be found all over the kingdom,—such as Odd Fellows, Merry Fellows, Eccentrics, Free and Easys, Lords and Commons, &c. &c., illustrious at Cheshire Cheeses, and Holes in the Wall; and often better than best for comfort. We must not forget one, however, of which we have read somewhere, called the Livers, which had bottles shaped like inverted cones, so that the wine would "stand" with nobody, but was forced to be always in circulation. The reader will not be surprised to hear, that these "Livers" were famous for dying before their time.

Johnson said, that a tavern chair was the "throne of human felicity." That to him it was, we have no doubt; and with admirable wit and sense he filled it. Yet the word "throne" betrays a defect in the right club notion. His felicity consisted in laying down the law, and having the best of the argument. There was too much in it of his illustrious namesake the poet. We suspect, however, that although Johnson was greatest among his great friends, he was pleasantest among his least. He had to make the most of them in his turn, and to set them a good example. He has the merit of having invented the word "clubable." Boswell, said he, is a "clubable man." He meant intelligent, social, and good tempered. These are the three great requisites for a clubbist; and it is better to miss the intelligence than the sociality, and the sociality than the good temper. The great end of a club is the refreshment to the spirits, after the cares of business or of home, whether those cares be of a bad or a good sort; and though intellect may be everything with some, and sociality with others, better is the merest puff of a tobacco-pipe with peace, than Johnson himself or Burke without it. We are for the Hum-Drums in preference to the Duellists; for a little noise with good fellowship to the Hum-Drums; for good fellowship and wit without the noise to anything. But if we cannot have all we desire in those respects, give us a few chatty, cordial people, neither geniuses nor fools, with whom the news of the day and questions of personal interest can be exchanged, with the certainty that there will at least be peace and harmony, if little wit. Intellect and wit enough can be got from books; perhaps too much of them may have been met with in the course of the day. But a club is the next thing before a pillow; and if it is to refresh you after the day's employment, it should do it in a manner that at all events dismisses you tranquilly to your repose for the night. We suspect, upon the whole, that the Street and Village Clubs have been most successful; meetings established by the natural course of things, and expecting nothing but a comparison of daily notes and a little cheerful refreshment. As to great Reform and Conservative Clubs, Athenæums, &c., they may be good for public objects, but publicity has nothing to do with the comfort suitable to the club proper; and those institutions in fact, club-wards, are but escapes from domesticity into cheapness and solitude. A man may be a great frequenter of them, and club with nothing but callers on business and a lonely dinner-table. The club to belong to, of all others, would be one composed of good-natured men of genius, such as Steele, Fielding, and Thomson, who had reflection enough for all subjects, enthusiasm enough to give them animation, good breeding enough to hinder the animation from becoming noisy, and humanity enough to make allowance for honest occasional departures from any rule whatever. Shakspeare would include such men in his all-comprehensive person; but we are not sure that he would not over-inform the club with intellect; set it too abundantly thinking; and besides, it is difficult, as modern clubbists, to take to the idea of a man of a distant period, with a different style of language, and retrospective meats and drinks. Otherwise Chaucer would surely be a perfect member; and who would not rejoice in the company of Suckling and Marvell?

We have selected the following clubs from the writings of Steele and Goldsmith, as exemplifying the three main varieties; the well-bred, humorsome, but intellectual club (for though Sir Roger de Coverley and Will Honeycomb make the principal figures in the account of it, it is to be recollected that the Spectator is there); the Trumpet Club in Shire Lane, frequented by the Tatler, which is the ordinary common-place club of smokers and old story-tellers, by way of opiate, bedwards; and the clubs of low life, which Goldsmith, as a cosmopolite, delighted to paint, and which had probably often seen him as a visitor, without suspecting that the simple-looking Irishman was a genius come to immortalize it. Steele's delineations are exquisite; but Goldsmith's are no less so.

THE SPECTATOR'S CLUB.*

BY STEELE.

THE first of our society is a gentleman of Worcestershire, of ancient descent, a baronet, his name Sir Roger de Coverley. His great-grandfather was inventor of that famous country-dance which is called after him. All who know that shire are very well acquainted with the parts and merits of Sir Roger. He is a gentleman that is very singular in his behavior, but his singularities proceed from his good sense, and are contradictions to the manners of the world, only as he thinks the world is in the wrong. However, this humor creates him no enemies, for he does nothing with sourness or obstinacy; and his being unconfined to modes and forms makes him but the readier and more capable to please and oblige all who know him. When he is in town he lives in Soho Square. It is said he keeps himself a bachelor by reason he was crossed in love by a perverse beautiful widow of the next county to him. Before this disappointment Sir Roger was what you call a fine gentleman, had often supped with my Lord Rochester and Sir George Etherege, fought a duel upon his first coming to town, and kicked Bully Dawson in a public coffee-house for calling him youngster.† But be-

---

* No. 2.

† This has been thought inconsistent with Sir Roger's character for simplicity; but it is not so. It only shows that simplicity is compatible with the imitation of anything in vogue during the outset of life. Collins, the poet, whose subsequent appearance Johnson de-

ing ill-used by the above-mentioned widow, he was very serious for a year and a half; and though, his temper being naturally jovial, he at last got over it, he grew careless of himself, and never dressed afterwards. He continues to wear a coat and doublet of the same cut that were in fashion at the time of his repulse, which, in his merry humors, he tells us has been in and out twelve times since he first wore it. 'Tis said Sir Roger grew humble in his desires after he had forgot this cruel beauty, insomuch that it is reported he has frequently offended in point of chastity with beggars and gipsies; but this is looked upon by his friends rather as a matter of raillery than truth. He is now in his fifty-sixth year, cheerful, gay, and hearty; keeps a good house both in town and country; a great lover of mankind; but there is such a mirthful cast in his behavior, that he is rather beloved than esteemed. His tenants grow rich; his servants look satisfied; all the young women profess love to him, and the young men are glad of his company. When he comes into a house he calls the servants by their names, and talks all the way up stairs to a visit. I must not omit, that Sir Roger is Justice of the Quorum; that he fills the chair at a Quarter Session with great ability; and three months ago gained universal applause by explaining a passage in the Game Act.

The gentleman next in esteem and authority among us is another bachelor, who is a member of the Inner Temple; a man of great probity, wit, and understanding; but he has chosen his place of residence rather to obey the direction of

scribes as "decent and manly," astonished his friends by the foppishness of his dress on his first coming to town; and Charles Fox, the simplest of men, was at one time a beau of the first fashion. At least he undertook to appear such. We suspect that the fopperies of Sir Roger, and of the poet, and the statesman, might all have been seen through by discerning eyes.

an old humorsome father, than in pursuit of his own inclinations. He was placed there to study the laws of the land, and is the most learned of any of the house in those of the stage. Aristotle and Longinus are much better understood by him than Littleton or Coke. The father sends up, every post, questions relating to marriage-articles, leases, and tenures, in the neighborhood; all which questions he agrees with an attorney to answer in the lump. He is studying the passions themselves, when he should be inquiring into the debates among men which arise from them. He knows the argument of each of the Orations of Demosthenes and Tully, but not one case in the reports of our own courts. No one ever took him for a fool; but none, except his most intimate friends, know he has a great deal of wit. This turn makes him at once both disinterested and agreeable. As few of his thoughts are drawn from business, they are most of them fit for publication. His taste for books is a little too just for the age lives in. He has read all, but approves of very few. His familiarity with the customs, manners, actions, and writings of the ancients, makes him a very delicate observer of what occurs to him in the present world. He is an excellent critic; and the time of the play is his hour of business. Exactly at five he passes through New Inn, crosses through Russell Court, and takes a turn at Will's* till the play begins. He has his shoes rubbed and his periwig powdered at the barber's, as you go in to the Rose.† It is for the good of the audience when he is at a play, for the actors have an ambition to please him.

* A coffee-house in Russell Street, Covent Garden, frequented by the wits. It occupied the south-west corner of Bow Street; and was the house that Dryden had frequented.

† The tavern mentioned in the pleasant story of the "Medicine" in the first volume of the *Tatler*, No. 2. We know not where it stood; probably in Rose Street, in the above neighborhood.

The person of next consideration is Sir Andrew Freeport, a merchant of great eminence in the city of London; a person of indefatigable industry, strong reason, and great experience. His notions of trade are noble and generous, and (as every rich man has some sly way of jesting, which would make no great figure were he not a rich man) he calls the sea the British Common. He is acquainted with commerce in all its parts, and will tell you that it is a stupid and barbarous way to extend dominion by arms; for true power is to be got by arts and industry. He will often argue, that if this part of our trade were well cultivated, we should gain from one nation; and if another, from another. I have heard him prove that diligence makes more lasting acquisitions than valor; and that sloth has ruined more nations than the sword. He abounds in several frugal maxims, amongst which the greatest favorite is "A penny saved is a penny got." A general trader of good sense is pleasanter company than a general scholar; and Sir Andrew having a natural unaffected eloquence, the perspicuity of his discourse gives the same pleasure that wit would in another man. He has made his fortune himself, and says that England may be richer than other kingdoms, by as plain methods as he himself is richer than other men; though, at the same time, I can say this of him, that there is not a point in the compass but blows home a ship in which he is an owner.

Next to Sir Andrew Freeport in the club-room sits Captain Sentry, a gentleman of great courage, good understanding, but of invincible modesty. He is one of those that deserve very well, but are very awkward at putting their talents within the observation of such as should take notice of them. He was some years a captain, and behaved with great gallantry in several engagements, and at several sieges; but, having a small estate of his own, and being next heir to Sir Roger, he has quitted a way of life in which no man can rise suitably to his merit who is not something of a courtier as well as a soldier. I have heard him often lament, that in a profession where merit is placed in so conspicuous a view, impudence should get the better of modesty. When he has talked to this purpose, I never heard him make a sour expression, but frankly confess that he left the world, because he was not fit for it. A strict honesty, and an even regular behavior, are in themselves obstacles to him that must press through crowds, who endeavor at the same end with himself—the favor of a commander. He will, however, in his way of talk, excuse generals for not disposing according to men's desert, or inquiring into it; for, says he, that great man who has a mind to help me, has as many to break through to come at me, as I have to come at him. Therefore he will conclude that the man who would make a figure, especially in a military way, must get over all false modesty, and assist his patron against the importunity of other pretenders, by a proper assurance in his own vindication. He says it is a civil cowardice to be backward in affecting what you ought to expect, as it is a military fear to be slow in attacking when it is your duty. With this candor does the gentlemen speak of himself and others. The same frankness runs through all his conversation. The military part of his life has furnished him with many adventures, in the relation of which he is very agreeable to the company; for he is never overbearing, though accustomed to command men in the utmost degree below him; nor ever too obsequious, from an habit of obeying men highly above him.

But that our society may not appear a set of humorists, unacquainted with the gallantries and pleasures of the age, we have among us the gallant Will Honeycomb, a gentleman who, according to his years, should be in the decline of his life, but having ever been very careful of his person, and always had a very easy fortune, Time has made but a very little impression upon him, either by wrinkles on his forehead or traces on his brain. His person is well turned, and of a good height He is very ready at that sort of discourse with which men usually entertain women. He has all his life dressed very well, and remembers habits as others do men. He can smile when one speaks to him. and laughs easily. He knows the history of every mode, and can inform you from which of the French king's wenches our wives and daughters had this manner of curling their hair, or that way of placing their hoods; whose frailty was covered with such a sort of petticoat, and whose vanity to show her foot made that part of the dress so short in such a year. In a word, all his conversation and knowledge have been in the female world. As other men of his age will take notice to you what such a minister said upon such and such an occasion, he will tell you, when the Duke of Monmouth danced at court, such a woman was then smitten; another was taken with him at the head of his troop in the park. In all these important relations, he has ever about the same time received a kind glance or blow of the fan from some celebrated beauty, mother of the present Lord Such-a-one. . . .

I cannot tell whether I am to account him whom I am next to speak of as one of our company, for he visits us but seldom; but when he does, he adds to every man else a new enjoyment of himself. He is a clergyman, a very philosophic man, of general learning, great sanctity of life, and the most exact good breeding. He has the misfortune to be of a very weak constitution, and consequently cannot accept of such cares and such business as preferments in his function would oblige him to. He is therefore among divines what a chamber counsellor is among lawyers. The probity of his mind, and the integrity of his life, create him followers; as being eloquent or loud advances others. He seldom introduces the subject he speaks upon; but we are so far gone in years, that he observes, when he is among us, an earnestness to have him fall on some divine topic, which he always treats with much authority, as one who has no interest in this world; as one who is hastening to the object of all his wishes, and conceives hope from his decays and infirmities. These are my ordinary companions.

THE CLUB OF THE TATLER.*

BY THE SAME.

"Habeo senectuti magnam gratiam, quæ mihi sermonis aviditatem auxit, potionis et cibi sustulit." TULL. DE SEN.

"I am much beholden to old age, which has increased my eagerness for conversation, in proportion as it has lessened my appetite of hunger and thirst."

AFTER having applied my mind with more than ordinary attention to my studies, it is my usual custom to relax and unbend it in the conversation of such as are rather easy than shining companions. This I find particularly necessary for me before I retire to rest, in order to draw my slumbers upon me by degrees, and fall asleep insensibly. This is the particular use I make of a set of heavy honest men, with whom I have passed many hours with much indolence, though not with great pleasure. Their conversation is a kind of preparative for sleep. It takes the mind down from its abstractions, leads it into the familiar traces of thought, and lulls it into that state of tranquillity which is the condition of a thinking man when he is but half awake. After this my reader will not be surprised to hear the account which I am about to give of a club of my own contemporaries, among

* No. 132.

whom I pass two or three hours every evening. This I look upon as taking my first nap before I go to bed. The truth of it is, I should think myself unjust to posterity, as well as to the society at the Trumpet,* of which I am a member, did not I in some part of my writings give an account of the persons among whom I have passed almost a sixth part of my time for these last forty years. Our club consisted originally of fifteen; but, partly by the severity of the law in arbitrary times, and partly by the natural effects of old age, we are at present reduced to a third part of that number; in which, however, we have this consolation, that the best company is said to consist of five persons. I must confess, besides the afore-mentioned benefit which I meet with in the conversation of this select society, I am not the less pleased with the company in which I find myself the greatest wit among them, and am heard as their oracle in all points of learning and difficulty.

Sir Jeoffry Notch, who is the oldest of the club, has been in possession of the right-hand chair time out of mind, and is the only man among us that has the liberty of stirring the fire. This, our foreman, is a gentleman of an ancient family that came to a great estate some years before he had discretion, and run it out in hounds, horses, and cock-fighting; for which reason he looks upon himself as an honest worthy gentleman, who has had misfortunes in the world, and calls every thriving man an upstart.

---

* The Trumpet was a public-house in the lane in which Steele, as the Tatler or Mr. Bickerstaff, pretended to live. This lane was no greater locality than Shire Lane, lately so called, close to Temple Bar, now Great Shire Lane; and the Trumpet is still extant as a public-house, called the Duke of York. Here, in the drawing-room (for the dignity's sake), we may fancy Major Matchlock and old Dick Reptile doling forth their respective insipidities.

Major Matchlock is the next senior, who served in the last civil wars, and has all the battles by heart. He does not think any action in Europe worth talking of since the fight of Marston Moor;* and every night tells us of his having been knocked off his horse at the rising of the London apprentices;† for which he is in great esteem amongst us.

Honest old Dick Reptile is the third of our society. He is a good-natured indolent man, who speaks little himself, but laughs at our jokes; and brings his young nephew along with him. a youth of eighteen years old, to show him good company, and give him a taste of the world. This young fellow sits generally silent, but whenever he opens his mouth, or laughs at anything that passes, he is constantly told by his uncle, after a jocular manner, " Ay, ay, Jack, you young men think us fools; but we old men know you are."

The greatest wit of our company, next to myself, is a Bencher of the neighboring Inn, who in his youth frequented the ordinaries about Charing Cross, and pretends to have been intimate with Jack Ogle.‡ He has about ten distichs of Hudibras without book, and never leaves the club until he has applied them all. If any modern wit be mentioned, or any town frolic spoken of, he shakes his head at the dulness of the present age, and tells us a story of Jack Ogle.

For my part, I am esteemed among them because they

---

* In 1644, where Cromwell's cavalry turned the day against Charles I.

† Probably in 1647, when they forced their way into the House of Commons with a petition signed by ten thousand citizens. But as the date of the club is 1709, the Major must have been a very old gentleman indeed, if his memory served him rightly.

‡ Jack Ogle was a wild fellow about town, whose sister is said to have been one of the mistresses of the Duke of York (James II.)

see I am something respected by others; though at the same time I understand by their behavior that I am considered by them as a man of a great deal of learning, but no knowledge of the world; insomuch that the Major sometimes, in the height of his military pride, calls me the philosopher; and Sir Jeoffry, no longer ago than last night, upon a dispute what day of the month it was then in Holland, pulled his pipe out of his mouth, and cried, "What does the scholar say to it?"

Our club meets precisely at six o'clock in the evening; but I did not come last night until half an hour after seven, by which means I escaped the battle of Naseby, which the Major usually begins at about three quarters after six. I found also that my good friend the Bencher had already spent three of his distichs, and only waited an opportunity to hear a sermon spoken of, that he might introduce the couplet* where "a stick" rhymes to "ecclesiastic." At my entrance into the room, they were naming a red petticoat and a cloak, by which I found that the Bencher had been diverting them with a story of Jack Ogle.†

I had no sooner taken my seat, but Sir Jeoffry, to show his good-will towards me, gave me a pipe of his own tobacco, and stirred up the fire. I look upon it as a point of morality

* In Hudibras.

† The story is thus given in the notes to the variorum edition of the Tatler, published in 1797. Ogle once rode "as a private gentleman, in the first troop of foot-guards, at that time under the command of the Duke of Monmouth. He had pawned his trooper's cloak, and to save appearances at a review, had borrowed his landlady's red petticoat, which he carried rolled up *en croupe* behind him. The Duke of Monmouth smoked it and willing to enjoy the confusion of a detection, gave order to *cloak all*, with which Ogle, after some hesitation, was obliged to comply. Although he could not *cloak*, he said he would *petticoat* with the best of them."--Vol. iii. p. 124.

to be obliged by those who endeavor to oblige me; and therefore, in requital for his kindness, and to set the conversation a-going, I took the best occasion I could to put him upon telling us the story of old Gantlett, which he always does with very particular concern. He traced up his descent on both sides for several generations, describing his diet and manner of life, with his several battles, and particularly the one in which he fell. This Gantlett was a game-cock, upon whose head the knight, in his youth, had won five hundred pounds and lost two thousand. This naturally set the Major upon the account of Edge-hill fight, and ended in a duel of Jack Ogle's.

Old Reptile was extremely attentive to all that was said, though it was the same he had heard every night for these twenty years, and upon all occasions winked upon his nephew to mind what passed.

This may suffice to give the world a taste of our innocent conversation, which we spun out till about ten of the clock, when my maid came with a lantern to light me home. I could not but reflect with myself, as I was going out, upon the talkative humor of old men, and the little figure which that part of life makes in one who cannot employ his natural propensity in discourses which would make him venerable. I must own it makes me very melancholy in company when I hear a young man begin a story; and have often observed, that one of a quarter of an hour long in a man of five-and-twenty, gathers circumstances every time he tells it, until it grows into a long Canterbury tale of two hours by the time he is threescore.

The only way of avoiding such a trifling and frivolous old age, is to lay up in our way to it such stores of knowledge and observation as make us useful and agreeable in our declining years. The mind of man in a long life will become a magazine of wisdom or folly, and will consequently discharge itself in something impertinent or improving. For which reason, as there is nothing more ridiculous than an old trifling story-teller, so there is nothing more venerable than one who has turned his experience to the entertainment and advantage of mankind.

In short, we, who are in the last stage of life, and are apt to indulge ourselves in talk, ought to consider if what we speak be worth being heard, and endeavor to make our discourse like that of Nestor, which Homer compares to the flowing of honey for its sweetness.

I am afraid I shall be thought guilty of this excess I am speaking of, when I cannot conclude without observing, that Milton certainly thought of this passage in Homer, when, in his description of an eloquent spirit, he says—

"His tongue dropped manna."*

---

* We cannot miss the opportunity of adding to this account of the members of the Trumpet Club, that of another associate, whose character is drawn by Steele in a previous number, and is one of the finest that ever proceeded from his pen. It shows his contempt of that absurdest of all the passions of mortality—Pride. The reader will take notice of the exquisite expression " insolent benevolence ;" and the " very insignificant fellow, but exceeding gracious."

" The most remarkable (he says) of the persons whose disturbance arises from Pride, and whom I shall use all possible diligence to cure, are such as are hidden in the appearance of quite contrary habits and dispositions. Among such, I shall in the first place take care of one who is under the most subtle species of pride that I have observed in my whole experience.

" This patient is a person for whom I have great respect, as being an old courtier and a friend of mine in my youth. The man has but a bare subsistence, just enough to pay his reckoning with us at the Trumpet; but, by having spent the beginning of his life in the hearing of great men and persons in power, he is always promising to do good

GOLDSMITH'S CLUBS.

FROM THE ESSAYS.

THE first club I entered upon coming to town was that of the Choice Spirits. The name was entirely suited to my taste; I was a lover of mirth, good-humor, and even sometimes of fun, from my childhood.

As no other passport was requisite but the payment of two shillings at the door, I introduced myself without farther ceremony to the members, who were already assembled, and had for some time begun upon business. The grand, with a mallet in his hand, presided at the head of the table. I could not avoid, upon my entrance, making use of all my skill in physiognomy, in order to discover that superiority of genius in men who had taken a title so superior to the rest of mankind. I expected to see the lines of every face marked with strong thinking; but, though I had some skill in this science, I could for my life discover nothing but a pert simper, fat or profound stupidity.

My speculations were soon interrupted by the grand, who

offices, to introduce every man he converses with into the world; will desire one of ten times his substance to let him see him sometimes, and hints to him that he does not forget him. He answers to matters of no consequence with great circumspection; but, however, maintains a general civility in his words and actions, and an insolent benevolence to all whom he has to do with. This he practises with a grave tone and air; and though I am his senior by twelve years, and richer by forty pounds per annum, he had yesterday the impudence to commend me to my face, and tell me 'he should always be ready to encourage me.' In a word, he is a very insignificant fellow, but exceeding gracious. The best return I can make him for his favors is to carry him myself to Bedlam, and see him well taken care of."—*Tatler*, No. 127.

had knocked down Mr. Spriggins for a song. I was upon this whispered by one of the company who sat next me, that I should now see something touched off to a nicety, for Mr. Spriggins was going to give us Mad Tom in all its glory. Mr. Spriggins endeavored to excuse himself; for, as he was to act a madman and a king, it was impossible to go through the part properly without a crown and chains. His excuses were over-ruled by a great majority, and with much vociferation. The president ordered up the jack-chain; and, instead of a crown, our performer covered his brows with an inverted jordan. After he had rattled his chain and shook his head, to the great delight of the whole company, he began his song. As I have heard few young fellows offer to sing in company that did not expose themselves, it was no great disappointment to me to find Mr. Spriggins among the number: however, not to seem an odd fish, I rose from my seat in rapture, cried out, "Bravo! encore!" and slapped the table as loud as any of the rest.

The gentleman who sat next me seemed highly pleased with my taste, and the ardor of my approbation; and, whispering, told me I had suffered an immense loss, for, had I come a few minutes sooner, I might have heard "Geeho Dobbin" sung in a tip-top manner, by the pimple-nosed spirit at the president's right elbow; but he was evaporated before I came.

As I was expressing my uneasiness at this disappointment, I found the attention of the company employed upon a fat figure, who, with a voice more rough than the Staffordshire giant's, was giving us the "Softly sweet, in Lydian measure," of Alexander's Feast. After a short pause of admiration, to this succeeded a Welsh dialogue, with the humors of Teague and Taffy: after that came on Old Jackson, with a story between every stanza; next was sung the Dust-

Cart, and then Solomon's Song. The glass began now to circulate pretty freely; those who were silent when sober would now be heard in their turn ; every man had his song, and he saw no reason why he should not be heard as well as any of the rest; one begged to be heard while he gave Death and the Lady in high taste ; another sung to a plate which he kept trundling on the edges; nothing was now heard but singing; voice rose above voice, and the whole became one universal shout, when the landlord came to acquaint the company that the reckoning was drunk out. Rabelais calls the moments in which a reckoning is mentioned, the most melancholy of our lives; never was so much noise so quickly quelled, as by this short but pathetic oration of our landlord. "Drunk out!" was echoed in a tone of discontent round the table ; "drunk out already! that was very odd! that so much punch could be drunk out already! impossible!" The landlord, however, seeming resolved not to retreat from his first assurances, the company was dissolved, and a president chosen for the night ensuing.

A friend of mine, to whom I was complaining some time after of the entertainment I have been describing, proposed to bring me to the club that he frequented, which he fancied would suit the gravity of my temper exactly. "We have, at the Muzzy Club," says he, "no riotous mirth, nor awkward ribaldry, no confusion or bawling, all is conducted with wisdom and decency ; besides, some of our members are worth forty thousand pounds, men of prudence and foresight every one of them ; these are the proper acquaintance, and to such I will to-night introduce you." I was charmed at the proposal. To be acquainted with men worth forty thousand pounds, and to talk wisdom the whole night, were offers that threw me into rapture.

At seven o'clock I was accordingly introduced by my

friend; not indeed to the company, for, though I made my best bow, they seemed insensible of my approach; but to the table at which they were sitting. Upon my entering the room, I could not avoid feeling a secret veneration, from the solemnity of the scene before me; the members kept a profound silence, each with a pipe in his mouth and a pewter pot in his hand, and with faces that might easily be construed into absolute wisdom. Happy society! thought I to myself, where the members think before they speak, deliver nothing rashly, but convey their thoughts to each other, pregnant with meaning, and matured by reflection.

In this pleasing speculation I continued a full half-hour, expecting each moment that somebody would begin to open his mouth. Every time the pipe was laid down, I expected it was to speak; but it was only to spit. At length, resolving to break the charm myself, and overcome their extreme diffidence, for to this I imputed their silence, I rubbed my hands, and, looking as wise as possible, observed that the nights began to grow a little coolish at this time of the year. This, as it was directed to no one of the company in particular, none thought himself obliged to answer; wherefore I continued still to rub my hands and look wise. My next effort was addressed to a gentleman who sat next me; to whom I observed that the beer was extremely good; my neighbor made no reply, but by a large puff of tobacco-smoke.

I now began to be uneasy in this dumb society, till one of them a little relieved me by observing, that bread had not risen these three weeks. "Ah!" says another, still keeping the pipe in his mouth, "that puts me in mind of a pleasant story about that—hem—very well; you must know—but, before I begin—sir, my service to you—where was I?"

My next club goes by the name of the Harmonical So

ciety; probably from that love of order and friendship which every person commends in institutions of this nature. The landlord was himself founder. The money spent is fourpence each, and they sometimes whip for a double reckoning. To this club few recommendations are requisite except the introductory fourpence and my landlord's good word, which as he gains by it, he never refuses.

We all here talked and behaved as everybody else usually does on his club-night. We discussed the topic of the day, drank each other's healths, snuffed the candles with our fingers, and filled our pipes from the same plate of tobacco. The company saluted each other in the common manner. Mr. Bellows-mender hoped Mr. Curry-comb-maker had not caught cold going home the last club-night; and he returned the compliment by hoping. that young Master Bellows-mender had got well again of the chincough. Dr. Twist told us a story of a parliament-man, with whom he was intimately acquainted; while the bagman, at the same time, was telling a better story of a noble lord, with whom he could do anything. A gentleman in a black wig and leather breeches, at the other end of the table was engaged in a long narrative of the ghost in Cock Lane;* he had read it in the papers of the day, and was telling it to some that sat next him who could not read. Near him, Mr. Dibbins was disputing on the old subject of religion with a Jew pedler over the table; while the president vainly knocked down Mr. Leathersides for a song. Besides the combination of these voices, which I could hear altogether, and which formed an upper part to the concert, there were several others playing under-parts by

* An impudent imposture of that day, in which it was pretended that a ghost scratched at a bed. Johnson was weak enough to be one of its grave investigators, and Churchill's *Ghost* was written in derision of it.

themselves, and endeavoring to fasten on some luckless neighbor's ear, who was himself bent upon the same design against some other.

We have often heard of the speech of a corporation, and this induced me to transcribe a speech of this club, taken in short-hand, word for word, as it was spoken by every member of the company. It may be necessary to observe, that the man who told us of the ghost had the loudest voice, and the longest story to tell; so that his continuing narrative filled every chasm in the conversation.

"So, sir, d'ye perceive me, the ghost giving three loud raps at the bed-post"—"Says my lord to me, my dear Smokeum, you know there is no man on the face of the yearth for whom I have so high"—"A false heretical opinion of all sound doctrine and good learning; for I'll tell it aloud and spare not, that"—"Silence for a song; Mr. Leathersides for a song"—"As I was walking upon the highway, I met a young damsel"—"'Then what brings you here?' said the parson to the ghost"—"Sanconiathon, Manetho, and Berosus" "The whole way from Islington turnpike to Dog-house bar" —"As for Abel Drugger, sir, he's low in it; my 'prentice boy has more of the gentleman than he"*—"For murder will out one time or another; and none but a ghost, you know, gentlemen, can"—"For my friend, whom you know, gentlemen, and who is a parliament-man, a man of consequence, a dear honest creature, to be sure; we were laughing last night at"—"Upon all his posterity, by simply, barely tasting"— "Sour grapes, as the fox said once when he could not reach them; and I'll, I'll tell you a story about that, that will make you burst your sides with laughing. A fox once"— "Will nobody listen to the song?"—"As I was walking upon

---

* A compliment to Goldsmith's friend, Garrick, in the part of *Abel Drugger*, which was a very low one.

the highway, I met a young damsel both buxom and gay"—" No ghost, gentlemen, can be murdered; nor did I ever hear of but one ghost killed in all my life, and that was ———" " Soul if I don't"—" Mr. Bellows-mender, I have the honor of drinking your very good health"—" Fire"— " Whizz"—" Blid"—" Tit"—" Rat"—" Trip"—the rest all riot, nonsense, and rapid confusion.

Were I to be angry at men for being fools (concludes Goldsmith, with touching pleasantry), I could here find ample room for declamation; but, alas! I have been a fool myself, and why should I be angry with them for being something so natural to every child of humanity?

Count Fathom's Adventure in the Lone Cottage.

BY SMOLLETT.

The *Adventures of Ferdinand Count Fathom* is one of those rare works of genius, in a very unusual sense of the epithet, which a reader of a well-constituted mind is at a loss whether to admire or to dislike. It is a history of such elaborate and unmitigated rascality, that one is surprised how the author's imagination could have consented to keep such a scoundrel company for so long a period. But there is one scene in it, which by universal consent is a masterpiece of interest; a mixture of the terrible and the probable that has often since been emulated, but never surpassed. It is to real life what the fragment of *Sir Bertrand* is to the ideal; and the writing is as fine as the conception. Smollett takes a delight in showing that the powers of his pen are equal to the most formidable occasions. He rejoices in "piling up an agony," especially on a victim not so courageous as himself; and by a principle of extremes meeting, a mischievous sarcasm, and strokes of humor itself, contribute to aggravate and envenom the impression of terror.

FATHOM departed from the village that same afternoon under the auspices of his conductor, and found himself benighted in the midst of a forest, far from the habitations of men. The darkness of the night, the silence and solitude of the place, the indistinct images of the trees that appeared on every side stretching their extravagant arms athwart the gloom, conspired with the dejection of spirits occasioned by his loss to disturb his fancy, and raise strange phantoms in his imagination. Although he was not naturally superstitious, his mind began to be invaded with an awful horror, that gradually prevailed over all the consolations of reason and philosophy; nor was his heart free from the terrors of assassination. In order to dissipate these disagreeable reveries, he had recourse to the conversation of his guide, by whom he was entertained with the history of divers travellers who had been robbed and murdered by ruffians, whose retreat was in the recesses of that very wood.

In the midst of this communication, which did not at all tend to the elevation of our hero's spirits, the conductor made an excuse for dropping behind, while our traveller jogged on in expectation of being joined again by him in a few minutes; he was, however, disappointed in that hope; the sound of the horse's feet by degrees grew more and more faint, and at last altogether died away. Alarmed at this circumstance, Fathom halted in the road, and listened with the most fearful attention; but his sense of hearing was saluted with naught but the dismal sighings of the trees, that seemed to foretell an approaching storm. Accordingly, the heavens contracted a more dreary aspect, the lightning began to gleam, the thunder to roll, and the tempest, raising its voice to a tremendous roar, descended in a torrent of rain.

In this emergency, the fortitude of our hero was almost quite overcome. So many concurring circumstances of danger and distress might have appalled the most undaunted breast; what impression then must they have made upon the mind of Ferdinand, who was by no means a man to set fear at defiance? Indeed he had well nigh lost the use of his reflection, and was actually invaded to the skin, before he could recollect himself so far as to quit the road, and seek for shelter among the thickets that surrounded him. Having rode some furlongs into the forest, he took his station under a tuft of tall trees, that screened him from the storm, and in that situation called a council with himself, to deliberate upon his next excursion. He persuaded himself that his guide had deserted him for the present, in order to give intelligence of a traveller to some gang of robbers with whom he was connected; and that he must of necessity fall a prey to those banditti, unless he should have the good fortune to elude their search, and disentangle himself from the mazes of the wood.

Harrowed with these apprehensions, he resolved to commit himself to the mercy of the hurricane, as of two evils the least, and penetrate straight forwards through some devious opening, until he should be delivered from the forest. For this purpose he turned his horse's head in a line quite contrary to the direction of the high road which he had left, on supposition that the robbers would pursue that tract in quest of him, and that they would never dream of his deserting the highway to traverse an unknown forest amidst the darkness of such a boisterous night. After he had continued in this progress through a succession of groves, and bogs, and thorns, and brakes, by which not only his clothes, but also his skin suffered in a grievous manner, while every nerve quivered with eagerness and dismay, he at length reached an open plain, and pursuing his course, in full hope of arriving at some village where his life would be safe, he descried a rushlight, at a distance, which he looked upon as the star of his good fortune; and riding towards it at full speed, arrived at the door of a lone cottage, into which he was admitted by an old woman, who, understanding he was a bewildered traveller, received him with great hospitality.

When he learned from his hostess that there was not another house within three leagues, and that she could accommodate him with a tolerable bed, and his horse with lodging and oats, he thanked Heaven for his good fortune in stumbling upon this humble habitation, and determined to pass the night under the protection of the old cottager, who gave him to understand, that her husband, who was a fagot-maker, had gone to the next town to dispose of his merchandise, and that in all probability he would not return till the next morning, on account of the tempestuous night. Ferdinand sounded the beldame with a thousand artful interrogations, and she answered with such an appearance of truth and simplicity, that he concluded his person was quite secure; and, after having been regaled with a dish of eggs and bacon, desired she would conduct him into the chamber where she proposed he should take his repose. He was accordingly ushered up by a sort of ladder into an apartment furnished with a standing bed, and almost half filled with trusses of straw. He seemed extremely well pleased with his lodging, which in reality exceeded his expectations; and his kind landlady, cautioning him against letting the candle approach the combustibles, took her leave, and locked the door on the outside.

Fathom, whose own principles taught him to be suspicious, and ever upon his guard against the treachery of his fellow-creatures, could have dispensed with this instance of her care in confining her guest to her chamber; and began to be seized with strange fancies, when he observed that there was no bolt on the inside of the door, by which he might secure himself from intrusion. In consequence of these suggestions, he proposed to take an accurate survey of every object in the apartment, and, in the course of his inquiry, had the mortification to find the dead body of a man, still warm, who had been lately stabbed, and concealed beneath several bundles of straw.

Such a discovery could not fail to fill the breast of our hero with unspeakable horror; for he concluded that he himself would undergo the same fate before morning, without the interposition of a miracle in his favor. In the first transports of his dread he ran to the window, with a view to escape by that outlet, and found his flight effectually obstructed by divers strong bars of iron. Then his heart began to palpitate, his hair to bristle up, and his knees to totter: his thoughts teemed with presages of death and destruction; his conscience rose up in judgment against him; and he underwent a severe paroxysm of dismay and distraction. His spirits were agitated into a state of fermentation that produced an energy akin to that which is inspired by brandy or other strong liquors; and, by an impulse that seemed supernatural, he was immediately hurried into measures for his own preservation.

What upon a less interesting occasion his imagination durst not propose, he now executed without scruple or remorse. He undressed the corpse that lay bleeding among the straw, and conveying it to the bed in his arms, deposited it in the attitude of a person who sleeps at his ease; then he extinguished the light, took possession of the place from whence the body had been removed, and, holding a pistol ready cocked in each hand, waited for the sequel with that determined purpose which is often the immediate production of despair. About midnight he heard the sound of feet ascending the ladder; the door was softly opened; he saw the shadow of two men stalking towards the bed; a dark lantern being unshrouded, directed their aim to the supposed sleeper; and he that held it thrust a poniard to his heart. The force of the blow made a compression on the chest, and a sort of groan issued from the windpipe of the defunct; the stroke was repeated without producing a repetition of the note, so that the assassins concluded the work was effectually done, and retired for the present, with a design to return and rifle the deceased at their leisure.

Never had our hero spent a moment in such agony as he felt during this operation. The whole surface of his body was covered with a cold sweat, and his nerves were relaxed with an universal palsy. In short, he remained in a trance, that in all probability contributed to his safety; for had he retained the use of his senses, he might have been discovered by the transports of his fear. The first use he made of his retrieved recollection, was to perceive that the assassins had left the door open in their retreat; and he would have instantly availed himself of this their neglect, by sallying out upon them at the hazard of his life, had not he been restrained by a conversation he overheard in the room below, importing that the ruffians were going to set out upon another expedition, in hopes of finding more prey. They accordingly departed, after having laid strong injunctions on the old woman to keep the door fast locked during their absence; and Ferdinand took his resolution without further delay. So soon as, by his conjecture, the robbers were at a sufficient distance from the house, he rose from his lurking-place, moved softly towards the bed, and rummaging the pockets of the deceased, found a purse well stored with ducats, of which, together with a silver watch and a diamond ring, he immediately possessed himself without scruple; and then, descending with great care and circumspection into the lower apartment, stood before the old beldame, before she had the least intimation of his approach.

Accustomed as she was to the trade of blood, the hoary hag did not behold this apparition without giving signs of infinite terror and astonishment. Believing it was no other than the spirit of her second guest, who had been murdered, she fell upon her knees, and began to recommend herself to the protection of the saints, crossing herself with as much devotion as if she had been entitled to the particular care and attention of Heaven. Nor did her anxiety abate when she was undeceived in this her supposition, and understood it was no phantom, but the real substance of the stranger; who, without staying to upbraid her with the enormity of her crimes, commanded her, on pain of immediate death, to produce his horse; to which being conducted, he set her on the saddle without delay, and mounting behind, invested her with the management of the reins, swearing, in a most peremptory tone, that the only chance for her life was in directing him to the next town; and that as soon as she should give him the least cause to doubt her fidelity in the performance of that task, he would on the instant act the part of her executioner.

This declaration had its effect on the withered Hecate, who, with many supplications for mercy and forgiveness, promised to guide him in safety to a certain village at the distance of two leagues, where he might lodge in security, and be provided with a fresh horse, or other conveniences for pursuing his route. On these conditions he told her she might deserve his clemency; and they accordingly took their departure together, she being placed astride upon the saddle, holding the bridle in one hand, and a switch in the other, and our adventurer sitting on the crupper, superintending her conduct, and keeping the muzzle of a pistol close at her ear. In this equipage they travelled across part of the same wood in which his guide had forsaken him: and it is not to be supposed that he passed his time in the most agreeable reverie, while he found himself involved in the labyrinth of those shades, which he considered as the haunts of robbery and assassination.

Common fear was a comfortable sensation to what he felt in this excursion. The first steps he had taken for his preservation were the effect of mere instinct, while his faculties were extinguished or suppressed by despair; but now, as his reflection began to recur, he was haunted by the most intolerable apprehensions. Every whisper of the wind through the thickets was swelled into the hoarse menaces of murder; the shaking of the boughs was construed into the brandishing of poniards; and every shadow of a tree became the apparition of a ruffian eager for blood. In short, at each of these occurrences he felt what was infinitely more tormenting than the stab of a real dagger; and at every fresh fillip of his fear, he acted as a remembrancer to his conductress in a new volley of imprecations, importing, that her life was absolutely connected with his opinion of his own safety.

Human nature could not long subsist under such complicated terror; but at last he found himself clear of the forest, and was blessed with a distant view of an inhabited place. He then began to exercise his thoughts on a new subject. He debated with himself whether he should make a parade of his intrepidity and public spirit, by disclosing his achievement, and surrendering his guide to the penalty of the law, or leave the old hag and her accomplice to the remorse of their own consciences, and proceed quietly on his journey to Paris, in undisturbed possession of the prize he had already obtained. This last step he determined to take upon recollecting, that, in the course of his information, the story of the murdered stranger would infallibly attract the attention of justice, and, in that case, the effects he had borrowed from the defunct must be refunded for the benefit of those who had a right to the succession. This was an argument which our adventurer could not resist: he foresaw that he should be stripped of his acquisition, which he looked upon as the fair fruits of his valor and sagacity; and moreover, be detained as an evidence against the robbers, to the manifest detriment of his affairs. Perhaps, too, he had motives of conscience that dissuaded him from bearing witness against a set of people whose principles did not much differ from his own.

Influenced by such considerations, he yielded to the first importunity of the beldame, whom he dismissed at a very small distance from the village, after he had earnestly exhorted her to quit such an atrocious course of life, and atone for her past crimes by sacrificing her associates to the demands of justice. She did not fail to vow a perfect reformation, and to prostrate herself before him for the favor she had found; then she betook herself to her habitation, with the full purpose of advising her fellow-murderers to repair with all despatch to the village and impeach our hero; who, wisely distrusting her professions, stayed no longer in the place than to hire a guide for the next stage, which brought him to the city of Chalons-Sur-Marne

The Hermit.

BY PARNELL.

We know not how it is with others, but we never think of *Parnell's Hermit* without tranquillizing and grateful feelings. Parnell was a true poet of a minor order; he saw nature for himself, though he wrote a book style; and this, and one or two other poems of his, such as the eclogue on *Health*, and the *Fairy Tale*, have inclined us to believe that there is something in the very name of "Parnell" peculiarly gentle and agreeable. Hermits themselves, in poetry, are almost always interesting and soothing people. We see nothing but their brooks, their solitude, and their resignation, their hermitage and their crust; and long to be like them, and play at loneliness.

> "And may at last my weary age
> Find out the peaceful hermitage,
> The hairy gown, and mossy cell,
> Where I may sit and rightly spell
> Of every star that heaven doth show,
> And every herb that sips the dew,
> Till old experience do attain
> To something like prophetic strain."

So, who does not love Goldsmith's *Edwin and Angelina*, and the gentle line with which it sets out?—

> "Turn, gentle hermit of the dale."

Drayton tears himself away with reluctance from a long list of herbs which he describes a hermit gathering, in his *Polyolbion*. The following are some of the verses. " The Hermit," he says,

> ———————" leads a sweet retired life.
> Suppose, 'twixt noon and night, (the sun his half-way wrought,)
> The shadows to be large, by his descending brought,
> Who with a fervent eye looks through the twyring* glades,
> And his dispersèd rays commixeth with the shades,
> Exhaling the milch† dew, which there had tarried long,
> And on the ranker grass till past the noon-stead hung;"

" 'Tis then," he says,

> ———"the hermit comes out of his homely cell,
> Where from all rude resort, he happily doth dwell;
> And in a little maund‡ (being made of osiers small),
> Which serveth him to do full many a thing withal,
> He very choicely sorts his simples, got abroad.
> Here finds he on an oak rheum-purging polypode;§
> And in some open place that to the sun doth lie,
> He fumitory gets, and eyebright for the eye;
> And from the falling-ill by five-leaf| doth restore,
> And melancholy cures by sovereign hellebore."

But Parnell's hermit is not only a proper hermit, with a " cave" for his " cell,"

> " His food the fruits, his drink the crystal well;"

he is a questioning philosopher. Resigned as he is to Providence, he is not without doubts as to its attributes, occasioned by the sufferings of virtue and the seeming triumphs of vice; and an angel is sent to restore peace to his mind. The way in which this is done, though it does not go into the permission of evil in the abstract (one of the secrets of good, which Heaven seems to keep in reserve for us, in order to enhance the joys of retrospection), furnishes, nevertheless, a far better and more Christian answer, than the assumptions of many a graver authority. It is not Parnell's own. The story is as old, at least, as the Koran, probably a great deal older; and has most likely

---

* Turning and winding.
† Soft. Perhaps in pastoral analogy with *milk*.
‡ Basket.
§ *Polypodium* (Many-foot). a *genus* of fern.
| Cinque-foil—*Potentilla* (from its medical powers)—a flower of the order *Rosaceæ*.

been told in the languages of all civilized countries. But Parnell's is the most pleasing version of it we know. The undertone of thought and wonder, on the hermit's part, is well preserved; the touches of scenery evince the author's taste for nature; and even the sweet monotony of the versification (so like Pope's, that he has been invidiously said to have had a hand in it), is not unsuitable to the cremetical ground-work of the subject and the lesson of resignation.

Parnell was a gentle clergyman, who, with all his inculcations of patience and retirement, found it difficult to reconcile himself to a desolate spot in Ireland, and impossible (it is said) to bear the loss of his wife. We often preach what we cannot practise, not out of hypocrisy, but from opposing frailties and unavailing desire. Parnell admired his hermit the more, because he could not settle down to his solitude and his bin of water. There is a touching passage about him in one of the letters of Swift. Bolingbroke's second wife was like the one that Parnell had lost. The poor poet saw her, for the first time, on a visit at Bolingbroke's house; and when she came into the room, Swift says, he could not take his eyes off her, and seemed very melancholy.

THE HERMIT.

FAR in a wild, unknown to public view,
From youth to age a reverend hermit grew;
The moss his bed, the cave his humble cell,
His food the fruits, his drink the crystal well;
Remote from men, with God he pass'd his days,
Prayer all his business, all his pleasure praise.

A life so sacred, such serene repose,
Seemed heaven itself, till one suggestion rose;
That vice should triumph, virtue vice obey,
This sprung some doubt of Providence's sway,
His hopes no more a certain prospect boast,
And all the tenor of his soul is lost.
So when a smooth expanse receives, imprest
Calm Nature's image on its watery breast,

Down bend the banks, the trees depending grow,
And skies beneath with answering colors glow:
But if a stone the gentle sea divide,
Swift ruffling circles curl on every side;
And glimmering fragments of a broken sun,
Banks, trees, and skies, in thick disorder run.
To clear this doubt, to know the world by sight,
To find if books, or swains, report it right,
(For yet by swains alone the world he knew,
Whose feet came wandering o'er the nightly dew,)
He quits his cell; the pilgrim staff he bore,
And fix'd the scallop in his hat before;
Then with the sun a rising journey went,
Sedate to think, and watching each event.

 The morn was wasted in the pathless grass,
And long and lonesome was the wild to pass;
But when the southern sun had warmed the day,
A youth came posting o'er a crossing way;
His raiment decent, his complexion fair,
And soft in graceful ringlets wav'd his hair.
Then, near approaching, "Father, hail!" he cried,
And "Hail, my son," the reverend sire replied;
Words followed words, from question answer flow'd,
And talk of various kind deceiv'd the road;
Till each with other pleas'd, and loth to part,
While in their age they differ, join in heart.
Thus stands an aged elm, in ivy bound;
Thus youthful ivy clasps an elm around.

 Now sunk the sun; the closing hour of day
Came onward, mantled o'er with sober gray;
Nature in silence bid the world repose,
When near the road a stately palace rose;

There, by the moon, through ranks of trees they pass,
Whose verdure crown'd their sloping sides of grass.
It chanc'd the noble master of the dome
Still made his house the wandering stranger's home;
Yet still the kindness, from a thirst of praise,
Prov'd the vain flourish of expensive ease.
The pair arrive; the liveried servants wait,
Their lord receives them at the pompous gate;
The table groans with costly piles of food,
And all is more than hospitably good.
Then led to rest, the day's long toil they drown,
Deep sunk in sleep, and silk, and heaps of down.
 At length 'tis morn, and at the dawn of day,
Along the wide canals the zephyrs play:
Fresh o'er the gay parterres the breezes creep,
And shake the neighboring wood to banish sleep.
Up rise the guests obedient to the call,
An early banquet deck'd the splendid hall;
Rich luscious wine a golden goblet grac'd,
Which the kind master forc'd the guests to taste.
Then pleas'd and thankful from the porch they go;
And, but the landlord, none had cause of woe:
His cup was vanished; for, in secret guise,
The younger guest purloin'd the glittering prize.
 As one who spies a serpent in his way,
Glistening and basking in the summer ray,
Disorder'd stops to shun the danger near,
Then walks with faintness on, and looks with fear;
So seem'd the sire, when far upon the road
The shining spoil his wily partner show'd.
He stopp'd with silence, walk'd with trembling heart,
And much he wish'd, but durst not ask to part;

Murmuring he lifts his eyes, and thinks it hard
That generous actions meet a base reward.

 While thus they pass, the sun his glory shrouds,
The changing skies hang out their sable clouds;
A sound in air presag'd approaching rain,
And beasts to covert scud across the plain.
Warn'd by the signs, the wandering pair retreat
To seek for shelter at a neighboring seat.
'Twas built with turrets on a rising ground,
And strong, and large, and unimproved around;
Its owner's temper timorous and severe,
Unkind and griping, caused a desert there.

 As near the miser's heavy doors they drew,
Fierce rising gusts with sudden fury blew;
The nimble lightning mix'd with showers began,
And o'er their heads loud rolling thunder ran.
Here long they knock, but knock or call in vain,
Driven by the wind, and batter'd by the rain.
At length some pity warm'd the master's breast
('Twas then his threshold first received a guest);
Slow creaking turns the door with jealous care,
And half he welcomes in the shivering pair:
One frugal fagot lights the naked walls,
And Nature's fervor through their limbs recalls;
Bread of the coarsest sort, with eager wine,*
(Each hardly granted) serv'd them both to dine;
And when the tempest first appear'd to cease,
A ready warning bid them part in peace.

 With still remark the pondering hermit view'd.
In one so rich, a life so poor and rude;

---

* The word *eager* is here used in its old sense of "sour"—*aigre*; and if we interpret "wine" accordingly, "eager wine" should be vinegar—*vin-aigre*.

And why should such within himself, he cried,
Lock the lost wealth a thousand want beside?
But what new marks of wonder soon took place
In every settling feature of his face,
When from his vest the young companion bore
The cup the generous landlord own'd before,
And paid profusely with the precious bowl
The stinted kindness of his churlish soul!

But now the clouds in airy tumult fly;
The sun emerging opes an azure sky;
A fresher green the smiling leaves display,
And, glittering as they tremble, cheer the day;
The weather courts them from the poor retreat,
And the glad master bolts the wary gate.

While hence they walk, the pilgrim's bosom wrought
With all the travel of uncertain thought;
His partner's acts without their cause appear,
'Twas there a vice, and seemed a madness here;
Detesting that, and pitying this, he goes,
Lost and confounded with the various shows.

Now night's dim shades again involve the sky,
Again the wanderers want a place to lie;
Again they search, and find a lodging nigh.
The soil improv'd around, the mansion neat,
And neither poorly low, nor idly great,
It seem'd to speak its master's turn of mind,
Content, and not to praise, but virtue kind.

Hither the walkers turn their weary feet,
Then bless the mansion, and the master greet;
Their greeting fair, bestow'd with modest guise,
The courteous master hears, and thus replies:
" Without a vain, without a grudging heart,
To him who gives us all, I yield a part;

From him you come, from him accept it here,
A frank and sober, more than costly cheer."
He spoke, and bid the welcome table spread,
They talk of virtue till the time of bed;
When the grave household round his hall repair,
Warn'd by a bell, and close the hours with prayer.

At length the world, renew'd by calm repose,
Was strong for toil; the dappled morn arose;
Before the pilgrims part, the younger crept
Near the clos'd cradle where an infant slept,
And writh'd its neck; the landlord's little pride,
O strange return! grew black, and gasp'd, and died.
Horror of horrors! what! his only son!
How look'd our hermit when the fact was done;
Not hell, though hell's black jaws in sunder part,
And breathe blue fire, could more assault his heart.

Confus'd, and struck with silence at the deed,
He flies; but, trembling, fails to fly with speed;
His steps the youth pursues; the country lay
Perplex'd with roads; a servant show'd the way;
A river cross'd the path, the passage o'er
Was nice to find; the servant trod before;
Long arms of oak an oaken bridge supplied,
And deep the waves beneath the bending glide;
The youth, who seem'd to watch a time to sin,
Approach'd the careless guide and thrust him in;
Plunging he falls, and rising, lifts his head,
Then flashing turns, and sinks among the dead.

Wild sparkling rage inflame the father's eyes,
He bursts the bands of fear, and madly cries,
" Detested wretch!"—but scarce his speech began,
When the strange partner seemed no longer man;

His youthful face grew more serenely sweet ;
His robe turn'd white, and flow'd upon his feet ;
Fair rounds of radiant points invest his hair ;
Celestial odors breathe through purpled air ;
And wings, whose colors glittered on the day,
Wide at his back their gradual plumes display ;
The form ethereal burst upon his sight,
And moves in all the majesty of light.
  Though loud at first the pilgrim's passion grew,
Sudden he gaz'd, and wist not what to do ;
Surprise in secret chains his words suspends,
And in a calm his settling temper ends.
But silence here the beauteous angel broke
(The voice of music ravish'd as he spoke).
  " Thy prayer, thy praise, thy life to vice unknown,
In sweet memorial rise before the throne ;
These charms success in our bright region find,
And force an angel down to calm thy mind ;
For this commission'd, I forsook the sky ;
Nay, cease to kneel, thy fellow-servant I.
  " Then know the truth of government divine,
And let these scruples be no longer thine.
  " The Maker justly claims that world he made,
In this the right of Providence is laid ;
Its sacred majesty through all depends
On using second means to work his ends :
'Tis thus, withdrawn in state from human eye,
The Power exerts his attributes on high ;
Your actions uses, nor controls your will.
And bids the doubting sons of men be still.
  " What strange events can strike with more surprise
Than those which lately struck thy wondering eyes ?

Yet, taught by these, confess the Almighty just,
And where you can't unriddle, learn to trust!

" The great, vain man, who far'd on costly food,
Whose life was too luxurious to be good,
Who made his ivory stands with goblets shine,
And forc'd his guests to morning draughts of wine,
Has, with the cup, the graceless custom lost,
And still he welcomes, but with less of cost.

" The mean, suspicious wretch, whose bolted door
Ne'er mov'd in duty to the wandering poor;
With him I left the cup, to teach his mind
That Heaven can bless, if mortals will be kind.
Conscious of wanting worth, he views the bowl,
And feels compassion touch his grateful soul.
Thus artists melt the sullen ore of lead,
With heaping coals of fire upon its head;
In the kind warmth the metal learns to glow,
And, loose from dross, the silver runs below.

" Long had our pious friend in virtue trod,
But now the child half wean'd his heart from God;
Child of his age, for him he liv'd in pain,
And measured back his steps to earth again.
To what excesses had his dotage run?
But God, to save the father, took the son.
To all, but thee, in fits he seemed to go,
And 'twas my ministry to deal the blow:
The poor fond parent, humbled in the dust,
Now owns, in tears, the punishment was just.

" But now had all his fortune felt a wrack,
Had that false servant sped in safety back:
This night his treasur'd heaps he meant to steal,
And what a fund of charity would fail!

Thus Heaven instructs thy mind : this trial o'er,
Depart in peace, resign, and sin no more."

On sounding pinions here the youth withdrew,
The sage stood wondering as the seraph flew.
Thus look'd Elisha, when, to mount on high,
His master took the chariot of the sky ;
The fiery pomp ascending left to view;
The prophet gaz'd, and wish'd to follow too.

The bending hermit here a prayer begun,
Lord ! as in heaven, on earth thy will be done:
Then, gladly turning, sought his ancient place,
And pass'd a life of piety and peace.

Peter Pounce's Dialogue with Parson Adams.

FROM FIELDING'S "JOSEPH ANDREWS."

THERE was once in great vogue a book called *Pamela, or Virtue Rewarded*, the object of which was to show how a servant-maid might be very virtuous, in the heavenly sense of the word, and very prosperous, in the worldly; a combination which, in the author's opinion, was effected by making her resist all the efforts of a vicious master to ruin her, and then accept his hand in marriage when he found he could obtain her in no other way. Society is so much advanced in reflection since the writing of that book, that a moral so bad would now meet with contempt from critics of all classes, even though recommended by as rare and affecting a genius as his who taught it, and who was no less a person than Samuel Richardson, author of *Clarissa Harlowe*. With much that is admirable and noble, there is a great deal of false morality even in *Clarissa*; a dangerous exaltation of the formal, and literal, and self-worshipping, above the heartier dictates of prudence itself. But the moral in Pamela (with leave of a great name, be it said), was a pure vulgar mistake. The master was a scoundrel to whom an honest girl ought not to have been given in marriage at all; and the heroine was a *prig* and a schemer, with no real respect for the virtues she professed, otherwise she would not have jumped at the first "honorable" offer from one who had done all he could to destroy her.

The healthier genius of Fielding saw the folly of these ethics; and, seasoning his wish to counteract them with a spice of no ill-natured malice against the author (who was in the habit of making another vulgar mistake, and applying that epithet to all who wrote of humble life not in his own manner, particularly Fielding himself), produced the exquisite novel of *Joseph Andrews*. In this, not his greatest, but in our opinion most delightful work, he has contrived, with a most unexpected, successful, and (to Richardson, we fear) most provoking admission of the value of his moral when put into right action, to make Joseph Andrews Pamela's own brother, both in blood and virtue; to maintain his manly character nevertheless, in spite of conventional jests and prejudices; and, at the same time, to show how little of her pretended purity and humility was in the sister, who in admirable keeping with the spirit of her matrimonial virtue, objects to her brother's marrying a girl in her own former condition of society, because it was lowering the family which her "dear Mr. B." had "raised." As a pleasant instance of Fielding's quickness and vivacity in small matters as well as great, this "Mr. B." of Richardson (for his name never appears in that author except as an initial) is assumed by Fielding to have been a Mr. "Booby." Mr. Booby's fine town-lady aunt, Lady B., thus becomes Lady Booby. She and her nephew enable us to see, that people of no real heart and goodness, whatever be their rank, riches, or gaiety, may deserve the appellation of fool, as well as humbler or more solemn pretenders; and this is one of the many instances, we think, in which an exception should be made in favor of those characteristical names of persons in works of fiction, to which critics make wholesale objection. Names of the kind often occur in real life, sometimes with ludicrous propriety; and if similar ones could be taken away from the novels in which we have been used to them, people would reasonably miss the *Boobies* palmed upon Richardson, the *Pickles* and *Bowlings* of Smollett, the *Snakes* and *Sir Anthony Absolutes* of Sheridan, and the *Marplots* and *Aimwells* of Centlivre and Farquhar. We confess we should be loth to lose even the *Dryasdusts* of Sir Walter, excessive as they may appear. Fortune herself, (not to say Nature) seems to take pleasure in these whims of cognomination. Who has not met with stout gentlemen of the name of Onslow and Heaviside; lively Miss Quicks, and languishing Mrs. Sweets?

Joseph Andrews is a footman who marries a maid-servant. They are excellent persons, and have a delicious friend in Mr. Abraham Adams, a country curate, who prefers his Æschylus to everything but his duty. He is one of the simplest but at the same time manliest of men; is anxious to read a man of the world his sermon on "vanity;" preaches patience under affliction, and is ready to lose his senses on the death of his little boy; in short, has "every virtue under heaven," except that of superiority to the common failings of humanity, or of being able to resist knocking a rascal down when he insults the innocent. He is very poor; and, agreeably to the notions of refinement in those days, is treated by the rich as if he were little better than a servant himself. Even their stewards think it a condescension to treat him on equal terms. In the following scene, which is one of the most exquisite in all novel-writing, the reader experiences a delightful triumph in seeing how a vulgar upstart of this class is led to betray his baseness while he thinks he is most exalting himself— Adams, on the other hand, rising and becoming glorious out of the depths of his humble honesty. The picture gives you such a vivid idea of the two men, that not having read it for some years, we had fancied, in the interval, that when Pounce throws the curate's hat after him out of the window, Fielding had represented Adams as clapping it triumphantly on his head, and snapping his fingers at him. But this is the way with fine writers. In suggesting more than they say, they write more than they do.

PETER POUNCE, being desirous of having some one to whom he might communicate his grandeur, told the parson he would convey him home in his chariot. This favor was, by Adams, with many bows and acknowledgments, accepted, though he afterwards said he ascended the chariot rather that he might not offend, than from any desire of riding in it, for that in his heart he preferred the pedestrian even to the vehicular expedition.

The chariot had not proceeded far before Mr Adams observed it was a very fine day.

"Aye, and a very fine country, too," answered Pounce.

"I should think so more," returned Adams, "if I had not lately travelled over the Downs, which I take to exceed this, and all other prospects in the universe."

"A fig for prospects," answered Pounce; "one acre here is worth ten there; for my part, I have no delight in the prospect of any land but my own."

"Sir," said Adams, "you can indulge yourself in many fine prospects of that kind."

"I thank God I have a little," replied the other, "with which I am content, and envy no man. I have a little, Mr. Adams, with which I do as much good as I can."

Adams answered, "That riches, without charity, were nothing worth; for that they were a blessing only to him who made them a blessing to others."

"You and I," said Peter, "have different notions of charity. I own, as it is generally used, I do not like the word, nor do I think it becomes one of us gentlemen; it is a mean, parson-like quality; though I would not infer that many parsons have it neither."

"Sir," said Adams, "my definition of charity is a generous disposition to relieve the distressed."

"There is something in that definition," answered Peter, "which I like well enough; it is, as you say, a disposition—and does not so much consist in the act as in the disposition to do it; but, alas! Mr. Adams, who are meant by the distressed? believe me, the distresses of mankind are mostly imaginary, and it would be rather folly than goodness to relieve them."

"Sure, sir," replied Adams, "hunger and thirst, cold and nakedness, and other distresses which attend the poor, can never be said to be imaginary evils."

"How can any man complain of hunger," said Pounce, "in a country where such excellent salads are to be gathered almost in every field?—or of thirst, where every stream and river produce such delicious potations?—and as for cold and nakedness, they are evils introduced by luxury and custom.

A man naturally wants clothes no more than a horse or any other animal; and there are whole nations who go without them. But these are things, perhaps, which you, who do not know the world.——"

"You will pardon me, sir," returned Adams; "I have read of the *Gymnosophists.*"

"A plague of your Jehosaphats," cried Peter; "the greatest fault in our constitution is the provision made for the poor, except that perhaps made for some others. Sir, I have not an estate which doth not contribute almost as much again to the poor as to the land-tax; and I do assure you I expect myself to come to the parish in the end."

To which Adams giving a dissenting smile, Peter thus proceeded:—"I fancy, Mr. Adams, you are one of those who imagine I am a lump of money; for there are many who I fancy believe that not only my pockets, but my whole clothes, are lined with bank bills; but, I assure you, you are all mistaken; I am not the man the world esteems me. If I can hold my head above water, it is all I can. I have injured myself by purchasing; I have been too liberal of my money. Indeed I fear my heir will find my affairs in a worse situation than they are reputed to be. Ah! he will have reason to wish I had loved money more and land less. Pray, my good neighbor, where should I have that quantity of money the world is so liberal to bestow on me? Where could I possibly, without I had stole it, acquire such a treasure?"

"Why truly," said Adams, "I have been always of your opinion; I have wondered, as well as yourself, with what confidence they could report such things of you, which have to me appeared as mere impossibilities; for you know, sir, and I have often heard you say it, that your wealth is of your own acquisition; and can it be credible that in your short time you should have amassed such a heap of treasure as these people will have you are worth? Indeed, had you inherited an estate like Sir Thomas Booby, which had descended in your family through many generations, they might have had a color for their assertions."

"Why, what do they say I am worth?" cries Peter, with a malicious sneer.

"Sir," answered Adams, "I have heard some aver you are not worth less than twenty thousand pounds." At which Peter frowned.

"Nay, sir," said Adams, "you ask me only the opinion of others; for my own part, I have always denied it, nor did I ever believe you could possibly be worth half that sum."

"However, Mr. Adams," said he, squeezing him by the hand, "I would not sell them all I am worth for double that sum; and as to what you believe, or they believe, I care not a fig. I am not poor, because you think me so, nor because you attempt to undervalue me in the country. I know the envy of mankind very well; but I thank heaven I am above them. It is true, my wealth is of my own acquisition. I have not an estate like Sir Thomas Booby, that hath descended in my family through many generations; but I know heirs of such estates, who are forced to travel about the country, like some people in torn cassocks, and might be glad to accept of a pitiful curacy, for what I know; yes, sir, as shabby fellows as yourself, whom no man of my figure, without that vice of good-nature about him, would suffer to ride in a chariot with him."

"Sir," said Adams, "I value not your chariot of a rush; and if I had known you had intended to affront me, I would have walked to the world's end on foot, ere I would have accepted a place in it. However, sir, I will soon rid you of that inconvenience!" And so saying, he opened the chariot door, without calling to the coachman, and leaped out into the highway, forgetting to take his hat along with him; which, however, Mr. Pounce threw after him with great violence.

Verses written at an Inn at Henley.

BY SHENSTONE.

"Shall I not take," said Falstaff, with an exquisite duplication of the personal pronoun, "*mine* ease at *mine* INN ?"

The question might induce us to fancy, that he had another abode; that it was as much as to say, "Must I go and encounter my difficulty at my lodgings?" But he meant it as an appeal to the expectations of everybody. Everybody, the moment he entered an inn, looked to being thoroughly at his ease; to possess comfort and security as surely as he did the things he paid for.

And this is the feeling we all have of an inn. It is not comparable with home, on the very gravest or the very gayest occasions; much less as a place to reside in; but as a place to visit, there is nothing like it. It is like being abroad and at home at the same time; abroad, in respect to the novelty; and at home, as regards doing what we please. We are not sufficiently used to it, to feel a thankless indifference; neither do we entertain such affection for it, as converts interest into anxiety.—But we do it injustice in writing sentences about it. There is nothing sententious at an inn (except on the window-panes); it is only free and easy. If you are wise, it is with mirth : if you run the whole round of philosophy with some "learned Theban" of a friend, it is after dinner, when the blood is running the finer round of cheerfulness, to which you feel that the other round is only subordinate. The top things throughout are the dinner, and the inn, and the reciprocity; and you only wish that all the world were as happy as yourselves, wondering that they are not so, and that everybody does not do as he pleases upon the strength of the "Rose and Crown" and universal benevolence.

By an inn, however, we do not mean any inn; no, not even with companions who can make us forget everything else; for on their account also we desire an inn perfect of its kind; and this, we take it, is an old inn that has been a country-house, with at least a bit of the old garden to it, parterres of flowers, lavender, &c., and good sized old-fashioned rooms, with smaller ones in corners, to choose according as you are few or many, or wish to be roomy or snug. Hazlitt, who loved to escape from his irritabilities into an inn, has noticed such a one in a charming passage. He is speaking of the delight of reading favorite authors.

"The last time," he says, "I tasted this luxury in its full perfection, was one day after a sultry day's walk between Farnham and Alton. I was fairly tired out; I walked into an inn-yard (I think at the latter place); I was shown by the waiter to what looked at first like common out-houses at the other end of it, but they turned out to be a suite of rooms, probably a hundred years old—the one I entered opened into an old-fashioned garden, embellished with beds of larkspur and a leaden Mercury; it was wainscoted, and there was a grave-looking dark-colored portrait of Charles II. hanging up over the tiled chimney-piece. I had *Love for Love* in my pocket, and began to read; coffee was brought in, in a silver coffee-pot; the cream, the bread and butter, everything was excellent, and the flavor of Congreve's style prevailed over all. I prolonged the entertainment till a late hour, and relished this divine comedy better even than when I used to see it played by Miss Mellon, as *Miss Prue;* Bob Palmer, as *Tattle;* and Bannister as honest *Ben.* This circumstance happened just five years ago, and it seems like yesterday. If I count my life so, by lustres, it will soon glide away; yet I shall not have to repine, if, while it lasts, it is enriched by a few such recollections."*

The Henley at which Shenstone wrote his lines on an inn was the Henley on the road to Stratford-on-Avon. Johnson slept at it one night with Boswell, and had quoted a stanza from the lines in the course of the day, when they were dining at an "excellent inn at Chapelhouse."

"We dined," Boswell says, "at an excellent inn at Chapelhouse, where he (Johnson) expatiated on the felicity of England in its taverns

* *Plain Speaker*, vol. i. p. 302.

and inns, and triumphed over the French for not having, in any perfection, the tavern life. 'There is no private house,' said he, 'in which people can enjoy themselves so well, as at a capital tavern. Let there be ever so great plenty of good things, ever so much grandeur, ever so much elegance, ever so much desire that everybody should be easy, in the nature of things it cannot be; there must always be some degree of care and anxiety. The master of the house is anxious to entertain his guests; the guests are anxious to be agreeable to him; and no man, but a very impudent dog indeed, can as freely command what is in another man's house, as if it were his own. Whereas, at a tavern, there is a general freedom from anxiety. You are sure you are welcome; and the more noise you make, the more trouble you give, the more good things you call for, the welcomer you are. No servants will attend you with the alacrity which waiters do, who are incited by the prospect of an immediate reward in proportion as they please. No, sir; there is nothing which has yet been contrived by men, by which so much happiness is produced as by a good tavern or inn.' He then repeated with great emotion Shenstone's lines:

> "'Whoe'er has travell'd life's dull round,
> Where'er his stages may have been,
> May sigh to think he still has found
> His warmest welcome at an inn.'"*

Johnson was so fond of this little poem, that Miss Reynolds (sister of Sir Joshua) said she had learnt it by heart from hearing him repeat it. Some exclusive admirers of great poetry would see nothing in it; but let them try to write as good a one, and they would discover that some portion of the poetical facility was necessary to express and modulate even thoughts like these.

> To thee, fair Freedom! I retire,
>   From flattery, cards, and dice, and din;
> Nor art thou found in mansions higher
>   Than the low cot or humble Inn.
>
> 'Tis here with boundless power I reign;
>   And every health which I begin

* Boswell, Murray's Edition, vol. vi. p. 81.

Converts dull port to bright champagne;
   Such freedom crowns it at an Inn.

I fly from pomp, I fly from plate!
   I fly from Falsehood's specious grin!
Freedom I love and form I hate,
   And choose my lodgings at an Inn.

Here, waiter, take my sordid ore,
   Which lackeys else might hope to win,
It buys what courts have not in store,
   It buys me freedom at an Inn.

Whoe'er has travelled life's dull round,
   Where'er his stages may have been,
May sigh to think he still has found
   The warmest welcome at an Inn.

Five Letters of Gray.

GRAY appears to us to be the best letter-writer in the language. Others equal him in particular qualities, and surpass him in amount of entertainment; but none are so nearly faultless. Chesterfield wants heart, and even his boasted "delicacy;" Bolingbroke and Pope want simplicity; Cowper is more lively than strong; Shenstone reminds you of too many rainy days, Swift of too many things which he affected to despise, Gibbon too much of the formalist and the *littérateur*. The most amusing of all our letter-writers are Walpole and Lady Mary Wortley Montagu; but though they had abundance of wit, sense, and animal spirits, you are not always sure of their veracity. Now, "the first quality in a companion," as Sir William Temple observes, "is truth;" and Gray's truth is as manifest as his other good qualities. He has sincerity, modesty, manliness (in spite of a somewhat effeminate body), learning, good-nature, playfulness, a perfect style; and if an air of pensiveness breathes over all, it is only of that resigned and contemplative sort which completes our sympathy with the writer.

Mark what he says in these letters about his sitting in the forest; about Southern; about lords and their school-days; about Shaftesbury; about having a "garding" of one's own; about Akenside compared with himself; about the Southampton Abbot, the Grand Duchess of Tuscany, &c. &c.; and about sunrise—wondering "whether anybody ever saw it before," he is so astonished at their not having said more on the subject.

Gray is the "melancholy Jaques" of English literature, without the sullenness or causticity. His melancholy is of the diviner sort of Milton and Beaumont and is always ready to assume a kindly cheerfulness.

TO HORACE WALPOLE *

[A FOX-HUNTER—A POET'S SOLITUDE—SOUTHERN THE DRAMATIST.]

September, 1737.

I WAS hindered in my last, and so could not give you all the trouble I would have done. The description of road which your coach-wheels have so often honored, it would be needless to give you. Suffice it, that I arrived safe at my uncle's, who is a great hunter in imagination. His dogs take up every chair in the house, so I am forced to stand at this present writing; and though the gout forbids him galloping after them in the field, yet he continues to regale his ears and nose with their comfortable noise and stink.† He holds me mighty cheap, I perceive, for walking when I should ride, and reading when I should hunt. My comfort amidst all this is, that I have, at the distance of half a mile, through a green lane, a forest (the vulgar call it a common), all my own; at least as good as so, for I spy no human thing in it but myself. It is a little chaos of mountains and precipices —mountains, it is true, that do not ascend much above the

---

* Walpole and Gray had been school-fellows at Eton; and, though differing greatly in some respects, had tastes alike in others, particularly a love for romantic fiction and Gothic architecture. Their differences were found to render them unsuitable as fellow-travellers, when they visited Italy; but they renewed their intercourse at home, and continued correspondents as long as Gray lived.

At the date of the letter before us, Walpole was a youth of twenty, residing with his father, Sir Robert, at Haughton; Gray, twenty-one, on a visit to an uncle, at Burnham, in Buckinghamshire. The reader will observe the mature manliness of his style.

† Some readers of the present day might suppose that coarse habits are here but coarsely described by the delicate young poet. But such language was not considered coarse in the time of Gray.

clouds; nor are the declivities quite so amazing as Dover cliff; but just such hills as people who love their necks as well as I do may venture to climb; and crags that give the eye as much pleasure as if they were dangerous. Both vale and hill are covered with most venerable beeches, and other very reverend vegetables,* that, like most other ancient people, are always dreaming out their old stories to the winds:

> " And as they bow their hoary tops, relate
> In murmuring sounds the dark decrees of fate;
> While visions, as poetic eyes avow,
> Cling to each leaf, and swarm on every bough."

At the foot of one of these squats me I (*il penseroso*), and there I grow to the trunk for a whole morning. The timorous hare and sportive squirrel gambol around me, like Adam in paradise, before he had an Eve; but I think he did not use to read Virgil, as I commonly do there. In this situation I often converse with my Horace, aloud too; that is, talk to you; but I do not remember that I ever heard you answer me. I beg pardon for taking all the conversation to myself; but it is entirely your own fault. We have old Mr. Southern† at a gentleman's house, a little way off, who often comes to see us; he is now seventy-seven years old, and has almost wholly lost his memory, but is as agreeable as an old man can be; at least I persuade myself so when I look at him, and think of Isabella and Oroonoko. I shall be in town in about three weeks. Adieu."

---

* "Reverend vegetable" is a phrase of Steele's for a common-place old man.

† Southern lived nine years longer. When he was a young man, he knew Dryden; and here is Gray, a youth, in company with Dryden's acquaintance. It is always pleasant to observe these links of celebrity

TO RICHARD WEST.*

[BAD SPIRITS—RECOLLECTIONS OF HUSBANDS AND STATESMEN AT SCHOOL.]

LONDON, May 27th, 1742.

MINE, you are to know, is a white melancholy, or rather leucocholy,† for the most part; which, though it seldom laughs, or dances, nor ever amounts to what one calls joy or pleasure, yet is a good easy sort of a state, and *ça ne laisse que de s'amuser*.‡ The only fault of it is insipidity; which is apt now and then to give a sort of *ennui*, which makes one form certain little wishes that signify nothing. But there is another sort, black indeed, which I have now and then felt, that has somewhat in it like Tertullian's rule of faith, "*credo quia impossibile est*,"§ for it believes, nay, is sure of everything that is unlikely, so it be but frightful; and, on the other hand, excludes and shuts its eyes to the most possible hopes, and everything that is pleasurable. From this, the Lord deliver us; for none but he and sun-shiny weather can do it. In hopes of enjoying this kind of weather, I am going into the country for a few weeks, but shall be never the nearer any society, so if you have any

---

* Son of the Lord Chancellor of Ireland, by a daughter of Bishop Burnet. His tastes were very like Gray's, and he promised to attain celebrity, but died of a consumption the year following the date of this letter, at the age of twenty-six.

† Melancholy signifying black choler, leucocholy would be white choler. Gray pleasantly coins the word for the occasion.

‡ Does nothing but trifle.

§ *I believe because it is impossible.* Gray might have added (and perhaps he meant to do so by what follows) that Tertullian, who was a cruel bigot, held another rule of faith, equally reasonable, namely, *I believe because it is horrible.*

charity you will contrive to write. My life is like Harry the Fourth's supper of hens: "*poulets à la broche, poulets en ragoût, poulets en hâchis, poulets en fricasées;*[*] reading here, reading there; nothing but books with different sauces. Do not let me lose my dessert then; for though that be reading too, yet it has a very different flavor. The May seems to be come since your invitation;[†] and I promise to bask in her beams, and dress me in her roses:

> "Et caput in vernâ semper habere rosâ."[‡]

I shall see Mr. ——— and his wife, nay, and his child too, for he has got a boy. Is it not odd to consider one's contemporaries in the grave light of husband and father? There are my Lords ——— and ———, they are statesmen; do not you remember them dirty boys playing at cricket? As for me, I am never a bit the older, nor the bigger, nor the wiser than I was then; no, not for having been beyond sea. Pray, how are you?

TO THE REVEREND NORTON NICHOLLS.

[BANTER OF FORMAL EXCUSES AND FINE EXORDIUMS—SOUTH-AMPTON—AN ABBOT—SUNRISE.]

Nov. 19, 1764.

I RECEIVED your letter at Southampton; and as I would wish to treat everybody according to their own rule and measure of good breeding, have, against my inclination, waited till now before I answered it, purely out of fear and

---

[*] Roast chicken, ragooed chicken, hashed chicken, fricaseed chicken.

[†] West had written an ode to May, addressed to his friend.

[‡] "And have my head forever in spring roses."
A line in "*Propertius*," lib. iii. v. 22.

respect, and an ingenuous diffidence in my own abilities. It you will not take this as an excuse, accept it at least as a well-turned period, which is always my principal concern.*

So I proceed to tell you, that my health is much improved by the sea. Not that I drank it, or bathed in it, as the common people do; no! I only walked by it, and looked upon it. The climate is remarkably mild, even in October and November; no snow has been seen to lie there for these thirty years past; the myrtles grow in the ground against the houses, Guernsey lilies bloom in every window; the town, clean and well-built, surrounded by its old stone walls, with their towers and gateways, stands at the point of a peninsula, and opens full south to an arm of the sea, which, having formed two beautiful bays on each hand of it stretches away in direct view, till it joins the British Channel. It is skirted on either side with gently rising grounds, clothed with thick wood; and directly across its mouth rise the high lands of the Isle of Wight at distance, but distinctly seen. In the bosom of the woods (concealed from profane eyes) lie hid the ruins of Nettley Abbey; there may be richer and greater houses of religion, but the abbot is content with his situation. See there, at the top of that hanging meadow, under the shade of those old trees that bend into a half-circle about it, he is walking slowly (good man!) and bidding his beads for the souls of his benefactors, interred in that venerable pile that lies beneath him. Beyond it (the meadow still descending) nods a thicket of oaks that mask the building, and have excluded a view too garish and luxuriant for a holy eye; only on either hand they leave an opening to the blue glittering sea. Did you not observe how, as that white sail shot by and was lost, he turned and crossed himself, to drive the tempter

---

* A banter probably of some apologetical formality on the part of Nicholls.

from him that had thrown that distraction in his way? I should tell you that the ferryman who rowed me, a lusty young fellow, told me that he would not for all the world pass a night at the Abbey (there were such things seen near it), though there was a power of money hid there. From thence I went to Salisbury, Wilton, and Stonehenge: but of these things I say no more. They will be published at the University press.

P.S.—I must not close my letter without giving you one principal event of my history; which was, that (in the course of my late tour) I set out one morning before five o'clock, the moon shining through a dark and misty autumnal air, and got to the sea-coast time enough to be at the sun's levee. I saw the clouds and dark vapors open gradually to right and left, rolling over one another in great smoky wreaths, and the tide (as it flowed gently in upon the sands) first whitening, then slightly tinged with gold and blue, and all at once a little line of insufferable brightness that (before I can write these five words) was grown to half an orb, and now to a whole one too glorious to be distinctly seen. It is very odd it makes no figure on paper; yet I shall remember it as long as the sun, or at least as long as I endure. I wonder whether anybody ever saw it before? I hardly believe it.

TO THE SAME.

[A MOTHER—SCENERY OF KENT.]

1765.

IT is a long time since, that I heard you were gone in hast into Yorkshire on account of your mother's illness; an the same letter informed me that she was recovered, otherwise I had then wrote to you only to beg you would take care of her, and to inform you that I had discovered a thing very little known, which is, that in one's whole life one can never have any more than a single mother. You may think this is obvious, and (what you call) a trite observation. You are a green gosling! I was at the same age (very near) as wise as you; and yet I never discovered this (with full evidence and conviction, I mean) till it was too late. It is thirteen years ago, and seems but as yesterday, and every day I live it sinks deeper into my heart. Many a corollary could I draw from this axiom for your use (not for my own), but I will leave you the merit of doing it for yourself. Pray tell me how your health is; I conclude it perfect, as I hear you offered yourself as a guide to Mr. Palgrave into the Sierra Morena of Yorkshire. For me, I passed the end of May, and all June, in Kent, not disagreeably. In the west part of it, from every eminence, the eye catches some long reach of the Thames or Medway, with all their shipping: in the east, the sea breaks in upon you, and mixes its white transient sails, and glittering blue expanse, with the deeper and brighter green of the woods and corn. This sentence is so fine I am quite ashamed, but no matter! You must translate it into prose. Palgrave, if he heard it, would cover his face with his pudding sleeve.* I do not tell you of the great and small beasts, and creeping things innumerable, that I met with, because you do not suspect that this world is inhabited by anything but men, and women, and clergy, and such two-legged cattle. Now I am here again, very disconsolate and all alone, for Mr. Brown is gone, and the cares of this world are coming thick upon me; you, I hope, are better off, riding and walking in the woods of Studley, &c &c. I must not wish for you here; besides, I am going to town at Michaelmas, by no means for amusement.

* He was a clergyman; rector of Palgrave and Thrandeston, in Suffolk.

TO THE SAME.

[HAVING A GARDEN OF ONE'S OWN—SHENSTONE—SECOND BANTER ON FORMAL APOLOGIES.

PEMBROKE COLLEGE, June 24th, 1769.

AND so you have a garden of your own, and you plant and transplant, and are dirty and amused. Are not you ashamed of yourself? Why, I have no such thing, you monster; nor ever shall be either dirty or amused as long as I live.* My gardens are in my windows, like those of a lodger up three pair of stairs in Petticoat Lane, or Camomile Street, and they go to bed regularly under the same roof that I do. Dear! how charming it must be to walk out in one's own *garding*, and sit on a bench in the open air, with a fountain and leaden statue, and a rolling-stone, and an arbor! Have a care of sore throats though, and the *agoe*.

However, be it known to you, though I have no garden, I have sold my estate,† and got a thousand guineas and fourscore pounds a-year for my old aunt, and a twenty-pound prize in the lottery, and Lord knows what arrears in the treasury, and am a rich fellow enough, go to: a fellow that hath had losses, and one that hath two gowns, and everything handsome about him;‡ and in a few days shall have new window-curtains: are you avized of that? Aye, and a new mattress to lie upon.

---

* This pleasantry becomes the more charming, when read in connection with some previous letters to Nicholls, which were in a strain of serious and somewhat remonstrating advice on carelessness in his affairs, though full of the most touching kindness.

† Some houses on the west side of Hand Alley, in Cornhill.

‡ From Dogberry's speech in *Much ado about Nothing*, Act iv. sc. 2

My Ode* has been rehearsed again and again, and the scholars have got scraps by heart. I expect to see it torn piecemeal in the North Briton,† before it is born. If you will come, you shall see it, and sing in it amidst a chorus from Salisbury and Gloucester music-meeting, great names there, and all well versed in Judas Maccabæus.‡ I wish it was once over, for then I immediately go for a few days to London, and so with Mr. Brown to Aston, though I fear it will rain the whole summer, and Skiddaw will be invisible and inaccessible to mortals.

I have got De la Lande's Voyage through Italy in eight volumes. He is a member of the Academy of Sciences, and pretty good to read. I have read, too, an octavo volume of Shenstone's Letters. Poor man! he was always wishing for money, for fame, and other distinctions; and his whole philosophy consisted in living against his will in retirement, and in a place which his taste had adorned, but which he only enjoyed when people of note came to see and commend it. His correspondence is about nothing else but this place and his own writings, with two or three neighboring clergymen who wrote verses too.§

---

* "On the Installation of the Duke of Grafton as Chancellor of the University of Cambridge."

† A periodical publication now forgotten.

‡ Handel's Oratorio of that name.

§ This is a true view of the weak side of Shenstone's character; and Gray, perhaps, confined himself to that side of it for some purpose connected with his correspondent. Otherwise Shenstone must inevitably have reaped great enjoyment from the lovely and surprising landscapes he created on his estate, which were the admiration of the best judges, and the site of his own gentle verse-making. Shenstone, like most people, was a different man under different phases of health. Gray was a warm admirer of the poem in these volumes, *The School-mistress*. He pronounced it "excellent in its kind, and masterly."

I have just found the beginning of a letter, which somebody had dropped: I should rather call it first-thoughts for the beginning of a letter, for there are many scratches and corrections. As I cannot use it myself (having got a beginning already of my own), I send it for your use on some great occasion.

" Dear Sir,

" After so long silence, the hopes of pardon, and prospect of forgiveness, might seem entirely extinct, or at least very remote, was I not truly sensible of your goodness and candor, which is the only asylum that my negligence can fly to, since every apology would prove insufficient to counterbalance it, or alleviate my fault: how then shall my deficiency presume to make so bold an attempt, or be able to suffer the hardships of so rough a campaign?" &c. &c. &c *

* See note *, p. 125.

Advantages of Cultivating a Taste for Pictures.

BY JONATHAN RICHARDSON.

JONATHAN RICHARDSON was a portrait-painter and critic in the time of Pope, whom he knew. He was esteemed in his art, and still more for his knowledge and admiration of art in others. He wrote treatises on Painting, notes on Milton, a poem in *Nichols's Collection*, evincing his inquiring and amiable turn of mind, called an *Address to the Morning Star*; and he was famous for his industry, early-rising, and the affection existing between him and his son. His writings have perhaps created more enthusiasm for pictures than those of any other man in England. He is not an accomplished writer, like Sir Joshua; nor has he the depth of Hazlitt; much less any of the transcendental insights of the promising critical genius who has lately made his appearance among us under the title of the "Oxford Graduate." His style is colloquial, to a degree of slovenliness: and, with the tendencies natural perhaps to his art in a professional point of view, he is too much inclined to confound prosperity with success. But he would interest us less if he did not pour forth all he thought. Candor, honesty, goodness, vivacity, and a considerable amount of taste and knowledge, constitute the charms of his writing. Sir Joshua respected him; Pope, who dabbled in painting himself, was attached to him; Hazlitt quoted him with delight.

The following remarks are on a subject which is yet far too little appreciated, but which is destined, we suspect, to play a great and delightful part in the universal world of civilization. "Knowledge is power;" but it is not only power to command (which is the sense in which the axiom is generally taken), it is also power to enjoy. Everybody who knows anything of anything, knows how much that knowledge adds to the sum of his ordinary satisfaction; what strength it gives him, what ennui and vacuity it saves him. The smallest botanist or geologist knows it, by the way-side; the least meteorologist, as he gazes at a rack of clouds. Pictures make themselves known at once, more or less; yet nobody, who has not in some measure thought on the subject as Richardson here teaches to think, has any conception how much is to be got out of a good picture, the more he knows of the art, and of nature. He learns to know everything which the painter intends; everything which he intimates; and thus to discover volumes of meaning and entertainment where others see little but a colored page. And the more we know of pictures, the more we come to value engravings, and to know what companions they can be made; what little treasures of art we may possess, even in those faint representations, compared with the nothing to be got out of the finest paintings by the eyes of ignorance.

And then there is the reflex of Painting itself on Nature; the grateful light which she throws in her turn on the source of her inspiration; so that the more we know of objects on canvas, the more we learn to know of the objects themselves, and thus become qualified to discern pictures in everything, and to be critics of our instructor. But Richardson has touched on this point also, and the reader must not be detained from him. We would only beg leave to add, by way of individual experience in such matters, without pretending to any remarkable insight into them, either natural or acquired, that Mr. Hazlitt, whom we had the pleasure of knowing, converted us from a wrong admiration of white cottages in landscapes to the right one of the honest old red; that Mr. Haydon (whom we will not call "unfortunate," even for his end, knowing what pleasure he got out of his art in life) was the first, in our youth, to give us an eye to the attitudes and groups of people in company; and that we have reason to regard the having been conversant with a house full of paintings during childhood as one of the blessings of our existence. We have never since entered a room of that sort without a tendency to hush and move softly, as if in the presence of things above the ordinary course of nature, of spirits left behind them by great men, looking at us with divine eyes, or informing the most beautiful visions of nature with art as wonderful. And we are so.

WHAT is beautiful and excellent, is naturally adapted to please: but all beauties and excellencies are not, naturally, seen. Most gentlemen see pictures and drawings as the generality of people see the heavens in a clear, starry night; they perceive a sort of beauty there, but such a one as produces no great pleasure in the mind; but when one considers the heavenly bodies as other worlds, and that there are an infinite number of these in the empire of God (Immensity), and worlds which our eyes, assisted by the best glasses, can never reach, and so far remote from the most distant of what we see, that these visible ones are as it were our neighbors, as the continent of France is to Great Britain; when one considers farther, that as there are inhabitants on this continent. though we see them not when we see *that*, it is altogether unreasonable to imagine that those innumerable worlds are uninhabited and desert; there must be beings there, some perhaps more, others less noble and excellent than man. When one thus views this vast prospect, the mind is otherwise affected than before, and feels a delight which common notions never can administer. So those who at present cannot comprehend there can be such pleasure in a good picture or drawing as connoisseurs pretend to find, may learn to see the same thing themselves; their eyes being once opened, they may be said to obtain a new sense; and new pleasures flow in as often as the objects of that superinduced sight present themselves, which (to people of condition especially) very frequently happens, or may be procured, whether here at home, or in their travels abroad. When a gentleman has learned to see the beauties and excellencies that are really in good pictures and drawings and which may be learnt by conversing with such, and applying himself to the consideration of them, he will look upon that with joy which he now passes over with very little pleasure, if not with indifference;

nay, a sketch, a scrabble of the hand of a great master, will be capable of administering to him a greater degree of pleasure than those who know it not by experience can have any conception of. Besides the graceful and noble attitudes, the beauty of colors and forms, and the fine effects of light and shadow, which none sees as a connoisseur does, such a one enters farther than any other can do into the beauties of the invention, expression, and other parts of the work he is considering. He sees strokes of art, contrivances, expedients, a delicacy and spirit, that others see not, or very imperfectly.

He sees what force of mind the great masters had to conceive ideas; what judgment to see things beautifully, or to imagine beauty from what they saw; and what a power their hands were endued withal, in a few strokes and with ease, to show to another what themselves conceived.

What is it that gives us pleasure in reading a history or poem, but that the mind is thereby furnished with a variety of images? And what distinguishes some authors, and sets them above the common level, but their knowing how to raise their subject? The Trojan or Peleponnesian wars would never have been thought of by us, if a Homer or Thucydides had not told the stories of them, who knew how to do it so as to fill the minds of their readers with great and delightful ideas. He who converses with the works of the best masters is always reading such admirable authors; and his mind consequently, in proportion, entertained and delighted with the histories, fables, characters, the ideas of magnificent buildings, fine prospects, &c.

And he sees these things in those different lights which the various manners of thinking of the several masters sets them; he sees them as they are represented by the capricious but vast genius of Leonardo da Vinci; the fierce and gigantic one of Michael Angelo; the divine and polite one of Raphael; the poetical fancy of Guido; the angelical mind of Corregio, or Parmegiano; the haughty, sullen, but accomplished Annibal, the learned Augustino Caracci.

A connoisseur hath this further advantage, that he not only sees beauties in pictures and paintings, which to common eyes are invisible; but he learns by these to see such in nature, in the exquisite forms and colors, the fine effects of lights, and shadows, and reflections, which in her are always to be found, and from whence he hath a pleasure which otherwise he could never have had, and which none with untaught eyes can possibly discern: he has a constant pleasure of this kind even in the most common things, and the most familiar to us, so that what people usually look upon with the utmost indifference, creates an home-felt delight in his mind. The noblest works of Raphael, the most ravishing music of Handel, the most masterly strokes of Milton, touch not people who are without discernment.

So, the beauties themselves of those all-perfect works of the great author of nature are not seen but by enlightened eyes, that is, those eyes which are taught to see; to those they appear far otherwise than before they were; so, so far otherwise! that *one* sees through a glass darkly (through the gross medium of ignorance); the *other*, that of a connoisseur, as when the angel had removed the film from Adam's eyes, and purged with euphrasy and rue, the visual nerve, seeth beauty divine and human, as far as human may, as we hope to see everything, still nearer to its true beauty and perfection, in a better state; when we shall " see what eye hath not seen, neither hath it entered the heart of man to conceive."

By conversing with the works of the best masters, our imaginations are impregnated with great and beautiful images, which present themselves on all occasions in reading an author, or ruminating upon some great action, ancient or modern; everything is raised, everything improved from what it would have been otherwise. Nay, those lovely images with which our minds are thus enriched, arise there continually, and give us pleasure, with or without any particular application.

What is rare and curious, exclusive of any other consideration, we naturally take pleasure in; because, as variable as our circumstances are, there is so much of repetition in life that more variety is still desirable. The works of the great masters would thus recommend themselves to us, though they had not that transcendent excellency that they have; they are such as are rarely seen; they are the works of a small number of the species in one little country of the world, and in a short space of time. But their excellency being put into the scale makes the rarity of them justly considerable. They are the works of men like whom none are now to be found, and when there will be, God only knows!

> "Art et guides, tout est dans les Champs Élysées."
> LA FONTAINE.

What the old man Melanthius says of Polygnotus (as he is cited by Plutarch in the life of Cimon), may, with a little alteration, be applied to these men in general; it is thus already translated:

> "This famous painter, at his own expense,
> Gave Athens beauty and magnificence;
> New life to all the heroes did impart;
> Embellish'd all the temples with his art;
> The splendor of the state restor'd again;
> And so he did oblige both gods and men."

What still adds to the rarity of the excellent works we

are speaking of is, their number must necessarily diminish by sudden accidents, or the slow, but certain injuries of time.

Another pleasure belonging to connoissance is when we find anything particular and curious; as the first thoughts of a master for some remarkable picture; the original of a work of a great master, the copy of which we have already by some other considerable hand; a drawing of a picture, or after an antique very famous, or which is now lost; or when we make some new acquisition upon reasonable terms, chiefly when we get for ourselves something we much desired, but could not hope to be masters of; when we make some new discovery, something that improves our knowledge in connoissance or painting, or otherwise; and abundance of such like incidents, and which very frequently happens to a diligent connoisseur.

The pleasure that arises from a knowledge of hands is not like, or equal to that of the other parts of the business of a connoisseur, but neither is this destitute of it. When one sees an admirable piece of art, it is part of the connoisseur to know to whom to attribute it, and then to know his history; which arises, I hope, from a natural justice in the human mind that loves and desires to pay a little tribute of gratitude where it discovers it to be due to that merit of another which it is actually enjoying. The custom of putting the author's portrait or life at the beginning of his book, is kindly giving us an opportunity of doing this.

When one is considering a picture or a drawing,* and at the same time thinks this was done by him who had many

---

* The passage here commencing is one enormously long sentence, continued to the words "these reflections," at p. 140. It may be supposed, however, to be very agreeably poured forth in the heat of conversation.

extraordinary endowments of body and mind, and was withal a virtuous man and a fine gentleman in his whole life, and still more at his death, expiring in the arms of one of the greatest princes of that age, Francis I., king of France, who loved him as a friend ;*—another is of him who lived a long and happy life beloved of the Emperor Charles V., and many others of the first princes of Europe ;†—when one has another in his hand, and thinks that this was done by one who so excelled in three arts, as that any one of them, in that degree he possessed them all, had rendered him worthy of immortality, and who moreover dared to contend with his sovereign (one of the haughtiest popes that ever was) upon a slight offered to him, and extricated himself with honor ;‡ —another is the work of that great self-formed, authentic genius, who was the model of supernatural grace ; who alone painted heaven, as surely it is ; and hath represented to human weakness the angelic nature ; this, too, by inspiration ! not having had any master, or none but whom he left quite out of sight in the earliest progresses of his divine pencil ; he even never saw the works of other great masters, having always confined himself to his native Lombardy, except one single one of Raphael, and a great one indeed that was, his St. Cecilia when brought to Bologna ; and then, after considering it with long attention, and the admiration it deserved, he had the spirit (and he had a right to that spirit) to say, " Well, I am a painter, too ;"§ he was so little known to the rest of Italy, that he passed till very lately, in the opinion of the world, for a low, poor, indigent creature, from the ill-information or malice of Vasari, always prejudiced against the Lombard painters, when his character was rescued from its affected obscurity, and his noble birth and connections, and splen-

* Leonardo da Vinci. † Titian.
‡ Michael Angelo. § Corregio.

did wealth, asserted beyond all possibility and dispute by the indefatigable industry of Ludiovico Antonio David, a Milanese painter, and published at Bologna;—another we shall consider as the work of him who restored painting when it was almost sunk; of him whom his art made honorable; but who neglecting and despising greatness with a sort of cynical pride, was treated suitably to the figure he gave himself, not to his intrinsic merit; which not having philosophy enough to bear, it broke his heart;* another is performed by one, who (on the contrary) was a fine gentleman, and of great magnificence, and was much honored by his own and foreign princes; who was a courtier, a statesman, and a painter; and so much all these, that when he acted in either character, that seemed to be his business, and the others his diversion;†—when one thus reflects, besides the pleasure arising from the beauties and excellencies of the work, the fine ideas it gives us of natural things, the noble way of thinking one finds in it, and the pleasing thoughts it may suggest to us, an additional pleasure results from these reflections.

But, oh! the pleasure! when a connoisseur and lover of art has before him a picture or drawing, of which he can say, this is the hand, these the thoughts of him who was one of the politest, best-natured gentlemen that ever was; who was beloved and assisted by the greatest wits, and the greatest men then at Rome, at a time when politeness and all those arts which make life taste truly agreeable, were carried to a greater height than at any period since the reign of Augustus: of him who lived in great fame, honor, and magnificence, and died universally lamented; and even missed a cardinal's hat only by dying a few months too soon; but was, above all, highly esteemed and favored by two popes, the only ones

---

* Caravaggio? † Rubens.

who filled the chair of St. Peter in his time;—one (in short) who could have been a Leonardo, a Michael Angelo, a Titian, a Corregio, a Parmegiano, an Annibal, a Rubens, or any other when he pleased, but none of them could ever have been a Raphael

Ode on a Distant Prospect of Eton College.

This poem has been noticed in our preface, and in the introduction to the Long Story. It is full of thought, tenderness, and music, and should make the writer beloved by all persons of reflection, especially those who know what it is to visit the scenes of their schooldays. They may not all regard them in the same melancholy light; but the melancholy light will cross them, and then Gray's lines will fall in upon the recollection, at once like a bitter and a balm.

YE distant spires, ye antique towers,
   That crown the watery glade,
Where grateful science still adores
   Her Henry's holy shade;
And ye that from the stately brow
Of Windsor's heights th' expanse below
   Of grove, of lawn, of mead survey,
Whose turf, whose shade, whose flowers among
Wanders the hoary Thames along
   His silver-winding way.

Ah, happy hills, ah, pleasing shade,
   Ah, fields beloved in vain,

Where once my careless childhood stray'd,
    A stranger yet to pain?
I feel the gales that from ye blow
A momentary bliss bestow,
    As waving fresh their gladsome wing
My weary soul they seem to soothe,
And, redolent of joy and youth,
    To breathe a second spring.

Say, father Thames, for thou hast seen
    Full many a sprightly race,
Disporting on thy margent green,
    The paths of pleasure trace,
Who foremost now delight to cleave
With pliant arm thy glassy wave?
    The captive linnet which enthrall?
What idle progeny succeed
To chase the rolling circle's speed,
    Or urge the flying ball?

While some, on earnest business bent,
    Their murmuring labors ply
Gainst graver hours, that bring constraint
    To sweeten liberty,
Some bold adventurers disdain
The limits of their little reign,
    And unknown regions dare descry;
Still as they run they look behind,
They hear a voice in every wind,
    And snatch a fearful joy.

Gay hope is theirs, by fancy fed,
    Less pleasing when possest;

The tear forgot as soon as shed,
    The sunshine of the breast:
Theirs, buxom health of rosy hue,
Wild wit, invention ever new,
    And lively cheer, of vigor born;
The thoughtless day, the easy night,
The spirits pure, the slumbers light,
    That fly th' approach of morn.

Alas, regardless of their doom,
    The little victims play!
No sense have they of ills to come,
    Nor care beyond to-day:
Yet see how all around them wait
The ministers of human fate,
    And black misfortune's baleful train;
Ah, show them where in ambush stand,
To seize their prey, the murderous band!
    Ah, tell them they are men!

These shall the fury passions tear,
    The vultures of the mind,
Disdainful anger, pallid fear,
    And shame that skulks behind;
Or pining love shall waste their youth
Or jealousy, with rankling tooth,
    That inly gnaws the secret heart;
And envy wan, and faded care,
Grim-visag'd comfortless despair,
    And sorrow's piercing dart.

Ambition this shall tempt to rise,
    Then whirl the wretch from high,

To bitter scorn a sacrifice,
   And grinning infamy;
The stings of falsehood those shall try,
And hard unkindness' alter'd eye,
   That mocks the tear it forc'd to flow;
And keen remorse, with blood defil'd,
And moody madness laughing wild
   Amidst severest woe.

Lo, in the vale of years beneath
   A grisly troop are seen,
The painful family of death,
   More hideous than their queen;
This racks the joints, this fires the veins,
That every laboring sinew strains,
   Those in the deeper vitals rage:
Lo, poverty, to fill the band,
That numbs the soul with icy hand,
   And slow consuming age.

To each his sufferings; all are men,
   Condemn'd alike to groan;
The tender for another's pain,
   The unfeeling for his own.
Yet, ah! why should they know their fate!
Since sorrow never comes too late,
   And happiness too swiftly flies:
Thought would destroy their paradise.—
No more. Where ignorance is bliss,
   'Tis folly to be wise.

A Long Story.

THE *Long Story* is so entitled in deprecation of any tedium which the reader might experience in perusing a personal adventure of the author's who was too sensitive on such points. He pleasantly pretends that he has omitted five hundred stanzas. The occasion of the poem was a visit paid him by two ladies, who did him the honor of being their own introducers. Gray was at the house of his aunt, in his native village of Stoke Pogeis, near Windsor. His mother was there also. The Viscountess Cobham,* who possessed the mansion-house of the place, wished to make the poet's acquaintance. The ladies in question undertook to break the ice for her. Not finding him at home, they left a card, intimating that they came to tell him of the good health of a Lady Brown, a friend of his. Shy and sequestered as he was, the poet returned the visit; and he takes the opportunity of describing the house, and complimenting its inmates.

Walpole said of Gray, that, however well he might write in moods altogether serious, his real forte was pleasantry. Undoubtedly Gray's pleasantry is of a more original cast than his seriousness; less indebted to that of his predecessors. Yet there is reason to believe that every thought which he transferred to paper had passed through his own mind, though his love of the writings of others too often induced him to express it in their words. Half his verses are centos; and yet we feel them to be rather sympathies than echoes. His *Ode on the Prospect of Eton College*, and his *Elegy in a Country Churchyard*, are the regrets of all his fellow-mortals, and of himself. Gray was a scholarly, thoughtful, affectionate man; a little effeminate in his hab-

* Sister of Pope's Lord Cobham, and subsequently Countess Temple.

its, owing to a feeble constitution; but manly in his judgments, and superior to every kind of sophistry and meanness.

Gray's pleasantry came to him through his melancholy, assisted by the general delicacy of his perceptions, and his willingness to be pleased. Though a little too cautious of committing his dignity, he was not one of those who "take a calamity for an affront." He was willing to give and to receive pleasure, and this is a disposition which Nature is sure to reward. In the *Long Story* we see him hesitating at first whether he should go to the "great house." He was not only loth to be disturbed in his sequestered habits; he was jealous of what might be thought of his humble independence, and his footing as a "gentleman." (He was the son of a scrivener.) But good-nature prevails, not unaccompanied by a willingness to find himself among ladies of rank and elegance; and though he might as well have dropped the circumstance of his secreting himself, he has made a charming picture both of the interview of the ladies with his mother and aunt (whom he pretends they pinched and "rummaged" like fairies), and of the great Elizabethan house, with its old associations,—things in which he delighted; for he was an antiquary with all the zest of a poet. The whole poem is full of picturesqueness, fancy, and wit.

IN Britain's isle, no matter where,
 An ancient pile of building stands;
The Huntingdons and Hattons there
 Employ'd the power of fairy hands

To raise the ceiling's fretted height,
 Each panel in achievements clothing,
Rich windows that exclude the light,
 And passages that lead to nothing.*

Full oft within the spacious walls,
 When he had fifty winters o'er him,

---

* A line that has become a favorite quotation with critics, especially as applied to passages in music.

My grave Lord-Keeper led the brawls;*
    The seal and maces danc'd before him.

His bushy beard and shoe-strings green,
    His high-crown'd hat and satin doublet,
Mov'd the stout heart of England's Queen,
    Though Pope and Spaniard could not trouble it.

What, in the very first beginning?
    Shame of the versifying tribe!
Your history whither are you spinning?
    Can you do nothing but describe?

A house there is (and that's enough)
    From whence one fatal morning issues
A brace of warriors, not in buff,
    But rustling in their silks and tissues.

The first† came *cap-à-pie* from France,
    Her conquering destiny fulfilling,
Whom meaner beauties eye askance,
    And vainly ape her art of killing.

---

* The brawl (*branle*) was a fashionable dance. The Lord Keeper is Sir Christopher Hatton, a handsome man, who is said to have danced himself into the office. It is unquestionable that he made way somehow into the heart of Elizabeth. Dancing, however, appears to have been so much admired by this great queen, that another and graver lawyer, Sir John Davies, no mean philosophical poet, who was also one of her most devoted panegyrists, divided his leisure thoughts between metrical treatises on the *Art of Dancing* and on the *Immortality of the Soul*. Biographers, by the way, tell us, that Hatton never possessed a house at Stoke Pogeis. Gray, however, says he did; and there he is in consequence, living forever.

† Lady Schaub.

The other Amazon* kind heav'n
  Had arm'd with spirit, wit, and satire;
But Cobham had the polish giv'n,
  And tipp'd her arrows with good-nature.

To celebrate her eyes, her air—
  Coarse panegyrics would but tease her:
Melissa is her *nom de guerre;*
  Alas! who would not wish to please her?

With bonnet blue, and capuchin,
  And aprons long, they hid their armor,
And veil'd their weapons bright and keen
  In pity to the country farmer.

Fame in the shape of Mr. P——t
  (By this time all the parish know it)
Had told that thereabouts there lurk'd
  A wicked imp they call'd a poet,†

Who prowl'd the country far and near,
  Bewitch'd the children of the peasants,
Dry'd up the cows and lam'd the deer,
  And suck'd the eggs and kill'd the pheasants.

My Lady, heard their joint petition,
  Swore, by her coronet and ermine,
She'd issue out her high commission
  To rid the manor of such vermin.

---

* Miss Harriett Speed. She was a descendant of the historian, and became the wife of the Sardinian ambassador, the Count de Veri.

† Mr. P—— was a Mr. *Purt* or *Purkt.* He is said to have been displeased with this allusion,—Mason thinks unreasonably; but nobody likes to be thought a gossip. Mason knew that Gray was a good-natured man; but of this, Mr. P. might not have been so sure.

The heroines undertook the task;
   Thro' lanes unknown, o'er stiles they ventur'd,
Rapp'd at the door, nor stay'd to ask,
   But bounce into the parlor enter'd.

The trembling family they daunt;
   They flirt, they sing, they laugh, they tattle;
Rummage his mother, pinch his aunt,
   And up stairs in a whirlwind rattle.

Each hole and cupboard they explore,
   Each creek and cranny of his chamber,
Run hurry-skurry round the floor,
   And o'er the bed and tester clamber;

Into the drawers and china pry,
   Papers and books, a huge imbroglio;
Under a tea-cup he might lie,
   Or creas'd, like dogs-ears, in a folio.

On the first marching of the troops,
   The Muses, hopeless of his pardon,
Conveyed him underneath their hoops
   To a small closet in the garden.

So Rumor says (who will, believe);
   But that they left the door ajar,
Where safe, and laughing in his sleeve,
   He heard the distant din of war.

Short was his joy; he little knew
   The power of magic was no fable;
Out of the window whisk they flew,
   But left a spell upon the table.

The words too eager to unriddle,
 The poet felt a strange disorder;
Transparent bird-lime form'd the middle,
 And chains invisible the border.

So cunning was the apparatus,
 The powerful pot-hooks did so move him,
That will-he, nill-he, to the great house
 He went as if the devil drove him.

Yet on his way (no sign of grace,
 For folks in fear are apt to pray)
To Phœbus he preferr'd his case,
 And begg'd his aid that dreadful day.

The godhead would have back'd his quarrel;
 But, with a blush, on recollection,
Own'd that his quiver and his laurel
 'Gainst four such eyes were no protection.

The court was set, the culprit there;
 Forth from their gloomy mansion creeping
The Lady Janes and Joans repair,
 And from the gallery stand peeping:

Such as in silence of the night
 Come (sweep) along some winding entry
(Styack* has often seen the sight),
 Or at the chapel-door stand sentry;

In peaked hoods and mantles tarnish'd,
 Sour visages enough to scare ye,
High dames of honor once that garnish'd
 The drawing-room of fierce Queen Mary!

* The housekeeper.

The peeress comes; the audience stare,
   And doff their hats with due submission;
She curt'sies, as she takes her chair,
   To all the people of condition.

The bard with many an artful fib
   Had in imagination fenc'd him,
Disprov'd the arguments of Squib,*
   And all that Groom† could urge against him;

But soon his rhetoric forsook him,
   When he the solemn hall had seen;
A sudden fit of ague shook him—
   He stood as mute as poor Macleane.‡

Yet something he was heard to mutter
   " How in the park, beneath an old tree,
Without design to hurt the butter,
   Or any malice to the poultry,

He once or twice had penn'd a sonnet,
   Yet hop'd that he might save his bacon;
Numbers would give their oath upon it,
   He ne'er was for a conj'rer taken."

The ghostly prudes with hagged face
   Already had condemn'd the sinner;
My Lady rose, and with a grace—
   She smil'd, and bid him come to dinner.

" Jesu Maria! Madam Bridget,
   Why what can the Viscountess mean?"

---

* The groom of the chamber.   † The steward.
‡ A famous highwayman who had just been executed.

Cry'd the square hoods in woful fidget;
  " The times are alter'd, quite and clean:

" Decorum's turn'd to mere civility!
  Her air and all her manners show it.
Commend me to her affability!
  Speak to a commoner and poet!"

         [*Here* 500 *Stanzas are lost.*]

And so God save our noble King,
  And guard us from long-winded lubbers,
That to eternity would sing,
  And keep my lady from her rubbers.

Sir Roger de Coverley.

FROM ADDISON'S PAPERS IN THE "SPECTATOR."

SIR ROGER DE COVERLEY is one of those truthful types of character, which, though created by the mind of man, yet, by the ordination of Nature herself (for Nature includes art among her works), outlasts the successive generations of flesh and blood which it represents. The individuals perish, and leave no memorial; nay, we hardly care to know them while living. We might find them tiresome. We feel that Nature has done well in making them; we are grateful for the race; especially on behalf of others, and of the poor; but we do not particularly see the value of their society; when, lo! in steps one of Nature's imitators—called men of genius—and, by the mere fact of producing a likeness of the species to the mind's eye, enchants us forever both with it and himself. A little philosophy may easily explain this; but perhaps a little more may still leave it among the most interesting of mysteries.

We have said a word elsewhere (see *Gradations of Clubs*) respecting the first invention of Sir Roger by Steele, and the compatibility of his early fopperies with a genuine simplicity. But unquestionably Addison took up the invention of Steele, and enriched and completed it in a way that left the invention itself at a distance. The whole of the following papers are from his exquisite pen. They render comment superfluous. One has nothing to do but repeat passages, and admire them.

SIR ROGER'S HOUSEHOLD ESTABLISHMENT.

HAVING often received an invitation from my friend Sir Roger de Coverley to pass away a month with him in the country, I last week accompanied him thither, and am settled with him for some time at his country-house, where I intend to form several of my ensuing speculations. Sir Roger, who is very well acquainted with my humor, lets me rise and go to bed when I please, dine at his own table or in my own chamber as I think fit, sit still and say nothing without bidding me be merry. When the gentlemen of the country come to see him, he only shows me at a distance. As I have been walking in his fields I have observed them stealing a sight of me over a hedge, and have heard the knight desiring them not to let me see them, for that I hated to be stared at.

I am the more at ease in Sir Roger's family, because it consists of sober and staid persons; for, as the knight is the best master in the world, he seldom changes his servants; and as he is beloved by all about, his servants never care for leaving him; by this means his domestics are all in years, and grown old with their master. You would take his valet-de-chambre for his brother; his butler is gray-headed, his groom is one of the gravest men that I have ever seen, and his coachman has the looks of a privy-councillor. You see the goodness of the master even in the old house-dog, and in a gray pad that is kept in the stable with great care and tenderness, out of regard for his past services, though he has been useless for several years.

I could not but observe, with a great deal of pleasure, the joy that appeared in the countenances of these ancient domestics upon my friend's arrival at his country-seat. Some of them could not refrain from tears at the sight of their old master; every one of them pressed forward to do something for him, and seemed discouraged if they were not employed. At the same time, the good old knight, with a mixture of a father and the master of a family, tempered the inquiries after his own affairs with several kind questions about themselves. This humanity and good-nature engages everybody to him, so that when he is pleasant upon any of them, all his family are in good-humor, and none so much as the person he diverts himself with. On the contrary, if he coughs, or betrays any infirmity of old age, it is easy for a stander-by to observe a secret concern in the looks of all his servants.

My worthy friend has put me under the particular care of his butler, who is a very prudent man, and, as well as the rest of his fellow-servants, wonderfully desirous of pleasing me, because they have often heard their master talk of me as his particular friend.

My chief companion, when Sir Roger is diverting himself in the woods or the fields, is a very venerable man who is ever with Sir Roger, and has lived at his house in the nature of a chaplain above thirty years. This gentleman is a person of good sense and some learning; of a very regular life and obliging conversation: he heartily loves Sir Roger, and knows that he is very much in the old knight's esteem, so that he lives in the family rather as a relation than as a dependant.

I have observed in several of my papers, that my friend Sir Roger, amidst all his good qualities, is something of an humorist; and that his virtues, as well as imperfections, are, as it were, tinged by a certain extravagance which makes them particularly *his*, and distinguishes them from those of other men. This cast of mind, as it is generally very innocent in itself, so it renders his conversation highly agreeable, and more delightful than the same degree of sense and virtue would appear in their ordinary colors. As I was walking with him last night, he asked me how I liked the good man I have just now mentioned? And without staying for an answer told me, "That he was afraid of being insulted with Latin and Greek at his own table; for which reason he desired a par ticular friend of his at the University to find him out a clergyman rather of plain sense than much learning; of a good aspect, a clear voice, a sociable temper, and, if possible, a man that understood a little of backgammon. My friend," says Sir Roger, " found me out this gentleman, who, besides the endowments required of him, is, they tell me, a good scholar, though he does not show it. I have given him the parsonage of the parish; and, because I know his value, have settled upon him a good annuity for life. If he outlives me, he shall find that he was higher in my esteem than perhaps he thinks he is. He has now been with me thirty years, and though he does not know I have taken notice of it, has never in all that time asked anything of me for himself, though he is every day soliciting me for something in behalf of one or other of my tenants his parishioners. There has not been a law-suit in the parish since he has lived among them: if any dispute arises, they apply themselves to him for the decision; if they do not acquiesce in his judgment, which I think never happened above once or twice at most, they appeal to me. At his first settling with me, I made him a present of all the good sermons that have been printed in English, and only begged of him, that every Sunday he would pronounce one of them in the pulpit. Accordingly, he has digested them into such a series, that they follow one another naturally, and make a continued series of practical divinity."

As Sir Roger was going on in his story, the gentleman we were talking of came up to us; and upon the knight asking him who preached to-morrow (for it was Saturday night), told us the Bishop of St. Asaph* in the morning, and Dr. South in the afternoon. He then showed us his list of preachers for the year, where I saw, with a great deal of pleasure, Archbishop Tillotson, Bishop Saunderson, Dr. Bar-

* Dr. Fleetwood, afterwards Bishop of Ely.

row, Dr. Calamy, with several living authors who have published discourses of practical divinity. I no sooner saw this venerable man in the pulpit, but I very much approved of my friend's insisting upon the qualifications of a good aspect and a clear voice ; for I was so charmed with the gracefulness of his figure and delivery, as well as with the discourses he pronounced, that I think I never passed any time more to my satisfaction. A sermon repeated after this manner, is like the composition of a poet in the mouth of a graceful actor.

I could heartily wish that more of our country clergy would follow this example ; and, instead of wasting their spirits in laborious compositions of their own, would endeavor after a handsome elocution, and all those other talents that are proper to enforce what has been penned by greater masters. This would not only be more easy to themselves, but more edifying to the people.

SIR ROGER'S BEHAVIOR IN CHURCH ON A SUNDAY.

I AM always very well pleased with a country Sunday, and think, if keeping holy the seventh day were only a human institution, it would be the best method that could have been thought of for the polishing and civilizing of mankind. It is certain the country people would soon degenerate into a kind of savages and barbarians, were there not such frequent returns of a stated time, in which the whole village meet together with their best faces, and in their cleanliest habits, to converse with one another upon indifferent subjects, hear their duties explained to them, and join together in adoration of the Supreme Being. Sunday clears away the rust of the whole week, not only as it refreshes in their minds the notions of religion, but as it puts both sexes upon appearing in their most agreeable forms, and exerting all such qualities as are apt to give them a figure in the eye of the village. A country fellow distinguishes himself as much in the churchyard as a citizen does upon 'Change, the whole parish politics being generally discussed there, either after sermon or before the bell rings.

My friend Sir Roger, being a good church-man, has beautified the inside of his church with several texts of his own choosing: he has likewise given a handsome pulpit-cloth, and railed in the communion-table at his own expense. He has often told me, that at his coming to his estate he found his parishioners very irregular; and that, in order to make them kneel and join in the responses, he gave every one of them a hassock and a common-prayer book; and at the same time employed an itinerant singing-master, who goes about the country for that purpose, to instruct them rightly in the tunes of the psalms; upon which they now very much value themselves, and outdo most of the country churches that I have ever heard.

As Sir Roger is landlord to the whole congregation, he keeps them in very good order, and will suffer nobody to sleep in it besides himself; for if by chance he has been surprised into a short nap at sermon, upon recovering out of it he stands up and looks about him, and if he sees anybody else nodding, either wakes them himself or sends his servants to them. Several other of the old knight's particularities break out upon these occasions; sometimes he will be lengthening out a verse in the singing-psalms, half a minute after the rest of the congregation have done with it; sometimes, when he is pleased with the matter of his devotion, he pronounces Amen three or four times to the same prayer; and sometimes stands up when everybody else is on their knees, to count the congregation, or see if any of his tenants are missing.

I was yesterday very much surprised to hear my old friend, in the midst of the service, calling out to one John Matthews to mind what he was about, and not disturb the congregation. This John Matthews, it seems, is remarkable for being an idle fellow, and at that time was kicking his heels for his diversion. This authority of the knight, though exerted in that odd manner which accompanies him in all circumstances of life, has a very good effect upon the parish, who are not polite enough to see anything ridiculous in his behavior; besides that the general good sense and worthiness of his character makes his friends observe these little singularities as foils that rather set off than blemish his good qualities.

As soon as the sermon is finished, nobody presumes to stir till Sir Roger is gone out of the church. The knight walks down from his seat in the chancel between a double row of his tenants, that stand bowing to him on each side, and every now and then inquires how such an one's wife, or mother, or son, or father do, whom he does not see at church; which is understood as a secret reprimand to the person that is absent.

The chaplain has often told me, that upon a catechizing day, when Sir Roger has been pleased with a boy that answers well, he has ordered a bible to be given him next day for his encouragement; and sometimes accompanies it with a flitch of bacon to his mother. Sir Roger has likewise added five pounds a-year to the clerk's place: and that he may encourage the young fellows to make themselves perfect in the church-service, has promised, upon the death of the present incumbent, who is very old, to bestow it according to merit.

The fair understanding between Sir Roger and his chaplain, and their mutual concurrence in doing good, is the more remarkable, because the very next village is famous for the differences and contentions that rise between the parson and the squire, who live in a perpetual state of war. The parson is always preaching at the squire, and the squire, to be revenged on the parson, never comes to church. The squire has made all his tenants atheists and tithe-stealers; while the parson instructs them every Sunday in the dignity of his order, and insinuates to them, in almost every sermon, that he is a better man than his patron. In short, matters are come to such an extremity, that the squire has not said his prayers either in public or private this half-year; and that the parson threatens him, if he does not mend his manners, to pray for him in the face of the whole congregation.

Feuds of this nature, though too frequent in the country, are very fatal to the ordinary people; who are so used to be dazzled with riches, that they pay as much deference to the understanding of a man of an estate, as of a man of learning; and are very hardly brought to regard any truth, how important soever it may be, that is preached to them, when they know there are several men of five hundred a-year who do not believe it.

SIR ROGER AND THE GIPSIES.

AS I was yesterday riding out in the fields with my friend Sir Roger, we saw at a little distance from us a troop of gipsies. Upon the first discovery of them, my friend was in some doubt whether he should not exert the justice of the peace upon such a band of lawless vagrants, but not having his clerk with him, who is a necessary counsellor on these oc casions, and fearing that his poultry might fare the worse for it, he let the thought drop; but, at the same time, gave me a particular account of the mischief they do in the country, in stealing people's goods and spoiling their servants. "If a stray piece of linen hangs on the hedge," says Sir Roger, "they are sure to have it; if the hog loses his way in the field, it is ten to one but he becomes their prey; our geese cannot live in peace for them; if a man prosecutes them with severity, his hen-roost is sure to pay for it: they generally straggle into these parts about this time of the year; and set the heads of our servant-maids so agog for husbands, that we do not expect to have any business done as it should be whilst they are in the country. I have an honest dairy-maid who crosses their hands with a piece of silver every summer, and never fails being promised the handsomest young fellow in the parish for her pains. Your friend the butler has been fool enough to be seduced by them, and although he is sure to lose a knife, a fork, or a spoon every time his fortune is told him, generally shuts himself up in the pantry with an old gipsy for about half an hour once in a twelvemonth. Sweethearts are the things they live upon, which they bestow very plentifully upon all those that apply themselves to them. You see now and then some handsome jades amongst them; the sluts have very often white teeth and black eyes."

Sir Roger observing that I listened with great attention to his account of a people who were so entirely new to me, told me, that if I would, they should tell us our fortunes. As I was very well pleased with the knight's proposal, we rid up and communicated our hands to them. A Cassandra of the crew, after having examined my lines very diligently, told me, that I loved a pretty maid in a corner, that I was a good woman's man, with some other particulars, which I do not think proper to relate. My friend Sir Roger alighted from his horse, and exposed his palm to two or three that stood by him; they crumpled it into all shapes, and diligently scanned every wrinkle that could be made in it; when one of them, who was older and more sun-burnt than the rest, told him, that he had a widow in his line of life: upon which the knight cried, "Go, go, you are an idle baggage;" and at the same time smiled upon me. The gipsy, finding he was not displeased in his heart, told him, after a farther inquiry into his hand, that his true-love was constant, and that she should dream of him to-night; my old friend cried pish, and bid her go on. The gipsy told him that he was a bachelor, but would not be so long; and that he was dearer to somebody than he thought: the knight still repeated "she was an idle baggage," and bid her go on. "Ah, master," says the gipsy, "that roguish leer of yours makes a pretty woman's heart ache; you han't that simper about the mouth for nothing." The uncouth gibberish with which all this was uttered, like the darkness of an oracle, made us more attentive to it. To be short, the knight left the money with her that he had crossed her hand with, and got up again on his horse.

As we were riding away, Sir Roger told me, that he knew several sensible people who believed these gipsies now and then foretold very strange things; and for half an hour together appeared more jocund than ordinary. In the height of his good-humor, meeting a common beggar on the road who was no conjurer, as he went to relieve him he found his pocket was picked; that being a kind of Palmistry at which this race of vermin are very dexterous.

I might here entertain my reader with historical remarks on this idle profligate people, who infest all the countries of Europe, and live in the midst of governments in a kind of Commonwealth by themselves. But instead of entering into observations of this nature, I shall fill the remaining part of my paper with a story which is still fresh in Holland, and was printed in one of our monthly accounts, about twenty years ago. "As the Trekschuyt or Hackney-boat which carries passengers from Leyden to Amsterdam, was putting off, a boy running along the side of the canal desired to be taken in, which the master refused, because the lad had not quite money enough to pay his fare. An eminent merchant, being pleased with the looks of the boy, and secretly touched with compassion towards him, paid the money for him, and ordered him to be taken on board. Upon talking with him afterwards, he found that he could speak readily in three or four languages, and learned upon further examination that he had been stolen away when he was a child by a gipsy, and had rambled ever since with a gang of those strollers up and down several parts of Europe. It happened that the merchant, whose heart seems to have inclined towards the boy by a secret kind of instinct, had himself lost a child some years before. The parents, after a long search for him, gave him for drowned in one of the canals with which that country abounds; and the mother was so afflicted at the loss of a fine boy, who was her only son, that she died for grief of it. Upon laying together all particulars, and examining the several moles and marks by which the mother used to describe the child when he was first missing, the boy proved to be the son of the merchant whose heart had so unaccountably melted at the sight of him. The lad was very well pleased to find a father who was so rich, and likely to leave him a good estate; the father, on the other hand, was not a little delighted to see a son return to him, whom he had given for lost, with such a strength of constitution, sharpness of understanding, and skill in languages.". Here the printed story leaves off; but if I may give credit to reports, our linguist, having received such extraordinary rudiments towards a good education, was afterwards trained up in everything that becomes a gentleman; wearing off, by little and little, all the vicious habits and practices that he had been used to in the course of his peregrinations : nay, it is said, that he has since been employed in foreign courts upon national business, with great reputation to himself and honor to those who sent him, and that he has visited several countries as a public minister, in which he formerly wandered as a gipsy.

SIR ROGER'S VISIT TO THE TOMBS IN WESTMINSTER ABBEY.

MY friend Sir Roger de Coverley told me t'other night, that he had been reading my paper upon Westminster Abbey, in which, says he, there are a great many ingenious fancies. He told me, at the same time, that he observed I had promised another paper upon the tombs, and that he should be glad to go and see them with me, not having visited them since he had read history. I could not imagine how this came into the knight's head, till I recollected he had been very busy all last summer upon Baker's Chronicle, which he has quoted several times in his disputes with Sir Andrew Freeport, since his last coming to town. Accordingly, I promised to call upon him the next morning, that we might go together to the abbey.

I found the knight under his butler's hands, who always shaves him. He was no sooner dressed, than he called for a glass of the Widow Truby's Water, which he told me he always drank before he went abroad. He recommended me to a dram of it at the same time, with so much heartiness, that I could not forbear drinking it. As soon as I had got it down, I found it very unpalatable; upon which the knight, observing that I had made several wry faces, told me that he knew I should not like it at first, but that it was the best thing in the world against the stone or gravel.

I could have wished indeed that he had acquainted me with the virtues of it sooner; but it was too late to complain, and I knew what he had done was out of good-will. Sir Roger told me further, that he got together a quantity of it upon the first news of the sickness being at Dantzick; when, of a sudden turning short to one of his servants who stood behind him, he bid him call a hackney coach, and take care it was an elderly man that drove it.

He then resumed his discourse upon Mrs. Truby's Water, telling me that the Widow Truby was one who did more good than all the doctors and apothecaries in the country; that she distilled every poppy that grew within five miles of her; that she distributed her water gratis among all sorts of people: to which the knight added that she had a very great jointure, and that the whole country would fain have it a match between him and her; "and truly," says Sir Roger, "if I had not been engaged, perhaps I could not have done better."

His discourse was broken off by his man's telling him he had called a coach. Upon our going to it, after having cast his eye upon the wheels, he asked the coachman if his axle-tree was good; upon the fellow's telling him he would warrant it, the knight turned to me, told me he looked like an honest man, and went in without further ceremony.

We had not gone far, when Sir Roger, popping out his head, called the coachman down from his box, and upon presenting himself at the window, asked him if he smoked. As I was considering what this would end in, he bid him stop by the way at any good tobacconist's, and take in a roll of their best Virginia. Nothing material happened in the remaining part of our journey, till we were set down at the west end of the abbey.

As we went up the body of the church, the knight pointed at the trophies upon one of the new monuments, and cried out, "A brave man, I warrant him!" Passing afterwards by Sir Cloudesly Shovel, he flung his hand that way, and cried, "Sir Cloudesly Shovel! a very gallant man." As we stood before Busby's tomb, the knight uttered himself again after the same manner: "Dr. Busby! a great man! he whipped my grandfather: a very great man! I should have gone to him myself, if I had not been a blockhead: a very great man!"

We were immediately conducted into the little chapel on the right hand. Sir Roger, planting himself at our historian's elbow, was very attentive to everything he said, particularly to the account he gave us of the lord who had cut off the King of Morocco's head. Among several other figures, he was very much pleased to see the statesman Cecil upon his knees: and concluding them all to be great men, was conducted to the figure which represents that martyr to good housewifery, who died by the prick of a needle. Upon our interpreter's telling us that she was maid of honor to Queen Elizabeth, the knight was very inquisitive about her name and family: and, after having regarded her finger for some time, "I wonder," says he, "that Sir Richard Baker has said nothing of her in his Chronicle."

We were then conveyed to the two coronation chairs, where my old friend, after having heard that the stone underneath the most ancient of them, which was brought from Scotland, was called Jacob's pillar, sat himself down in the chair, and, looking like the figure of an old Gothic king, asked our interpreter, what authority they had to say that Jacob had ever been in Scotland? The fellow, instead of returning him an answer, told him that he begged his honor would pay his forfeit. I could observe Sir Roger a little ruffled upon being thus trepanned; but our guide not insisting on his demand, the knight soon recovered his good-humor, and whispered in my ear, that if Will Wimble were with us, and saw those chairs, it would go hard but he would get a tobacco-stopper out of one or t'other of them.

Sir Roger, in the next place, laid his hand upon Edward the Third's sword, and leaning upon the pummel of it, gave us the whole history of the Black Prince; concluding, that in Sir Richard Baker's opinion, Edward the Third was one of the greatest princes that ever sat upon the English throne.

We were then shown Edward the Confessor's tomb; upon which Sir Roger acquainted us, that he was the first who touched for the evil; and afterwards Henry the Fourth's, upon which he shook his head, and told us there was fine reading in the casualties of that reign.

Our conductor then pointed out that monument where there is the figure of one of our English kings without a head; and upon giving us to know, that the head, which was of beaten silver, had been stolen away several years since; "Some Whig, I'll warrant you," said Sir Roger; "you ought to lock up your kings better: they will carry off the body too, if you don't take care."

The glorious names of Henry the Fifth and Queen Elizabeth gave the knight great opportunities of shining, and of doing justice to Sir Richard Baker, who, as our knight observed with some surprise, had a great many kings in him whose monuments he had not seen in the abbey.

For my own part, I could not but be pleased to see the knight show such an honest passion for the glory of his country, and such a respectful gratitude for the memory of its princes.

I must not omit, that the benevolence of my good old

friend which flows out towards every one he converses with, made him very kind to our interpreter, whom he looked upon as an extraordinary man; for which reason he shook him by the hand at parting, telling him that he should be very glad to see him at his lodgings in Norfolk Buildings, and talk over these matters with him more at leisure.

Manners of the French.

About thirty years ago a volume appeared from the pen of a traveller in France, which set "all the world" in England upon going to that country, and living on the charming "banks of the Loire;" a river not so well known then, as it has lately been, for an ugly trick it has of overflowing its banks, and frightening its Paradisaical inhabitants out of their wits. We allude to the travels of Lieutenant-Colonel Pinckney, an officer in the American service, who made the greater part of his tour in company with another American gentleman and two French ladies, one of whom was his friend's wife. This circumstance will account for the different modes in which he speaks of himself in the following extracts, one of them implying that he was alone Our extracts are what the reviewers would call "favorable specimens;" that is, of French character; and we make them advisedly such, for neighborly purposes. Englishmen like to see favorable specimens of their own travellers in the accounts given of them by Frenchmen; and we therefore do as we would be done by. Both Englishmen and Frenchmen have faults to mend and customs to get rid of; and they cannot do better than by regarding with kindness what is best on both sides.

THE main purpose of my journey (says the gallant Colonel) being rather to see the manners of the people, than the brick and mortar of the towns, I had formed a resolution to seek the necessary refreshment as seldom as possible at inns, and as often as possible in the houses of the humbler farmers, and the better kind of peasantry. About fifteen miles from Calais my horse and myself were looking out for something of this kind, and one shortly appeared about three hundred yards on the left side of the road. It was a cottage in the midst of a garden, and the whole surrounded by a hedge, which looked delightfully green and refreshing. The garden was all in flower and bloom. The walls of the cottage were robed in the same livery of nature. I had seen such cottages in Kent and Devonshire, but in no other part of the world. The inhabitants were simple people, small farmers, having about ten or fifteen acres of land. Some grass was immediately cut for my horse, and the coffee which I produced from my pocket was speedily set before me, with cakes, wine, some meat, and cheese—the French peasantry having no idea of what we call tea. Throwing the windows up, so as to enjoy the scenery and freshness of the garden; sitting upon one chair, and resting a leg upon the other; alternately pouring out my coffee, and reading a pocket edition of Thomson's *Seasons*, I enjoyed one of those moments which gave a zest to life; I felt happy, and in peace and in love with all around me.

Proceeding upon my journey, two miles on the Calais side of Boulogne I fell in with an overturned chaise, which the postilion was trying to raise. The vehicle was a *chaise de poste*, the ordinary travelling carriage of the country, and a thing in a civilized country wretched beyond conception. It was drawn by three horses, one in the shafts, and one on each side. The postillion had ridden on the one on the driving side; he was a little punch fellow, and in a pair of boots like fire-buckets. The travellers consisted of an old French lady and gentleman; madame in a high crimped cap, and stiff long whalebone stays. Monsieur informed me very courteously of the cause of the accident, whilst madame alternately curtsied to me, and menaced and scolded the postilion.

A single cart, and a wagon, were all the vehicles that I saw between Boulogne and Abbeville. In England, in the same space, I should have seen a dozen or score.

Not being pressed for time, the beauty of a scene at some little distance from the road-side tempted me to enter into a bye-lane, and take a nearer view of it. A village church, embosomed in a chestnut-wood, just rose above the trees on the top of a hill; the setting sun was on its casements, and the foliage of the wood was burnished by the golden reflection. The distant hum of the village green was just audible; but not so the French horn, which echoed in full melody through the groves. Having rode about half a mile through a narrow sequestered lane, which strongly reminded me of the half-green and half-trodden bye-roads in Warwickshire, I came to the bottom of the hill, on the brow and summit of which the village and church were situated. I now saw whence the sound of the horn proceeded. On the left of the road was an ancient chateau, situated in a park or very extensive meadow, and ornamented as well by some venerable trees, as by a circular fence of flowering shrubs, guarded on the outside by a paling on a raised mound. The park or meadow having been newly mown, had an air at once ornamented and natural. A party of ladies were collected under a patch of trees situated in the middle of the lawn. I stopped at the gate to look at them, thinking myself unperceived; but in the same moment the gate was opened to me by a gentleman and two ladies, who were walking the round. An explanation was now necessary, and was accordingly given. The gentleman informed me, upon his part, that the chateau belonged to Mons. St. Quentin, a member of the French senate, and a judge of the district; that he had a party of friends with him upon the occasion of his lady's birthday, that they were about to begin dancing, and that Mons. St. Quentin would highly congratulate himself on my accidental arrival. One of the ladies, having previously apologized and left us, had seemingly explained to Mons. St. Quentin the main circumstance belonging to me; for he now appeared, and repeated the invitation in his own person. The ladies added their kind importunities. I dismounted, gave my horse to a servant in waiting, and joined this happy and elegant party—for such it really was.

I had now, for the first time, an opportunity of forming an opinion of French beauty, the assemblage of ladies being very numerous, and all of them most elegantly dressed. Travelling, and the imitative arts, have given a most surprising uniformity to all the fashions of dress and ornament; and whatever may be said to the contrary, there is a very slight difference between the scenes of a French and English polite assembly. If anything, however, be distinguishable, it is more in degree than in substance. The French fashions, as I saw them here, differed in no other point from what I had seen in London, but in degree. The ladies were certainly more exposed about the necks, and their hair was dressed with more fancy; but the form was in almost everything the same. The most elegant novelty was a hat, which doubled up like a fan, so that the ladies carried it in their hands. There were more colored than white muslins; a variety which had a very pretty effect amongst the trees and flowers. The same observation applies to the gentlemen. Their dresses were made as in England; but the pattern of the cloth, or some appendage to it, was different. One gentleman habited in a grass-colored silk coat, had very much the appearance of Beau Mordecai in the farce: the ladies, however, seemed to admire him; and in some conversation with him I found him, in spite of his coat, a very well-informed man. There were likewise three or four fancy dresses; a Dian, a wood-nymph, and a sweet girl playing upon a flute, habited according to a picture of Calypso by David. On the whole, there was certainly more fancy, more taste, and more elegance, than in an English party of the same description; though there was not so many handsome women as would have been the proportion of such an assembly in England.

From La Fleche to Angers, and thence to Ancennis, the country is a complete garden. The hills were covered with vines; every wood had its chateau, and every village its church. The peasantry were clean and happy, the children cheerful and healthful looking, and the greater part of the younger women spirited and handsome. There was a great plenty of fruit; and as we passed through the villages, it was invariably brought to us, and almost as invariably any pecuniary return refused with a retreating curtsey. One sweet girl, a young peasant, with eyes and complexion which would be esteemed handsome even in Philadelphia, having made Mr. Young and myself an offering of this kind, replied very prettily to our offer of money, that the women of La Fleche never sold either grapes or water; as much as to say that the one was as plentiful as the other. Some of these young girls were dressed not only neatly but tastily. Straw hats are the manufacture of the province; few of them, therefore, but had a straw bonnet, and few of these bonnets were without ribbons or flowers.

We remained at Oudon till near sunset, when we resumed our road to Ancennis, where we intended to sleep. As this was only a distance of seven miles, we took it very leisurely, sometimes riding and sometimes walking. The evening was as beautiful as is usual in the southern parts of

Europe at this season of the year. The road was most romantically recluse, and so serpentine as never to be visible beyond a hundred yards. The nightingales were singing in the adjoining woods. The road, moreover, was bordered on each side by lofty hedges, intermingled with fruit-trees, and even vines in full bearing. At every half-mile a crossroad, branching from the main one, led into the recesses of the country, or to some castle or villa on the high grounds which look to the river. At some of these bye-ways were very curious inscriptions, painted on narrow boards affixed to a tree. Such were, "The way to 'My Heart's Content' is half a league up this road, and then turn to the right, and keep on till you reach it." And another, "The way to 'Love's Hermitage' is up this lane, till you come to the cherry-tree by the side of a chalk-pit, where there is another direction." Mademoiselle Sillery informed me, that these kind of inscriptions were characteristic of the banks of the Loire.

"The inhabitants along the whole of the course of this river," said she, "have the reputation, from time immemorial, of being all native poets; and the reputation, like some prophecies, has perhaps been the means of realizing itself. You do not perhaps know that the Loire is called in the provinces the River of Love: and doubtless its beautiful banks, its green meadows, and its woody recesses, have what the musicians would call a symphony of tone with that passion." I have translated this sentence verbally from my note-book, as it may give some idea of Mademoiselle Sillery. If ever a figure was formed to inspire the passion of which she spoke, it was this lady. Many days and years must pass over before I forget our walk on the green road from Oudon to Ancennis—one of the sweetest, softest scenes in France.

We entered the forest of Ancennis as the sun was setting This forest is celebrated, in every ancient French ballad, as being the haunt of fairies, and the scene of the ancient archery of the provinces of Bretagne and Anjou. The road through it was over a green turf, in which the marks of a wheel were scarcely visible. The forest on each side was very thick. At short intervals, narrow footpaths struck into the wood. Our carriage had been sent before to Ancenis, and we were walking merrily on, when the well-known sound of the French horn arrested our steps and attention. Mademoiselle Sillery immediately guessed it to proceed from a company of archers; and in a few moments her conjecture was verified by the appearance of two ladies and a gentleman, who issued from one of the narrow paths. The ladies, who were merely running from the gentleman, were very tastily habited in the favorite French dress after the Dian of David; whilst the blue silk jacket and hunting-cap of the gentleman gave him the appearance of a groom about to ride a race. Our appearance necessarily took their attention; and after an exchange of salutes, but in which no names were mentioned on either side, they invited us to accompany them to their party, who were refreshing themselves in an adjoining dell. "We have had a party at archery," said one of them, "and Madame St. Amande has won the silver bugle and bow. The party is now at supper, after which we go to the chateau to dance. Perhaps you will not suffer us to repent having met you, by refusing to accompany us." Mademoiselle Sillery was very eager to accept this invitation, and looked rather blank when Mrs. Young declined it, as she wished to proceed on her road as quickly as possible. "You will at least accompany us, merely to see the party." "By all means," said Mademoiselle Sillery. "I must really regret that I cannot," said Mrs. Young. "If it must be so," resumed the lady who was inviting us, "let us exchange tokens, and we may meet again." This proposal, so perfectly new to me, was accepted: the fair archers gave our ladies their pearl crescents, which had the appearance of being of considerable value. Madame Young returned something which I did not see: Mademoiselle Sillery gave a silver Cupid, which had served her for an essence-bottle. The gentleman then shaking hands with us, and the ladies embracing each other, we parted mutually satisfied. "Who are these ladies?" demanded I. "You know them as well as we do," replied Mademoiselle Sillery. "And is it thus," said I, "that you receive all strangers indiscriminately?" "Yes," replied she, "all strangers of a certain condition. Where they are evidently of our own rank, we know of no reserve. Indeed, why should we? It is to general advantage to be pleased, and to please each other." "But you embraced them as if you really felt an affection for them." "And I did feel that affection for them," said she, "as long as I was with them. I would have done them every service in my power, and would even have made sacrifices to serve them." "And yet if you were to see them again, you would perhaps not know them." "Very possibly," replied she. "But I can see no reason why every affection should be necessarily permanent. We never pretend to permanence. We are certainly transient, but not insincere."

In this conversation we reached Ancennis, a village on a green surrounded by forests. Some of the cottages, as we saw them by moonlight, seemed most delightfully situated; and the village had altogether that air of quietness and of rural retreat, which characterizes the scenery of the Loire. Our horses having preceded us by an hour or more, everything was prepared for us when we reached our inn. A turkey had been put down to roast, and I entered the kitchen in time to prevent its being spoilt by French cookery. Mademoiselle Sillery had the table provided in an instant with silver forks and table-linen. Had a Parisian seen a table thus set out at Ancenis, without knowing that we had brought all these requisites with us, he would not have credited his senses. The inns in France along the banks of the Loire are less deficient in substantial comforts than in these ornamental appendages. Poultry is everywhere cheap, and in great plenty; but a French inn-keeper has no idea of a table-cloth, and still less of a clean one. He will give you food and a feather-bed, but you must provide yourselves with sheets and table-cloths.

A House and Grounds.

FROM COWLEY, SIR WILLIAM TEMPLE, LADY WINCHILSEA,
AND MACKENZIE.

"I've often wished that I had clear,
For life, six hundred pounds a-year,
A handsome house to lodge a friend,
A river at my garden's end,
A terrace walk, and half a rood
Of land set out to plant a wood."

FEW indeed are the persons that in the course of their lives have not entertained wishes of the like sort. Sometimes they have realized them; sometimes been disappointed by the realization itself. In the latter case, the fault is neither in the wish nor in the things wished for. The wish is good, if only as a pleasure of the imagination and an encouragement to the means for attaining its object; and the things are found to be very good indeed, by those whose temperaments and habits qualify them for the enjoyment. Stories of unhappy millionaires who retire only to find the country tedious, of tallow-chandlers who yearn for their melting days, and even of poets discontented with their "groves," prove but the want of previous fitness, or of sufficient good health. The tallow-chandler should have cultivated something besides long-sixes, and the poet should not have sate reading about his groves till the state of his biliary vessels hindered his enjoyment when he got them.* There is, however, a great deal of difference in those cases. That of the tallow-chandler, if he knows nothing but tallow and is not in a patient state of health, is hopeless, for he is neither clever nor poor enough to be able to go and help the village carpenter. He must needs quit his roses for the melting-tub, and in very desperation grows richer than he was before. But the love of groves and gardens being a habit of the poet's mind, he bears ill-health better with them than without them; complaint itself comforts him more than it does other men, for he complains in verse; and it is not to be supposed that Shenstone, with all his desire of visitors, and Cowley, with all his child-like disappointments as to "rustic innocence," did not pass many happy, or at least many soothing, days in their country abodes. Shenstone, in particular, must have largely partaken of the pleasures of a creator, for he invented the lovely scenes about his house, and saw to their execution.

It would be a good work in some writer to collect instances of this kind of disappointment and the reverse, and show how entirely each was to be attributed to particular circumstances, and not to that universal doom so falsely predicated of all human expectations. Great names prove nothing against counter-examples. Solomon himself may have been disappointed; but it was not because he was the "wisest of men;" it was because he had been too rich and luxurious, and so far one of the foolishest. We do not find that his brother philosopher, Epicurus, was disappointed; for he was poor and temperate, and thus was enabled to enjoy his garden to the last. There have been abdicated monarchs who wished to resume their thrones—royal tallow-chandlers who could not do without their melting levee-days; but such was not the case with Diocletian, who had a taste for gardening. On the contrary, he told the ambassadors who came to tempt him back to power, that if they knew what pleasure he took in his "cabbages," they would hate to go back themselves. Swift, who imitated from Horace the verses at the head of this article, would never have been happy in retirement, for he had a restless blood, and his good consisted in the attainment of power. He must have written with greater zest the lines a little further on:—

> "But here a grievance seems to lie,
> All this is mine but till I die;
> I can't but think 'twould sound more clever,
> To me and to my heirs forever."

But his friend Pope set up his rest early in life at Twickenham, and never desired to leave it. Ill-health itself in him was luckily of a kind that made him tranquil. The author of the *Seasons* never tired of the country. White of Selborne never tired of it. Both found incessant occupation in watching the proceedings of the Nature they loved.

It must be observed of Thomson, however, that he lived so near town as to be able to visit it whenever he chose. His house was at beautiful Richmond. I doubt not he would have been happy anywhere with a few trees and friends; but he liked a play also, and streets, and human movement. He would fain not go so far from London as not to be able to interchange the delights of town and country. And why should anybody that can help it? The loveliest country can be found within that reasonable distance, especially in these days of railroads. You may bury yourself in as healthy, if not as wide, a solitude as if you were in the Highlands; and, in an hour or two, you can enhance the pleasures of returning to it, by a book of your own buying, or a toy for your children. To resign forever the convenience and pleasures of intercourse with a great city would be desired by few; and it would be least of all desired (except under very particular circumstances) by those who can enjoy the country most; because the power to discern, and the disposition to be pleased, are equally the secrets of the enjoyment in both cases. These, and a congenial occupation, will make a conscientious man happy anywhere if he has decent health; and if he is sickly, no earthly comforts can supply the want of them, no, not even the affection of those about him: for what is affection, if it show nothing but the good hearts of those who feel it, and is wasted on a thankless temper? Acquirement of information, benignity, something to do, and as many things as possible to love, these are the secrets of happiness in town or country. If White of Selborne had been a town instead of a country clergyman, he would have told us all about the birds in the city as well as the suburbs. We should have had the best reason given us why lime-trees flourish in London smoke; lists of flowers for our windows would have been furnished us, together with their times of blooming; we should have been told of the Ratopolis under ground, as well as of the dray-horses above it; and perhaps the discoverer of the double *spiracula* in the noses of stags would have found out the reason why tallow-chandlers have no noses at all.

Now, what sort of house would most take the fancy of readers who enjoy a book like the present? We mean for repose and comfort, apart from the nobler and severer pleasures (very rare ones) arising from discharging the duties belonging to a large estate. Certainly not the house belonging to such an estate; not a house like Pliny's, the size and " set out" of which it is a labor to read of; not the cold southern halls of the Romans or Italians, unfit for this climate; nor an ancient Greek, nor modern Eastern house, with the women's apartments imprisoned off from the rest; nor an old French chateau (except in Mrs. Radcliffe's romances)—for though pretty to read of, as belonging to the Montmorencys or the Rambouillets, it was inconvenient inside, and had formal grounds without; nor the lumbering old German house, such as Goethe describes it, though habit and love may have sanctified all these; no, nor even the princely palace of Chatsworth, though it be as full of taste as the owner, and of fragrance from conservatories as of blessings from the poor. Comfortable rooms, doubtless, are to be found in that palace; nay, snug ones; for the height of taste implies the height of good sense; and such a nest and corner-loving mood of the mind as that epithet designates, we may be sure is not unprovided for. Yet the corner still is in the great house; is a part of it; cannot get rid of it; is shouldered and (of any other such mansion you might say) scorned by it. We must have been used to such houses all our lives (which is seldom the case with those whose luxuries lie in books), otherwise we cannot settle ourselves comfortably in idea to the extent and responsibilities of all those suits of apartments, those corridors, pillars, galleries, looks out and looks in, and to the visitations of the steward. It is not a house, but a set of houses thrown into one; not a nest, but a range under cover; not a privacy, but a publicity and an empire! Admiration and blessing be upon it, for it is the great house of a good man and his large heart fits it well; and yet assuredly, in the eyes of us lovers of nooks and books, the idea of him never seems so happy as when it contracts its princely dimensions, and stoops into such cottage rooms as some in which we have had the pleasure of beholding him.

But we must not digress in this manner, with an impertinence however respectful.

The house to be desiderated by the lover of books in ordinary, is a warm, cosy, picturesque, irregular house, either old but not fragile, or new but built upon some good principle; a house possessing, nevertheless, modern comforts; neither big enough to require riches, nor small enough to cause inconvenience; more open to the sun than otherwise; yet with trees about it, and the sight of more; a prospect on one of the sides, to give it a sense of freedom, but a closer scene in front, to insure the sense of snugness; a garden neither wild nor formal; or rather two gardens, if possible, though not of expensive size; one to remind him of the time of his ancestors, a "trim garden," with pattern beds of flowers, lavender, &c., and a terrace—the other of a freer sort, with a shrubbery, and turf and trees; a bowling-green by all means; (what sane person would be without a bowling-green?) a rookery; a dove-cote; a brook; a paddock; a heath for air; hill and dale for variety; walks in a forest, trunks of trees for seats; towers "embosomed" in their companions; pastures, cottages; a town not far off; an abbey close by; mountains in the distance; a glimpse of sails in a river, but not large sails; a combination, in short, of all which is the most——

But hold. One twentieth part of all this will suffice, if the air be good, and the neighbors congenial; a cottage, an old farm-house, anything solid and not ugly, always excepting the mere modern house, which looks like a barrack, or like a workhouse, or like a chapel, or like a square box with holes cut into it for windows, or a great bit of cheese or hearth-stone, or yellow ochre. It has a gravel walk up to the door, and a bit of unhappy creeper trying to live upon it; and (under any possible circumstances of quittal) is a disgrace to inhabit.

As to the garden, the only absolute *sine qua non* is a few good brilliant beds of flowers, some grass, some shade, and a bank. But if there is a bee-hive in a corner it is better; and if there is a bee-hive, there ought to be a brook, provided it is clear, and the soil gravelly.

> "There, in some covert, by a brook,
> Where no profaner eye may look,
> Hide me from day's garish eye;
> While the bee with honied thigh,
> That at her flowery work doth sing,
> And the waters murmuring,
> With such concert as they keep,
> Entice the dewy-feather'd sleep."

Beware, though, as Gray says, "of *agues*." It is good in the land of poetry, to sleep by a brook; but in Middlesex it is best to do it in one's chamber. The best place to take a nap in, out of doors, in this lovely but moist country, is a hay-field.

But we are detaining the reader from the houses and gardens provided for him by his books. What signify any others, while the enjoyment of these is upon us? May-Fair or Saint Mary Axe can alike rejoice in them. The least luxurious room in a street, provided there be but quiet enough to read by, or imagination enough to forget one's self, enables us to be put in possession of a paradise.

We shall begin with the modest retreat desiderated by Cowley, and the eulogy which he has delivered on gardens in general. His style is as sweet and sincere as his wishes. The poetical portion of his essay is addressed to the famous English country gentleman and sylvan patriot, his friend Evelyn, who realized all and more than the sensitive poet did, because his means were greater and his complexion more healthy. But Cowley must have had delicious moments both in fancy and possession; and if there be gardens in heaven resembling those on earth (which some have thought, and which is not so unheavenly a notion as many that are held divine), his innocent heart is surely the inhabitant of one of the best of them.

THOUGHTS OF COWLEY ON A GARDEN.

FROM A LETTER TO EVELYN.

I NEVER had any other desire so strong, and so like to covetousness, as that one which I have had always, that I might be master at last of a small house and large garden, with very moderate conveniences joined to them, and there dedicate the remainder of my life, only to the culture of them, and study of nature;

"And there (with no design beyond my wall) whole and entire to lie,
In no unactive ease, and no unglorious poverty."

Or, as Virgil has said, shorter and better for me, that I might there

"Studiis florere ignobilis oti;"*

though I could wish that he had rather said, "Nobilis oti," when he spoke of his own.

* [Take studious flower in undistinguished ease.]

THOUGHTS OF COWLEY ON A GARDEN.

Among many other arts and excellences which you enjoy, I am glad to find this favorite of mine the most predominant. I know nobody that possesses more private happiness than you do in your garden; and yet no man who makes his happiness more public, by a free communication of the art and knowledge of it to others. All that I myself am able yet to do, is only to recommend to mankind the search of that felicity, which you instruct them how to find out and to enjoy.

Happy art thou, whom God does bless
With the full choice of thine own happiness;
    And happier yet, because thou'rt blest
    With prudence how to choose the best.
In books and gardens, thou hast plac'd aright
    (Things which thou well dost understand,
And both dost make with thy laborious hand)
    Thy noble innocent delight:
And in thy virtuous wife, where thou again dost meet
    Both pleasures more refin'd and sweet,
    The fairest garden in her looks,
    And in her mind the wisest books.
Oh, who would change these soft, yet solid joys,
    For empty shows, and senseless noise;
    And all which rank ambition breeds,
Which seem such beauteous flowers, and are such poisonous
    weeds?

When Epicurus to the world had taught
    That pleasure was the chiefest good,
(And was perhaps i' th' right, if rightly understood),
    His life he to his doctrine brought,
And in a garden's shade that sovereign pleasure sought:

Whoever a true epicure would be,
May there find cheap and virtuous luxury
Vitellius' table, which did hold
As many creatures as the ark of old,
That fiscal table to which every day
All countries did a constant tribute pay,
Could nothing more delicious afford,
    Than nature's liberality
Help'd with a little art and industry
Allows the meanest gard'ner's board.
The wanton taste no fish or fowl can choose,
For which the grape or melon she would lose
Though all th' inhabitants of sea and air
Be listed in the glutton's bill of fare,
    Yet still the fruits of earth we see
Plac'd the third story high in all her luxury.

Where does the wisdom and the power divine
In a more bright and sweet reflection shine,—
Where do we finer strokes and colors see
Of the Creator's real poetry,
    Than when we with attention look
Upon the third day's volume of the book?
If we could open and intend our eye,
    We all, like Moses, should espy,
Ev'n in a bush, the radiant Deity.
But we despise these his inferior ways
(Though no less full of miracle and praise) :
    Upon the flowers of heaven we gaze;
The stars of earth no wonder in us raise,
    Though these perhaps do, more than they,
    The life of mankind sway.
Although no part of mighty nature be

More stor'd with beauty, power and mystery,
Yet, to encourage human industry,
God has so order'd, that no other part
Such space and such dominion leaves for art.

We nowhere art do so triumphant see,
  As when it grafts or buds the tree :
In other things we count it to excel,
If it a docile scholar can appear
To nature, and but imitate her well ;
It over-rules and is her master here.
It imitates her Maker's power divine,
And changes her sometimes and sometimes does refine
It does, like grace, the fallen tree restore,
To its blest state of Paradise before.
Who would not joy to see his conquering hand
O'er all the vegetable world command ?
And the wild giants of the wood receive
  What law he's pleas'd to give ?
He bids th' ill-natur'd crab produce
The gentler apple's winy juice,
The golden fruit that worthy is
Of Galatea's purple kiss :
He does the savage hawthorn teach
To bear the medlar and the pear ;
He bids the rustic plum to rear
A noble trunk, and be a peach.
Even Daphne's coyness he doth mock,
And weds the cherry to her stock.
Though she refus'd Apollo's suit,
  Even she, that chaste and virgin tree,
  Now wonders at herself to see
That she's a mother made, and blushes in her fruit.

Methinks I see great Dioclesian walk
In the Salonian garden's noble shade,
Which by his own imperial hands was made;
I see him smile (methinks) as he does talk
With th' ambassadors who come in vain
    T' entice him to a throne again.
If I, my friends (said he), should to you show
All the delights which in these gardens grow,
'Tis likelier much that you should with me stay,
Than 'tis that you should carry me away.
And trust me not, my friends, if every day
    I walk not here with more delight
Than ever, after the most happy fight,
In triumph to the capitol I rode,
To thank the gods, and to be thought, myself, almost a god.

    A noble finish that, to a sometimes prosaical, often poetical, and always engaging and thoughtful effusion.
    The garden possessed by Cowley's friend Evelyn was at his seat of Sayes Court, Deptford. It contained, among other beauties, an enormous hedge of holly, which made a glorious show in winter time with its shining red berries. The Czar Peter, who came to England in Evelyn's time, and occupied his house, took delight (by way of procuring himself a strong Russian sensation), in being drawn through this hedge " in a wheel-barrow !" He left it in sad condition accordingly, to the disgust and lamentation of the owner. The garden cuts rather a formal and solemn figure, to modern eyes, in the engravings that remain of it. But such engravings can suggest little of color and movement of flowers and the breathing trees; and our ancestors had more reason to admire those old orderly creations of theirs than modern improvement allows. We are too apt to suppose that one thing cannot be good, because another is better; or that an improvement cannot too often reject what it might include or ameliorate. There was no want of enthusiasm in the admirers of the old style, whether they were right or wrong. Hear what an arbiter of taste in the next age said of it, the famous Sir William Temple. He was an honest

statesman and mild Epicurean philosopher, in the real sense of that designation; that is to say, temperate and reflecting, and fonder of a garden and the friends about him than of anything else. He was a great cultivator of fruit. He had the rare pleasure of obtaining the retirement he loved; first at Sheen, near Richmond, in Surrey, which is the place alluded to in the following "Thoughts on Retirement;" and, secondly, at Moor Park, near Farnham, in the same county—a residence probably named after the Moor Park which he eulogizes in the subsequent description of a garden. In the garden of his house at Farnham he directed that his heart should be buried; and it was. The sun-dial, under which he desired it might be deposited, is still remaining.

SIR WILLIAM TEMPLE'S THOUGHTS ON RETIREMENT.

FROM ONE OF HIS LETTERS.

AS the country life, and this part of it more particularly (gardening), were the inclination of my youth itself, so they are the pleasure of my age; and I can truly say, that, among many great employments that have fallen to my share, I have never asked or sought for any one of them, but often endeavored to escape from them into the ease and freedom of a private scene, where a man may go his own way and his own pace, in the common paths or circles of life.

> "Inter cuncta leges et per cunctabere doctos
> Qua ratione queas traducere leniter ævum,
> Quid minuat curæ, quid te tibi reddet amicum;
> Quid pure tranquillet, honos, an dulce lucellum,
> An secretum iter, et fallentis semita vitæ."

> But above all the learned read, and ask
> By what means you may gently pass your age,
> What lessens care, what makes thee thine own friend,
> What truly calms the mind; honor, or wealth,
> Or else a private path of stealing life

These are the questions that a man ought at least to ask himself, whether he asks others or no, and to choose his course of life rather by his own humor and temper, than by common accidents, or advice of friends; at least if the Spanish proverb be true, That a fool knows more in his own house than a wise man in another's.

The measure of choosing well is, whether a man likes what he has chosen; which, I thank God, is what has befallen me; and though among the follies of my life, building and planting have not been the least, and have cost me more than I have the confidence to own, yet they have been fully recompensed by the sweetness and satisfaction of this retreat, where, since my resolution taken of never entering again into any public employments, I have passed five years without ever going once to town, though I am almost in sight of it and have a house there always ready to receive me. Nor has this been any sort of affectation, as some have thought it, but a mere want of desire or humor to make so small a remove: for when I am in this corner, I can truly say with Horace,

> "Me quoties reficit gelidus Digentia rivus,
> Quid sentire putas, quid credis, amice, precari?
> Sit mihi, quod nunc est, etiam minus, ut mihi vivam
> Quod superest ævi, si quid superesse volunt Di.
> Sit bona librorum, et provisæ frugis in annum
> Copia, ne fluitem dubiæ spe pendulus horæ;
> Hoc satis est orare Jovem, qui donat et aufert."

> Me when the cold Digentian stream revives,
> What does my friend believe I think or ask?
> Let me yet less possess, so I may live,
> Whate'er of life remains, unto myself.
> May I have books enough, and one year's store,
> Not to depend upon each doubtful hour;
> This is enough of mighty Jove to pray,
> Who, as he pleases, gives and takes away.

AN OLD ENGLISH GARDEN OF THE SEVEN-TEENTH CENTURY.

FROM THE ESSAYS OF SIR WILLIAM TEMPLE.

THE perfectest figure of a garden I ever saw, either at home or abroad, was that of Moor Park in Hertfordshire, when I knew it about thirty years ago. It was made by the Countess of Bedford, esteemed among the greatest wits of her time, and celebrated by Dr. Donne. I will describe it for a model to those that meet with such a situation, and are above the regards of common expense. It lies on the side of a hill (upon which the house stands), but not very steep. The length of the house, where the best rooms and of most use or pleasure are, lies upon the breadth of the garden. The great parlor opens into the middle of a terras gravel-walk that lies even with it, and which may be, as I remember, about three hundred paces long, and broad in proportion; the border set with standard laurels, and at large distances, which have the beauty of orange-trees, out of flower and fruit. From this walk are three descents by many stone steps, in the middle and at each end, into a very large parterre. This is divided into quarters by gravel-walks, and adorned by two fountains and eight statues in the several quarters. At the end of the terras-walk are two summer-houses, and the sides of the parterre are ranged with two large cloisters, open to the garden, upon arches of stone, and ending with two other summer-houses even with the cloisters, which are paved with stone, and designed for walks of shade, there being none other in the whole parterre. Over these two cloisters are two terrasses covered with lead, and fenced with balusters; and the passage into these airy walks is out of the two summer-houses at the end of the first terras-walk. The cloister facing the south is covered with vines, and would have been proper for an orange-house, and the other for myrtles, or other more common greens,* and had, I doubt not, been cast for that purpose, if this piece of gardening had been in as much vogue as it is now.

From the middle of the parterre is a descent by many steps, flying on each side of a grotto that lies between them (covered with lead, and flat) into the lower garden, which is all fruit-trees, ranged about the several quarters of a wilderness which is very shady. The walks here are all green, the grotto embellished with figures of shell-rock-work, fountains, and water-works. If the hill had not ended with the lower garden, and the wall were not bounded by a common way that goes through the park, they might have added a third quarter of all greens; but this want is supplied by a garden on the other side the house, which is all of that sort, very wild very shady, and adorned with rough rock-work and fountains.

This was Moor Park when I was acquainted with it, and the sweetest place, I think, that I have seen in my life, either before or since, at home or abroad. What it is now I can give little account, having passed through several hands that have made great changes in gardens as well as houses; but the remembrance of what it was is too pleasant ever to forget.

The taste of Sir William Temple in gardening prevailed more or less up to the time of George the Third; but though Milton had in some degree countenanced it, or appeared to do so, in the couplet in which he speaks of

"Retired leisure,
That in *trim* gardens takes his pleasure,"

yet the very universality of right feeling natural to a poet could not help running out of such bounds, when he came to describe a garden fit for paradise. Spenser had set him the example in his "Bower of

* *Greens* formerly meant plants in general.

Bliss;" and Tasso, who is supposed to have drawn from some actual gardens in his own time, had set Spenser himself the example in his beautiful account of the bowers of Armida. The probability is, that in all great ages Nature had spoken on the subject, in particular instances, to the feelings of genius. Even the Chinese are thought to have anticipated the modern taste, though with their usual semi-barbarous mixture of clumsy magnificence and petty details; possibly not always so much so, as the startled invidiousness of their betters has supposed. The Chinese, at all events, are very fond of flowers, and show a truly poetical appreciation of their merits, as may be seen in the charming novel of *Ju-Kiao-Li*. Milton's garden of Eden made a great impression, when Addison dug it up for the general benefit in his articles on the great poet in the *Spectator*. Pope's good sense was naturally on the side of it; and Shenstone gave into it with practical and masterly enthusiasm. Hence the rise of what is called landscape gardening. The new taste ran a little wild at first in the hands of "Kent and Nature;" then incurred another danger in more mechanical hands; but has finally become the best that ever existed, by the combination of a liberal feeling for nature with the avowed and local reasonableness of art. Gardens are now adapted to places, to climates, and to the demands of the presence of a house; that is to say, to the compromise which the house naturally tends to make between something like the orderliness and comfort inside of it, and the nature which art goes forth to meet. This is the reason why we have said we should like to have two gardens, if possible: one modified from the old terraces and parterres and formal groves of our ancestors, and the other from the wildness of "Kent and Nature." If required to choose between the two, we should say, Give us anything comprising a few trees, a few flowers, a plot of grass, a bench, and seclusion;—anything in which we could pace up and down, sit when we pleased, see a little brilliant color, a good deal of green, and not be overlooked. Whatever did this best, we should like best, whether made by art or nature.

There was a lady in the time of Pope, a true poetess (if she had but known it and taken pains), Lady Winchilsea, a friend of his, who had as thorough a taste for seclusion on the romantic side as ever existed. Her maiden name was Kingsmill; her husband the fifth Earl of Winchilsea, of the same family that now possess the title. Anne Kingsmill was an open-hearted, excellent creature; she made a loving friend and wife; is one of the very few original observers of nature (as Wordsworth has remarked) who appeared in an artificial age; and deserves to have been gathered into collections of English verse far more than half of our minor poets. We will give a taste or two of this lady's style from her poem on the subject of retirement, and then conclude the present department of our book with two papers out of the periodical works of Mackenzie, worthy to have been read by herself, and more suited to the desires of readers in general. There is a great deal more of the poem, all creditable to the writer's turn of mind, but not choice enough in style for a book of selection. We beg the reader's admiration for the burden at the close of each paragraph.

PETITION FOR AN ABSOLUTE RETREAT.

FROM A POEM BY THE COUNTESS OF WINCHILSEA.

GIVE me, O indulgent Fate,
Give me yet before I die,
A sweet, but absolute retreat,
'Mongst paths so lost, and trees so high,
That the world may ne'er invade,
Through such windings and such shade,
My unshaken liberty.
 No intruders thither come,
Who visit but to be from home;
None who their vain moments pass
Only studious of their glass.
News, that charm to listening ears,
That false alarm to hopes and fears,
That common theme for every fop
From the statesman to the shop,
In these coverts ne'er be spread;
Of who's deceas'd or who's to wed
Be no tidings thither brought;
But silent as a midnight thought,

Where the world may ne'er invade,
Be those windings and that shade.
   Courteous Fate! afford me there
A table spread, without my care,
With what the neighb'ring fields impart,
Whose cleanliness be all its art.
When of old the calf was drest
(Though to make an angel's feast)
In the plain, unstudied sauce
Nor truffle, nor morillia was,
Nor cou'd the mighty patriarch's board
One far-fetch'd ortolan afford.
Courteous Fate, then give me there
Only plain and wholesome fare.
Fruits indeed (wou'd Heaven bestow)
All that did in Eden grow,
All, but the *forbidden tree,*
Wou'd be coveted by me;
Grapes with juice so crowded up,
As breaking thro' the native cup;
Figs (yet growing) candy'd o'er
By the sun's attracting pow'r;
Cherries, with the downy peach,
All within my easy reach;
Whilst creeping near the humble ground
Shou'd the strawberry be found,
Springing wheresoe'er I stray'd
Thro' those windings and that shade.
   Give me there (since Heaven has shown
It was not good to be alone)
A partner suited to my mind,
Solitary, pleas'd, and kind;

Who, partially, may something see
Preferr'd to all the world in me;
Slighting, by my humble side,
Fame and splendor, wealth and pride.
When but two the earth possest,
'Twas their happiest days, and best;
They by business, nor by wars,
They by no domestic cares,
From each other e'er were drawn,
But in some grove or flow'ry lawn
Spent the swiftly flying time,
Spent their own and nature's prime
In love, that only passion given
To perfect man, whilst friends with Heaven
Rage, and jealousy, and hate,
Transports of his fallen state,
When by Satan's wiles betray'd,
Fly those windings, and that shade!
Let me then, indulgent Fate!
Let me still in my retreat
From all roving thoughts be freed,
Or aims that may contention breed;
Nor be my endeavors led
By goods that perish with the dead!
Fitly might the life of man
Be indeed esteem'd a span,
If the present moment were
Of delight his only share;
If no other joys he knew
Than what round about him grew:
But as those whose stars would trace
From a subterranean place,

Through some engine lift their eyes
To the outward glorious skies;
So th' immortal spirit may,
When descended to our clay,
From a rightly govern'd frame
View the height from whence she came;
To her Paradise be caught,
And things unutterable taught.
Give me, then, in that retreat,
Give me, O indulgent Fate!
For all pleasures left behind,
Contemplations of the mind.
Let the fair, the gay, the vain,
Courtship and applause obtain;
Let th' ambitious rule the earth;
Let the giddy fool have mirth;
Give the epicure his dish,
Every one their several wish;
Whilst my transports I employ
On that more extensive joy,
When all Heaven shall be survey'd
From those windings and that shade.

An old Country House and an old Lady.

FROM MACKENZIE'S "LOUNGER," NO. 87.

The old lady described in the following charming paper of Mackenzie (which was a favorite with Sir Walter Scott), is not of so large-minded an order as Lady Winchilsea, but she has as good a heart; is very touching and pleasant; and her abode suits her admirably. It is the remnant of something that would have been greater in a greater age. We fancy her countenance to have been one that would have reminded us of the charming old face in Drayton:

> "Ev'n in the aged'st face where beauty once did dwell,
> And Nature in the least but seemed to excel,
> Time cannot make such waste, but something will appear
> To show some little tract of delicacy there."
>
> *Polyolbion.*

The reader, perhaps, hardly requires to be told that Mackenzie, whose writings have been gathered into the British classics, was a Scottish gentleman, bred to the bar, who in his youth wrote the once popular novel called the *Man of Feeling*, and died not long ago at a reverend age, universally regretted. He was the editor and principal writer of the two periodical works called the *Mirror* and *Lounger*, to which several of the reigning Scottish wits contributed. He was not a very original or powerful writer, but he was a very shrewd, elegant, and pleasing one, a happy offset from Addison; and he sometimes showed great pathos. His stories of *La Roche* and *Louisa Venoni* are among the most affecting in the world, and free from the somewhat morbid softness of his novel. We are the happier in being able to do this tardy, though very unnecessary justice to the merits of a good man and a graceful essayist, because in the petulance and presumption of youth we had mistaken our incompetence to judge them for the measure of their pretensions.

I HAVE long cultivated a talent very fortunate for a man of my disposition, that of travelling in my easy chair; of transporting myself, without stirring from my parlor, to distant places and to absent friends; of drawing scenes in my mind's eye; and of peopling them with the groups of fancy, or the society of remembrance. When I have sometimes lately felt the dreariness of the town, deserted by my acquaintance; when I have returned from the coffee-house, where the boxes were unoccupied, and strolled out from my accustomed walk, which even the lame beggar had left, I was fain to shut myself up in my room, order a dish of my best tea (for there is a sort of melancholy which disposes one to make much of one's self), and calling up the powers of memory and imagination, leave the solitary town for a solitude more interesting, which my younger days enjoyed in the country, which I think, and if I am wrong I do not wish to be undeceived, was the most Elysian spot in the world.

'Twas at an old lady's, a relation and godmother of mine, where a particular incident occasioned my being left during the vacation of two successive seasons. Her house was formed out of the remains of an old Gothic castle, of which one tower was still almost entire; it was tenanted by kindly daws and swallows. Beneath, in a modernized part of the house, resided the mistress of the mansion. The house was skirted by a few majestic elms and beeches, and the stumps of several others showed that once they had been more numerous. To the west a clump of firs covered a rugged rocky dell, where the rooks claimed a prescriptive seignory. Through this a dashing rivulet forced its way, which afterwards grew quiet in its progress; and gurgling gently through a piece of downy meadow-ground, crossed the bottom of the garden, where a little rustic paling enclosed a washing-green, and a wicker seat, fronting the south, was placed for the accommodation of the old lady, whose lesser tour, when her fields did not require a visit, used to terminate in this spot. Here, too, were ranged the hives for her bees, whose hum, in a still warm sunshine, soothed the good old lady's indolence, while their proverbial industry was sometimes quoted for the instruction of her washers. The brook ran brawling through some underwood on the outside of the garden, and soon after formed a little cascade, which fell into the river that winded through a valley in front of the house. When hay-making or harvest was going on, my godmother took her long stick in her hand, and overlooked the labors of the mowers or reapers; though I believe there was little thrift in the superintendency, as the visit generally cost her a draught of beer or a dram, to encourage their diligence.

Within doors she had so able an assistant, that her labor was little. In that department an old man-servant was her minister, the father of my Peter, who serves me not the less faithfully that we have gathered nuts together in my godmother's hazel-bank. This old butler (I call him by his title of honor, though in truth he had many subordinate offices) had originally enlisted with her husband, who went into the army a youth (though he afterwards married and became a country gentleman), had been his servant abroad, and attended him during his last illness at home. His best hat, which he wore on Sundays, with a scarlet waistcoat of his master's, had still a cockade in it.

Her husband's books were in a room at the top of a screw staircase, which had scarce been opened since his death; but her own library, for Sabbath or rainy days, was ranged in a little book-press in the parlor. It consisted, so far as I can remember, of several volumes of sermons, a *Concordance*, *Thomas à Kempis*, *Antoninus's Meditations*, the works of the author of the *Whole Duty of Man*, and a translation of *Boethius;* the original editions of the *Spectator* and *Guardian*, *Cowley's Poems* (of which I had lost a volume soon after I first came about her house), *Baker's Chronicle*, *Burnet's History of his own Times*, *Lamb's Royal Cookery*, *Abercromby's Scots Warriors*, and *Nisbet's Heraldry*.

The subject of the last-mentioned book was my godmother's strong ground; and she could disentangle a point of genealogy beyond any one I ever knew. She had an excellent memory for anecdotes; and her stories, though sometimes long, were never tiresome; for she had been a woman of great beauty and accomplishment in her youth, and had kept such company as made the drama of her stories respectable and interesting. She spoke frequently of such of her own family as she remembered when a child, but scarcely ever of those she had lost, though one could see she thought of them often. She had buried a beloved husband and four children. Her youngest, Edward, "her beautiful her brave," fell in Flanders, and was not entombed with his ancestors. His picture, done when a child, an artless red and white portrait, smelling at a nosegay, but very like withal, hung at her bed-side, and his sword and gorget were crossed under it. When she spoke of a soldier, it was in a style above her usual simplicity; there was a sort of swell in her language, which sometimes a tear (for her age had not lost the privilege of tears) made still more eloquent. She kept her sorrows, like her devotions that solaced them, sacred to herself. They threw nothing of gloom over her deportment; a gentle shade only, like the fleckered clouds of summer, that increase, not diminish, the benignity of the season.

She had few neighbors, and still fewer visitors; but her reception of such as did visit her was cordial in the extreme. She pressed a little too much, perhaps; but there was so much heart and good-will in her importunity, as made her good things seem better than those of any other table. Nor was her attention confined only to the good fare of her guests, though it might have flattered her vanity more than that of most exhibitors of good dinners, because the cookery was generally directed by herself. Their servants lived as well in her hall, and their horses in her stable. She looked after the airing of their sheets, and saw their fires mended if the night was cold. Her old butler, who rose betimes, would never suffer anybody to mount his horse fasting.

The parson of the parish was her guest every Sunday, and said prayers in the evening. To say truth, he was no great genius, nor much a scholar. I believe my godmother knew rather more of divinity than he did; but she received from him information of another sort: he told her who were the poor, the sick, the dying of the parish, and she had some assistance, some comfort for them all.

I could draw the old lady at this moment! dressed in gray, with a clean white hood nicely plaited (for she was somewhat finical about the neatness of her person), sitting in her straight-backed elbow-chair, which stood in a large window, scooped out of the thickness of the ancient wall. The middle panes of the window were of painted glass—the story of Joseph and his brethren. On the outside waved a honeysuckle tree, which often threw its shade across her book or her work; but she would not allow it to be cut down. "It has stood there many a day," said she, "and we old inhabi tants should bear with one another." Methinks I see her thus seated, her spectacles on, but raised a little on her brow for a pause of explanation, their shagreen case laid between the leaves of a silver-clasped family Bible. On one side, her bell and snuff-box; on the other, her knitting apparatus in a blue damask bag.—Between her and the fire an old Spanish pointer, that had formerly been her son Edward's, teased, but not teased out of his gravity, by a little terrier of mine.—All this is before me, and I am a hundred miles from town, its inhabitants, and its business. In town I may have seen such a figure: but the country scenery around, like the tasteful frame of an excellent picture, gives it a heightening, a relief, which it would lose in any other situation.

Some of my readers, perhaps, will look with little relish on the portrait. I know it is an egotism in me to talk of its value; but over this dish of tea, and in such a temper of mind, one is given to egotism. It will be only adding another to say, that when I recall the rural scene of the good old lady's abode, her simple, her innocent, her useful employments, the afflictions she sustained in this world, the comforts she drew from another, I feel a serenity of soul, a benignity of affections, which I am sure confer happiness, and I think must promote virtue.

This delightful paper appears to have had its just effect on the readers of the *Lounger*. It produced some pleasant remarks from a correspondent who signed himself "Urbanus;" and these remarks produced a letter from the Editor himself, under the signature of "Adrastus," which contains a sort of character of an Old Gentleman to match that of the Old Lady, and has also a tone of reflection that will sensibly affect most readers, especially those at a similar time of life.

LOVE OF THE COUNTRY IN THE DECLINE OF LIFE.

FROM THE SAME, NO. 93.

SIR.—I, as well as your correspondent Urbanus, was very much pleased with your late paper on the moral use of the country, and the portrait of the excellent lady it contained. I am an old man, sir, but thank God, with all my faculties and feelings entire and alive about me; and your description recalled to my memory some worthy characters with which my youth was acquainted, and which, I am inclined to believe. I should find it a little difficult, were I even disposed to look out for them, to supply now. At my time of life, friends are a treasure which the fortunate may have preserved, but the most fortunate can hardly acquire; and if I am not mistaken in my opinion of the present race, there are not many friendships among them which I would be solicitous to acquire or they will be likely to preserve. It is not of their little irregularities or imprudencies I complain; I know these must always be expected and pardoned in the young; and there are few of us old people who can recollect our youthful days without having some things of that sort to blush for. No, Mr. Lounger, it is their prudence, their wisdom, their foresight, their policy, I find fault with. They put on the livery of the world so early, and have so few of the weaknesses of feeling or of fancy! To this cause I impute the want of that rural sentiment which your correspondent Urbanus seems to suppose is banished only from the country retreats of town dissipation, from the abodes of fashionable and frivolous people, who carry all the follies and pleasures of a city into scenes destined for rural simplicity and rural enjoyment. But in truth, sir, the people of the country themselves, who never knew fashionable life, or city dissipation, have now exchanged the simple-hearted pleasures which in my younger days were common among them, for ideas of a much more selfish sort. Most of my young acquaintance there (and I spend at least eight months of the year in the country) are really arrived at that prudent way of estimating things which we used to be diverted with in Hudibras:

> "For what's the value of a thing,
> But as much money as 'twill bring?"

Their ambition, their love, their friendship, all have this tendency; and their no-ambition, their no-love, their no-friendship, or, in one word, their indifference about every object from which some worldly advantage is not to be drawn, is equally observable on the other hand. On such a disposition, Mr. Lounger, what impression is to be made by rural objects or rural scenery? The visions which these paint in fancy, or the tender ties they have on remembrance, cannot find room in an imagination or a heart made callous by selfish and interested indifference. 'Tis with regret rather than resentment that I perceive this sort of turn so prevalent among the young people of my acquaintance, or those with whom I am connected. I have now, alas! no child of my own in whom I can either lament such a failing, or be proud of the want of it.

I think myself happy, sir, that, even at my advanced period of life, I am still susceptible of such impressions as those which our 87th Number imputes to rural contemplation. At this season, above all others, methinks they are to be enjoyed. Now in this fading time of the year, when the flush of vegetation and the glow of maturity is past, when the fields put on a sober or rather saddened appearance, I look on the well-known scenery around my country dwelling, as I would on a friend fallen from the pride of prosperity to a more humble and more interesting situation. The withering grass that whistles on the unsheltered bank; the fallen leaves strewed over the woodland path; the silence of the almost naked copse, which not long ago rung with the music of the birds; the flocking of their little tribes that seem mute with the dread of ills to come; the querulous call of the partridge in the bare brown field, and the soft low song of the redbreast from the household shed; this pensive landscape, with these plaintive accompaniments, dimmed by a gray October sky, which we look on with the thoughts of its shortened and still shortening light; all this presses on my bosom a certain still and gentle melancholy, which I would not part with for all the pleasure that mirth could give, for all the luxury that wealth could buy.

You say, truly, in one of your late papers, that poetry is almost extinguished among us: it is one of my old-fashioned propensities to be fond of poetry, to be delighted with its descriptions, to be affected by its sentiments. I find genuine poetry a sort of opening to the feelings of my mind, to which my own expression could not give vent; I see in its descriptions a picture more lively and better composed, than my own less distinct and less vivid ideas of the objects around me could furnish. It is with such impressions that I read the following lines of Thomson's Autumn introductive of the solemn and beautiful apostrophe to philosophic melancholy:—

> " But see the fading many-color'd woods,
> Shade deepening over shade, the country round
> Imbrown; a crowded umbrage, dusk and dun,
> Of every hue, from wan declining green
> To sooty dark. These now the lonesome muse,
> Low whispering, lead into their leaf-strown walks,
> And give the season in its latest view.

> "Meantime, light-shadowing all, a sober calm
> Fleeces unbounded ether; whose least wave
> Stands tremulous, uncertain where to turn
> The gentle current; while illumined wide
> The dewy-skirted clouds imbibe the sun,
> And through their lucid veil his soften'd force
> Shed o'er the peaceful world. Then is the time,
> For those whom wisdom and whom nature charm,
> To steal themselves from the degenerate crowd,
> And soar above this little scene of things;
> To tread low-thoughted vice beneath their feet,
> To soothe the throbbing passions into peace,
> And woo lone quiet in her silent walks."

About this time three years, sir, I had the misfortune to lose a daughter, the last survivor of my family, whom her mother, dying at her birth, left a legacy to my tenderness, who closed a life of the most exemplary goodness, of the most tender filial duty, of the warmest benevolence, of the most exalted piety, by a very gradual but not unperceived decay.

When I think on the returning season of this calamity, when I see the last fading flowers of autumn, which my Harriet used to gather with a kind of sympathetic sadness, and hear the small chirping note of the flocking linnets, which she used to make me observe as the elegy of the year! when I have drawn her picture in the midst of this rural scenery, and then reflected on her many virtues and accomplishments, on her early and unceasing attention to myself, her gentle and winning manners to every one around her; when I remember her resignation during the progress of her disorder, her unshaken and sublime piety in its latest stages; when these recollections filled my mind, in conjunction with the drooping images of the season, and the sense of my own waning period of life I feel a mixture of sadness and of com posure, of humility and of elevation of spirit, which I think, sir, a man would ill exchange for any degree of unfeeling prudence, or of worldly wisdom and indifference.

The attachment to rural objects is like that family affection which a warm and uncorrupted mind preserves for its relations and early acquaintance. In a town, the lively partiality and predilections for these relations or friends is weakened or lost in the general intercourse of the multitude around us. In a town, external objects are so common, so unappropriated to ourselves, and are so liable to change and to decay, that we cannot feel any close or permanent connection with them. In the country we remember them unchanged for a long space of time, and for that space known and frequented by scarce any but ourselves. "Methinks I should hate," says a young lady, the child of fiction, yet drawn with many features like that excellent girl I lost, "methinks I should hate to have been born in a town. When I say my native brook, or my native hill, I talk of friends, of whom the remembrance warms my heart." When the memory of persons we dearly loved is connected with the view of those objects, they have then a double link to the soul. It were tender enough for me to view some ancient trees that form my common evening walk, did I only remember what I was when I first sported under their shade, and what I am when I rest under it now; but it is doubly tender when I think of those with whom I have walked there; of her whom but a few summers ago I saw beneath those beeches, smiling in health, and beauty, and happiness, her present days lighted up with innocence and mirth, and her future drawn in the flattering colors of fancy and of hope.

But I know not why I should trouble you with this recital of the situation and feelings of an individual, or indeed why I should have written to you at all, except that I catched a sort of congenial spirit from your 87th Number, and was led by the letter of Urbanus to compare your description of a personage in former times with those whose sentiments I sometimes hear in the present days. I am not sure that these have gained in point of substance what they have lost in point of imagination. Power, and wealth, and luxury, are relative terms; and if address, and prudence, and policy, can only acquire us our share, we shall not account ourselves more powerful, more rich, or more luxurious, than when in the little we possessed we were still equal to those around us. But if we have narrowed the sources of internal comfort and internal enjoyment,—if we have debased the powers of purity of the mind,—if we have blunted the sympathy or contracted the affections of the heart, we have lost some of that treasure which was absolutely our own, and derived not its value from comparative estimation. Above all, if we have allowed the prudence or the interests of this world to shut out from our souls the view or the hopes of a better, we have quenched that light which would have cheered the darkness of affliction and the evening of old age, which at this moment, Mr. Lounger (for like an old man I must come back to myself), I feel restoring me my virtuous friends, my loved relations, my dearest child!—I am, &c.   ADRASTUS.

Two Sonnets, and an Inscription on a Spring.

BY THOMAS WARTON.

IT is curious that Warton, who was by no means a great poet, should have written some of the most favorite sonnets in the language. The reason is, that they were upon subjects he understood, and that the writer was in earnest. Upon most, indeed upon any occasions, Warton's mind was not sufficiently active or excitable to be moved into much eloquence of expression. The Fellow of Trinity College, Oxford, was a luxurious Protestant monk, who found something to minister to his satisfaction in everything around him, Gothic architecture, books, country walks, &c., not omitting the club-room and the pipe; but he was content, in general, to admire them through the medium of the thoughts of others, and so let the companions of his mind speak for him. He was susceptible, however, of strong general impressions; and as these, in the instances before us, were made by his favorite subjects, they are given with corresponding truth. Almost all his sonnets (they are only nine), but especially these two, notwithstanding conventional phrases, have elegance, simplicity, and a touching fervor. Nobody had written on the particular topics before him, at least not poetically; so that his modesty was not tempted into imitation. It makes us regret that he did not oftener take up new subjects, especially when we see the original eye for nature which is discernible even in his half centos from the poets he admired. It must be allowed, nevertheless, that the good comfortable collegian was made rather to feel sentiment in others, than to express it in his own sturdy person.

INSCRIPTION OVER A CALM AND CLEAR SPRING.

HERE quench your thirst, and mark in me
 An emblem of true charity;
Who, while my bounty I bestow.
Am neither heard, nor seen, to flow.

WRITTEN IN A BLANK LEAF OF DUGDALE'S "MONASTICON."*

DEEM not devoid of elegance the sage,
 By fancy's genuine feelings unbeguil'd,
Of painful pedantry the poring child,
Who turns of these proud domes th' historic page,
Now sunk by time and Henry's fiercer rage.
Think'st thou the warbling muses never smil'd
On his lone hours?   Ingenuous views engage
His thoughts, on themes, unclassic falsely styl'd,
Intent.   While cloistered piety displays
Her mouldering rolls, the piercing eye explores
New manners and the pomp of elder days,
Whence culls the pensive bard his pictured stores.
Nor rough, nor barren, are the winding ways
Of hoar antiquity, but strewn with flowers.

WRITTEN AFTER SEEING WILTON HOUSE.†

FROM Pembroke's princely dome, where mimic art
 Decks with a magic hand the dazzling bowers,
Its living hues where the warm pencil pours,
And breathing forms from the rude marble start,

---

* The *Monasticon* is an account of the monasteries existing in England before the Reformation.

† The seat of the Pembroke family; where there was, and is, a fine collection of pictures.

How to life's humbler scene can I depart,
My breast all glowing from those gorgeous towers?
In my low cell how cheat the sullen hours?
Vain the complaint. For fancy can impart
(To fate superior and to fortune's doom)
Whate'er adorns the stately storied hall.
She, 'mid the dungeon's solitary gloom,
Can dress the graces in their Attic pall;
Bid the green landskip's vernal beauty bloom,
And in bright trophies clothe the twilight wall.

Descriptions of Night.

FROM THE NOTES TO OSSIAN.

The dispute respecting the merits and authenticity of the poems of Ossian has long settled down, we believe, into an admission of the former, and a conclusion that Macpherson invented them, assisted by traditional fragments. It is a pity Macpherson ever suffered the dispute to take place; for it has left him a doubtful reputation both for genius and honesty, when perhaps nobody would have questioned either. The fragments may have excelled the inventions; but hardly any one, except a man of genius, could have put them so well together, notwithstanding the violation of times and manners. There is a great deal of repetition and monotony; yet somehow these faults themselves contribute to the welcome part of the impression. They affect us like the dreariness of the heaths and the moaning of the winds. But the work would not have stood its ground, and gained the admirers it has, did it not possess positive beauties; veins of genuine feeling and imagination. It is understood that an Italian translation was a favorite with Bonaparte and his officers during the early republican times. The present king of Sweden, Oscar Bernadotte, is said, we believe, to have been named after the son of Ossian. But even these illustrious testimonies to its merit are unnecessary after the single one of Gray, who in his Letters repeatedly expresses his admiration, particularly of the passages before us. We shall extract his notice of them by way of argument as well as critique. It is hardly requisite to mention, that Macpherson does not attribute these passages to Ossian. He has put them in a note, and says they were written by some imitator "a thousand years afterwards!" Gray takes no notice of this; nor shall we. If they are not of the same manufacture as the rest, ghost is not like ghost, nor a wind a wind.

Observe how beautifully Gray talks of the gust of wind "recollecting itself," and resembling the voice of a spirit.

"I have received," he says to his friend Mr. Stonhewer, "another Scotch packet with a third specimen, inferior in kind (because it is merely description), but full of nature and noble wild imagination. Five bards pass the night at the castle of a chief (himself a principal bard); each goes in his turn to observe the face of things, and returns with an extempore picture of the changes he has seen (it is an October night, the harvest month of the Highlands). This is the whole plan; yet there is a contrivance, and a preparation of ideas, that you would not expect. The oddest thing is, that every one of them sees ghosts (more or less). The idea that struck me and surprised me most, is the following:—One of them (describing a storm of wind and rain) says,

> "Ghosts ride on the tempest to-night;
> Sweet is their voice between the gusts of wind;
> Their songs are of other worlds!"

Did you never observe (while rocking winds are piping loud) that pause, as the gust is recollecting itself, and rising upon the ear in a shrill and plaintive note, like the swell of an Æolian harp? I do assure you there is nothing in the world so like the voice of a spirit. Thomson had an ear sometimes: he was not deaf to this; and has described it gloriously, but given it another different turn, and of more horror. I cannot repeat the lines: it is in his Winter. There is another very fine picture in one of them. It describes the breaking of the clouds after the storm, before it is settled into a calm, and when the moon is seen by short intervals.

> "The waves are tumbling on the lake,
> And lash the rocky sides,
> The boat is brimful in the cove,
> The oars on the rocking tide.
> Sad sits a maid beneath a cliff,
> And eyes the rolling stream;
> Her lover promised to come.
> She saw his boat (when it was evening) on the lake;
> Are these his groans on the gale?
> Is this his broken boat on the shore?"

Note, that Gray has written out these sentences in distinct lines, as though they had been metrically disposed in the original, and not prose. And indeed it is difficult not to discern a music in them, or to think they want a music of any other sort. But the effect would be different in long compositions.

FIRST BARD.

NIGHT is dull and dark. The clouds rest on the hills. No star with green trembling beam, no moon, looks from the sky. I hear the blast in the wood; but I hear it distant far. The stream of the valley murmurs; but its murmur is sullen and sad. From the tree at the grave of the dead the long-howling owl is heard. I see a dim form on the plain! It is a ghost! it fades, it flies. Some funeral shall pass this way; the meteor marks the path.

The distant dog is howling from the hut of the hill The stag lies on the mountain moss: the hind is at his side She hears the wind in its branching horns. She starts, but lies again.

The roe is in the cleft of the rock: the heath-cock's head is beneath his wing. No beast, no bird is abroad, but the owl and the howling fox. She on a leafless tree; he in a cloud on the hill.

Dark, panting, trembling, sad, the traveller has lost his way. Through shrubs, through thorns, he goes along the gurgling rill. He fears the rock and the fen. He fears the ghost of night. The old tree groans to the blast; the falling branch resounds. The wind drives the withered burs, clung together, along the grass. It is the light tread of a ghost! He trembles amidst the night.

Dark, dusky, howling is night, cloudy, windy, and full of ghosts! The dead are abroad! My friends, receive me from the night.

SECOND BARD.

The wind is up. The shower descends. The spirit of the mountain shrieks. Woods fall from high. Windows flap. The growing river roars. The traveller attempts the ford. Hark! that shriek! he dies! The storm drives the horse from the hill, the goat, the lowing cow. They tremble as drives the shower, beside the mouldering bank.

The hunter starts from sleep, in his lonely hut; he wakes the fire decayed. His wet dogs smoke around him. He fills the chinks with heath. Loud roar two mountain-streams which meet beside his booth.

Sad on the side of a hill the wandering shepherd sits. The tree resounds above him. The stream roars down the rock. He waits for the rising moon to guide him to his home.

Ghosts ride on the storm to-night. Sweet is their voice between the squalls of wind. Their songs are of other worlds.

The rain is past. The dry wind blows. Streams roar, and windows flap. Cold drops fall from the roof. I see the starry sky. But the shower gathers again. The west is gloomy and dark. Night is stormy and dismal; receive me, my friends, from night.

THIRD BARD.

The wind still sounds between the hills, and whistles through the grass of the rock. The firs fall from their place. The turfy hut is torn. The clouds, divided, fly over the sky, and show the burning stars. The meteor, token of death! flies sparkling through the gloom. It rests on the hill. I see the withered fern, the dark-browed rock, the fallen oak. Who is that in his shroud beneath the tree, by the stream?

The waves dark tumble on the lake, and lash its rocky sides. The boat is brimful in the cove; the oars on the rocking tide. A maid sits sad before the rock, and eyes the rolling stream. Her lover promised to come. She saw his boat, when yet it was light, on the lake. Is this his broken boat on the shore? Are these his groans on the wind?

Hark! the hail rattles around. The flaky snow descends. The tops of the hills are white. The stormy winds abate. Various is the night and cold; receive me, my friends, from night.

FOURTH BARD.

Night is calm and fair: blue, starry, settled is night! The winds, with the clouds, are gone. They sink behind the hill. The moon is upon the mountains. Trees glister: streams shine on the rock. Bright rolls the settled lake: bright the stream of the vale.

I see the trees overturned; the shocks of corn on the plain. The wakeful hind rebuilds the shocks, and whistles on the distant field.

Calm, settled, fair is night! Who comes from the place of the dead? That form with the robe of snow-white arms, and dark-brown hair! It is the daughter of the chief of the people: she that lately fell! Come, let us view thee, O maid! thou that hast been the delight of heroes! The blast drives the phantom away: white without form, it ascends the hill.

The breezes drive the blue mist slowly over the narrow

vale. It rises on the hill, and joins its head to heaven. Night is settled, calm, blue, starry, bright with the moon. Receive me not, my friends, for lovely is the night.

FIFTH BARD.

Night is calm, but dreary. The moon is in a cloud in the west. Slow moves that pale beam along the shaded hill. The distant wave is heard. The torrent murmurs on the rock. The cock is heard from the booth. More than half the night is past. The housewife, groping in the gloom, rekindles the settled fire. The hunter thinks that day approaches, and calls his bounding dogs. He ascends the hill, and whistles on his way. A blast removes the cloud: he sees the starry plough of the north. Much of the night is to pass. He nods by the mossy rock.

Hark! the whirlwind is in the wood. A low murmur in the vale! It is the mighty army of the dead, returning from the air.

The moon rests behind the hill. The beam is still on that lofty rock. Long are the shadows of the trees. Now it is dark over all. Night is dreary, silent, and dark; receive me, my friends, from night.

THE CHIEF.

Let clouds rest on the hills, spirits fly, and travellers fear. Let the winds of the woods arise, the sounding storms descend. Roar streams, and windows flap, and green-winged meteors fly! Rise the pale moon from behind her hills, or enclose her head in clouds! Night is alike to me, stormy or gloomy the sky. Night flies before the beam, when it is poured on the hill The young day returns from his clouds, but we return no more.

Where are our chiefs of old? Where our kings of mighty name? The fields of their battles are silent. Scarce their mossy tombs remain. We shall also be forgot. This lofty house shall fall. Our sons shall not behold the ruins in grass. They shall ask of the aged, "Where stood the walls of our fathers?"

Raise the song, and strike the harp; send round the shells of joy. Suspend a hundred tapers on high. Youths and maids begin the dance. Let some graybeard be near me, to tell the deeds of other times; of kings renowned in our land, of chiefs we behold no more. Thus let the night pass, until morning shall appear in our hall. Then let the bow be at hand, the dogs, the youths of the chase. We shall ascend the hill with day, and awake the deer.

Retirement and Death of a Statesman.

PASSAGES SELECTED FROM TROTTER'S MEMOIRS OF FOX.

Politics have nothing to do with this volume. The reader will have seen, that the questions between Whig and Tory are of no more concern to us, in these delightful lands of compilation, than any other interference which should limit their extent and freedom. There have been amiable and large-hearted men on both sides. Mr. Fox was one of them; and we repeat these accounts of him, as we should of any other human being under the like circumstances, because they suit this portion of our work, and the whole genial intention of it.

Mr. Trotter's book has some faults of style, but not in the passages extracted. He has given a valuable report of the way in which the great statesman passed his time at Saint Anne's Hill; and the account of his own feelings, while occupied in waiting his patron's last hour, especially during the visit to the dressing-room once occupied by the Duchess of Devonshire, is very striking. Saint Anne's Hill is in the neighborhood of Chertsey.

ST. Anne's Hill is delightfully situated; it commands a rich and extensive prospect. The house is embowered in trees, resting on the side of a hill, its grounds declining gracefully to a road, which bounds them at bottom. Some fine trees are grouped round the house, and three remarkably beautiful ones stand on the lawn; while a profusion of shrubs are distributed throughout with taste and judgment. Here

Mr. Fox was the tranquil and happy possessor of about thirty acres, and the inmate of a small but pleasant mansion. The simplicity and benignity of his manners, speaking the integrity of his character, soon dispelled those feelings of awe, which one naturally experiences on approaching what is very exalted.

The domestic life of Mr. Fox was equally regular and agreeable. In summer he rose between six and seven; in winter before eight. The assiduous care and excellent management of Mrs. Fox rendered his rural mansion the abode of peace, elegance, and order, and had long procured her the gratitude and esteem of those private friends whose visits to Mr. Fox, in his retirement at St. Anne's Hill, made them witnesses of this amiable woman's conduct. I confess I carried with me some of the vulgar prejudices respecting this great man! How completely was I undeceived! After breakfast, which took place between eight and nine in summer, and at a little after nine in winter, he usually read some Italian author with Mrs. Fox, and then spent the time preceding dinner at his literary studies, in which the Greek poets bore a principal part.

A frugal but plentiful dinner took place at three, or half-past two, in summer, and at four in winter; and a few glasses of wine were followed by coffee. The evening was dedicated to walking and conversation till tea-time, when reading aloud in history commenced, and continued till near ten. A light supper of fruit, pastry, or something very trifling, finished the day; and at half-past ten the family were gone to rest.

At breakfast the newspaper was read, commonly by Mr. Fox, as well as the letters which had arrived; for such was the noble confidence of his mind, that he concealed nothing from his domestic circle, unless it were the faults or the secrets of his friends. At such times, when the political topics of the day were naturally introduced by the paper. I never could observe the least acrimony or anger against that party which so sedulously, and indeed successfully, had labored to exclude him from the management of affairs, by misrepresentations of his motives, rather than by refutations of his arguments.

In private conversation, I think, he was rather averse to political discussion, generally preferring subjects connected with natural history, in any of its branches: above all, dwelling with delight on classical and poetical subjects. It is not to be supposed, however, that, where the interests and happiness of millions were concerned, he preserved a cold silence.

About the end of May, Mrs. Fox mentioned slightly to me that Mr. Fox was unwell; but at this time there was no alarm or apprehension. In the beginning of June I received a message from her, requesting me to come to him, as he had expressed a wish for me to read to him, if I was disengaged. It was in the evening, and I found him reclining upon a couch, uneasy and languid. It seemed to me so sudden an attack, that I was surprised and shocked. He requested me to read some of the Æneid to him, and desired me to turn to the fourth book: this was his favorite part. The tone of melancholy with which that book commences, was pleasing to his mind: he appeared relieved, and to forget his uneasiness and pains; but I felt this recurrence to Virgil as a mournful omen of a great attack upon his system, and that he was already looking to abstract himself from noise, and tumult, and politics. Henceforth his illness rapidly increased, and was pronounced a dropsy! I have reason to think that he turned his thoughts very soon to retirement at St. Anne's Hill, as he found the pressure of business insupportably harassing; and I have ever had in mind those lines, as very applicable to him at this time:—

> "And as an hare, whom hounds and horns pursue,
> Pants to the goal, from whence at first she flew,
> I still had hopes—my long vexations past—
> *Here to return,* and die (at home) at last."

Another of these symptoms of melancholy foreboding, I thought, was shown in his manner at Holland House. Mrs. Fox, he, and I, drove there several times before his illness confined him, and when exercise was strongly urged. He looked around him the last day he was there with a farewell tenderness that struck me very much. It was the place where he had spent his youthful days. Every lawn, garden, tree, and walk, were viewed by him with peculiar affection. He pointed out its beauties to me, and, in particular, showed me a green lane or avenue, which his mother, the late Lady Holland, had made by shutting up a road. He was a very exquisite judge of the picturesque, and had mentioned to me how beautiful this road had become, since converted into an alley. He raised his eyes in the house, looking around, and was earnest in pointing out everything he liked and remembered.

Soon, however, his illness very alarmingly increased; he suffered dreadful pains, and often rose from dinner with intolerable suffering. His temper never changed, and was always serene and sweet: it was amazing to behold so much distressing anguish, and so great equanimity. His friends, alarmed, crowded round him, as well as those relatives who, in a peculiar degree, knew his value and affectionate nature.

Mrs. Fox, whose unwearied attentions were the chief comfort of the sufferer, and myself, read aloud a great deal to him. Crabbe's poems, in manuscript, pleased him a great deal; in particular, the little episode of Phœbe Dawson. He did not, however, hear them all read, and there are parts in which he would have suggested alterations. We thus read, relieving each other, a great number of novels to him. He now saw very few persons. In truth, he had now every reason to do so.—visitors fatigued and oppressed him. He languished for St. Anne's Hill, and there all his hopes and wishes centered; he thought of a private life, and of resigning his office, and we had hopes that he might be restored sufficiently to enjoy health by abstaining from business. The Duke of Devonshire offered him the use of Chiswick House as a resting-place, from whence, if he gained strength enough, he might proceed to St. Anne's. Preparations for his departure began, therefore, to be made, which he saw with visible and unfeigned pleasure.

Two or three days before he was removed to Chiswick House, Mr. Fox sent for me, and with marked hesitation and anxiety, as if he much wished it, and yet was unwilling to ask it, informed me of his plan of going to Chiswick House, requesting me to form one of the family there. There was no occasion to request me; duty, affection, and gratitude, would have carried me wherever he went. About the end of July, Mrs. Fox and he went there, and on the following day I joined them. No mercenary hand approached him. Mrs. Fox hung over him every day with vigilant and tender affection: when exhausted I took her place; and at night, as his disorder grew grievously oppressive, a confidential servant and myself shared the watching and labors between us. I took the first part, because I read to him, as well as gave him medicine or nourishment.

We continued our reading of *Johnson's Lives of the Poets*. How often at midnight, as he listened with avidity, and made the remarks that occurred, he apologized to me for keeping me from my rest, but, still delighted with our reading, would say, "Well, you may go on a little more," as I assured him that I liked the reading aloud. At these times he would do

RETIREMENT AND DEATH OF A STATESMAN. 219

fend Johnson, when I blamed his severity and unwillingness to allow, and incapacity to appreciate, poetical merit,—would refer me to his life of Savage, and plainly showed much partiality for Johnson. Of Dryden, he was a warm and almost enthusiastic admirer. He conversed a great deal about that great English poet; and indeed I never perceived, at any time, a stronger relish for, or admiration of, the poets, than at this afflicting period. I generally read to him till three or four in the morning, and then retired for a few hours: he showed always great uneasiness at my sitting up, but evidently was soothed and gratified by my being with him. At first he apologized for my preparing the nourishment, which required to be warmed in the night; but seeing how sincerely I was devoted to him, he ceased to make any remark. Once he asked me, at midnight, when preparing chicken panade for him, "Does this amuse you? I hope it does." He was so far from exacting attendance, that he received every little good office, every proper and necessary attention, as a favor and kindness done him. So unvitiated by commerce with mankind, so tender, so alive to all the charms of friendship, was this excellent man's heart! His anxiety also, lest Mrs. Fox's health should suffer, was uniformly great till the day he expired.

Lord Holland and General Fitzpatrick, as he grew worse, came and resided at Chiswick House entirely. Miss Fox also remained there. Thus he had around him, every day, all he loved most; and the overwhelming pressure of his disorder was as much as possible relieved by the converse and sight of cherished relatives and friends. Lord Holland showed how much he valued such an uncle. He never left him;—the hopes of power or common allurements of ambition, had no effect upon him. His affectionate attention to Mr. Fox, and his kindness to all who assisted that great man, were endearing in a high degree. Miss Fox—calm and resigned, grieving, without uttering a word—would sit at the foot of his bed, and often reminded me of the fine heads of females, done by masterly hands, to express sorrow, dignity, and faith in God.

There was now a plaintiveness in his manner very interesting, but no way derogating from his fortitude and calmness. He did not affect the stoic. He bore his pains as a Christian and a man. Till the last day, however, I do not think he conceived himself in danger. A few days before the termination of his mortal career, he said to me at night, " Holland thinks me worse than I am ;" and, in fact, the appearances were singularly delusive not a week before he expired. In the day, he arose and walked a little, and his looks were not ghastly or alarming by any means. Often did he latterly walk to his window to gaze on the berries of the mountain ash, which hung clustering on a young tree at Chiswick House; every morning he returned to look at it he would praise it, as the morning breeze, rustling, shook the berries and leaves; but then the golden sun, which played upon them, and the fresh air that comes with the dawn, were to me almost heart-sickening, though once so delightful: he whom I so much cherished and esteemed,—whose kindness had been ever unremitting and unostentatious,—he whose society was to me happiness and peace,—was not long to enjoy this sun and this morning air. His last look on that mountain-ash was his farewell to nature.

I continued to read aloud to him every night, and as he occasionally dropt asleep, I was then left to the awful meditations incident to such a situation. No person was awake beside myself; the lofty rooms and hall of Chiswick House were silent, and the world reposed. In one of those melancholy pauses, I walked about for a few moments, and found myself involuntarily and accidentally in the late Duchess of Devonshire's dressing-room. Everything was as that amiable and accomplished lady had left it: the music-book still open, the books not restored to their places, a chair as if she had but just left it, and every mark of a recent inhabitant in this elegant apartment. The Duchess had died in May, and Mr. Fox had very severely felt her loss. Half-opened notes lay scattered about. The night was solemn and still; and at that moment, had some floating sound of music vibrated through the air, I cannot tell to what my feelings would have been wrought. Never had I experienced so strong a sensation of the transitory nature of life, of the vanity of a fleeting world! I stood scarce breathing,—heard nothing,—listened. Scarcely knowing how I left the dressing-room, I returned. All was still. Mr. Fox slept quietly. I was deluded into a tranquil joy to find him still alive, and breathing without difficulty. His countenance was always serene in sleep: no troubled dreams ever agitated or distorted it,—it was the transcript of his guileless mind.

Mr. Fox expired between five and six in the afternoon of the 13th of September, 1806. The Tower guns were firing for the capture of Buenos Ayres, as he was breathing his last.

Gray's Elegy in a Country Churchyard.

We desire to say as little as possible about this affecting and noble poem. It is so sweet, so true, and so universally appreciated, that we feel inclined to be as silent before it, as if listening to the wind over the graves. It is the fit conclusion for our book, both in the subject and spirit—serious, calm, and hopeful.

The epitaph is on the author; and never did a man speak of himself with a truth more beautifully combining dignity with humility, a sense of all that he felt worthy and all that he felt weak. We suspect, that the "cross'd in love" of the previous lines might very well apply to Gray. He had secret griefs of some kind, perhaps of disease, perhaps of sympathy with a good mother, and distress at having a bad father (for such, alas! was the case); but whatever they were, we may be sure that they were those of a good and kind man.

The poem before us is as sweet as if written by Coleridge, and as pious and universal as if religion had uttered it, undisturbed by polemics. It is a quintessence of humanity.

THE curfew tolls the knell of parting day,
  The lowing herd winds slowly o'er the lea,
The ploughman homeward plods his weary way,
  And leaves the world to darkness and to me.

Now fades the glimmering landscape on the sight
  And all the air a solemn stillness holds,

Save where the beetle wheels his droning flight,
    And drowsy tinklings lull the distant folds;

Save that from yonder ivy-mantled tower,
    The moping owl does to the moon complain
Of such as, wandering near her secret bower,
    Molest her ancient solitary reign.

Beneath those rugged elms, that yew-tree's shade,
    Where heaves the turf in many a mouldering heap,
Each in his narrow cell forever laid,
    The rude forefathers of the hamlet sleep.

The breezy call of incense-breathing morn,
    The swallow twittering from the straw-built shed,
The cock's shrill clarion, or the echoing horn,
    No more shall rouse them from their lowly bed.

For them no more the blazing hearth shall burn,
    Or busy housewife ply her evening care;
No children run to lisp their sire's return,
    Or climb his knees the envied kiss to share.

Oft did the harvest to their sickle yield;
    Their furrow oft the stubborn glebe has broke;
How jocund did they drive their team afield!
    How bow'd the woods beneath their sturdy stroke!

Let not ambition mock their useful toil,
    Their homely joys, and destiny obscure;
Nor grandeur hear, with a disdainful smile,
    The short and simple annals of the poor.

The boast of heraldry, the pomp of power,
    And all that beauty, all that wealth e'er gave,

Await alike the inevitable hour—
    The paths of glory lead but to the grave.

Nor you, ye proud, impute to these the fault,
    If memory o'er their tomb no trophies raise,
Where, through the long-drawn aisle and fretted vault,
    The pealing anthem swells the note of praise.

Can storied urn or animated bust
    Back to its mansion call the fleeting breath?
Can honor's voice provoke the silent dust,
    Or flattery soothe the dull cold ear of death?

Perhaps in this neglected spot is laid
    Some heart once pregnant with celestial fire,
Hands that the rod of empire might have sway'd
    Or wak'd to ecstasy the living lyre.

But knowledge to their eyes her ample page,
    Rich with the spoils of time, did ne'er unroll;
Chill penury repress'd their noble rage,
    And froze the genial current of the soul.

Full many a gem of purest ray serene
    The dark unfathom'd caves of ocean bear;
Full many a flower is born to blush unseen,
    And waste its sweetness in the desert air.

Some village Hampden, that, with dauntless breast,
    The little tyrant of his fields withstood,
Some mute inglorious Milton here may rest,
    Some Cromwell, guiltless of his country's blood.

Th' applause of listening senates to command,
    The threats of pain and ruin to despise,

To scatter plenty o'er a smiling land,
    And read their history in a nation's eyes,

Their lot forbade; nor circumscrib'd alone
    Their growing virtues, but their crimes confin'd;
Forbade to wade through slaughter to a throne,
    And shut the gates of mercy on mankind;

The struggling pangs of conscious truth to hide,
    To quench the blushes of ingenuous shame,
Or heap the shrine of luxury and pride
    With incense kindled at the muse's flame.

Far from the madding crowd's ignoble strife
    Their sober wishes never learnt to stray;
Along the cool sequester'd vale of life
    They kept the noiseless tenor of their way.

Yet e'en these bones from insult to protect,
    Some frail memorial still erected nigh,
With uncouth rhymes and shapeless sculpture deck'd,
    Implores the passing tribute of a sigh.

Their name, their years, spelt by th' unletter'd muse,
    The place of fame and elegy supply;
And many a holy text around she strews,
    That teach the rustic moralist to die.

For who to dumb forgetfulness a prey,
    This pleasing anxious being e'er resign'd,
Left the warm precincts of the cheerful day,
    Nor cast one longing, lingering look behind?

On some fond breast the parting soul relies,
    Some pious hand the closing eye requires;
Ev'n from the tomb the voice of nature cries,
    Ev'n in our ashes live their wonted fires.

For thee, who, mindful of th' unhonor'd dead,
   Dost in these lines their artless tale relate,
If chance, by lonely contemplation led,
   Some kindred spirit shall inquire thy fate,

Haply some hoary-headed swain may say,
   " Oft have we seen him, at the peep of dawn,
Brushing with hasty steps the dews away,
   To meet the sun upon the upland lawn.

" There, at the foot of yonder nodding beech,
   That wreathes its old fantastic roots so high,
His listless length at noontide would he stretch,
   And pore upon the brook that bubbles by.

" Hard by yon wood, now smiling as in scorn,
   Muttering his wayward fancies, he would rove,
Now drooping woful wan, like one forlorn,
   Or craz'd with care, or cross'd in hopeless love.

" One morn I miss'd him on the custom'd hill,
   Along the heath, and near his favorite tree:
Another came; nor yet beside the rill,
   Nor up the lawn, nor at the wood was he;

" The next with dirges due, in sad array,
   Slow through the churchyard path we saw him borne—
Approach and read (for thou canst read) the lay
   'Graved on the stone beneath yon aged thorn."

The Epitaph.

Here rests his head upon the lap of earth,
   A youth to fortune and to fame unknown;
Fair science frown'd not on his humble birth,
   And melancholy mark'd him for her own.

Large was his bounty, and his soul sincere,
    Heaven did a recompense as largely send;
He gave to misery all he had—a tear;
    He gain'd from Heaven ('twas all he wish'd) a friend.

No farther seek his merits to disclose,
    Or draw his frailties from their dread abode
(There they alike in trembling hope repose),
    The bosom of his Father and his God.

THE END

www.ingramcontent.com/pod-product-compliance
Lightning Source LLC
Chambersburg PA
CBHW022136300426
44115CB00006B/204